Library of
Davidson College

JOHN ADAMS SPEAKING

POUND'S SOURCES FOR THE ADAMS CANTOS

by

Frederick K. Sanders

UNIVERSITY OF MAINE PRESS
ORONO, MAINE

811
P87c-xa

Copyright © by the National Poetry Foundation, Inc. and the University of Maine Press

Library of Congress Catalog Number: 75-620003
ISBN 0-915032-00-7   81-3295

PROLOGUE

Pound said more than once that *The Cantos* would be "a poem containing history." Unhappily, his words have led a large contingent of critics to suppose that one of the poet's main concerns must then be that of an historian. The argument of such critics in their more querulous moments goes like this: if a poet is going to make historical judgments his business must be the same as that of the professional historian: he must study all the sources and discriminatingly weigh the evidence important and trivial until that moment when he can say, "I have the answer. This is it." He should then set forth his findings with appropriate documentation and make a considered judgment. Such critics misunderstand both the poet and his poetry, as well as Pound's intent in presenting historical characters. Pound's intent, in fact, is quite different from the intent of analytical historians. It is different in particular with John Adams, second president of the United States.

From six thousand pages of letters, documents, memoirs, and reflections written by John Adams, Ezra Pound excerpted eighty pages which he wove into the twenty-five hundred line fabric of poetry known as "The Adams Cantos." The excerpts vary in length from a few words to several lines and give hundreds of candid glimpses of John Adams in a variety of moments during a ninety-year life. The man himself is put on record: here we have John Adams speaking and acting; we do not have someone else's opinions about his speaking and acting. One dramatic gesture is sometimes worth thousands of words: the gesture for black power made by an Olympic gold-medal winner speaks louder than volumes of commentary about and after the fact. The gestures and acts of John Adams as selected and presented by Pound speak as loudly.

Pound's technique all through The Cantos is to present both ideas and men in action. By this technique he presents the truth, not speculation about the truth. In this way he builds dramatic intensity into the poem. But as in grand opera, levels of intensity vary from the quiet of recitative to the climax of great lyric cadenza, so the levels of intensity ebb and flow in *The Cantos,* as a whole and in its parts.

This technique of presentation has respectable antecedents back in the pre-Raphaelite era of the 19th Century. The many ceremonies and gestures of Water Pater as developed by the Symbolists, Vitalists, and Decadents are antecedents of the acts of Stephen Daedalus who might himself enjoy burning with a hard gem-like flame from moment to evanescent moment. In *Stephen Hero* [New York, 1955, p. 211] we read: "By an epiphany he meant a sudden spiritual manifestation whether in the vulgarity of speech or of gesture or in a memorable phase of the mind itself. He believed that it was for the man of letters to record these epiphanies with extreme care seeing that they themselves are the most delicate and evanescent of moments." Out of such speculations evolves Eliot's "objective correlative," couched in highly dramatic and climatic terms as the end of an intentionally and emotionally charged chain of events. Concurrently (1910-20) Pound's concepts develop from Imagism to the image-in-action, to the ideogramic method, to the vortex, to the final mature practice in *The Cantos.* Pound defined the image in-action as "that which presents an intellectual and emotional complex in an instant of time." Later he said, "The ideogramic method consists of presenting one facet and then another until at some point one gets off the dead and desensitized surface of the reader's mind, onto a part that will register." [*Guide to Kulchur,* p. 51] This idea is not far from Pater's famous creed at the end of *The Renaissance* where he is concerned with revitalizing the habit-desensitized mind into states of joy: "The service . . . of speculative culture towards the human spirit is to rouse, to startle it into sharp and eager observation." Relating the "image" to the vortex, Pound said: "The image is not an idea. It is a radiant node or cluster; it is what I can, and must perforce, call a VORTEX, from which, and through which, and into which ideas are constantly rushing." So, "The Adams Cantos" add up to a large vortex just as each of its several parts is a smaller vortex. The stunning result is the image of an Adams dramatically different from the image previously made by analytical historians. And there is no doubt about the truth of the new image: word by word and line by line this is what Adams said, wrote, and thought.

For Pound is dedicated to the truth about men and history. In fact one of his main concerns in "The Adams Cantos" is to rid the record of the detritus of prejudice, cliche, and propaganda and get to the man himself. Pound's intent is to use the epiphany, the image-in-action, the ideogram, the vortex, and at times the entire chain of action in the objective correlative so as to paint as complete a picture of John Adams and his age as possible in 2500 lines of poetry: to picture him in courageous and dynamic moments as well as in moments of weakness and depression. We see him in dramatic moments as a boy, youth, student, husband, father, farmer, teacher, lawyer, philosopher, revolutionary, economist, anti-theologian, critic, author, ambassador, vice president, president, and elder-statesman. Among the founding fathers he is a fully rounded man, and like Odysseus or Sigismundo a "live man" among many "duds." We see all the major historical figures in *The Cantos* in various moods, but since much more space is devoted to John Adams than to any of the others, we see him in many more moods than we see the others: happy, sad, exhuberant, determined, depressed, hopeful, discouraged, ecstatic, wistful, longing, angry, proud, humble, selfconscious, courageous, jealous, suspicious, triumphant, self-effacing, placid, and resigned—to list but a few. These roles, gestures, moods, and attitudes are the "gists and piths" of the man himself: John Adams in action.

One of Pound's gists and piths about literature in general reached a characteristic slogan form during the twenties: "Great literature is simply language charged with meaning to the utmost possible degree." He repeats this definition in *ABC of Reading* (p. 36) and follows it with a comment on the German word *Dichten* which he says equals *condensare*. Then he says: "I begin with poetry because it is the most concentrated form of verbal expression." And we know that *Dichtung* means "poetry." Many Pound critics, even those who admire his poetry most, find that he concentrates verbal expression to a point where the text becomes difficult to understand if not downright unintelligible. But the difficulties one has in reading *The Cantos* come not from an abstruse symbolism or from any other type of ambiguity. *The Cantos* seem difficult only when readers lack the kind of knowledge Pound believed a select audience ought to have about the great moments in human history. For "The Adams Cantos" this means the history of the American Revolution. Pound thought it was preposterous that biographies and collections of sayings and writing were easily available about or by Marx, Lenin, and Stalin, sometimes in paperback for 5 or 10 cents, while the lives and works of many of the founding fathers and great presidents of the United States were either not available or available only in huge tomes at exhorbitant cost, thus denying them even to so select an audience as readers of great poetry, who are more likely to be poor than rich.

In America and England, especially, great poets write for a very small audience. But that audience criss-crosses all class, racial, or religious boundaries. Many readers of great poetry come from or live among the masses. But any idea that great poetry is written for or read by the masses is both sentimental romanticism and intellectual dishonesty. By its very nature great art limits its audience which for poetry may be 1 person in 100,000. It is this select audience that Pound believes should have (or should take the trouble to obtain) the kind of knowledge which would make *The Cantos* comprehensible.

Pound does not expect the masses either to know or care about the truth or ideals of the American Revolution and the motivation of its Sons of Liberty. He does expect those dedicated to building and maintaining civilization—people who care about freedom, democracy, and the poetry which strengthens these—either to know or to discover enough facts to make the poetry clear. These lines may at first seem enigmatic:

>   barber's boy ragging the sentinel
>   so Capn Preston etc/
>   lower order with billets of wood and 'just roving'
>   force in fact of a right sez Chawles Fwancis
>   at the same time, and in Louses of parleymoot. . .
>   so fatal a precision of aim,
>   sojers aiming??
>   Gent standing in his doorway got 2 balls in the arm
>   and five deaders 'never Cadmus. . .' etc

Young lawyer John Adams agreed to defend Captain Preston and the British soldiers in what is known as the Boston Massacre case and thereby participated in the most unpopular act a Son of Liberty could be guilty of. But when one understands why he did it and what his defense meant to the whole concept of the rule of law rather than rule of men we see the old time history-book fairy tales in a new light and the truth in a powerful new focus. The poetry is not difficult but our lack of knowledge makes it seems difficult.

If one were to encounter these lines of supposed verse in the year 2200 they would doubtless seem bewildering:

>   Mist over the Potomac
>   Athena turned away
>   Beclouds the Watergate.
>
>   Eyebrows twist and jowls shake
>   Dean: At that point in time
>
>   A figures slouches eyes fixed on the sand
>   Alone near the waves off San Clemente
>
>   TK deadpans the image floating in air
>   The words echo and reecho
>
>   across the land at that point
>
>   At that point
>   At that point
>   in time.

But today they would be as clear to almost anyone in the world with a television set as the Capn Preston lines would be to anyone in the American Colonies in 1770-1772 while the trial went on. We can say "No American should ever forget the implications of Watergate." Pound would agree. He would also insist that every educated American should know the truth about those events of the American Revolution pointed to in "The Adams Cantos." But we do lack this knowledge and we need help in obtaining it. Frederick Sanders has given us the first needed help by searching out and presenting in more detail the exact sources Pound used in writing them. By putting the 80 pages of poetry back into the letters and documents from which they came, he has given us over 550 pages of text. And he follows the trail of the poet. He presents the letters and documents without comment, letting them speak for themselves. When Pound wrote "The Adams Cantos," John Adams had been relegated by historians to a minor role among the founders of the republic. As second president, he was considered responsible for the collapse of federalism and short-sighted (or grudgingly praised) for avoiding war with France. Pound's "excernment" gives us a quite different picture. He is now seen as one of the most important forces in the whole American Revolutionary movement: in fact, *the* most important among the "Sons of Liberty.*

During the time Pound was composing "The Adams Cantos," he wrote: "To escape a word or a set of words loaded up with dead association Frobenius uses the term Paideuma for the tangle or complex of the inrooted ideas of any period. [*Guide to Kulchur* p. 57]. In a word, "The Adams Cantos" are a paideuma, not only for John Adams but for the tangle or complex of the inrooted ideas of the whole revolutionary period. In extending the 80 pages to over 550 pages, Mr. Sanders in *John Adams Speaking* has elaborated and dramatised this paideuma. Our previous dead ideas and cliches are swept away and we are left with wholly refocused images and new ideas about the American Revolution and John Adams as founding father, President, and elder statesman of the United States of America.

Carroll R. Terrell
Orono, 1975

*Pound's picture engaged the interest of Catherine Drinker Bowen whose book, *John Adams and the American Revolution,* 1950, continued the process. She helped restore him to his rightful place of importance as the main force in solving the legal and governmental problems which made the *Declaration of Independence* possible. In years of letter writing to leaders in all the colonies, Adams painstakingly prescribed the machinery to elect local governments, constituent assemblies, and delegates to the Continental Congresses so that a total governmental infra-structure was in place to carry on the revolution after the Declaration. It was Adams alone among the other New England delegates who saw that the only way the colonies would act together would be by having a non-New Englander as

General of the Armies. Against great odds, he nominated Washington and campaigned to get him elected. Until the correspondence between Bowen and Pound is published, we cannot assess the importance of "The Adams Cantos" on her attitude. We may only note that most items in the introduction she wrote for her book had received fifteen years earlier a special emphasis in Pound. Since Bowen's book, the process of restoring Adams to his rightful place has gone on slowly but steadily. See especially Page Smith, Vol. I *John Adams 1735-1784,* and Vol. II *John Adams 1784-1826 (New York, 1962).*

JOHN ADAMS SPEAKING:

POUND'S SOURCES FOR THE ADAMS CANTOS

by

Frederick K. Sanders

TO

KAREN and SEAN

CONTENTS

PREFACE	i
INTRODUCTION	1
LIST OF WORKS CITED	47
THE SOURCES	49
CANTO LXII	50
CANTO LXIII	108
CANTO LXIV	128
CANTO LXV	174
CANTO LXVI	265
CANTO LXVII	302
CANTO LXVIII	356
CANTO LXIX	400
CANTO LXX	428
CANTO LXXI	459
APPENDIX A: CHRONOLOGY	507
APPENDIX B: A NOTE ON THE TEXT	521

PREFACE

Readers who have made their own search for the sources of Ezra Pound's "Adams Cantos" in the Charles Francis Adams edition of the *Works of John Adams* know how rich are the rewards of the search. Following Pound's lead, one meets John Adams on his own terms and finds him to be what Pound says he is, *pater patriae*--in many ways a man uniquely deserving that title. His intelligence and honesty animate the story his writings tell about his prodigious public service of more than forty years in a way that the biographer's art finally cannot do, even in so masterful a biography as that of Page Smith. Pound is surely correct to take us back to the writings of John Adams himself.

Two works not listed in the bibliography below have special interest for the reader of the "Adams Cantos." The first is *The Adams-Jefferson Letters*, edited in two volumes by Lester J. Cappon (Chapel Hill: Univ. of North Carolina Press, 1959), the authoritative edition of the correspondence that Pound has characterized as "a shrine and a monument" to civilization in America.

The second, essential for anyone using the Charles Francis Adams edition of the *Works of John Adams*, is the monumental publication of *The Adams Papers* by the Belknap Press of Harvard University Press under the direction of L. H. Butterfield, Editor in Chief. Although Charles Francis Adams proved himself a particularly conscientious and scholarly editor for his time, his edition of his grandfather's papers is not without problems. These are described in the "Introduction" to Volume I of the *Diary and Autobiography of John Adams*, ed. L. H. Butterfield,

Leonard C. Faber, and Wendell D. Garrett (Cambridge, Mass.: Harvard Univ. Press, 1961), xxvii-xxx; xlvii-lii, an informative discussion of the nature of the text Pound was working with. When completed, the publication of the writings of John Adams in The Adams Papers will provide a definitive text against which to compare that of the Charles Francis Adams edition.

The already published volumes supplement the older edition in important ways. For example, full accounts of the significant legal cases of Adams mentioned by Pound in the "Adams Cantos" may be found in Legal Papers of John Adams, edited in three volumes by L. Kinvin Wroth and Hiller B. Zobel (Cambridge, Mass.: Harvard Univ. Press, 1965), with commentary explaining the courts and judicial practices of his day, and, in Volume III, a chronology of Adams's legal career up to the time of his departure for France in February of 1778. The Adams Papers also offers, in its prefaces and introductions, editorial notes and documentation, a wealth of information helpful to the reader of the "Adams Cantos." Especially useful are the brief biographical notes identifying the minor figures whose names turn up in the writings of John Adams because of some association he had with them. In this regard the John Adams volumes in The Adams Papers are singularly valuable.

ACKNOWLEDGEMENTS

The first time I heard Ezra Pound discussed as a major artist was eighteen years ago in an undergraduate class at Wofford College taught by Professor Vincent Miller. At that time Pound himself was still incarcerated at St. Elizabeth's, in Washington, D. C., and in a new textbook from a large American publishing house the editors were bluntly announcing to students this about the Cantos:

> Learning rubs shoulders too often with sham and pretense; and one may regard as sheer impudence the perversions of British and American history, the garbled interpolation of obscure literary works in several languages, including Chinese ideograms, and the private jokes.*

To draw Pound in caricature seemed the habit of the times, for it was easier to mock him than to read him. But Vincent Miller asked students to read Pound, and in classroom discussions directed with a sensitivity and wisdom that deserve to be called Socratic, he showed that the way Pound articulates his concerns in the Cantos makes sense—that the poem is intelligible. I owe my first and oldest debt to him.

I am also indebted to Professor Ward Pafford, who, when he was teaching in the English Department at Emory University, encouraged my interest in Pound at a critical time during my graduate work; to Mr. Andrew Lytle, for the opportunity he gave me to write about Pound; to Professor Robert H. West of the University of Georgia, for his support of my work during my four years of residence there; to Professor Edward F. Krickel, whose comprehensive knowledge of literature, history, and philosophy has, in the conversations of friendship over the years, greatly contributed to my understanding of Pound; and to Professor Marion Montgomery, a friend and judicious critic who saw the original version of the present work take shape as a dissertation and, in directing it, met all requests for assistance, even those that inconvenienced him, with exemplary promptness, thoroughness, and kindness.

My thanks are also due Dr. Richard Harwell, Director of Libraries, and Ms. Edna Earle Brown, Associate Director of Libraries at Georgia Southern College; Dean Hardy M. Edwards, Jr., and Associate Dean Thomas H. Rogers of the University of Georgia Graduate School, and Mr. John W. Bonner, Jr., Special Collections Librarian at University of Georgia. I am grateful to Professor Lawrence Huff, Head of the Department of English, Journalism, and Philosophy at Georgia Southern College, for his kindness in assigning me a schedule that gave me valuable time for

---

* The American Tradition in Literature, ed. Sculley Bradley, Richmond Croom Beatty, and E. Hudson Long (New York: Norton, 1956), II, 882.

correcting and revising the typescript. For their assistance in the preparation of the typescript, I thank Ms. Jane Brown and Ms. Sharon Bennett.

My wife, Donna, for her contributions to the completion of this task, has my gratitude beyond measure.

I owe a special debt to Princess Mary de Rachewiltz, who encouraged me to seek publication of the present work, and to Professor Carroll F. Terrell, whose generous efforts on its behalf have led to its publication.

A documented version of the discussion of Canto 70 (pp. 23-38, below) has previously appeared in <u>Paideuma</u>.

Frederick K. Sanders
Georgia Southern College
Statesboro, Georgia

INTRODUCTION

The Cantos of Ezra Pound, published in 1970 by New Directions, brings together in one volume, with pages numbered consecutively from beginning to end for the first time in an American edition, all previously published segments of Pound's long poem. In this form the poem, consisting of Cantos 1-117 (Cantos 72-73 have never been published), runs to a length of 802 pages. Eighty pages, or one-tenth of the poem (Cantos 62-71), Pound devotes to the career of John Adams,

>   pater patriae
>   the man who at certain points
>   made us
>   at certain points
>   saved us
>   by fairness, honesty and straight moving,[1]

an act of homage by the poet important for several distinctive reasons.

The first reason has to do with the most controversial episode of Pound's life. The broadcasts Pound made on Rome Radio, starting in 1941, led to his indictment in July, 1943,

---

[1] Ezra Pound, "Canto LXII," in The Cantos of Ezra Pound (New York: New Directions, 1970), p. 350. I shall follow the practice of Daniel D. Pearlman in The Barb of Time (New York: Oxford Univ. Press, 1969) and use Arabic numerals to identify the various cantos mentioned in the text, but in formal citations I will use the Roman numeral designations as they appear in the 1970 New Directions edition of the Cantos.

for treason against the United States. The indictment read, in part, that Pound had committed

> .... each and every one of the overt acts herein described for the purpose of and with the intent to adhere to and give aid and comfort to the Kingdom of Italy, and its military allies, enemies of the United States, and the said defendent Ezra Pound committed each and every one of the said overt acts contrary to his duty of allegiance to the United States and to the form of the statute in such case made and provided and against the peace and dignity of the United States.[2]

Whether the charges in the indictment are true or not,[3] what is undeniably true is that this poet, charged with acting "contrary to his duty of allegiance to the United States," had spent considerable time during the preceding decade attempting to show those Americans who would listen that the experience of the nation's founding belonged not simply to an archeological past but to the twentieth century as well.

Early in 1933 Pound was writing to William Bird, publisher of Three Mountains Press in Paris, "I observe that you are a follerer ov Alex Hamilton, whereas T. J. is my cherished forebear."[4] Jefferson was, indeed, the first of

---

[2] Charles Norman, *Ezra Pound*, revised ed. (New York: Funk & Wagnalls, 1969), p. 388.

[3] Mary de Rachewiltz, Pound's daughter, wrote in *Esquire*, April 1966, p. 116: "This is no time to go over the press of those days, but there is one refrain that still gets repeated: he broadcast for Mussolini. So we shall have to insist: he did not broadcast for Mussolini. There should be a difference between making propaganda for a dictator and expressing personal ideas."

[4] *The Letters of Ezra Pound*, ed. D. D. Paige (New York: Harcourt, 1950), p. 243.

the great American leaders to whom Pound gave detailed attention, a fact confirmed by his publication in 1935 of <u>Jefferson</u> <u>and/or</u> <u>Mussolini</u>,[5] along with the publication the preceding year of <u>Eleven</u> <u>New</u> <u>Cantos</u>: <u>XXXI-XLI</u>,[6] the first three cantos of which are based upon Jefferson's correspondence, including portions of the Jefferson-Adams correspondence. As William Vasse has noted, "Thomas Jefferson, the most important personality of Cantos XXXI-XXXIII, is characterized by the diversity and flexibility of his personal culture."[7] But even then Pound was looking at more than Jefferson alone, for he had based Canto 34 on writings of John Quincy Adams and Canto 37 on writings of Martin Van Buren.[8] In fact, Pound had had occasion to write Harriet Monroe in September

---

[5] <u>Jefferson</u> <u>and/or</u> <u>Mussolini</u> (London: Stanley Nott, 1935).

[6] In the 1970 edition of the <u>Cantos</u> these eleven cantos appear on pp. 153-206.

[7] William Vasse, "American History and the Cantos," <u>The Pound Newsletter</u>, No. 5, ed. John Edwards (Department of English, Univ. of California at Berkeley, January, 1955), p. 15. Mr. Vasse also writes: "In the early cantos of American history John Adams is made subordinate to Jefferson; he plays a secondary role in the Adams-Jefferson correspondence, and, although Canto XXXII outlines many of the issues which are analyzed at length in the Adams Cantos, the personality of John Adams is never precisely defined in this canto."

[8] Vasse, p. 14: ". . . the John Quincy Adams canto (XXXIV) comes out of the selected edition of <u>The Diary of John Quincy Adams, 1794-1845</u> (New York, 1928); the Martin Van Buren canto (XXXVII) comes from <u>The Autobiography of Martin Van Buren</u> (Washington, D. C., 1920) . . . ."

of 1933 to reassure her about the importance of the Martin Van Buren canto.[9] Jefferson was not the only statesman whose writings Pound believed should be valued.

Nevertheless it was Jefferson, and, later, John Adams, who stood at the center of the American experience, according to Pound. The most elaborate prose discussion Pound offers of the cardinal importance of these two men is to be found in his magnificent essay of 1937 on the Jefferson-Adams correspondence.[10] Pound thought that the United States as a nation would inevitably decay--a process already well advanced, he felt--unless its people made a serious attempt to regain the kind of understanding out of which the country was born by tracing that understanding back to its origins, that is to say, most specifically, back to Jefferson and Adams. Irrespective of whether or not Pound sensed the prospect of American involvement in a European war as early as 1933, or 1937, and long before there was even a remote possibility of Pound's broadcasting from Rome, he believed that Americans had lost their hold upon the essential meanings of

---

[9] Pound, Letters, p. 247: "Anyhow Van Buren was a national hero, and the young ought to know it. Also this canto continues after the Adams. Printed separate, it will be clearer than if I pubd. 35 and 36 next.
"Consider that Van's autobiography lay unprinted from 1860 or so down to 1920, probably because people who knew of it were too god damn stupid to understand it."

[10] Ezra Pound, "The Jefferson-Adams Letters as a Shrine and a Monument," in Impact: Essays on Ignorance and the Decline of American Civilization (Chicago: Regnery, 1960), pp. 166-183.

the American experience, meanings available in the writings of John Quincy Adams and of Martin Van Buren, but especially in the writings of Jefferson and John Adams. In a letter dated 15 October 1938 Pound wrote to John Crowe Ransom of his concern about the deleterious effects of a concept of American "literature" that excluded the writings of the Founding Fathers:

> As final enquiry: are you ready for a revival of American culture considering it as something specifically grown from the nucleus of the American Founders, present in the Adams, Jefferson correspondence; not limited to belles lettres and American or colonial imitation of European literary models, but active in all departments of thought, and tackling the problems which give life to epos and Elizabethan plays, without rendering either Homer or Bard of Avon dry doctrinaires?[11]

Jefferson and Adams--of all the Founding Fathers, those are the two Pound singled out.

If Jefferson's paradigmatic value lay in his immense personal culture, an example of the range of matters about which a civilized man concerns himself, the paradigmatic value of John Adams lay in his singular commitment to facing, articulating, and solving the tough theoretical and practical problems of making a new government, and of making that new government work. With the publication of <u>Guide to Kulchur</u> in 1938 Pound explicitly acknowledged his recognition of the special importance of John Adams in relation to Jefferson:

> The tragedy of the U. S. A. over 160 years is the decline of Adamses. More and more we cd., if we

---

[11] Pound, <u>Letters</u>, p. 319.

examined events, see that John Adams had the corrective for Jefferson.[12]

Pound does not, in the passage following that statement, go on to tell in what way he thought "that John Adams had the corrective for Jefferson." His explanation came two years later, with the publication of Cantos 62-71, the "Adams Cantos," which he based upon the ten-volume edition of the Works of John Adams edited by Charles Francis Adams,[13] and where he allowed John Adams for the most part to speak for himself.

The "Adams Cantos" constitute the most elaborate tribute, so far as I know, that has ever been accorded John Adams by a major artist. One is tempted to say that these cantos form the kind of tribute only an American artist would have wanted to make. Pound seems to have thought of his labors with the Adams material partly in this way, for he wrote to Hubert Creekmore a now-famous letter, dated simply February, 1939, in which he remarked:

> I don't have to try to be American. Merrymount, Braintree, Quincy, all I believe in or by, what had been "a plantation named Weston's."
> Vide also the host in Longfellow's "Wayside Inn." Wall ornament there mentioned still at my parents'. Am I American? Yes, and buggar the present state of the country, the utter betrayal of the American

---

[12] Ezra Pound, Guide to Kulchur (New York: New Directions, n.d.), p. 254. "Decline of the Adamses" is the title Pound gives the chapter from which this remark is taken.

[13] The Works of John Adams, ed. Charles Francis Adams, 10 vols., (Boston: Little and Brown, 1850-1856). Volume I of this edition is a biography of John Adams by the editor.

> Constitution, the filth of the Universities, and the ---- system of publication whereby you can buy Lenin, Trotsky (the messiest mutt of the lot), Stalin for 10 cents and 25 cents, and it takes <u>seven</u> years to get a set of John Adams at about 30 dollars. Van Buren's autobiog not printed till 1920.
> An Ars Poetica might in time evolve from the <u>Ta Hio</u>. Note esp. my "Mencius" in last summer's <u>Criterion</u>. And as to "am I American"; wait for Cantos <u>62/71</u> now here in rough typescript.[14]

The poet who began broadcasting on Rome Radio in 1941 his vituperative criticisms of the leadership of Franklin Roosevelt and of American involvement in World War II and for his broadcasts found himself charged with treason against the United States was the poet of the "Adams Cantos," a man who thought of himself as "American" to the bone.

The English critic G. S. Fraser has written of this portion of the <u>Cantos</u> that Pound devoted a

> long section to John Adams, the second President of the United States, and in a sense almost the father of a dynasty, as an example of what the good ruler, seeking to lay the foundations of a stable community, should be. These Adams cantos, which came out in 1940, are a great expression of American patriotism; it is tragic to think that their author, five years later, was nearly put on trial for his life for high treason.[15]

The very paradox of Pound's situation in the 1940's as described by Mr. Fraser is one reason why the content of the "Adams Cantos" would seem to deserve more than a casual glance.

The second reason for emphasizing Pound's homage to John

---

[14] Pound, <u>Letters</u>, p. 322.

[15] <u>Ezra Pound</u> (New York: Grove, 1961), p. 70.

Adams is that those who have written extended commentary on the *Cantos* have devoted relatively little attention, either hostile or favorable, specifically to the "Adams Cantos." Hugh Kenner, in his landmark study of 1951, described the function of the Adams material in this way:

> When we read in Canto LXII,
>> Routledge was elegant
> 'said nothing not hackneyed six months before'
>> wrote J. A. to his wife,
>
> it is less important to know who Routledge was and what he talked about on what occasion, than to apprehend the quality and energy of John Adams's critical mind. Impatience of platitude and exact knowledge of what <u>was</u> hackneyed six months before are qualities sufficiently rare in statesmen to justify the chisel-cut effected by these lines. The structural units in the Adams Cantos are generally very small, brief intellectual manifestations of this kind.[16]

Mr. Kenner goes on to observe that the principle which guides Pound's selection and abbreviation of passages from the works of John Adams allows Pound to achieve an intelligible pattern:

> The intended analogy is with the Confucian Analects, of which Pound, remarking 'Points define a periphery,' has noted that they 'should be considered rather as definitions of words,' as Adams' quotation defines one aspect of 'elegance.'[17]

These remarks two decades ago on the "Adams Cantos" pointed to a way of understanding that portion of the *Cantos*, but Mr. Kenner did not provide a detailed or systematic discussion of the "Adams Cantos" as a group, his book being designed to fulfill a different role.

---

[16] *The Poetry of Ezra Pound* (London: Faber, 1951), p. 219.

[17] Kenner, p. 219.

A distinctively valuable discussion of the *Cantos* appeared in 1958. Written by Clark Emery and titled *Ideas Into Action*, it remains, after more than a decade, a cogent and illuminating examination of some of the tough problems in the poem. Because Mr. Emery finds the *Cantos* on the whole to be a coherent artistic success, and because he gives more attention than is usual for Pound critics to the importance of the "Adams Cantos" in the complete poem, his reservations about the "Adams Cantos" deserve quotation:

> My objection . . . is not to the quality of the lines but to the method by which the Adams cantos are developed. They are altogether too crowded with fragments; they require too much shifting between the poem and Pound's source to become as meaningful as one would like; they lack continuity, do not flow; and there is too little variety and relief from focus upon Adams. Pound seems to have over-run limits here as (or so it seems to me) Joyce did in the question-answer sequence (pp. 650 *et seq.*) of *Ulysses*.[18]

In calling attention to the close relationship of the poem to its sources, Mr. Emery identifies the primary reason for the present study, which brings together the lines of the poem and Pound's sources in a way that permits a reader to see for himself what relationship exists between them.

However debatable the appropriateness of Mr. Emery's other observations about the "Adams Cantos," his comment concerning the relationship of the poetry to its sources was to be picked up and seconded by George Dekker five

---

[18] *Ideas into Action* (Coral Gables: Univ. of Miami Press, 1958), p. 177.

years later. After noting the usefulness of Mr. Kenner's idea that the "Adams Cantos" in a sense are analogous to the Analects of Confucius, Mr. Dekker remarked that even so, differences in the two works do not allow a very exact comparison, and he proceeded to make the same essential criticism as did Mr. Emery:

> Though clearly related to the political situation which existed during Confucius's lifetime, the problems and personalities in the Analects appear to have undergone a salutary simplification--so that they are by no means embedded in the history of a particular province during a particular period. The Adams Cantos are inevitably very different in character: they are, unmistakably, extracts from a fuller context and therefore less self-sufficient than the Analects; and they are very much embedded in the history of a particular province during a particular period.[19]

However, the larger difficulty of overall strategy in these cantos, according to Mr. Dekker, is the true indication of the basic failure of the sequence:

> Pound's problem, then, is somehow to liberate Adams from his historical context--and thus give his observations a general significance and force--but, at the same time, to reveal Adams's role in shaping American governmental policy and practice. The difficulty of such a task is manifest, and Pound does not overcome it.[20]

Largely for this reason, Mr. Dekker writes that these cantos "cannot be accepted without major reservations."[21] He does

---

[19] The Cantos of Ezra Pound (New York: Barnes and Noble, 1963), p. 184.

[20] Dekker, pp. 184-185.

[21] Dekker, p. 183.

regard the Chinese cantos (52-61), by contrast, to be a more satisfactory sequence. Mr. Dekker's criticism is relevant, but the seven pages devoted to the "Adams Cantos" do not add up to a detailed analysis.

The passage by G. S. Fraser quoted earlier suggests that he sees the "Adams Cantos" in a favorable light, but he comments on them only in a general way, and only in passing. Noel Stock, when he wrote Poet in Exile, gave one chapter to the subject of "Pound as Historian," and another to "An American Tradition," but in the first his eye is primarily on Canto 37, and at no point in the book do the "Adams Cantos" receive extended discussion.[22]

However, the same year that Poet in Exile appeared, another study of Pound was published whose dust jacket specifically advertised it as a book which "breaks new ground in comparing critically Pound's treatment of certain sources (particularly John Adams's diaries and letters in the Cantos) with their originals, and spends more time in elucidating these sources than have most previous critics of Pound." The book was Donald Davie's Ezra Pound: Poet as Sculptor,

---

[22] Poet in Exile (New York: Barnes and Noble, 1964), pp. 194-219. In a later book, Reading the Cantos (London: Routledge, 1967), Mr. Stock noted that the "Adams Cantos" sequence "is one of the most forbidding, on the face of it, but successful, in the whole work" (p. 67). Unlike Mr. Dekker, Mr. Stock finds these cantos, even with the various flaws he sees in them, more satisfactory than the Chinese cantos. He devotes less than a dozen pages to the appearance of John Adams in the Cantos, however.

one of the important Pound studies of the decade. True enough, Mr. Davie did devote three pages to the "Adams Cantos," and a little over three pages more to Pound's 1937 essay on the Jefferson-Adams correspondence.[23] But the full seven pages, taken together, still did not allow enough space for very much new ground to be broken.[24] Mr. Davie probably did not write the dust jacket description. What he did write

---

[23] *Ezra Pound: Poet as Sculptor* (New York: Oxford Univ. Press, 1964), pp. 161-167.

[24] The limited scope of Mr. Davie's investigation of the "Adams Cantos" may be suggested by his reference (p. 164) to William Vasse's article on the American history cantos (see footnote 7, above): "Cantos 52 to 71 were published early in 1940, and William Vasse, who has usefully tabulated all their numerous misspellings and apparent errors of transcription [actually Mr. Vasse lists errors only in the "Adams Cantos"], says indulgently, 'Many are of the kind to suggest a typographical error, not caught in the proofreading, perhaps because of the rush and uncertainty of things at that time.'"
  Mr. Vasse included, on p. 19 of his article, a list of names and dates in the "Adams Cantos" that an examination of the sources shows to be inaccurate. He chose not to include other kinds of textual deviations, and although he did say (p. 18) he had recorded "all instances" of errors in names and dates, a few such errors, for understandable reasons, did escape his notice. The misspelled proper names are corrected in the Edwards and Vasse *Annotated Index to the Cantos of Ezra Pound* (Berkeley: Univ. of California Press, 1959), but the *Index* does not include, except in a few instances, other textual deviations.
  One example of an uncorrected error may be found in Canto 65, line 29, on page 379 of the 1970 edition of the *Cantos*. There Pound quotes the date "17 May '83." The actual date in the sources, as a reader of this study will discover, is "17 June 1783." The other textual errors are much like this one, and although they vary in importance, none seems crucial to the overall pattern of the "Adams Cantos."
  Mr. Vasse's list is a helpful beginning, but it does not include all errors. Mr. Davie, whose book otherwise has much to recommend it, appears to have been unaware of this fact.
  For further comment on the text of the "Adams Cantos," see footnote 41, below, and Appendix B.

about the "Adams Cantos" was highly critical for the reason he gave in the following statement: "Pound's cuts and compressions and juxtapositions make a non-sensical hurly-burly of Adams's life, a life that was harried indeed but admirably purposeful."[25] Mr. Davie's discussion of the "Adams Cantos" is so limited, though, that his assertion rests upon very little demonstration.

The Influence of Ezra Pound, by K. L. Goodwin, with the particular focus suggested by its title, treats the "Adams Cantos" only in relation to what William Carlos Williams was doing in Paterson, Books II and IV, and the "Adams Cantos," even then, get only the briefest mention.[26]

In The Barb of Time, by Daniel D. Pearlman, the "Adams Cantos" fare little better. This splendid book, subtitled "on the Unity of Ezra Pound's Cantos," provides an elaborate and intelligent investigation of the Chinese cantos (52-61) which were published at the same time as the "Adams Cantos." Having finished his account of the Chinese cantos, Mr. Pearlman turns to the "Adams Cantos" and writes:

> Earlier in this chapter I discussed the Adams Cantos as a continuation of the dynastic theme of the Chinese cantos. Although the Adams Cantos are logically called for in the scheme of the poem, I feel that Pound has treated the subject in excessive detail and at disproportionate length, so that after the Chinese cantos the

---

[25] Davie, p. 163.

[26] The Influence of Ezra Pound (New York: Oxford Univ. Press, 1966), pp. 154-156.

Adams section figures as an anti-climactic bulge which even the relatively open form of the *Cantos* can ill assimilate.[27]

The result of this evaluation is that even in Mr. Pearlman's fine book, devoted wholly to the *Cantos* and to the method of exegesis, a reader will discover little more than a general summarizing commentary, on a dozen or so scattered pages, concerning the content of the "Adams Cantos."

Others have looked into the "Adams Cantos." For example, an unpublished Master's thesis written by Charles Allen Case offers, in addition to thirty-four pages of annotations of selected passages, a brief but helpful introductory discussion.[28] Still, in all, the "Adams Cantos" have yet to receive the kind of detailed attention one would think appropriate for so prominent a section of the *Cantos*.

Pound himself has clearly stated his own view of the importance of the "Adams Cantos." He wrote in a letter to Mrs. Lulu Cunningham of Hailey, Idaho: "I suppose my best book is Cantos 52/71/ and probably the one before it, ('Kulch, or Ez) Guide to Kulchur' which the publishers blush to print with its real title, is the best prose."[29] One could dismiss

---

[27] *The Barb of Time* (New York: Oxford Univ. Press, 1969), pp. 231-232.

[28] "Ezra Pound's 'Adams Cantos': A Commentary and Annotations," (unpublished master's thesis, Univ. of South Carolina, 1968).

[29] Norman, p. 375. No date for this letter is given, but Mr. Norman quotes it in a chapter titled "The 1939 Visit."

such a remark, of course, as the thoroughly predictable statement of an artist who would be foolish to say that any work other than his most recent is his best. But one cannot deny the presence of the "Adams Cantos" in the Cantos, eighty pages of eight hundred, a major part of the structure of the entire poem, though in relation to other sections of the Cantos, a comparatively unexamined part.

The third reason for calling attention to the "Adams Cantos," and perhaps the most significant reason of all, is that the very people who should have been concerned with the career of John Adams--the historians--have been demonstrably slow about devoting their labors to his story. A characteristic omission occurs in the "Preface" to A Pocket History of the United States, by Allan Nevins and Henry Steele Commager. There the authors write:

> Our mountain passes are as picturesque as feudal castles, our town meetings as majestic as royal courts, the swarming of peoples into the interior is as exciting as the expansion of the Normans or the Saracens, and our national heroes--Washington, Jefferson, Lincoln--can stand comparison with the heroes of any other people.[30]

Admittedly this book was written as a compact popular history for the layman, and in it no American statesman has very detailed consideration. Admittedly, too, if one were singling out the first rank of American statesmen from all the rest,

---

[30] A Pocket History of the United States, 5th ed., revised and enlarged (New York: Washington Square Press, 1968), vi.

or if one were reaching for the "national" heroes most easily recognized by the generality of Americans, one would surely name Washington, Jefferson, and Lincoln. Nevertheless, the fact is that a reader cannot find in this history any discussion revealing the extent of the influence John Adams exerted upon the successful resolution of many of the theoretical and practical problems faced by the nation in its early years.[31]

Certain historians themselves have remarked the neglect of John Adams. In 1957, in an important essay on John Adams, Clinton Rossiter wrote:

> I should like to make such an assessment of John Adams of Massachusetts, whose legacy to modern America has rested too long in the vaults of indifference and hostility. Adams is rarely admitted, except as an afterthought, to the inmost circle with Washington, Jefferson, Franklin, Hamilton, Marshall, Lincoln, and Lee; and even when admitted he is left standing by himself, shy and perplexing, over to one side.[32]

The list of names mentioned by Mr. Rossiter is worth noting, for when Daniel J. Boorstin in 1958 published The Americans: The Colonial Experience, he was able to cite, in his bibliography, a monumental, multi-volume biography for four of the Founders--Washington, Jefferson, Franklin, and Marshall--but

---

[31] Perhaps one should remark that Nevins and Commager, while omitting much, do give special mention to the success of John Adams in avoiding war with France in 1800 (see A Pocket History, p. 131), a matter of particular importance to John Adams himself, and to Pound in the "Adams Cantos."

[32] Clinton Rossiter, "The Legacy of John Adams," The Yale Review, 46 (1957), 528-529.

not for John Adams.[33]

By 1962 Page Smith had published his two-volume study, John Adams, a work that did meet the need for a major biography of John Adams even though it had, and has, important limitations. Like Mr. Rossiter, Mr. Smith also observed that John Adams had attracted less attention than his "distinguished contemporaries," and noted only two twentieth-century biographies, Gilbert Chinard's Honest John Adams (1933), and Catherine Drinker Bowen's John Adams and the American Revolution (1950), the second of which he called a "novelized biography."[34] The neglect of John Adams, wrote Mr. Smith, may have been partly the result of the inaccessibility of the papers of Adams prior to 1954, although he did not feel this to have been the only reason:

> But beyond the inaccessibility of the papers of John Adams there was the perhaps ultimately more important fact that Adams was an uncongenial figure during the period when America's counterparts of the "Whig historians" dominated the field of historical writing in the United States. Americans have preferred other heroes--Washington, Jefferson and Hamilton among them--to the prickly and outspoken New Englander.[35]

In view of the acknowledgement by such historians as these of the lack of recognition accorded John Adams by twentieth-

---

[33] The Americans: The Colonial Experience (New York: Vintage-Knopf, 1958), pp. 376-377.

[34] John Adams (Garden City, N. Y.: Doubleday, 1962), II, p. 1139.

[35] Smith, II, p. 1139.

century historians, it is all the more extraordinary that Ezra Pound, three decades ago, should have perceived in his own way the importance of John Adams, and created out of that perception a permanent tribute to John Adams in his Cantos, the major work of his career.

Certainly the fact of Pound's tribute to John Adams deserves to be noted, but the content of that tribute, finally, is what must concern the reader of the Cantos. The present study deals directly with the content of the "Adams Cantos," and to that matter the discussion now turns.

The most useful account of the overall pattern of the "Adams Cantos" is still to be found in William Vasse's article in the Pound Newsletter of 1955. Mr. Vasse points out that in these cantos the material "is almost invariably arranged in the same chronological sequence as in its source."[36] He goes on to describe the distribution of the Adams material in the "Adams Cantos," and one can, using this information but substituting the page numbers of the most recent edition of the Cantos for those of the edition Mr. Vasse had available, arrange his findings in the following manner:

"Adams Cantos"   The Works of John Adams
pp. 341-352   Volume I: a biography of John Adams by Charles Francis Adams, who used as his opening chapters the completed portion of a projected biography by John Quincy Adams.

---

[36] Vasse, p. 14.

"Adams Cantos"	The Works of John Adams
pp. 352-381	Volumes II, III: the diary and autobiography of John Adams, as well as an autobiographical account titled "Travels and Negotiations."
pp. 381-396	Volumes III, IV, VI: this part is "derived from Adams' political writings, from his Defense of the Constitution [sic], Discourses on Davilla [sic], and articles published in the Boston Gazette; the most comprehensive statement of Adams' political ideas is found in this section of the Adams Cantos."[37]
pp. 396-410	Volumes VII, VIII, IX: "Adams' state papers and correspondence" appear on these pages.[38]
pp. 410-421	Volumes IX, X: this portion comes "from Adams' private correspondence; this section provides a retrospective view of almost all the foregoing events as Adams reflects upon his past actions."[39]

Although Pound does present the Adams material as it appears in the normal numerical sequence of the volumes of The Works of John Adams, his presentation does not result in a single linear chronological account of the career of John Adams. The Charles Francis Adams edition of the Adams

---

[37] Vasse, p. 18. Note that Volume V, a part of the Defence of the Constitutions, is the only one of the ten volumes Pound does not draw from.

[38] Vasse, p. 18.

[39] Vasse, p. 18. I have identified the sources in the Adams material somewhat more precisely than Mr. Vasse does, and in one not very important instance I have corrected Mr. Vasse's account: the political writings of John Adams, as Pound has referred to them, run one page beyond the endpoint indicated by Mr. Vasse. But his divisions are otherwise accurate, and his descriptions of the divisions, appropriate. One should perhaps add that Pound does use material in the appendices of the various volumes, too.

material has, not unexpectedly, certain natural and inevitable repetitions in it. The biography by Charles Francis Adams (Volume I) tells of the mission of John Adams to Holland. John Adams himself deals with that mission in his diary (Volume III), in his official correspondence (Volumes VII, VIII), and in his private correspondence (Volume IX). Consequently, the numerical order of the volumes afforded Pound an excellent opportunity to develop thematic repetitions that would emphasize the crucial events in the story he had to tell. As Mr. Vasse observes:

> The same method of restatement [evident in references to John Adams's mission to Holland] is used to focus attention upon all Adams' most important activities: his defense of Captain Preston, his battles with Vergennes, his preoccupation with the construction of a constitution, his interest in a navy, his battles to save the North Atlantic fishing grounds for the United States. In the same manner those events which, in Pound's consideration, were the most important to the nation are emphasized by repetition: the Stamp Act, the writs of assistance, the Boston Massacre, the Continental Congresses, the Paris Treaty conference.[40]

This passage by Mr. Vasse is, I believe, an admirably succinct account of what Pound emphasizes in the overall pattern of the "Adams Cantos."

A reader unfamiliar with Pound's sources would have little difficulty recognizing these key episodes and events to which Pound calls attention, and such a reader, should he have some general knowledge of the history of the period if not a detailed knowledge of Pound's sources, would perceive

[40] Vasse, p. 17.

the basic clarity of the story of John Adams as Pound recounts it. But not knowing the sources, the reader cannot know in exactly what way Pound has combined the historical records and correspondence he draws upon.

For example, the reader will find in Canto 68 the following passage:

> It is certain that a loan of money is very much wanted
> affly/ to Master Johnnie
> and believe me with gt/ esteem, Sir
> B, Franklin[41]

Since the passage immediately preceding ends with mention of the signatures to a different letter, these lines appear to belong together, a reference to a single new item. An obvious function of the complimentary closing of Franklin's letter is that of indicating the formal courtesy maintained by Franklin and John Adams despite the lack of a cordial relationship between the two men during their work together in Europe. The statement concerning a loan hardly seems out of place--indeed, thematically it is certainly not out of place--so important was the problem of a loan to the various

---

[41] See page 398, lines 1-4, in the 1970 edition of the Cantos. The comma following the "B" of Franklin's name is another example of the condition the text of the American edition of the "Adams Cantos" is in. The punctuation looks like a typographical error: an abbreviation, if punctuated at all, is normally followed by a period. The English edition of The Cantos of Ezra Pound (London: Faber, 1964) does print the punctuation as a period (see page 419, line 14). Such errors as the present one and the one discussed earlier (in footnote 24, above) suggest the need for a corrected text. Additional examples in the "Adams Cantos" of textual deviations from the sources may be found in Appendix B.

American emissaries in Europe during these years. But the reader would be mistaken if he assumed that the four lines come from the same source. The first line, referring to a loan, occurs in a letter John Adams wrote to the Marquis de La Fayette on 21 February 1779. Benjamin Franklin wrote his letter to John Adams on 3 April 1779; in it he mentioned no loan whatever. In the sources this distinction is clear, but not in the poem.

Does it matter? In this instance, I believe not. The story of John Adams concerns issues and personalities, and Pound, throughout, emphasizes the issues swirling about Adams as much as he does the personalities Adams encountered. The reference to the need for a loan keeps before the reader the subject to which Pound is to devote the last half of Canto 68 and much of Canto 69: the persistent and ultimately successful efforts of John Adams to secure a loan in Holland. Here the issue is more important than the person to whom the issue is mentioned, and although a reader unfamiliar with Pound's sources would not be aware of how Pound has combined his materials in this passage, he would probably recognize, having read the earlier cantos of the sequence, the thematic relevance of the references to a loan and to the conventional courtesies appearing in Benjamin Franklin's correspondence.

In other passages, however, a familiarity with Pound's sources completes for the reader meanings that would otherwise be relatively inaccessible to him in the reading of the Poundian lines on the page. The concluding forty-four lines of Canto 70 will illustrate what I mean.[42] Perhaps the most useful approach to this discussion would be to attempt to recreate how an alert reader, having Pound's sources conveniently within reach, might experience reading such a passage.

When the reader comes upon the lines that begin this passage,

<pre>
populariser, dépopulariser
                to popularize Mr Jefferson
and dépopulariser General Washington, all on system,
</pre>

he would quite rightly suspect the appearance of the French words there to be an indication that the lines describe a French view of American domestic politics. He would not necessarily be certain, however, because, for one thing, he would know that the French were not alone in using the French language, it being the language of international diplomacy. Furthermore, the twenty-two lines immediately following make no direct reference to the French by name, and the immediately preceding line refers not to the French but to the success of John Adams in winning recognition for the United States in Holland. Still, having read through Canto 70 up to that point, he would have good reason to believe his initial suspicion correct.

---

[42] In the 1970 edition of the Cantos the concluding forty-four lines of Canto 70 begin with the passage at the top of page 412. Canto 70 itself begins on page 409.

The reader would note that, after all, Canto 70 did open with references to a series of difficult problems John Adams as President faced in dealing with the French--references sharply emphasized by the first four lines of the canto:

> 'My situation almost the only one in the world
>   where firmness and patience are useless'
>   J. A. vice-president and president of the senate
>   1791.

For nothing served John Adams, and, in consequence, his country, better than the qualities of firmness and patience which he as vice-president had found so useless, in resolving the conflict with France without war despite the contrary advice of some of his closest advisors during his term as President.

Although the reader unfamiliar with Pound's sources would probably not know that the line "set our seamen ashore at St Jago de Cuba" refers to American sailors left stranded after capture by French privateers, he would undoubtedly recognize the name Talleyrand, the mention of the notorious XYZ affair in which Talleyrand attempted to secure a bribe from the United States in return for a favorable treaty with France, and perhaps even the reference to the French rejection of Charles Cotesworth Pinckney's diplomatic mission to France in 1797, a very provocative action on the part of the French government. If the reader be at all acquainted with American domestic politics during the presidency of Adams, he would know that followers of Hamilton were not displeased at the prospect of war with France, and he would recognize the roles of two of them, McHenry and Pickering, in advising Adams on the subject. He would know, too, that the decision of Adams to assign William Vans Murray as a replacement for Pinckney at the diplomatic post in France, in spite of the opposition it received from members of Adams's own party, did bring the dispute between the two nations to a satisfactory conclusion without war.

All these references, appearing as they do on the first page of Canto 70, suggest to the reader that one major theme of Canto 70 is what could be called the "French theme": John Adams and France. In many ways John Adams defined himself as a statesman and political philosopher more by his "opposition" relationship to France than ever he did by his "opposition" relationship to England. Though his career in national affairs began when he found himself cast in the role of England's adversary and, subsequently, France's ally, Adams always thought of himself as a man of English ancestry engaged in the task of showing his English contemporaries that they had forsaken their own cherished traditions. He had no illusions whatever about the actual reasons for France's declared philanthropic interest in the American struggle for independence, realizing that to France any action leading to the dismembering of the British empire served French interests, nor did he have illusions about the limits of the "philanthropy" France was willing to extend his struggling nation. Although Adams early recognized that for necessary practical reasons France was an ally of crucial but finally limited importance to the United States in winning its independence, he nevertheless believed that France was of little or no value to his country as a model for political institutions. True enough, the opening page of Canto 70, with its repeated emphasis upon the troubles President John Adams had with France in the years 1797-1799, presents only one dimension of Adams's relationship with France, but it does make clear, beyond the shadow of a doubt, that the poet is inviting the reader to direct his attention to the role France played in the career of John Adams, and in so doing, it gives plausibility to the reader's expectation, even if he does not know Pound's sources, that the passage about "popularizing" Mr. Jefferson concerns the French. And if the reader were aware that Mr. Jefferson was at the time America's most famous Francophile, he would be all the more confirmed in his view.

Now when the reader does turn to Pound's sources, having come upon the lines

<u>populariser</u>, <u>dépopulariser</u>
                          to popularize Mr Jefferson
and <u>dépopulariser</u> General Washington, all on system,

he discovers, first of all, that his supposition is correct; the passage is taken from an evaluation by John Adams of the French view of American domestic politics:

> They [the French] consider nobody but themselves. Their apparent respect and real contempt for all men and all nations but Frenchmen, are proverbial among themselves. They think it is in their power to give

characters and destroy characters as they please, and
they have no other rule but to give reputation to their
tools, and to destroy the reputation of all who will not
be their tools. Their efforts to 'populariser'
Jefferson, and to 'dépopulariser' Washington, are all
upon this principle. To a Frenchman the most important
man in the world is himself, and the most important
nation is France. He thinks that France ought to govern
all nations, and that he ought to govern France. Every
man and nation that agrees to this, he is willing to
'populariser'; every man or nation that disputes or
doubts it, he will 'dépopulariser,' if he can.

Secondly, the reader sees that Adams's remarks appear in a letter dated 30 March 1797, a date which places the writing of this passage during Adams's term as President and thereby ties it in with the various references to the French on the canto's opening page. A further examination of Pound's sources for the canto indicates that the preceding forty-nine lines all come from correspondence written before 1783 and the lines following, running to the end of the canto, all appear in correspondence written before February of 1791. Pound, then, has introduced the quoted passage out of chronological sequence. Just how much out of sequence the passage is becomes even more clear when the reader notices that the quoted passage is not in the same volume of the Adams writings as are those of the Poundian lines surrounding it, for after line 35 of Canto 70 all the lines following are taken from material found in volume IX, with the single exception of these particular three lines, which come from a letter found in volume VIII. With the evidence of the sources before him, the reader concludes that Pound had to have chosen that place for the quoted passage: a fact suggesting that the arrangement of the material in the "Adams Cantos" is actually less random than the reader may suppose.

Placed where they are in Canto 70, what do the lines accomplish? Here extended quotation is required to show the pattern of meaning.

```
    I must be
         (whole of french policy)
      within scent of
         (merely to string us along to keep us from)
 5    the sea
         (sinking entirely, to have us strong enough for their
      purpose, but not strong enough for our own, to prevent us
      from obtaining consideration in Europe.  Hence my pleasure
            in having set up a standard in Holland.
10    populariser, dépopulariser
                 to popularize Mr Jefferson
      and dépopulariser General Washington, all on system.
                 were our interest the same as theirs
      we might better trust them, yet not entirely
15    for they do not understand even their own.
```

With the sources before him the reader sees that Pound has combined two letters of John Adams in lines 1-8 above, in counterpointing an expression of yearning on the part of Adams for certain private pleasures with his thoroughly unsentimental awareness, as a statesman with important public responsibilities, of being engaged in a difficult diplomatic contest with the French. Thus the success of John Adams's mission to Holland, mentioned next, stands not only as an important contribution to victory over England but also as an implicit diplomatic victory over France, because the consideration Adams got for the new United States in Holland was almost entirely the result of his own personal efforts and initiative, pursued in spite of French attempts to impede his labors.

Having earlier noted in the sources the dates of the remarks--lines 1-8 having been written at different times in 1782; lines 10-12 having been written in 1797; lines 13-15, in 1783--the reader now sees that the insertion of lines 10-12 out of chronological sequence emphasizes the duration of the diplomatic struggle in which Adams found France an adversary. The dates also indicate that the conflicts were not caused by disagreement with a single regime that just happened to be at odds with American interests at a certain time, for the span of fifteen years encapsulated by these dates reaches from the royalist ministry of Louis XVI to the Directory during the French Revolution, and, in Adams's own career, from his diplomatic mission at the French court to his tenure as President. The reader can follow fairly easily the thematic continuity of the direct references to France as he reads through Canto 70, but he will not know--cannot know-- the significance that emerges from the dates of the various passages until he begins to investigate Pound's sources, for Pound himself only occasionally supplies the dates of the material.

Yet the great importance of the sources for the reader of the "Adams Cantos" is finally less what the sources reveal about chronology, valuable though such information can be, than what they reveal about the thematic threads of which the sequence is woven. For example, upon turning to the sources, the reader finds that lines 13-15 above appear in a letter John Adams wrote to Arthur Lee on 12 April 1783, and he discovers, again, that if he had assumed the antecedent of the third person pronouns in those lines to be "the French," the sources prove him correct. Adams had written to Lee:

> I think, however, you cannot too soon send a minister to London to arrange finally a system of commerce, and to watch over all your interests in that country. French politics are now incessantly at work in England, and we may depend upon it they labor less for our good than their own. If our interests were the same with theirs, we might better trust them; yet not entirely, for they do not understand their own interests so well as we do ours.

Interestingly enough, the first part of the passage—the part concerning the tactical decisions of diplomacy: the same kind of concerns Pound shows Adams dealing with at the beginning of the canto—is what Pound chooses not to bring before the reader. Instead, Pound focuses on Adams's remark about the difference between American and French interests, and, more to the point, on his judgment that the French did not really understand their own interests as well as the Americans did theirs, the latter observation being edited by Pound to give exclusive attention to the French theme. The effect of Pound's choice, the reader perceives, is to elevate the French theme now to the level of the philosophical implications of political decisions, for though he still does not ignore the practical consequences of political actions, Pound clearly emphasizes John Adams's awareness of the philosophical dimension of political life in the last forty or so lines of the canto, and these lines 13-15 begin to modify the focus. Here, too, the date 1783 is not without its significance, since it places Adams's remarks about the French a scant six years before the chaos of the French Revolution, the event that provides the context of the next reference to France twenty lines later.

But before the reader gets to that passage, he will come to the line "Court as putrid as Amsterdam, divine science of politics," which keeps in view Adams's hardheaded realism in recognizing the contrast between ideal political principles and their inevitable corruption in practice. A look at the sources reveals that Pound has once more inserted material out of chronological order, evidence suggesting that he "placed" the line at that point for a reason. In the letter to James Warren, dated 17 June 1782, from which the line is taken, Adams had written:

> Perhaps you will say that the air of a Court is as putrid as that of Amsterdam. In a moral and political sense, perhaps; but I am determined that the bad morals and false politics of other people shall no longer affect my repose of mind nor disturb my physical constitution. . . .
> . . . It is, however, the real employment of a statesman to play such a game [as if nations were pieces in a game of chess] sometimes; a sublime one, truly; enough to make a man serious, however addicted to sport. Politics are the divine science, after all. How is it possible that any man should ever think of making it subservient to his own little passions and mean private interests?

The reader recognizes that Pound's compressed rendering of this passage picks up the previous reference to the importance of understanding correctly what one's true political interests are by calling attention to the lofty concept John Adams had of the deeper meanings of political life, meanings that, in his view, require diligent study from the man who would comprehend them. Thus the line sets up the collocation that follows of Adams's insistence that few people really want to study the meanings of political matters with his observation about the actual French experience with constitution-making during their Revolution.

This juxtaposition is clear in the Poundian lines, which include, in this instance, the date of the letter from which they come, making it perfectly obvious that Adams is talking about the France of the Revolution:

> 'Their constitution, experiment, I KNOW
> that France can not be long governed by it.'
>   To Price, 19 April 1790
> aim of my life has been to be useful, how small in
> any nation the number who comprehend ANY
> system of constitution or administration
>   and these few do not unite.

Significantly, like Edmund Burke who published his criticism of the French Revolution, <u>Reflections</u> <u>on</u> <u>the</u> <u>Revolution</u> <u>in</u> <u>France</u>, in November of 1790, before the Terror, before anyone really had clear evidence of how badly wrong the Revolution was to go, John Adams also found himself very early expressing objections to the drift of the French revolutionary enterprise. But what is it about the French constitution that has convinced Adams, with the French Revolution but nine months old, that France could not be governed by it? The reader, based on his recollection of Adams's ideas on government in his <u>Defence</u>, found in Cantos 67 and 68, may shrewdly deduce the answer to that question, but whether he does or not, he finds, when he turns to the sources, that here the sources explicitly complete the meaning of the Poundian lines:

> The constitution [of France] is but an experiment, and must and will be altered. I know it to be impossible that France should be long governed by it. If the sovereignty is to reside in one assembly, the king, princes of the blood, and principal quality, will govern it at their pleasure as long as they can agree; when they differ, they will go to war, and act over again all the tragedies of Valois, Bourbons, Lorraines, Guises, and Colignis, two hundred years ago. . . .
> I thank you, Sir, for your kind compliment. As it has been the great aim of my life to be useful, if I had any reason to think I was so, as you seem to suppose, it would make me happy. . . . It is incredible how small is the number, in any nation, of those who comprehend any system of constitution or administration, and those few it is wholly impossible to unite.

In fact, the reader discovers that an investigation of Pound's sources becomes all the more essential as he confronts the concluding ten lines of Canto 70 which further fuse together the concern for careful study of political institutions with the example of political practices in France during the Revolution.

Before the poet sounds again these two notes, he gives John Adams a chance to affirm his own most fundamental principle of government: "I am for balance." Beside that statement Pound places the Chinese ideogram for "pivot," an ideogram whose pictorial effect is to assert the presence of "balance." This ideogram, the only one in the canto, like those in the other cantos of the sequence, reminds the reader that Pound believes John Adams to have been a governor-statesman in the Confucian tradition. Beyond the significance of having Adams's statement here brought together with the ideogram, the reader must turn to Pound's sources to see how directly that statement connects with the earlier lines about the French constitution:

> I am for a balance between the legislative and executive powers, and I am for enabling the executive to be at all times capable of maintaining the balance between the Senate and House, or in other words, between the aristocratical and democratical interests.

Once more the date of the letter to Benjamin Rush in which these remarks occur, 1790, establishes the French Revolution present in the background.

When the reader examines in the sources the passage from which the next lines are taken,

> and know not how it is but mankind have an aversion
>   to any study of government,

he then realizes how carefully Pound has pulled together his various thematic threads--the need to study government, the principle of government that Adams felt such study would reveal, and the evidence that the French leaders have failed to undertake such study:

> I know not how it is, but mankind have an aversion to the study of the science of government. Is it because the subject is dry? To me, no romance is more entertaining. Those who take the lead in revolutions are seldom well-informed, and they commonly take more pains to inflame their own passions and those of society, than to discover truth; and very few of those who have just ideas have the courage to pursue them.

But John Adams was too astute an observer of human behavior during his public career to believe the French unique in neglecting to give the study of government the attention it deserves, and Pound, who often found himself no less critical of his countrymen than John Adams sometimes was, carefully prevents the formation of any such impression when next he picks up the French theme.

The reader unfamiliar with Pound's sources, however, will more than likely read right over the next appearance of the French theme without recognizing it at all, for the line "nec lupo committere agnum," out of context, is surely one of the most puzzling lines in the canto. Even when the reader translates the Latin--"nor entrust a lamb to a wolf"--he still does not know, without considering the passage from which Pound took the line, exactly what subject the line focuses. A look at Pound's sources identifies its link with the French theme:

> In this country the pendulum has vibrated too far to the popular side, driven by men without experience or judgment, and horrid ravages have been made upon property by arbitrary multitudes or majorities of multitudes. France has severe trials to endure from the same cause. Both have found, or will find, that to place property at the mercy of a majority who have no property, is '<u>committere agnum lupo</u>.' My fundamental maxim of government is, never to trust the lamb to the custody of the wolf.

Having read that passage (from a letter John Adams wrote Thomas Brand-Hollis on 11 June 1790), the reader once more sees convincing evidence of the care with which the poet has selected and arranged his materials. The reference to the importance of property in the above passage reminds the reader of an earlier line in Canto 70: "power follows balance of land." When the reader turns to the source for that line, he discovers there a superb statement of a concept which Adams had learned from James Harrington's <u>Oceana</u> (1656) and which, to Adams, was fundamental to stable political order:

> Harrington has shown that power always follows property. This I believe to be as infallible a maxim in politics, as that action and reaction are equal, is in mechanics. Nay, I believe we may advance one step farther, and affirm that the balance of power in a society, accompanies the balance of property in land. The only possible way, then, of preserving the balance of power on the side of equal liberty and public virtue, is to make the acquisition of land easy to every member of society; to make a division of the land into small quantities so that the multitude may be possessed of landed estates. If the multitude is possessed of the balance of real estate, the multitude will have the balance of power, and in that case the multitude will take care of the liberty, virtue, and interest of the multitude, in all acts of government.

In this passage from a letter John Adams wrote to James Sullivan on 26 May 1776--the date gives an idea of how early in his career John Adams was committed to principles he enunciated in correspondence with Brand-Hollis fourteen years later--the various references to balance--balance of power, balance of property--direct the reader's attention back to the line with the Chinese ideogram at the end of the canto, and thus enlarge the concept of "balance" that Adams explains in the letter from which Pound excerpted the statement: "I am for balance."

As Pound concludes the canto, he again focuses on Adams's sobering judgment that few people desire to do what Adams himself had been willing to do in reading Harrington, for example--that is, undertake the kind of study of governments necessary to give an individual knowledge of a sound concept of government:

> But, as you observe, the feelings of mankind are so much against any rational theory [of government], that I find my labor [in writing the <u>Defence</u>] has all been in vain, and it is not worth while to take any more pains upon the subject.

That passage, the source of the line "so they are against any rational theory," indicates that at the time of writing, 23 January 1791, Adams was explaining to John Trumbull why he thought it unnecessary for him to devote any additional time to his <u>Defence</u>. In Pound's poem the reference to a passage concerning the <u>Defence</u> has the additional function of completing the French theme in the canto, for, the reader will remember, Adams wrote <u>A Defence of the Constitutions of Government of the United States of America</u> in reply to an attack by Turgot, one of the men whose thought later influenced the French Revolution, upon Adams's idea of balance--what we have come to call "checks and balances"--in government.

One further observation seems appropriate: although the French theme in the canto ends on a note of melancholy, at the conclusion of the canto itself Pound has John Adams express an emphatic personal affirmation. The final two references to the French theme in Canto 70 are framed by the lines "DUM SPIRO/ . . . DUM SPIRO AMO," meaning "while

I breathe/ . . . while I breathe, I love." These lines effectively place in perspective Adams's acknowledgement of the essential quality that can survive even if an individual suffers public disappointments: in this context, the apparent failure of his <u>Defence</u> to interest people in the study of government so important, to Adams, in achieving a stable civic order. The lines have unusual significance because they state the position Pound himself is to come to eight years later in the <u>Pisan Cantos</u>, most notably in the eloquent lyric conclusion of Canto 81:

> What thou lovest well remains,
>   the rest is dross
> What thou lov'st well shall not be reft from thee
> What thou lov'st well is thy true heritage.

The paradigmatic value of the career of John Adams consists of more than the political story alone.

    I have gone into some detail in discussing the French theme of Canto 70 to illustrate how a knowledge of Pound's sources contributes to a reader's understanding of the "Adams Cantos." Even an alert reader of these cantos would miss certain of the poet's uses of chronology and, perhaps more importantly, would miss the poet's development of themes in lines and passages with submerged connections that become visible upon an examination of the sources. The sources help make better sense out of the sense already there, in the Poundian lines. This kind of elaborate study of each one of the "Adams Cantos" lies beyond the province of the present book. However, I have begun a companion volume which will offer just such a study of the individual cantos in the sequence.

This present study has two purposes. The first purpose is to identify the passages throughout the ten-volume Works of John Adams that Pound has abbreviated, edited, or referred to in the "Adams Cantos." The textual material in the ten volumes runs to nearly six thousand pages, and Pound has selected from and abbreviated this material to produce eighty pages of poetry. Nearly all of the more than 2500 lines that make up the "Adams Cantos" have a clearly recognizable source, identifiable by volume and page number, in the Works of John Adams. This study allows a reader to go to the Works and locate, with a minimum of search, the source of any specific line. Only a handful of exceptions exist.

The second purpose is to quote the exact passage--sentence or paragraph--from which Pound has taken the lines of the "Adams Cantos," so that a reader, without having to have a set of the ten-volume Works of John Adams at hand, can see just how Pound has used the material he was working with.

Although not an interpretive study, an unavoidable problem of interpretation did appear in bringing the source material together. My basic idea was to place the Poundian lines back into the smallest possible word unit that would suggest the original context. But what was the smallest possible word unit? For the sake of consistency, I have chosen to quote at least the complete sentence from which the Poundian line has been taken, and in virtually all instances I have observed this practice. There are exceptions. For example, where John Adams recorded in his diary whole conversations in one long sentence, using the semi-colon to connect clause after clause, I have quoted the relevant clauses and not the entire sentence.

Many times the single sentence from which Pound had taken some part simply did not adequately contain enough of the context to stand by itself. Occasionally the problem was that of picking up a pronoun antecedent in an earlier sentence. Where possible, I have inserted the appropriate identification, in brackets, within the quotation, but frequently the easiest procedure has been to quote the earlier sentence (or sentences) leading to what Pound has used in addition to that particular sentence itself.

In certain instances the source of the Poundian line is a passage whose significance would not be clear without extensive quotation. A good example is the source of the line "des Noailles 18 million louis a year from the crown" that appears in Canto 65. Pound takes this line from John Adams's account of the family to which the young Marquis de La Fayette belonged. This family, des Noailles, was famous for, among other things, its unusual sense of commitment to service on behalf of what might be called the "public good," and Adams describes how La Fayette, in serving with Washington, was continuing a venerable family tradition. The Poundian line leads back to that account but does not contain it, although once a reader sees what lies behind the line it takes on greater meaning. The long quotation provides the full context.

In determining all citations, long and short, I have been guided by my own judgment of what would be the smallest possible word unit necessary to suggest the original context of the Poundian line, always preferring too full, rather than too brief, a quotation. Still, deciding the length of a citation is a matter of interpretation, and doubtless on occasion a reader will disagree with my choices. I have identified the location of each citation at the end of the quoted passage. Any interested reader with a question should consult, as a check on both the "Adams Cantos" and the present work, the actual passage in the Works of John Adams for himself.

A word about format. All page numbers given at the top left margin refer to the pages of the "Adams Cantos" as printed in the 1970 New Directions edition of The Cantos of Ezra Pound.

The numbers in parentheses on the left side of the page refer to the lines on that particular page of the "Adams Cantos" identified at the top left margin. No edition of the Cantos has been published with line numbers. For that reason I have numbered the lines from top to bottom of each page, always starting again at line number one on each new page. For the sake of consistency I have counted each word printed on a separate line as a line of its own, and have numbered it accordingly.

The basic source of the "Adams Cantos," *The Works of John Adams*, edited by Charles Francis Adams, I have abbreviated throughout the following pages as *WJA*, with volume and page numbers after.

The writings of John Adams, done in a variety of circumstances for a number of different reasons, reveal that he seldom missed an opportunity to record his observations or those of people with whom he associated. He kept a diary; he kept notes of the debates of the Continental Congress. For newspapers he wrote controversial papers on behalf of the cause of independence, signing his name now as "Novanglus," now as "Clarendon." In correspondence he was a tireless explainer, here and abroad, of the patriot cause and of the concept of government which he believed gave the best hope for a stable public order. The latter concern led him finally to write his major work, *A Defence of the Constitutions of Government of the United States*, his answer, in three volumes, to an attack by Turgot (who preferred a simple central authority) upon the idea of a distribution of governmental power through a system of checks and balances, which idea Adams had labored so hard to see incorporated in the new state constitutions. He wrote an account of his European diplomatic missions; he wrote an autobiography. All these writings come together to tell one story: the commitment of John Adams to the survival and success of the new nation he had helped create.

I could have identified all citations by volume and page number alone. But that arrangement would have inadequately reflected not only the pattern and order of John Adams's life as a whole, but also the number of separate occasions on which Adams found himself sorting and evaluating meanings of experiences in relation to his larger commitments. Because Charles Francis Adams, in editing the Adams writings, inserts extracts from the correspondence, or from the autobiography, or whatever, at places where the added material might throw another light on the particular event or episode at hand, one often finds before him more than a single perspective of the same event when he confronts the view of John Adams at the time, and of John Adams in retrospect. Therefore, to emphasize the separateness of the entries, I have given, along with volume and page number, the specific source from among the Adams papers, as indicated by Charles Francis Adams.

An unavoidable clutter tends to result from providing so much identification. To minimize the clutter, I have abbreviated, in the following manner, some of the titles of the separate writings of John Adams that Pound has drawn from.

D. "Diary."

Notes/Debates — "Notes of Debates in the Continental Congress, in 1775 and 1776."

Travels/Negotiations — "Travels and Negotiations": see WJA, III, headnote p. 89.

Dissertation — "A Dissertation on the Canon and Feudal Law," printed in the Boston Gazette in August of 1765.

Instructions — "Instructions of the Town of Braintree to their Representative, 1765," printed in the Boston Gazette of 14 October 1765.

Clarendon — "The Earl of Clarendon to William Pym," a series of articles written by John Adams in answer to papers published in the London Evening Post in August of 1765 and in the Boston Evening Post the following November, in support of the Loyalist cause, and signed with the name William Pym. The Boston Gazette published Adams's articles in January of 1766.

Winthrop — "Governor Winthrop to Governor Bradford," articles written by John Adams and printed in the Boston Gazette in January and February of 1767, concerning, among other things, whether or not a ruler has the right to decide the legality of elections.

Boston Instructions — "Instructions of the Town of Boston to their Representatives, 17 June, 1768; 15 May, 1769."

Judiciary — See WJA, III, pp. 513ff. In the controversy over the independence of the judiciary, John Adams, replying to papers by William Brattle published in the Massachusetts Gazette, contributed a series of papers in January and February of 1773 to the Boston Gazette. Charles Francis Adams has brought these papers together here under the title "Independence of the Judiciary."

Thoughts/ Government	"Thoughts on Government: Applicable to the Present State of the American Colonies," the famous letter John Adams wrote at the request of George Wythe in January of 1776 and later that year printed by John Dunlap of Philadelphia.
Defence	*A Defence of the Constitutions of Government of the United States of America, Against the Attack of M. Turgot, in His Letter to Dr. Price, Dated the Twenty-Second Day of March, 1778*, written by John Adams in three volumes in the years 1786-1787, in defence of the various state constitutions and not of the federal constitution, which did not exist at the time of writing.
Davila	*Discourses on Davila: A Series of Papers on Political History*, begun by John Adams in 1788 while he was Vice-President of the United States and first published at Philadelphia in the *Gazette of the United States* as a sequel to his *Defence*.
Twenty-Six Letters	"Twenty-Six Letters upon Interesting Subjects Respecting the Revolution of America," letters written at the request of Mr. Calkoen, a prominent Amsterdam lawyer, by John Adams in 1780 while he was in Holland, to explain the cause of independence in America.
L.	All correspondence is abbreviated L. (letter) with the correspondents' names following.

The one indispensible reference work for anyone studying the *Cantos* is the *Annotated Index to the CANTOS of Ezra Pound: Cantos I-LXXXIV*, edited by John Hamilton Edwards and William W. Vasse. In this book a reader will find all of the proper names appearing in the "Adams Cantos" identified, all the foreign words and phrases translated, and the Chinese ideograms explained. The book also contains a chronology of important dates that relate to or appear in the Cantos, including the "Adams Cantos." For references to this work I have used the abbreviation Index.

LIST OF WORKS CITED

Adams, John. *The Works of John Adams*. Ed. with a biography and notes by Charles Francis Adams. 10 vols. Boston: Little and Brown, 1850-1856.

Boorstin, Daniel J. *The Americans: The Colonial Experience*. Vintage Paperbacks. New York: Knopf, 1958.

Case, Charles Allen. "Ezra Pound's 'Adams Cantos': A Commentary and Annotations." Unpublished master's thesis. Univ. of South Carolina, 1968.

Davie, Donald. *Ezra Pound: Poet as Sculptor*. New York: Oxford Univ. Press, 1964.

Dekker, George. *The Cantos of Ezra Pound*. New York: Barnes and Noble, 1963.

de Rachewiltz, Mary. "Ezra Pound at Eighty." *Esquire*, April 1966, pp. 115-116; 178-180.

Edwards, John Hamilton, and William W. Vasse, eds. *Annotated Index to the Cantos of Ezra Pound: Cantos I-LXXXIV*. Berkeley and Los Angeles: Univ. of California Press, 1959.

Emery, Clark. *Ideas into Action*. Coral Gables: Univ. of Miami Press, 1958.

Fraser, G. S. *Ezra Pound*. New York: Grove Press, 1961.

Goodwin, K. L. *The Influence of Ezra Pound*. New York: Oxford Univ. Press, 1966.

Kenner, Hugh. *The Poetry of Ezra Pound*. London: Faber, 1951.

Nevins, Allan, and Henry Steele Commager. *A Pocket History of the United States*. 5th ed., revised and enlarged. New York: Washington Square Press, 1968.

Norman, Charles. *Ezra Pound*. Revised ed. New York: Funk and Wagnalls, 1969.

Pearlman, Daniel D. *The Barb of Time: On the Unity of Ezra Pound's Cantos*. New York: Oxford Univ. Press, 1969.

Pound, Ezra. *The Cantos of Ezra Pound*. New York: New Directions, 1970.

_____. *The Cantos of Ezra Pound*. London: Faber, 1964.

_____. *Guide to Kulchur*. New York: New Directions, n.d.

_____. "The Jefferson-Adams Letters as a Shrine and a Monument." *Impact: Essays on Ignorance and the Decline of American Civilization*. Ed. Noel Stock. Chicago: Regnery, 1960.

_____. *Jefferson and/or Mussolini: L'Idea Statale Fascism as I Have Seen It*. London: Stanley Nott, 1935.

_____. *The Letters of Ezra Pound*. Ed. D. D. Paige. New York: Harcourt, 1950.

Rossiter, Clinton. "The Legacy of John Adams." *The Yale Review*, 46 (1957), 528-550.

Smith, Page. *John Adams*. 2 vols. Garden City, N. Y.: Doubleday, 1962.

Stock, Noel. *Poet in Exile*. New York: Barnes and Noble, 1964.

_____. *Reading the Cantos*. London: Routledge, 1967.

Vasse, William. "American History and the Cantos." *The Pound Newsletter*, No. 5, ed. John Hamilton Edwards (Department of English, Univ. of California at Berkeley, January, 1955), pp. 13-19.

THE SOURCES

CANTO LXII

p. 341

(1-5) "Hence if it should turn out that he has fallen into any essential error, or been guilty of material injustice, he trusts that he may be acquitted of evil intention in the beginning, or inclination to persevere in it against evidence. Should any such be shown to him, he stands ready to acknowledge it with candor and to correct it with cheerfulness.

". . . This [effect of new material to rectify impressions of earlier events] is particularly true in regard to the motives of action, which governed the policy of the great nations of Europe during the Revolution, as well as to those which controlled the course of Mr. Adams's own administration afterwards." ("Preface," C. F. Adams, WJA, I, vi-vii)

(6-11) "The first charter of the Colony of Massachusetts Bay was granted by Charles the First, and bears date the 4th of March, in the fourth year of his reign, 1629. It recites letters-patent of James the First, dated 3 November, in the eighteenth year of his reign, 1620, granting to the Council established at Plymouth, in the county of Devon, for the planting, ruling, ordering, and governing of New England, in America, all that part of America, from latitude 40° to 48°,

p. 341 (cont.)

and through the main lands from sea to sea. Then, that the Plymouth Council, by deed indented 19 March, 1628, conveyed to Sir Henry Rosewell, Sir John Young, knights, Thomas Southcott, John Humphrey, John Endicott, and Symon Whetcomb, their heirs and associates forever, all that part of New England, lying between three miles south of Charles, and three miles north of Merrimack rivers. Charles, therefore, at the petition of the grantees, and of others whom they had associated unto them, grants to them the same lands, and constitutes them a body <u>corporate</u> <u>politique</u>, in fact and name, by the name of the Governor and Companie of the Massachusetts Bay in New England.

"Among the grantees of this charter is a person by the name of THOMAS ADAMS." (<u>WJA</u>, I, p. 3)

(12) "John Winthrop was elected governor [at meeting of 20 October 1629], John Humphrey, deputy-governor, and eighteen assistants; of whom Thomas Adams was the last." (<u>WJA</u>, I, p. 4)

(13) Pound's comment.

(14) "The petition of the inhabitants of Mount Wollaston was voted, and granted them to be a town, according to the agreement with Boston, and the town is to be called Braintree." (<u>WJA</u>, I, p. 5)

p. 341 (cont.)

(15)   "Hutchinson says that, in 1625, one Captain Wollaston, with about thirty persons, began a plantation near Weston's, which had been abandoned; that no mention is made of a patent to Wollaston; that Morton changed the name of Mount Wollaston to Merry Mount; and that the people of Plymouth seized him, to send him to England." (WJA, I, p. 4)

(16)   "In the records of the town of Boston, the following entry occurs:--

"'24th day, 12th month, 1640. Granted to Henry Adams, for ten heads, forty acres, upon the same covenant of three shillings per acre.'" (WJA, I, p. 5, n. 3)

(17)   "By the records of the town of Braintree, it appears that this Henry Adams was buried on the 8th of October, 1646." (WJA, I, p. 6)

(17-19) "The brewery was probably commenced by the first Henry. It was continued by his son, Joseph, and formed the business of his life. At the age of twenty-four he married a wife of sixteen, and at his decease, after a lapse of more than forty years, left the malting establishment to his youngest son." (WJA, I, p. 11)

(20)   "John Adams, born 19 October, 1735." (WJA, I,

p. 341 (cont.)

p. 12) The inscription on the marble tablet at the tomb of John Adams records his birth date as $\frac{19}{30}$ October, 1735. (<u>WJA</u>, I, p. 643)

(21)   "His condition, as the teacher of a school [a grammar-school in Worcester, 1755], was not and could not be a permanent establishment. Its emoluments gave but a bare and scanty subsistence." (<u>WJA</u>, I, p. 22)

(22)   "The Calvinistic doctrines of election, reprobation, and the atonement are so repulsive to human reason that they can never obtain the assent of the mind, but through the medium of the passions; and the master passion of orthodoxy is <u>fear</u>. Calvinism has no other agent." (<u>WJA</u>, I, p. 39)

(23-26) "'I perceived very clearly, as I thought, that the study of theology, and the pursuit of it as a profession, would involve me in endless altercations, and make my life miserable, without any prospect of doing any good to my fellow-men.'" (<u>WJA</u>, I, p. 42)

(27)   "The ground which, from his first introduction to public life, he took in the controversy between the colonies and Great Britain, was that the Parliament could not lawfully tax the colonies. His whole soul was in the cause. But to

p. 341 (cont.)

him it was not less the cause of order and of justice than of liberty." (WJA, I, p. 80)

(28)   "Yet Burke and Gibbon, the finest minds of their age, though differing in almost every thing else, have concurred in presenting to posterity, in the most attractive forms, the public men of these times as belonging in the front rank of British statesmen. Such a beautifier of imperfect figures is the illusive mirror of national pride!" (WJA, I, p. 92)

(29-32)   "His [Lord North's] voice turned the scale in favor of the policy pursued, so that on him, next to George the Third, must the greatest share of responsibility for what followed, rest. It was the same middle path, the perpetual resource of second-rate statesmen, which his Rockingham predecessors had equally tried to tread. [Lord North had argued that the duty on paper, paint, and glass, products of British industry, should be repealed so that their sale might be promoted. But tea, he argued, was another matter.] . . . 'But with tea, the case is different. It is not produced within the British islands. The London factor has no interest in it beyond the charges of forwarding it from the producer to the consumer, both out of the limits of Great Britain. The tax falls on them; and, being collected from

p. 341 (cont.)

the colonists, may very properly become a source of revenue, out of which the officers of their governments, civil and judicial, can be made, in pursuance of the original design, to derive a support wholly independent of their good-will.'" (WJA, I, p. 94) The word tcha in line 31 and the Chinese ideogram both mean "tea." (Index, p. 271)

p. 342

(1-2)   "Such was the exposition made by the new premier, purblind to the rights of a continent, whilst he applied a microscope to the interests of a few hundred manufacturers and merchants of London." (WJA, I, p. 95)

(3-8)   "Still less had the premier imagined that whilst he was calmly assuring his followers of the approaching dispersion of further opposition, events were happening which marked significantly enough the fact that the eyes of the American colonist no longer saw in the British soldier either a brother in arms, or a protector of his hearthstone. To be sure, the town of Boston in New England, relatively to the densely populated metropolis on the Thames, was but a speck. Scarcely sixteen thousand souls could be counted within its limits, and the times had not, for many years, favored an increase. . . . Whatever restraints had been put upon their trade by the mother country, in pursuance of the

p. 342 (cont.)

selfish commercial theories of that age, had been observed where there had been no temptation to break through them, and tacitly set aside where their interests had prompted a different course. And this had been done so long with impunity, that habits of mind favorable to entire personal freedom had been formed even among a large class who seldom get so far as to an analysis of principles." (WJA, I, pp. 95-96)

(9-12) "At about nine o'clock of the night on which Lord North declared himself impassible to menace, a single sentry was slowly pacing his walk before the door of the small custom-house in King Street, then, as ever since, the commercial centre of the town of Boston. It was moonlight, and a light coating of fresh snow had just been added to the surface of the ground, commonly covered at that time of the year with the condensed remnants of the winter's ice. There had been noise and commotion in the streets, particularly in Cornhill, now Washington Street, and at Murray's barracks, in what is now Brattle Street, where the twenty-ninth regiment was stationed." (WJA, I, p. 97)

(12-17) "In this case, it was a barber's boy whose thoughtless impertinence opened the floodgates of passion in the town. The resentment of the sentinal and the complaints

p. 342 (cont.)

of the boy drew the attention of stragglers, on the watch for causes of offence, to the soldier's isolated condition, which soon brought his fears to the point of calling upon his comrades for support. A corporal and six men of the guard, under the direction of Captain Preston, came to his relief, and ranged themselves in a semi-circle in front of his post. The movement could not take place without exciting observation, the effect of which was the collection around them of forty or fifty of the lower order of town's people, who had been roving the streets armed with billets of wood until they began to gather around the main-guard, scarcely averse to the prospect of a quarrel. . . . This was the first protest against the application of force to the settlement of a question of right. This comparatively slight disturbance, going on by the peaceful light of the moon in a deserted street of an obscure town, was the solution of the problem which had been presented on the same night to the selected representatives of the nation, assembled in one of the ancient and populous and splendid capitals of the world." (WJA, I, p. 98)

(18) "So fatal a precision of aim, indicating not a little malignity, though it seems never to have attracted notice, is one of the most singular circumstances attending the affray." (WJA, I, p. 99)

p. 342 (cont.)

(19)   Pound's comment.

(20-22) "Five men fell mortally wounded, two of them receiving two balls each. Six more were wounded, one of whom, a gentleman, standing at his own door, observing the scene, received two balls in his arm. . . . The drops of blood then shed in Boston were like the dragon's teeth of ancient fable--the seeds, from which spring up the multitudes who would recognize no arbitration but the deadly one of the battle-field." (<u>WJA</u>, I, p. 99)

(23-24) "It was not as a politician, but as a lawyer, that John Adams was first drawn into public life. The patriotic party stood in need of a legal adviser at all times, but never more than now, that they were summoned to contend with the shrewdness and the skill of [Governor] Hutchinson, just transferred from the highest judicial to the highest civil post of the province. . . . Be this as it may, the fact is certain that, from this date, whether in or out of public station, John Adams was looked to as a guide in those measures in which questions involving professional knowledge were to be discussed with the authorities representing the crown." (<u>WJA</u>, I, p. 107)

(25-26) "Somewhere about 1740, Colonel Bladen, a member

p. 342 (cont.)

of the board of trade and plantations, had seen, in the form then practised, beginning, 'Be it enacted by the Governor, Council, and House of Representatives <u>in General Court assembled, and by authority of the same</u>,' words of fear to the prerogative of the monarch of Great Britain. So he obtained an order, to be placed in the standing instructions of the governor, that the ominous terms should henceforward no longer appear. And they had been accordingly disused until now, when the House had revived them." (WJA, I, p. 108)

(27) "One [committee on which John Adams served] was directed to mature a plan for the encouragement of arts, agriculture, manufactures, and commerce, to be reported at the next session." (WJA, I, p. 109)

(28) "'I have endeavored,' he said, 'to produce the best authorities, and to give you the rules of law in their words; for I desire not to advance any thing of my own.'" (WJA, I, p. 112) Lines 28-35, p. 342, and lines 1-14, p. 343, all deal with John Adams's defence of Captain Preston and the British soldiers following the Boston "massacre."

(29-35) "'If Heaven, in its anger, shall ever permit the time to come when, by means of an abandoned ad-
p. 343   ministration at home, and the outrages of the
(1-2)   soldiery here, the bond of parental affection

p. 343 (cont.)

and filial duty between Britain and the colonies shall be dissolved, when we shall be shaken loose from the shackles of the common law and our allegiance, and reduced to a state of nature, the American and British soldier must fight it out upon the principles of the law of nature and of nations. . . . Till then, however, we must try causes in the tribunals of justice, by the law of the land. . . .

"'. . . If an assault was made to endanger their lives, the law is clear; they [British soldiers] had a right to kill in their own defence. If it was not so severe as to endanger their lives, yet if they were assaulted at all, struck and abused by blows of any sort, by snowballs, oyster-shells, cinders, clubs, or sticks of any kind, this was a provocation, for which the law reduces the offence of killing down to manslaughter, in consideration of those passions in our nature which cannot be eradicated.'" (WJA, I, p. 113)

(2-3)   Pound's comment.

(4)   "They [the two soldiers found guilty of manslaughter] immediately prayed for the benefit of clergy, according to the old forms of the English law, which was at once granted; and having been publicly burnt in the hand, agreeably to the sentence pronounced by the court, they were, likewise, suffered to depart." (WJA, I, p. 114)

p. 343 (cont.)

(5-8)   Pound's comment.

(9-10)   "'The law, in all vicissitudes of government, fluctuations of the passions, or flights of enthusiasm, will preserve a steady undeviating course. It will not bend to the uncertain wishes, imaginations, and wanton tempers of men.'" (<u>WJA</u>, I, p. 113)

(11)   "'"The law [in the words of Algernon Sidney] no passion can disturb. 'Tis void of desire and fear, lust and anger. 'Tis <u>mens sine affectu</u>, written reason, retaining some measure of the divine perfection."'" (<u>WJA</u>, I, p. 114) The Latin phrase <u>mens sine affectu</u> means "a mind without feeling (passion)." (<u>Index</u>, p. 142)

(12-14)   Pound's comment.

(15)   "'Bad laws,' said Burke of his own country, Great Britain, 'are the worst sort of tyranny. In such a country as this, they are of all bad things the worst; worse, by far, than anywhere else; and they derive a particular malignity even from the wisdom and soundness of the rest of our institutions.'" (<u>WJA</u>, I, pp. 120-121)

(16-17)   "It [the written reply of uncertain authorship to

p. 343 (cont.)

Governor Hutchinson's speech about obligatory allegiance to Britain] disputed the right, thus far generally conceded in Christendom, of seizing the lands occupied by the heathen, by virtue of authority vested in the head of the Catholic Church, and granting them to any Christian monarch whose subjects might be the first to discover them." (WJA, I, pp. 121-122)

(17-20) "'If our government be considered as merely feudatory, we are subject to the king's absolute will, and there is no authority of Parliament, as the sovereign authority of the British empire.'" (WJA, I, p. 126)

(21-23) "'"Every subject is presumed by law to be sworn to the king, which is to his natural person," says Lord Coke. "The allegiance is due to his natural body;" and he says: "In the reign of Edward the Second, the Spencers, the father and the son, to cover the treason hatched in their hearts, invented this damnable and damned opinion, that homage and oath of allegiance was more by reason of the king's crown, that is, of his politic capacity, than by reason of the person of the king; upon which opinion, they inferred execrable and detestable consequents." The judges of England, all but one, in the case of the union between Scotland and England, declared that "allegiance followeth

p. 343 (cont.)

the natural person, not the politic," and "to prove the allegiance to be tied to the body natural of the king, and not to the body politic, the Lord Coke cited the phrases of divers statutes mentioning our natural liege sovereign."'" (WJA, I, pp. 127-128)

(24) "'The question appears to us to be no other than whether we are subjects of absolute unlimited power, or of a free government formed on the principles of the English constitution.'" (WJA, I, p. 129)

(25) "The mercantile and manufacturing temper of Great Britain regarded the people of the colonies not as friends and brethren, but as strangers who might be made tributaries." (WJA, I, p. 132)

(26-27) "'I see,' said the judge [Trowbridge] to him [John Adams], 'you are determined to explore the constitution, and bring to life all its dormant and latent powers, in defence of your liberties, as you understand them.' To which he replied, that 'he should be very happy if the constitution could carry them safely through all their difficulties, without having recourse to higher powers not written.' It was doubtless in this spirit that his advice was taken by his friends, and the necessary measures accordingly prepared, by

p. 343 (cont.)

which to present Peter Oliver, chief justice of the superior court, guilty of high crimes and misdemeanors, as set forth in the proper forms of impeachment. The result was, that they were adopted by a vote of ninety-two members of the House against only eight dissentients." (<u>WJA</u>, I, pp. 138-139)

(28-29) Pound's statement of the quarrel over the independence of the judiciary. See the following passage: "But although the man [Oliver] was about to be removed, it was by no means clear that the absolute system which he had contributed to introduce would not become gradually confirmed by time. The judges of the superior court had betrayed no reluctance to the proposed change of the source of their emoluments from an uncertain and capricious legislature assembly to the steady patronage of the crown." (<u>WJA</u>, I, pp. 135-136; see also pp. 116-118)

(30) "When those who had been drawn to act as jurymen were summoned to qualify in the usual form, not a man could be found to consent. Each individual, as his name was called, assigned as his reason for declining, that the presiding officer, having been charged with high crimes and misdemeanors in office, by the legislative power of the province, could not be recognized as a suitable person to hold the court, whilst the charges remained unacted upon." (<u>WJA</u>, I, p. 139)

p. 343 (cont.)

(31-34) Pound's comment.

p. 344

(1-2) "'Boston, 12 May, 1774. . . . It is expensive keeping a family here, and there is no prospect of any business in my way in this town this whole summer. I don't receive a shilling a week.'" (<u>WJA</u>, I, p. 143)

(3-4) "Soon afterwards, despairing of his ability to control that body [House of Representatives], whilst yet protected by the charter, he [General Gage] adjourned it until the 7th of June, just a week after the new acts of parliament were to go into operation, under which it was prescribed to meet, not at Boston, but in Salem. . . . Just as he was taking measures to repair his error, on the seventeenth of June, a day memorable in the annals of Massachusetts for more than one event, the signal for action was given in the House by a motion, that the doorkeeper keep the doors closed against all passage in or out. Immediately, one hundred and twenty-nine members being present, resolutions were presented, among other things, approving of a meeting of what were designated as <u>committees</u> from the several colonies of America, at Philadelphia, on the 1st of September, 'to consult upon wise and proper measures to be recommended to all the colonies for the recovery and estab-

p. 344 (cont.)
lishment of their just rights and liberties, civil and religious, and the restoration of union and harmony between the two countries, most ardently desired by all good men,' and nominating James Bowdoin, Thomas Cushing, Samuel Adams, John Adams, and Robert Treat Paine, to serve as the committee in behalf of Massachusetts." (WJA, I, pp. 144-145)

(5-6)   "'I wander alone and ponder,' he [John Adams in his 'Diary'] says; 'I muse, I mope, I ruminate. I am often in reveries and brown studies. The objects before me are too grand and multifarious for my comprehension. We have not men fit for the times.'" (WJA, I, p. 148) The French phrase Pound has added, le personnel manque, means "the personnel is lacking." (Index, p. 122)

(7)   "'I pray God for your health [L. John Adams to his wife], and entreat you to rouse your whole attention to the family, the stock, the farm, the dairy. Let every article of expense, which can possibly be spared, be retrenched.'" (WJA, I, p. 150)

(8-11)   "Their non-importation, non-exportation, and non-consumption agreement can scarcely be defended on any grounds. . . .

"Mr. Adams was not one of those who had the smallest

p. 344 (cont.)

faith in this measure, as an instrument of reconciliation. He would have preferred to limit the pledge to non-exportation, without quite seeing the injurious operation of that. He assented to the whole because others, believing in its efficacy, demanded it, and because he thus sealed a bond of union with them for greater ends in the future." (<u>WJA</u>, I, pp. 163-164)

(12-13) "'Resolved, that the foundation of English liberty and of all free government is a right in the people to participate in their legislative council; and as the English colonists are not represented, and from their local and other circumstances cannot be properly represented in the British Parliament, they are entitled to a free and exclusive power of legislation in their several provincial legislatures, where their right of representation can alone be preserved, in all cases of taxation and internal polity, subject only to the negative of their sovereign, in such manner as has been heretofore used and accustomed. But, <u>from the necessity of the case</u>, and a regard to the mutual interests of both countries, we cheerfully consent to the operation of such acts of parliament as are, <u>bona fide</u>, restrained to the regulation of our external commerce, for the purpose of securing the commercial advantages of the whole empire to the mother country, and the commercial benefits of its respective members; excluding

p. 344 (cont.)

every idea of taxation, internal or external, for raising a revenue on the subjects in America without their consent.'" (WJA, I, pp. 161-162) This resolution was passed at the first Continental Congress.

(13-15) "The history of countries like China and Japan proves clearly enough that it is by no means essential to national existence that they should trade with outside nations at all, however promotive this may be of their wealth and prosperity." (WJA, I, p. 163)

(16-17) "Mr. Adams, stimulated the more, perhaps, by the suspicion that it was his old friend, Sewall, who was writing [the "Massachusettensis" papers], took up the gauntlet which had thus been thrown down, and the elaborate papers of Novanglus, in the Boston Gazette, were the result. They appeared weekly throughout the winter of 1774 and until cut off by the appeal to that very different species of arbitration first attempted at Lexington and Concord." (WJA, I, p. 166)

(18) "In all civil convulsions, there is a class of men who put off taking a side as long as they can, for the purpose of saving a chance to solve the interesting question, which will prove the strongest. This naturally leads them to

p. 344 (cont.)

oppose, with all their might, any and every measure likely to precipitate their decision. Already, at the first congress, both the Adamses had been marked by these persons as partisans of extreme, if not treasonable opinions." (WJA, I, p. 171)

(19-20) "He [John Adams] exerted himself in determining the selection of the other general officers, claiming the second rank for New England in the person of Artemas Ward, but not unwilling to concede the third to Charles Lee, though a stranger and but yesterday an officer in the army of the British king; in maturing the form of commission and the instructions for the commander-in-chief; and, lastly, in superintending the preparation of the continental bills of credit which were to serve the purposes of money during the earlier stages of the struggle." (WJA, I, p. 178)

(21-22) "Not many days elapsed before an opportunity occurred for pressing upon congress one of his favorite measures. On the 3d of October, the delegates of Rhode Island had presented the resolutions of their General Assembly, instructing them to use their influence to procure the establishment of a fleet at the expense of the continent. This naked proposition was at once met with a storm of ridicule, in which Samuel Chase, Dr. Zubly, of Georgia, J. Rutledge, and even one of the Massachusetts delegates, took an active

p. 344 (cont.)

part. . . .

". . . For, on the 11th of December, congress, having been well prepared by the debates on the former proposition, came to a determination to appoint a large committee to devise ways and means for furnishing the colonies with a naval armament." (WJA, I, pp. 187-188)

(23-24) "In this way [through the publication of John Adams's pamphlet "Thoughts on Government" and similar writings not formally published] his sentiments were so extensively diffused as materially to guide the public mind in the construction of many of the State constitutions. The immediate effect was particularly visible in those adopted by New York and North Carolina, the last of which remained unchanged for sixty years, and at the time of its amendment, in 1836, was the only one left of the constitutions adopted at the Revolution; and the remoter influence has remained to these times." (WJA, I, p. 209) The pamphlet "Thoughts on Government" may be found in WJA, IV, pp. 193-200.

(25-29) "Conservative by temperament and education, he [John Adams] applied his mind to the task of saving whatever experience had proved to be valuable in the British constitutional forms, and cutting off only those portions which were not adapted to the feelings, manners, habits, and

p. 344 (cont.)

principles of a young nation oppressed by no burdens transmitted from a ruder age, and deranged by no abuses, the offspring of barbarous force. . . .

"It is to be particularly noted, however, in speaking of the various letters written by Mr. Adams at this time, that they all agree in one thing, and that is, in viewing the States as nations wholly independent of each other, and needing no bond of union stronger than a single federal assembly of representatives fairly apportioned, with authority sacredly confined to cases of war, trade, disputes between the States, the post-office, and the common territories. This shows that the writer had not yet devoted so much thought to this branch of the subject as it required. . . . That republican jealousy which seeks to cut off all power from fear of abuses, sometimes does quite as much harm as if it created a despotism." (WJA, I, pp. 210-211)

(30-35) "It is probable that the period embraced between the 9th of February, the day of his return to Philadelphia, and the end of this year, was the most laborious and exciting of Mr. Adams's long life. . . . He felt, not that three millions of men were to declare their own emancipation, but that a nation was to come into being for a life of centuries. . . . On the 12th of April he wrote to his wife much in the spirit of his letter to Gates, that the point, then only

p. 344 (cont.)

hoped for, had at last been gained. 'The ports are opened wide enough at last, and privateers are allowed to prey upon British trade. This is not independency, you know. What is? Why, <u>government</u> <u>in</u> <u>every</u> <u>colony</u>, <u>a</u> <u>confederation</u> <u>among</u> <u>them</u> <u>all</u>, <u>and</u> <u>treaties</u> <u>with</u> <u>foreign</u> <u>nations</u> to acknowledge us a sovereign State, and all that.'" (<u>WJA</u>, I, p. 213)

p. 345

(1)   This line, with the preceding line 35, p. 344, is Pound's repeat of lines 33-34, p. 344.

(2-3)   "'Whereas his Britannic Majesty [stated the preamble of the resolution, both of which John Adams helped draft, in which the second Congress recommended that the colonies adopt their own governments according to the best interests of their constituents], in conjunction with the lords and commons of Great Britain, has, by a late act of parliament, excluded the inhabitants of these United Colonies from the protection of his crown; and, whereas, no answer whatever to the humble petitions of the colonies for redress of grievances and reconciliation with Great Britain has been or is likely to be given; but the whole force of that kingdom, aided by foreign mercenaries, is to be exerted for the destruction of the good people of these colonies; and, whereas, it appears absolutely irreconcilable to reason and good

p. 345 (cont.)

conscience for the people of these colonies now to take the oaths and affirmations necessary for the support of any government under the crown of Great Britain, and it is necessary that the exercise of every kind of authority under the said crown should be totally suppressed, and all the powers of government exerted under the authority of the people of the colonies, for the preservation of internal peace, virtue, and good order, as well as for the defence of their lives, liberties, and properties against the hostile invasions and cruel depredations of their enemies; therefore, resolved,' &c." (WJA, I, p. 218)

(4)   "'Yesterday [L. John Adams to his friend General Palmer] the Gordian knot was cut. If such a resolution had been passed twelve months ago, as it ought to have been, and it was not my fault that it was not, how different would have been our situation! The advantages of such a measure were pointed out very particularly twelve months ago. But then we must petition and negotiate, and the people were not ripe! I believe they were as ripe then as they are now.'" (WJA, I, p. 218) I have been unable to identify the reference to the date "May 12th" in this line. Pound may perhaps be referring back to the letter John Adams wrote his wife on 12 May 1774 (Cantos, p. 344, lines 1-2: see p. 65, above) after the Superior Court had closed following the impeach-

p. 345 (cont.)

ment of Peter Oliver. The people's support of Oliver's impeachment may be part of John Adams's reason for believing that the "people" were "ripe" earlier.

(5)   "The movement [in which the second Congress agreed to the formal discussion of independence] took place, accordingly, on the 7th of June. . . .

"'Certain resolutions respecting independency being moved and seconded,--

"'Resolved, that the consideration of them be referred till tomorrow morning; and that the members be enjoined to attend punctually at ten o'clock, in order to take the same into their consideration.'"   (WJA, I, p. 221)

(6-8)   "'That all persons, members of or owing allegiance to any of the United Colonies [stated the resolution proposed by what was called the "committee on spies," of which John Adams was a member, and adopted by Congress], as before described, who shall levy war against any of the said colonies within the same, or be adherent to the king of Great Britain, or other enemies of the said colonies, or any of them, within the same, giving to him or them aid and comfort, are guilty of treason against such colony. . . .

"'Resolved, that it be recommended to the several legislatures of the United Colonies to pass laws for punishing,

p. 345 (cont.)

in such manner as they shall think fit, persons who shall counterfeit, or aid or abet in counterfeiting, the continental bills of credit, or who shall pass any such bill in payment, knowing the same to be counterfeit.'" (WJA, I, p. 225)

(9)   Pound's comment. The two Latin words (orationem and elegantissimam) mean, respectively, "oration," and "very elegant." (Index, p. 160 and p. 58)

(10)   "The debating talent must be admitted to have preponderated on the opposite side. It claimed John Dickinson and James Wilson, of Pennsylvania; Robert R. Livingston, of New York, and Edward Rutledge, of South Carolina; the latter, described by Patrick Henry as the most elegant speaker in the first congress." (WJA, I, pp. 227-228)

(11 & 13) "Yet great as the impression [made by John Adams] was upon others, it is very clear that he never looked upon himself as having done much more than usual. In a letter, addressed to Samuel Chase, on the evening after the debate, he speaks of it all as an idle waste of time, for that nothing had been said which had not been hackneyed in that room for six months before." (WJA, I, p. 229)

p. 345 (cont.)

(12 & 14-15) "'And the new governments we are assuming [L. John Adams to his wife], in every part, will require a purification from our vices, and an augmentation of our virtues, or they will be no blessings. The people will have unbounded power, and the people are extremely addicted to corruption and venality as well as the great. But I must submit all my hopes and fears to an overruling Providence, in which, unfashionable as the faith may be, I firmly believe.'" (<u>WJA</u>, I, pp. 230-231)

(16)   Pound's comment. The German words <u>Schicksal</u>, <u>sagt</u> <u>der</u> <u>Fuhrer</u> mean "Destiny, says the Fuhrer." (<u>Index</u>, p. 194)

(17)   "'The second day of July, 1776, will be the most memorable epocha [wrote John Adams to his wife in the same letter mentioned in lines 14-15] in the history of America. I am apt to believe that it will be celebrated by succeeding generations as the great anniversary festival. It ought to be commemorated as the day of deliverance, by solemn acts of devotion to God Almighty. It ought to be solemnized with pomp and parade, with shows, games, sports, guns, bells, bonfires, and illuminations, from one end of this continent to the other, from this time forward, forevermore.'" (<u>WJA</u>, I, p. 232)

p. 345 (cont.)

(18)   "Several passages [of Thomas Jefferson's draft of the Declaration of Independence] were altered in deference to the lingering hopes of reconciliation of some, or to the tender consciences of others, but the tenacity of Mr. Adams saved its substance, which will remain to a distant future, to inspire a far more perfect system of liberty than any social community has ever yet, in its practice, carried out." (WJA, I, p. 233)

(19)   "The rugged will may be broken in small islands, or in cities and their immediate dependencies, where the surface can be measured by a physical force, but it escapes from subjection in the indefinite expanse of a continent. This consideration alone made the Declaration of Independence a reasonable act, without reference to the amount of aid which it might secure from the favor or the rivalry of foreign powers." (WJA, I, p. 234)

(20-21) "It [the mission of Lord Howe] forms a part of a series of inadequate concessions, always coming a day too late, which will render the policy of Lord North ever a memorable lesson to statesmen." (WJA, I, p. 239) The Latin word sero means "too late." (Index, p. 196)

(22)   "Indeed, throughout this history, it was the fate

p. 345 (cont.)
of that country [Great Britain] never to be in season with any measure, either of restraint or conciliation." (<u>WJA</u>, I, p. 240)

(22) "It [the form of a treaty the Congress would propose to foreign powers] was composed of articles purely commercial in their nature, and contemplated no connection beyond a reciprocation of the benefits of trade, and a mutual assurance of protection against the annoyances likely to interrupt it." (<u>WJA</u>, I, p. 241)

(23) "In Virginia, and in New England, the population had been the most exclusively derived from Great Britain; but it had come from very opposite classes of its society. The one had emigrated during a period, when the passions both in church and state had been stimulated to the utmost. They cherished the extreme ideas of the extreme reformers, as little idolaters of the crown as of the hierarchy. The other had borne the impress of the cavalier, holding his loyalty as a sentiment rather than a principle, revering the authority of the church, and the established order of ranks in the state, though never surrendering that spirit of personal independence which yet characterizes the higher classes of the mother country." (<u>WJA</u>, I, p. 243)

p. 345 (cont.)

(24) "Adventurers of all sorts [in France] crowded around him [Silas Deane], ready to offer their valuable services to the great cause of liberty at a much higher price than they could get by remaining to serve despotism at home." (<u>WJA</u>, I, p. 249)

(25-28) "'You should have numbered your regiments [L. John Adams to James Warren of Massachusetts], and arranged all your officers according to their rank, and transmitted the accounts to congress, at least to your delegates here. I assure you I have suffered much for want of this information. . . .

"'Another subject, of great importance, we ought to have been informed of. I mean your navy. We ought to have known the number of your armed vessels, their tonnage, their number of guns, weight of metal, number of men, officers' names, ranks and characters. In short, you should have given us your complete army and navy lists.'" (<u>WJA</u>, I, pp. 253-254)

(29-30) "The army, although at heart patriotic, was all the time filled with personal jealousies and discontents, which nothing kept within reasonable bounds but the impassible moderation of Washington. Herein it was that he saved the country, far more than by any act of his military

p. 345 (cont.)

campaigns." (WJA, I, p. 265)

(31)   "He [John Adams] likewise stood alone [among delegates from states north of Virginia] in voting for a representation apportioned to population, each delegate of which should have a separate vote. Again he so stood in favor of a representation proportioned to the annual contributions of the States to the federal treasury." (WJA, I, p. 269)

(32-33)   "'I never can think we shall finally fail of success [wrote an unidentified member of the Congress] while Heaven continues to the congress the life and abilities of Mr. John Adams. He is equal to the controversy in all its stages. He stood upon the shoulders of the whole congress when reconciliation was the wish of all America. He was equally conspicuous in cutting the knot which tied the colonies to Great Britain. In a word, I deliver to you the opinion of every man in the House, when I add that he possesses the clearest head and firmest heart of any man in the congress.'" (WJA, I, p. 273)

(34)   Pound's comment. The Greek word THUMON means "soul, life, strength, courage, mind." (Index, p. 222)

(35)   "'Dr. Franklin's age alarms us [L. James Lovell

p. 345 (cont.)

to John Adams, urging Adams to accept the commission to the court of France]. We want one man of inflexible integrity on the embassy.'" (<u>WJA</u>, I, p. 275)

p. 346

(1)   "He [John Adams] reached Bordeaux in safety, was received with honors, and immediately passed on to Paris, where he arrived on the 8th of April, 1778." (<u>WJA</u>, I, p. 277)

(2-4)   "The ethics of Franklin permitted of the enjoyment of advantages, obtained at the expense of others, that might come by passively permitting them to happen or even by indirectly promoting them. . . . Yet if rigid moral analysis [of even famous countrymen such as Benjamin Franklin] be not the purpose of historical writing, there is no more value in it than in the fictions of mythological antiquity." (<u>WJA</u>, I, p. 319)

(5)   "Among them, the persons with whom he established the most permanent and valuable relations were John Luzac, conductor of the Gazette at Leyden, and Cerisier, who set on foot a magazine entitled the <u>Politique</u> <u>Hollandais</u>. . . .

". . . It seems that this gentleman, by the name of Calkoen [a prominent Amsterdam lawyer], took the opportunity

p. 346 (cont.)

to address to him [John Adams] a series of questions, involving all the principal points of inquiry touching the history of the people of the United States, their character, and their ability to maintain their stand. But inasmuch as both parties experienced some embarrassment from the want of a common language to explain their meaning so fully as they wished, and as it occurred to Mr. Adams that the information which Mr. Calkoen had sought to obtain would be likely to be useful to many Dutch people, he procured the questions committed to writing, so that he might append a brief but clear answer to each in its order, and give the whole to the press, for the public information. This was accordingly done." (WJA, I, pp. 330-331) These answers, published under the title of "Twenty-six Letters upon interesting subjects respecting the Revolution of America," may be found in WJA, VII, pp. 265-312.

(6)   "The reception of the powers to open a loan in the absence of Mr. Laurens, was the signal for Mr. Adams to turn his efforts in that direction. He immediately set about inquiries of the leading brokers in Amsterdam, as to the probability of obtaining the aid of influential houses to effect the object." (WJA, I, p. 331)

(6-7)   "Two events just now came in, however, to

p. 346 (cont.)

exercise no unimportant influence upon his operations. One of them was the capitulation of Lord Cornwallis, the official account of which was transmitted directly to Mr. Adams by General Washington. The other was the arrival of still another commission, and instructions from congress to propose to the States General a treaty of triple alliance between France, Holland, and the United States. This measure had been initiated by Mr. Adams in a suggestion made to the Duke de la Vauguyon, the French envoy at the Hague, who had thought so well of it as to recommend it to the notice of his government." (WJA, I, pp. 343-344)

(8)   "The members [De Ruyter and others] of that party still cherished the ancient memories of the national freedom, though they were without the vigor necessary to raise it into a present reality." (WJA, I, p. 345)

(9-10)   "'Les amis de la France devaient toujours crier la liberté.' Flassan describes this as the policy of the court of Versailles under Louis the Fifteenth. From that quarter it was a cry and nothing else, as well in Holland as in America." (WJA, I, p. 345n) The French words Pound uses, doivent toujours crier la liberté,--amis de la France, mean "(they) ought always to cry Liberty,--friends of France." (Index, p. 53)

p. 346 (cont.)

(11-13) "Hence it was rather with the acquiescence than the full approval of the Duke de Vauguyon, that, in consonance with the suggestions of leading patriots, and especially the bold Van der Capellen, he [John Adams] made up his mind to take a daring step, which might indeed accomplish his great object [persuading the Dutch to acknowledge the independence of the United States], but which, on the other hand, if it failed, would inevitably, for the time, detract seriously from his reputation, and render chances of success, afterwards, more desperate than ever.

"Every thing having been accordingly arranged, on the 8th of January, 1782, Mr. Adams commenced a series of formal visits, in person, to the chief officers, and the deputies of each city, in the States General, at the Hague, in which he respectfully reminded them of the memorial he had addressed to them, asking for the recognition of his country, to which he had not yet received any reply. He then stated the object of his visit to be to demand a CATEGORICAL ANSWER, in order that he might transmit it, without delay, to his government. . . . In many of the great towns, such as Leyden, Rotterdam, Amsterdam, Haerlem, Utrecht, Zwol, petitions were gotten up, setting forth, at more or less length, reasons why the provincial States, to which they respectively belonged, should be instructed early to declare in favor of granting Mr. Adams's demand." (<u>WJA</u>, I, pp. 346-347)

p. 346 (cont.)

(14-21) "Zealand and Overyssel were not long in following, and in the same week of April the three other States, Groningen, Utrecht, and Guelderland, declared themselves. No sooner was the deci..on of the last State received than the States General proceeded to act. And thus it happened that on the 19th of April, exactly one year from the date of Mr. Adams's first memorial, an anniversary otherwise memorable in the commencement of the American struggle, the delegates, having received their instructions, directed, unanimously, the following record to be placed on their journals:--

"'Deliberated by resumption upon the address and the ulterior address made by Mr. Adams, the 4th of May, 1781, and the 9th of January of the current year, to the President of the Assembly of their High Mightinesses, to present to their High Mightinesses his letters of credence, in the name of the United States of North America, and by which ulterior address the said Mr. Adams has demanded a categorical answer, to the end to be able to acquaint his constituents thereof; it has been thought fit and resolved that Mr. Adams shall be admitted and acknowledged in quality of envoy of the United States of North America to their High Mightinesses, as he is admitted and acknowledged by the present.'

"Three days after the adoption of this resolution, Mr. Adams was introduced to the Stadtholder; and the next day, to the States General, as the accredited minister of the new

p. 346 (cont.)

nation, the United States of America; after which the Duke de la Vauguyon made a formal entertainment for the ministers representing the other European States, and Mr. Adams was there presented to each of them as a new and recognized member of the corps diplomatique at the Hague." (WJA, I, pp. 348-349)

(22-23) "His [John Adams's] activity had formed the literary connections, through which alone an opening could be made for him, a stranger equally to the language and manners of the [Dutch] people, to reach their ears or their hearts." (WJA, I, p. 349)

(23-25) "And nowhere is this [skillful judgment of John Adams in pursuing public goals] made to appear more strikingly than in his correspondence with M. Dumas and others through whom he acted during the period now under consideration in Holland." (WJA, I, p. 350)

(25)   "'It [L. John Adams to his wife concerning the American embassy in Holland] has not only prevailed with a minister or an absolute court to fall in with the national prejudice, but without money, without friends, and in opposition to mean intrigue, it has carried its cause, by the still small voice of reason and persuasion, triumphantly against

p. 346 (cont.)

the uninterrupted opposition of family connections, court influence, and aristocratical despotism.'" (WJA, I, p. 350)

(26-30) "So long as the recognition of the United States had remained in doubt, even though the current of events had been removing more and more every prospect of the reestablishment of the authority of Great Britain, there was little heart among the moneyed men to undertake, or the people at large to second any pecuniary advances. But now that the States General had decided to give countenance to the new nation, Mr. Adams felt the difference, in the reception of offers from several of the most responsible houses in Holland to undertake a loan. . . . It is enough here to say that through the activity of three houses, Messrs. Willink, Van Staphorst, and De la Lande & Fynje, a sum of five millions of guilders was obtained, at a moment when it was of essential service in maintaining the overstrained credit of the United States.

". . . From the date of the first successful loan until Mr. Adams returned to America, in 1788, he kept up his relations with the bankers of Amsterdam, and through them succeeded in procuring successive advances, which carried his country safely over the interval of disorder previous to the consolidation of the federal government." (WJA, I, pp. 350-351)

p. 346 (cont.)

(31)   "At last, on the 7th of October, 1782, the last hand was put to the papers, and Mr. Adams had the satisfaction of sending Mr. Livingston for ratification the second alliance entered into by the United States as a sovereign power [with Holland]." (WJA, I, p. 352)

(31-34) "There were no arts or disguises, no flattery or fawning, no profligacy or corruption put in use [by John Adams during his diplomatic mission to Holland] to further the result. It was an honest victory of principle gained by skilfully enlisting in a just cause the confidence and sympathy of a nation. And it was won by a man who up to the fortieth year of his life had scarcely crossed the borders of the small province in America within which he was born, and who had had no opportunities to profit of those lessons on the radiant theatres of the world, which even the republican poet of England was willing to admit, in his time, to be

    'Best school of best experience, quickest insight
    In all things that to greatest actions lead.'"

(WJA, I, p. 352)

p. 347

(1-2)   "'The post-boy (who, upon asking where I would be carried, was answered "to the best inn in London [to which John Adams had journeyed in 1783], for all are alike unknown

p. 347 (cont.)

to me,") carried us to the Adelphi buildings in the Strand. Whether it was the boy's cunning, or whether it was mere chance, I know not, but I found myself in a street which was marked John's Street. The postilion turned a corner, and I was in Adam's Street. He turned another corner, and I was in John Adam's Street!'" (WJA, I, p. 403)

(3-5) "'I will sum up all upon this subject in the words of one of the most active and extensive among the printers and booksellers to me. "Sir," said he, "the men of learning are all stark mad. There are in this city at least one hundred men of the best education, the best classical students, the most accomplished writers, any one of whom I can hire for one guinea a day to go into my closet and write for me whatever I please, for or against any man or any cause. It is indifferent to them whether they write pro or con."'" (WJA, I, p. 404)

(6) "'Here, also [at Sir Ashton Lever's museum], I saw Sir Ashton and some other knights, his friends, practising the ancient, but, as I thought, long forgotten art of archery.'" (WJA, I, p. 407)

(7) "'I succeeded also in that [borrowing additional money in Holland]; which preserved our credit till my return

p. 347 (cont.)

to America, in 1788, and till the new government came into operation and found itself rich enough.'" (<u>WJA</u>, I, p. 412)

(8-13) "'We were rowed in the water till we came to the ice, when the skipper and his men, to the number of eight or ten, perhaps, leaped out upon the ice, and hauled the boat up after them, when the passengers were required to get out and walk upon the ice, while the boatmen dragged the boat upon her runners. Presently, they would come to a spot where the ice was thin and brittle, when all would give way, and down went the boat into the water. . . .

"'I had ridden on horseback often to congress, over roads and across ferries, of which the present generation have no idea; and once, in 1777, in the dead of winter, from Braintree to Baltimore, five hundred miles, upon a trotting horse, as Dean Swift boasted that he had done, or could do. I had been three days in the Gulf Stream, in 1778, in a furious hurricane and a storm of thunder and lightning, which struck down our men upon deck, and cracked our mainmast; when the oldest officers and stoutest seamen stood aghast, at their last prayers, dreading every moment that a butt would start, and all perish. . . . I had passed the mountains in Spain, in the winter, among ice and snow, partly on muleback and partly on foot; yet I never suffered so much in any of these situations as in that jaunt from Bath to Amsterdam,

p. 347 (cont.)

in January, 1784.'" (WJA, I, pp. 411-412)

(14)   "And instead of dishonoring the humble name of his [George the Third's] American auditor [John Adams, visiting Parliament], that name was henceforth to go out indelibly graven by his act upon the list of those who, by upholding fundamental principles at critical moments, originate the beneficial movements of the world!" (WJA, I, p. 413)

(15-16) "Paris was just then [in the summer of 1784 when Mrs. Adams joined her husband there] in that stage of transition from the old to the new, which is apt to quicken whatever there may be of sprightly in society, without having yet materially impaired its stability. Literature and philosophy had become the rage even in fashionable circles." (WJA, I, p. 415)

(17-19) "This treaty [executed by the United States and adopted by Frederick the Great of Prussia] is sufficiently remarkable to merit to be distinguished from every other yet made. Free trade, freedom of neutrals, respect for individual property of enemies at sea, the abolition of privateering, and the limitation over the power to confiscate contraband of war, were new and bold steps in the progress of international civilization." (WJA, I, p. 416)

p. 347 (cont.)

(20-21) "Unfortunately the United States, at the time when they executed this treaty, were in a situation in which its provisions, if generally adopted, would have effectually protected their interests from the haughty domination of the sea, assumed by their ancient mistress. Hence their philanthropy was not wholly free from suspicion of incidental benefit to ensue to themselves." (<u>WJA</u>, I, p. 417)

(22) "On the 24th of February, 1785, congress, not insensible of the injury committed by the revocation of his former commission, elected him [John Adams] to the post of Envoy to the court of St. James's. . . . The Duke of Dorset, then the British ambassador at Paris, remarked to him, that 'he would be stared at a great deal.'" (<u>WJA</u>, I, p. 418)

(23-24) "The pamphlet of Lord Sheffield [which argued for and resulted in exclusion, by temporary acts of Parliament, in 1783, of the United States from trade with other British colonies] had its effect upon the formation and adoption of the federal constitution of 1788. Thus it often happens with nations that think to make a gain out of the embarrassments and miseries of their neighbors. . . . Lord Sheffield's interference must be classed among the secondary misfortunes which befell Great Britain in the disastrous record of the American war; whilst, among the people of America, it deserves

p. 347 (cont.)

to be remembered with satisfaction as a conversion of what was intended to be a poison into a health-producing medicine." (<u>WJA</u>, I, p. 423)

(25-30) "'If the system [of government] attempted to be defended in these letters [John Adams's recently published work, <u>A Defence of the Constitutions of the United States of America against the attack of M. Turgot</u>] is not the system of the wisest men among us, I shall tremble for the consequences, and wish myself in any obscure hole in the world [L. John Adams to his brother-in-law, Richard Cranch, 15 January 1787]. I am myself as clearly satisfied of the infallible truth of the doctrines there contained as I am of any demonstration in Euclid; and if our countrymen are bent upon any wild schemes inconsistent with the substance of it, the sooner they remove me out of their sight the better; for I can be of no service to them in promoting their views. . . .

"'I lament that it is so hasty a production. . . . But the disturbances in New England [about the kind of federal constitution to adopt] made it necessary to publish immediately, in order to do any good. . . . By the hurry and precipitation with which this work was undertaken, conducted and completed, I have been obliged to be too inattentive both to method and the ornaments of style for the present taste of our countrymen; for I perceive that taste and

p. 347 (cont.)

elegance are the cry. This appears to me like establishing manufactures of lace, fringe, and embroidery in a country, before there are any of silk, velvet, or cloth. Our countrymen are by no means advanced enough in solid science and learning, in mathematics and philosophy, in Greek and Latin, to devote so much of their time to rhetoric. . . . I am no enemy to elegance, but I say no man has a right to think of elegance till he has secured substance; nor then, to seek more of it than he can afford.

"'"Libertatem, amicitiam, fidem, praecipua humani animi bona"--these are essential to human happiness. Finery of every kind may be dispensed with, until it can be reconciled to the other.'" (WJA, I, pp. 432-433) The Latin words Pound uses, Libertatem Amicitiam Fidem, mean "Liberty, Friendship, Loyalty," and became part of John Adams's motto. (Index, p. 123)

(31)   "The commercial and moneyed interests, which were the first to feel it [the national prosperity], at once rallied around Mr. Hamilton [Alexander Hamilton, Washington's Secretary of the Treasury] as their benefactor, and they never deserted him afterwards. A new power arose, that of the fundholders, the rapid increase of which inspired Mr. Jefferson with alarm and a determination to resist it." (WJA, I, p. 452)

p. 347 (cont.)

(32-33) "'Our anti-federal scribblers are so fond of rotation, that they seem disposed to remove their abuse from me to the President [L. John Adams to his wife, 2 January 1794].'" (WJA, I, p. 460)

(34-35) "'Congress have been together more than two months, and have done nothing; and will continue sitting
p. 348 two months longer, and do little. I, for my part,
(1-3) am wearied to death with ennui. Obliged to be punctual by my habits, confined to my seat [as Vice-President presiding over the Senate], as in a prison, to see nothing done, hear nothing said, and to say and do nothing. . . .

"'. . . Borrowing of banks for a trading capital is very unmercantile [L. John Adams to his wife, 8 February 1794].'" (WJA, I, pp. 465-466)

(4) "'I have one comfort; that in thought, word, or deed I have never encouraged a war. I will persevere in doing all in my power to prevent it. If it is forced on us by England, or even if it is brought on us by our own imprudence, I must stand or fall with my country [L. John Adams to his wife, 27 March 1794].'" (WJA, I, p. 469)

(5) "'You cannot imagine [L. John Adams to his wife, 19 April 1794] what horror some persons are in, lest peace

p. 348 (cont.)

[of United States with warring European nations, Britain and France especially] should continue. The prospect of peace throws them into distress.'" (WJA, I, p. 471)

(6-7)   "'While I confess the necessity of it, and see its importance in giving strength to our government at home and consideration to our country abroad, I lament the introduction of taxes and expenses which will accumulate a perpetual debt and lead to future revolutions [L. John Adams to his wife, 5 May 1794].'" (WJA, I, p. 473)

(8-18)   "'Mr. Adet was presented to the President on Tuesday, and, accompanied by the Secretary of State, made me a visit immediately after his audience. I was not at home, but in Senate. On Wednesday morning I returned his visit at Oeller's hotel.

"'He [Mr. Adet, the French envoy] is not a friend to clubs--announced to the President the entire annihilation of factions in France, &c.

"'His Excellency, Governor Jay, returned yesterday to New York. He has been very sociable and in fine spirits. His health is improving. We have no chief justice as yet nominated. It is happy that Mr. Jay's election [as governor of the state of New York] was over before the treaty [that he had negotiated with England] was published; for the parties

p. 348 (cont.)

against him would have quarrelled with the treaty, right or wrong, that they might give a color to their animosity against him [L. John Adams to his wife, 18 June 1795].'" (<u>WJA</u>, I, p. 479)

(19)   "'Both the public dispatches and private letters of our dear boys are the delight of all who read them. No public minister has ever given greater satisfaction, than Mr. [John Quincy] Adams has hitherto. His prudence, caution, and penetration are as much approved as the elegance of his style is admired [L. John Adams to his wife, 23 June 1795].'" (<u>WJA</u>, I, p. 480)

(20)   "Thus far, the troubles of the times had not pressed heavily upon the mind of Mr. Adams, because his situation, excepting upon rare occasions, dictated inactivity, whilst it favored the preservation of a serenity highly propitious to his powers of observation. It is this which gives so much zest to the familiar correspondence with his wife, from which extracts have been freely given. They will now be continued down to the moment when these feelings begin to change. The first symptom of this is to be traced in the operation of the disturbed state of affairs upon the mind of the President [Washington]." (<u>WJA</u>, I, p. 482)

p. 348 (cont.)

(21-29) "'Happy is the country to be rid of Randolph [Edmund Randolph, the Secretary of State, whose integrity had been compromised by the revelation of a secret correspondence between himself and M. Fauchet, the French envoy*]; but where shall be found good men and true to fill the offices of government? . . . The President offered the office of State to several gentlemen who declined; to Mr. Patterson, Mr. King, Mr. Henry, of Virginia, Mr. Charles Cotesworth Pinckney, of South Carolina, and three others whose names I do not recollect. He has not been able to find any one to accept the war office. The expenses of living at the seat of government are so exorbitant, so far beyond all proportion to the salaries, and the sure reward of integrity in the discharge of public functions is such obloquy, contempt, and insult, that no man of any feeling is willing to renounce his home, forsake his property and profession for the sake of removing to Philadelphia, where he is almost sure of disgrace and ruin.

"'Where these things will end, I know not. In perfect secrecy between you and me, I must tell you that now I

---

* President Washington had appointed Colonel Timothy Pickering to fill temporarily the vacant post of Secretary of State. When he could find no other man to accept a permanent appointment, he was compelled to keep Colonel Pickering in that position. Colonel Pickering later became a difficult problem for John Adams as President. (See <u>WJA</u>, I, pp. 481-482)

p. 348 (cont.)

believe the President will retire. . . . But in that case [of a situation in which Adams might find himself lacking public confidence and unable to support the government in higher office], I ought not to serve in my present place [as Vice-President] under another, especially if that other should entertain sentiments so opposite to mine as to endanger the peace of the nation. It will be a dangerous crisis in public affairs, if the President and Vice-President should be in opposite boxes [L. John Adams to his wife, 7 January 1796].'" (WJA, I, pp. 483-484)

(30-32) "During the period now under consideration, the highest class of ability in the country was habitually enlisted in the production of elaborate dissertations for the newspapers upon the great topics of the day. These were commonly printed at all the central points, and being assiduously read by the people, exercised a strong influence upon their modes of thought and action." (WJA, I, p. 485)

(33-35) "'I hate to live in Philadelphia in summer, and I hate still more to relinquish my farm. I hate speeches, messages, addresses and answers, proclamations, and such affected, studied, constrained things. I hate levees and drawing-rooms. I hate to speak to a thousand people to whom I have nothing to say. Yet all this I can do. But I am too

p. 348 (cont.)

old to continue more than one; or, at most, more than two heats; and that is scarcely time enough to form, conduct, and complete any very useful system [L. John Adams to his wife, 1 March 1796].'" (WJA, I, p. 487)

p. 349

(1-6)   "'Alas! I am not Amphion. I have been thirty years singing and whistling among my rocks, and not one would ever move without money. I have been twenty years saying, if not singing, preaching, if not playing:—

> "From various discords to create
> The music of a well-tuned state,
> And the soft, silent harmony that springs
> From sacred union and consent of things,"

but an uncomplying world will not regard my uncouth discourses. I cannot sing nor play. If I had eloquence, or humor, or irony, or satire, or the harp or lyre of Amphion, how much good could I do to the world!

"'. . . If Mr. Jefferson should be President, I believe I must put up as a candidate for the House. But this is my vanity. . . . I declare, however, if I were in that House, I would drive out of it some demons that haunt it. There are false doctrines and false jealousies predominant there, at times, that it would be easy to exorcise [L. John Adams to his wife, 13 March 1796].'" (WJA, I, pp. 488-489)

(6-11)   "The retirement of President Washington removed

p. 349 (cont.)

the last check upon the fury of parties. . . . The individual whom the opposition would sustain, with marked unanimity, was Thomas Jefferson. . . . The federalists, on the other hand, enjoyed no such advantage [of unanimity]. A portion of them, embracing many of the active and intelligent leaders in the Northern and Eastern States, reposed implicit confidence in Alexander Hamilton. But they were reluctantly compelled to admit that that confidence was not shared by the people at large, and that an attempt to oppose him to Mr. Jefferson would be futile." (WJA, I, pp. 490-491)

(12)   "The fact is now beyond dispute, that an indirect and clandestine effort was made at this election to set aside the person who had been openly accepted as the candidate of the federal party [John Adams], in favor of another individual of whom nobody had thought in connection with the first office. This attempt was originated by Mr. [Alexander] Hamilton, and carried on through his particular friends in and out of New England." (WJA, I, p. 492)

(13)   "No President, since 1796 [when Pennsylvania's electors voted, with few exceptions, for Thomas Jefferson and for Aaron Burr], has been chosen by the popular voice, whom she [Pennsylvania] had not first designated by her wishes and her electoral votes." (WJA, I, p. 494)

p. 349 (cont.)

(14-16) "'Giles says, "the point is settled. The V. P. will be President. He is undoubtedly chosen. The old man will make a good President, too." (There's for you.) "But we shall have to <u>check</u> him a little now and then. That will be all." . . .

"'There have been manoeuvres and combinations in this election that would surprise you [L. John Adams to his wife, 12 December 1796].'" (<u>WJA</u>, I, pp. 495-496)

(17-19) "'. . . if a love of science and letters, and a wish to patronize every rational effort to encourage schools, colleges, universities, academies, and every institution for propagating knowledge, virtue, and religion among all classes of the people, not only for their benign influence on the happiness of life in all its stages and classes, and of society in all its forms, but as the only means of preserving our constitution from its natural enemies, the spirit of sophistry, the spirit of party, the spirit of intrigue, profligacy, and corruption, and the pestilence of foreign influence, which is the angel of destruction to elective governments. . . .'" (<u>WJA</u>, I, p. 505) This passage, from John Adams's Inaugural Address, is contained "in one of the longest sentences in the language [according to Charles Francis Adams]," and in that sentence is "his [John Adams's] whole creed." (See <u>WJA</u>, I, p. 504)

p. 349 (cont.)

(20)   "Chief Justice Ellsworth administered the oath, and with great energy [L. John Adams to his wife the day following his inauguration].'"   (WJA, I, p. 507)

(21-22) "And his [Napoleon's] victorious march in Italy was the sign under which the usurping section hoped to hold their power, maugre all resistance. . . . Napoleon's successes opened a paradise of jobs from army contractors, besides placing the Directory in a situation to dictate their own terms to weaker nations. . . . And particularly unfortunate chance to the United States, not yet strong enough to make their anger a cause of fear, whilst their commerce, which was growing to whiten every sea, presented a rich prey wherewith to fatten the officials of the hour [in France]!" (WJA, I, pp. 512-513)

(23-24) "It can only be accounted for by knowing the fact that at this very time Mr. Hamilton had become a party to a grand project of revolution in South America, conceived years before in the fertile brain of Francisco de Miranda, but now taking the form of a political combination, the details of which are found singularly to correspond with this feature of the plan submitted to the President [Adams] by Mr. McHenry [Secretary of War in the administration of John Adams]." (WJA, I, p. 523)

104

p. 349 (cont.)

(25-30) "But they [difficulties of form] had been at last somewhat skilfully surmounted by the preparation, on the part of M. Talleyrand, of a dispatch, addressed to M. Pichon, in which, whilst reiterating the professions of a desire to come to a good understanding with America, he managed to introduce a promise, in the very words that had been used by the President [Adams], to wit, that a new envoy, if sent, would be 'received as the representative of a great, free, powerful, and independent nation.' This dispatch, thus prepared, was placed in the hands of M. Pichon to be by him delivered to Mr. [William Vans] Murray, and by him, in turn, transmitted to the government of the United States. . . .

"Should he [John Adams] call his cabinet into his consultation, and prepare them for the adoption of a new measure of negotiation?

". . . The presentation of it in the cabinet would lead to a warm protest, and to the necessity of either persevering against an opposition profiting of the tactics of delay to become concerted in the Senate, or of abandoning the measure altogether.

". . . There was but one way. He ought to send to the Senate a communication nominating a minister to go to France; and the person must be the individual through whom the overtures for accomodation had been transmitted, William Vans Murray, now minister at the Hague. On the 18th of February,

p. 349 (cont.)

accordingly, the members of the Senate, not one of whom had a suspicion of what was coming, were astounded by the reception of a message from the President [Adams], covering the dispatch of Talleyrand to M. Pichon, as the motive to his decision to nominate Mr. Murray. The terms used by him were most carefully guarded in every particular, assuming no risk in trusting too readily the professions of M. Talleyrand, and providing that no advance should be made beyond the appointment, until further assurances, the most unequivocal, should be publicly and officially given by France that the minister now nominated would be honorably received." (WJA, I, pp. 542-543)

(31-32) "'I do not remember that I was ever vindictive in my life, though I have often been very wroth. I am not very angry now, nor much vexed or fretted. The mission [of William Vans Murray to France] came across the views of many, and stirred the passions of more. This I knew was unavoidable [L. John Adams to his wife, 22 February 1799].'" (WJA, I, p. 545)

(33-34) "He roused the country to war, solely as a measure of defence, and to deter France from further persevering in her aggressions." (WJA, I, p. 541) "Ready for war, if France continued faithless, he was not less ready for peace the

p. 349 (cont.)

moment she showed signs of returning reason." (WJA, I, p. 550) Both references are to John Adams.

(35)   "Some time in the spring of 1798, there had taken place in Northampton County, in Pennsylvania, as
p. 350   has already been mentioned, an armed resistance
(1)   to the levy of the direct tax, which spread into two or three of the neighboring counties, and for a few days assumed an appearance so alarming as to justify the President's proclamation and orders to equip a military force to put it down. The mere apparition of this force proved sufficient to effect the object. The men who had taken the lead in the disorders, being deserted by their fellows, were made prisoners, and handed over for trial to the courts. The principal one was a person by name John Fries, who was found with arms in his hands, acting as a chief, although he seems to have possessed few qualities to recommend him for any such elevation. . . ." (WJA, I, p. 571)

"In this case [of Fries] the cabinet could not complain that they had not been consulted at every step. But that seems to have made no difference in the feeling with which at least one of the disaffected viewed the direction of the President, given the next day, that a pardon should be made out for all the offenders." (WJA, I, p. 573)

p. 350 (cont.)

(2-9) "He [John Adams] had formed his own opinions of the policy of Mr. Hamilton and his friends, which had impaired his confidence in them, not less than theirs had become impaired in him. The measure which they had first proposed to him under the name of <u>cooperation</u> with Great Britain, he now fully believed to have been intended only as a preliminary to an alliance, offensive and defensive, which would have shut out all prospect of further preserving a neutrality in the wars of Europe. . . . Cool and collected when summoned to act in public on any emergency, he was seldom in the habit of resisting his natural impetuosity in the less guarded hours of private intercourse and familiar conversation. Then it was, that he would give to his language the full impress of his vehement will. . . . He charged the hostility, waged by Mr. Hamilton and his friends against himself to their disappointment, in failing to establish through his aid the desired connection with Great Britain, against France." (<u>WJA</u>, I, pp. 577-578)

(10-24) Pound's comment. The caricatured names in line 10 refer to James McHenry ("Snot"), Timothy Pickering ("Bott"?), and Oliver Wolcott ("Cott"?). See <u>Index</u>, pp. 201, 23, and 45, respectively.

The Spanish word <u>ARRIBA</u> in line 24 means "hail!" (<u>Index</u>, p. 11)

CANTO LXIII

p. 351

(1-2)   "The gravest of them [the charges against John Adams published under the title "Letter from Alexander Hamilton, concerning the Public Conduct and Character of John Adams, Esq., President of the United States," and released by Hamilton in an attempt to weaken the leadership of Adams in the Federalist party] were founded upon the determination of Mr. Adams to initiate the mission of Mr. Murray to France without consulting his cabinet; upon his perseverance in afterwards dispatching Messrs. Ellsworth and Davie, in opposition to the better judgment of Mr. Hamilton and his friends; and upon his pardon of John Fries, who according to them should rather have been hanged." (WJA, I, p. 583)

(3)   "A publication [the "Letter from Alexander Hamilton"], having for its object the destruction of the public character of a man who had spent twenty-five years of his life in stations of the highest responsibility, in some of which he had acquitted himself so honorably as to have extorted even from its author both praise and support, needed the most convincing proof of very grave offences against the public good in order to make it justifiable before the world." (WJA, I, pp. 582-583) The words "treaties put through and

p. 351 (cont.)

loans raised" seem to be Pound's comment, very likely referring to John Adams's service to his country during his Holland mission.

(4-6) "Without possessing abilities of the first class, General [Charles Cotesworth] Pinckney [whom Hamilton had chosen to oppose John Adams among the Federalists] had owed the respect which followed him in life quite as much to his integrity and nice sense of personal honor, as to the creditable manner in which he acquitted himself of his duties. . . . Unwilling to subject himself to the remotest suspicion of bad faith, after the reception of Mr. Hamilton's pamphlet admitted of a possible inference of collusion, he insisted upon standing or falling upon the same ticket inseparably with Mr. Adams." (WJA, I, p. 588)

(7) "The source of this error [of Alexander Hamilton in believing that he could match the intrigue of his enemy, Aaron Burr] is to be traced to a deficiency in early moral foundations, the effects of which, here and there, make themselves visible, breaking out of the folds of a noble nature throughout his career, but especially towards its close. It was this which substituted the false idol of honor, as worshipped in the society of his day, for the eternal law of God; which impelled him to justify himself against a charge

p. 351 (cont.)

ol peculation of the public money at the expense of a public confession of what to him seemed the more venial offence of aiding to corrupt an immortal soul; which led him into the clandestine relations with the cabinet officers of Mr. Adams, and the ultimate breach of confidence he made such awkward attempts to hide; which prompted that application to the upright John Jay, marked by the latter with so significant a condemnation; and, lastly, which, in the vain idea of the importance to his ulterior schemes, of retaining the regards of superficial men, drove him, against his most solemn convictions of duty, to the act that presented him unanealed for the final sentence of his Maker." (WJA, I, p. 589)

(8-9)   "'Here [in the new capitol at Washington, where John Adams was making his last speech to Congress], and throughout our country, may simple manners, pure morals, and true religion flourish forever!'" (WJA, I, p. 592)

(10)   "On the 4th of March, 1801, the day upon which Mr. Jefferson was inaugurated President of the United States, Mr. Adams retired from public life, after an uninterrupted course of service of six and twenty years, in a greater variety of trusts than fell to the share of any other American of his time." (WJA, I, p. 599)

p. 351 (cont.)

(11)   "A few old and tried friends sent [to John Adams after his retirement from public office] kind expressions of their warm regard, which he acknowledged in the same spirit, but the crowd who had solicited favors, so long as there were any to grant, moved on according to immemorial usage, towards the newly-created fountain of supply [President Thomas Jefferson]." (WJA, I, p. 603)

(12-15)   "Yet in the ardor of their [certain Massachusetts Federalists'] hostility to Mr. Jefferson, they were ready to overlook a great deal. Besides, the alienation of Mr. [John Quincy] Adams might be more dangerous to their ascendency than an attempt to conciliate him by a show of confidence. . . .

". . . By assenting to his [John Quincy Adams's] election to one of the places, a way was made for the attainment of the other by Colonel Pickering [John Adams's former opponent]. The consequence was the election of the two to sit as colleagues representing Massachusetts in the federal Senate." (WJA, I, pp. 607-608)

(16)   "It is highly honorable to Mr. Jefferson, that his active and unsolicited testimony, generously given to the value of the public services of his ancient opponent, and extensively spread among the large class over whose minds his

p. 351 (cont.)

authority was yet unbounded, had a great effect in accelerating this change [in the public attitude toward John Adams, a change beginning at about the time James Monroe was elected to the Presidency in 1817]. It was a cheering consolation to the declining days of the old statesman, whose integrity not even his most bitter enemies had ever really disputed, the prospect of losing which had at an earlier moment filled his mind with anxiety and gloom." (<u>WJA</u>, I, p. 622)

(17-19) "'Whereas, the Honorable John Adams, a member of this Convention, and elected the President thereof, has for more than half a century devoted the great powers of his mind, and his profound wisdom and learning, to the service of his country and mankind:

"'In fearlessly vindicating the rights of the North American provinces against the usurpation and encroachments of the superintendent government:

"'In diffusing a knowledge of the principles of civil liberty among his fellow-subjects, and exciting them to a firm and resolute defence of the privileges of freemen:

"'In early conceiving, asserting, and maintaining the justice and practicability of establishing the independence of the United States of America: . . .

"'In negotiating the treaty of peace, which secured forever the sovereignty of the United States, and in defeating

p. 351 (cont.)

all attempts to prevent it; and especially in preserving in that treaty the vital interests of the New England States: . . .

"'Resolved, That a committee of twelve be appointed by the chair, to communicate this proceeding to the Honorable John Adams, to inform him of his election to preside in this body [the Massachusetts Convention for the revision of the state constitution which Adams had influenced so greatly forty years earlier], and to introduce him to the chair of this Convention.'" (WJA, I, pp. 625-626) John Adams, then age 86, was obliged to decline the honor tendered him in this Resolution presented him by the Massachusetts Convention.

(20-23) "'New York, 4 March, 1825. . . . It is to your glory, Sir, that your son [John Quincy Adams] has proved himself worthy of your instructions, your wisdom, and your experience, and become confessedly the fittest and most deserving object to succeed, after time has restored the empire of reason, his father in the highest confidence and trust of a great and free people.

"'I remain, Sir, (changed with the times, tempora mutantur, since 1798, and notwithstanding my trial of the Sedition Law [for editing the "Bee," a Connecticut newspaper that attacked John Adams's administration],) with the most sincere deference, esteem, and veneration, and desirous of

p. 351 (cont.)

contributing my mite to the consolations of a political Simeon, Your very obed't humble servant, CHARLES HOLT.'" (<u>WJA</u>, I, pp. 631-632)

(24-26) "'Washington, 9 February, 1825. MY DEAR AND HONORED FATHER,--The inclosed note from Mr. King will inform you of the event of this day [John Quincy Adams's election to the Presidency of the United States on the first ballot of the House of Representatives], upon which I can only offer <u>you</u> my congratulations, and ask your blessings and prayers. Your affectionate and dutiful son, JOHN QUINCY ADAMS.'" (<u>WJA</u>, I, p. 632)

(27-29) "The brilliant fictions of Walter Scott, then in the height of their popularity, the sea stories of Cooper, and even the exaggerated, but vigorous poetry of Byron, were all welcome [and read to John Adams in his ninetieth year by members of his family], in the intervals when he could not obtain what he better relished, the reminiscences of contemporaries, or the speculations of more profound writers in England and France." (<u>WJA</u>, I, p. 633)

(30) "In Mr. Adams's vocabulary, the word <u>property</u> meant land. He had no confidence in the permanence of any thing else, hence he left little else behind him. The opinion

p. 351 (cont.)

was inherited by his son, John Quincy Adams, who, in consequence, purchased, at the settlement of the estate agreeably to the will, the lands his father left." (<u>WJA</u>, I, p. 639)

(31)   "'From lives thus spent thy earthly duties learn;
From fancy's dreams to active virtue turn:
Let Freedom, Friendship, Faith, thy soul engage,
And serve, like them, thy country and thy age.'"

The above lines are taken from the inscription at the tomb of John and Abigail Adams. (<u>WJA</u>, I, p. 644)

(32)   "'The Catholics thought him [Benjamin Franklin] almost a Catholic. The Church of England claimed

p. 352   him as one of them. The Presbyterians thought him

(1-3)   half a Presbyterian, and the Friends believed him a wet Quaker. The dissenting clergymen in England and America were among the most distinguished asserters and propagators of his renown. Indeed, all sects considered him, and I believe justly, a friend to unlimited toleration in matters of religion [John Adams in <u>The Boston Patriot</u>, 15 May 1811].'" (<u>WJA</u>, I, "Appendix B," p. 661)

(4)   "'To condense all the rays of this glory [of the invention of the lightning rod by Benjamin Franklin] to a focus, to sum it up in a single line, to impress it on every mind and transmit it to all posterity, a motto was devised for his picture, and soon became familiar to the memory of

p. 352 (cont.)

every school-boy who understood a word of Latin:--

    "'"Eripuit coelo fulmen sceptrumque tyrannis."'"

Thus it appeared at first, and the author of it was held in a mysterious obscurity. But, after some time, M. Turgot altered it to

    "'"Eripuit coelo fulmen; mox sceptra tyrannis."'"

By the first line, the rulers of Great Britain and their arbitrary oppressions of the Colonies were alone understood. By the second was intimated that Mr. Franklin was soon to destroy or at least to dethrone all kings and abolish all monarchical governments. This, it cannot be disguised, flattered at that time the ruling popular passion of all Europe [John Adams in The Boston Patriot, 15 May 1811].'" (WJA, I, "Appendix B," p. 662)

(5)   "'Such was the real character, and so much more formidable was the artificial character of Dr. Franklin, when he entered into partnership with the Count de Vergennes, the most powerful minister of State in Europe, to destroy the character and power of a poor man almost without name [John Adams], unknown in the European world, born and educated in the American wilderness, out of which he had never set his foot till 1778. Thanks to the wisdom, virtue, dignity, and fortitude of congress, all their arts were defeated in America [John Adams in The Boston Patriot, 15 May 1811].'" (WJA, I, "Appendix B," p. 663)

p. 352 (cont.)

(6)   Pound's comment. Volume II of the Charles Francis Adams edition of the writings of John Adams includes a "Diary," the "Notes" John Adams recorded of the debates in the Continental Congresses of 1775 and 1776, a portion of an "Autobiography," as well as several "Appendices."

(7)   "I long to be a master of Greek and Latin. I long to prosecute the mathematical and philosophical sciences. I long to know a little of ethics and moral philosophy. But I have no books, no time, no friends." (D. 24 April 1756: <u>WJA</u>, II, p. 13)

(8)   "Drank tea at the Colonel's. Not one new idea this week." (D. 14 May 1756: <u>WJA</u>, II, p. 17)

(9)   "[Sir Geoffrey] Amherst, who had arrived at Boston from the conquest of Louisburg, marched with his army of four thousand men across the country, and halted a few days at Worcester, having encamped his army on the hill behind the present court house. Here we had an opportunity of seeing him, his officers and army. The officers were very social, spent their evenings and took their suppers with such of the inhabitants as were able to invite them, and entertained us with their music and their dances. Many of them were Scotchmen in their plaids, and their music was delightful;

p. 352 (cont.)

even the bagpipe was not disagreeable." (Autobiography, 1757: WJA, II, p. 33)

(10) "Chores, chat, tobacco, tea, steal away time; but I am resolved to translate Justinian and his commentator's notes by daylight, and read Gilbert's Tenures by night, till I am master of both, and I will meddle with no other book in this chamber on a week day; on a Sunday I will read the Enquiry into the Nature of the Human Soul, and for amusement, I will sometimes read Ovid's Art of Love to Mrs. Savil. This shall be my method." (D. 5 October 1758: WJA, II, p. 37)

(11-15) "Rode to Boston; arrived about half after ten; went into the court house and sat down by Mr. Paine, at the lawyers' table. . . .

"However, I attended court steadily all day, and at night went to consort with Samuel Quincy and Dr. Gardiner. There I saw the most spacious and elegant room, the gayest company of gentlemen, and the finest row of ladies that ever I saw; but the weather was so dull, and I so disordered, that I could not make one half the observations that I wanted to make." (D. 24 October 1758: WJA, II, p. 45)

(15-20) "Then Mr. Gridley inquired what method of study I had pursued, what Latin books I read, what Greek, what

p. 352 (cont.)

French? what I had read upon rhetoric? Then he took his common-place book and gave me Lord Hales's advice to a student of the common law; and when I had read that, he gave me Lord C. J. Reeve's advice to his nephew, in the study of the common law. Then he gave me a letter from Dr. Dickins, Regius Professor of Law at the University of Cambridge, to him, pointing out a method of studying the civil law; then he turned to a letter he wrote to Judge Lightfoot, Judge of the Admiralty in Rhode Island, directing to a method of studying the admiralty law. . . . 'I have a few pieces of advice to give you, Mr. Adams. One is, to puruse the study of the law, rather than the gain of it; pursue the gain of it enough to keep out of the briers, but give your main attention to the study of it.'" (D. 25 October 1758: WJA, II, p. 46)

(20-22) "His advice made so deep an impression on my mind, that I believe no lawyer in America ever did so much business as I did afterwards, in the seventeen years that I passed in the practice at the bar, for so little profit." (Autobiography: WJA, II, p. 46n)

(23-29) "'You [said Gridley] must conquer the Institutes. The road of science is much easier now than it was when I set out; I began with Coke-Littleton, and broke through.' I asked his advice about studying Greek. He answered, 'It

p. 352 (cont.)

is a matter of mere curiosity.' After this long and familiar conversation, we went to court, attended all day, and in the evening I went to ask Mr. Thacher's concurrence with the bar; drank tea and spent the whole evening—upon original sin, origin of evil, the plan of the universe, and at last upon law. . . . Thacher thinks this county is full." (D. 25 October 1758: WJA, II, p. 47)

(30-33) "Mr. Gridley lent me Van Muyden's Compendiosa Institutionum Justiniani Tractatio in Usum Col-
p. 353   legiorum, Editio tertia prioribus auctior et emen-
(1)   datior. Pax Artium Altrix. After I have mastered this, I must read Hoppius's Commentary on Justinian. The design of this book is to explain the technical terms, and to settle the divisions and distributions of the civil law. By the way, this is the first thing a student ought to aim at, namely, distinct ideas under the terms, and a clear apprehension of the divisions and distributions of the science. This is one of the principal excellencies of Hawkins's Pleas of the Crown, and it is the very end of this book of Van Muyden." (D. 26 October 1758: WJA, II, p. 48) The Chinese ideogram emphasizes that Van Muyden's book illustrates a Confucian concern for terminology. The ideogram (cheng) means "to regulate + the name: to define the correct terms; to rectify the names or terms: a true definition." (Index, p. 269)

p. 353 (cont.)

(1-2) "I was desirous of seeking the law as well as I could in its fountains, and I obtained as much knowledge as I could of Bracton, Britton, Fleta and Glanville; but I suffered very much for want of books, which determined me to furnish myself at any sacrifice with a proper library; and accordingly, by degrees, I procured the best library of law in the State." (Autobiography: WJA, II, p. 50, n. 2)

(2-3) "Had he [James Putnam, the Worcester lawyer who accepted John Adams as a law pupil] given me, now and then, a few hints concerning practice, I should be able to judge better at this hour than I can now. I have reason to complain of him; but it is my destiny to dig treasures with my own fingers; nobody will lend me or sell me a pickaxe." (D. 18 December 1758: WJA, II, p. 52)

(4-5) "Yesterday and to-day I have read aloud Tully's four Orations against Catiline. The sweetness and grandeur of his sounds, and the harmony of his humbers, give pleasure enough to reward the reading, if one understood none of his meaning. Besides, I find it a noble exercise; it exercises my lungs, raises my spirits, opens my pores, quickens the circulations, and so contributes much to health." (D. 21 December 1758: WJA, II, pp. 52-53)

p. 353 (cont.)

(6-7) "Ruggles's grandeur consists in the quickness of his apprehension, steadiness of his attention, the boldness and strength of his thoughts and expressions, his strict honor, conscious superiority, contempt of meanness, &c. People approach him with dread and terror." (D. 8 April 1759?: <u>WJA</u>, II, p. 67)

(8-9) "Timothy Ruggles, a person, who, with the exception of Hutchinson, probably staked more of influence and property upon his activity on the loyal side than anybody in Massachusetts. At this time he was keeping a tavern and practising law in Sandwich, dividing the business of that section of the colony with the elder Otis; but he soon afterwards removed to Hardwick, in the county of Worcester, and became the political combatant of the younger Otis in the General Court. He was the President of the Congress of 1765, refused to sign the address which it adopted, and received, therefor, the censure of the House. He subsequently took an active part in organizing the loyalists in the field. He died in Nova Scotia in 1798. <u>Sabine's American Loyalists</u>." (Editor's note, <u>WJA</u>, II, p. 67n)

(10-11) "Is not variety more agreeable and profitable, too? Read one book one hour; then think an hour; then exercise an hour; then read another book an hour; then dine,

p. 353 (cont.)

smoke, walk, cut wood; read aloud another hour, then think, &c; and thus spend the whole day in perpetual variation, from reading to thinking, exercise, company, &c." (D. 8 April 1759?: <u>WJA</u>, II, p. 69)

(12-13) Pound's interpolation. From Cavalcanti's <u>Donna mi prega</u>, the Italian words <u>in quella parte/ dove sta memora</u> mean "in that part/ where the memory is." (<u>Index</u>, p. 100)

(13-15) "These are all wild, extravagant, loose opinions and expressions; he [Oxenbridge Thacher] expresses himself as wildly as Colonel Chandler--wild flights; he has not considered that these crude thoughts and wild expressions are catched and treasured as proofs of his character." (D. 8 April 1759?: <u>WJA</u>, II, pp. 74-75) Colonel Chandler was "a leader of the Boston pre-Revolutionary troops with which John Adams sometimes served." (<u>Index</u>, p. 34)

(16-24) "The next time Mr. Franklin was in Boston, Mr. [Edmund] Quincy waited on him to thank him for his slips; 'but I am sorry, sir, to give you so much trouble.' 'O, sir,' says Franklin, 'the trouble is nothing to me, if the vines do but succeed in your province. However, I was obliged to take more pains than I expected, when I saw you. I had been told that the vines were in the city, but I found none, and was

p. 353 (cont.)

obliged to send up to a village, seventy miles from the city, for them.' Thus, he took the trouble to hunt over the city, and not finding vines there, he sends seventy miles into the country, and then sends one bundle by water, and, lest they should miscarry, another by land, to a gentleman whom he owed nothing and was but little acquainted with, purely for the sake of doing good in the world by propagating the Rhenish vines through these provinces." (D. 26 May 1760: WJA, II, p. 81)

(24-25) "Arose very late. A cold, rainy, north-easterly storm, of several days continuance. Read Timon of Athens, the man-hater, in the evening, at the Doctor's." (D. 6 June 1760: WJA, II, p. 87)

(26-27) "In short, I never shall shine till some animating occasion calls forth all my powers. I find that the mind must be agitated with some passion, either love, fear, hope, &c., before she will do her best." (D. 10 June 1760: WJA, II, pp. 87-88) The Latin word IRA in line 26 means "anger." (Index, p. 101)

(28) Pound's interpolation. From Cavalcanti's Donna mi prega, the Italian words la qual manda fuoco mean "which sends fire." (Index, p. 118)

p. 353 (cont.)

(29-30) "These dirty and ridiculous litigations have been multiplied, in this town, till the very earth groans and the stones cry out. The town is become infamous for them throughout the county. I have absolutely heard it used as a proverb in several parts of the province,--'As litigious as Braintree.'" (D. 19 June 1760: <u>WJA</u>, II, p. 90)

(31-32) "Mr. Gridley, about fifteen months since, advised me to read an Institute of the Canon Law; and that advice lay broiling in my head till last week, when I borrowed the book. I am very glad that he gave and I took the advice, for it will explain many things in ecclesiastical history, and open that system of fraud, bigotry, nonsense, impudence, and superstition, on which the papal usurpations are founded, besides increasing my skill in the Latin tongue, and my acquaintance with civil law; for, in many respect the canon is grafted on the civil." (D. 27 January 1761: <u>WJA</u>, II, p. 116)

(32-34) "This Institute is a curious monument of priestly ambition, avarice, and subtlety. 'Tis a system of sacerdotal guile." (D. 9 February 1761: <u>WJA</u>, II, p. 117)

(35)   "I have heard men every day for fifty years boasting, 'Our constitution is the first under heaven. We are governed by our own laws. No tyrant can

p. 354   lord it over us. The king is as accountable for
(1-2)   his conduct as the subject. No government that ever existed was so essentially free; every man is his own monarch; his will or the will of his agent, and no other, can bind him.' All these gallant, blustering speeches I have heard in words, and I never failed to raise a horse laugh; for observe the pleasant course of these things." (D. 21 March 1761?: WJA, II, p. 121) This quotation comes from what the editor identifies as "Another article written for the newspapers." (WJA, II, p. 120n)

(3-9)   "The king sent instructions to his custom house officers to carry the acts of trade and navigation into strict execution. An inferior officer of the customs, in Salem, whose name was Cockle, petitioned the justices of the superior court, at their session in November (1760) for the county of Essex, to grant him writs of assistants, according to some provision in one of the acts of trade which had not been executed, to authorize him to break open ships, shops, cellars, houses, &c., to search for prohibited goods and merchandises, on which duties had not been paid. Some objection was made to this motion; and Mr. Stephen Sewall, who was then Chief Justice of that court, and a zealous friend of liberty, expressed some doubts of the legality and constitutionality of the writ, and of the power of the court to grant it. The court ordered the question to be argued at

p. 354 (cont.)

Boston, in February Term, 1761. . . .

"In February, Mr. James Otis, junior, a lawyer of Boston, and a son of Colonel Otis of Barnstable, appeared, at the request of the merchants in Boston, in opposition to the writ. . . . Mr. Oxenbridge Thacher, whose amiable manners and pure principles united to a very easy and musical eloquence made him very popular, was united with Otis; and Mr. Gridley alone appeared for Cockle, the petitioner, in support of the writ. . . . The views of the English government towards the colonies, and the views of the colonies towards the English government, from the first of our history to that time, appeared to me to have been directly in opposition to each other, and were now, by the imprudence of administration, brought to a collision. England, proud of its power, and holding us in contempt, would never give up its pretensions. The Americans, devoutly attached to their liberties, would never submit, at least without an entire devastation of the country and a general destruction of their lives. A contest appeared to me to be opened, to which I could foresee no end, and which would render my life a burden, and property, industry, and every thing insecure." (Autobiography: WJA, II, pp. 124, n. 1-125n)

CANTO LXIV

p. 355

(1)   "In pursuance of my plan of reforming the practice of sheriffs and pettifoggers in the country, I procured of all the justices in Braintree,—John Quincy, Edmund Quincy, Josiah Quincy, and Joseph Crosby,—a recommendation of my brother to Stephen Greenleaf, sheriff of the county, and a certificate of his character; upon receiving which, Mr. Greenleaf readily gave him a deputation. He was young, loved riding, and discharged his duties with skill and fidelity; but his disposition was so tender, that he often assisted his debtors with his own purse and credit, and upon the whole, to say the least, was nothing the richer for his office." (Autobiography: WJA, II, p. 129n)

(2-4)   "'Oliver [Cromwell] was successful, but not prudent nor honest, nor laudable, nor imitable.'" (D. 10 September 1761: WJA, II, p. 132) This was the judgment of Rev. Anthony Wibird, the Congregationalist minister at Braintree.

(5-11)   "I last night read through both of Dr. Donne's Satires versified by Pope. Was most struck with these lines:

p. 355 (cont.)

>'Bear me, some god! Oh! quickly bear me hence,
>To wholesome solitude, the nurse of sense,
>Where contemplation prunes her ruffled wings,
>And the free soul looks down to pity kings.'

"'Prayer.' A posture; hands uplifted, and eyes. A very proper prayer for me to make when I am in Boston. 'Solitude' is a personage in a clean, wholesome dress, the 'nurse' and nourisher of sense. 'Contemplation,' a personage. 'Prunes,' picks, smooths. Is she an angel or a bird?-- 'ruffled,' rumpled, rugged, uneven, tumbled;--'free soul,' not enslaved, unshackled, no bondage, no subjection; 'looks down,' pities George, Louis, Frederick, Philip, Charles, &c." (D. 18 October 1761: <u>WJA</u>, II, p. 132)

(12-16) "A secluded and beautiful spot almost surrounded by water, in which Deacon, afterwards called General Palmer, well known at this time, as well as subsequently, as a member of the Committee of Safety in the Revolution, had established himself among a colony of glassblowers from Germany, come to undertake the manufacture of that article in America." (Editor's note, <u>WJA</u>, II, p. 136, n. 4)

(17-21) "Returned to Mr. Borland's, dined, and afternoon rode to Germantown, where we spent our evening. Deacon Palmer showed us his lucern growing in his garden, of which he has cut, as he tells us, four crops this year. The Deacon had his lucern seeds of Mr. Greenleaf of Abington,

p. 355 (cont.)

who had his of Judge Oliver. . . . The cut of the lucern was exact enough; the pod in which the seeds are is an odd thing, a kind of ram's-horn or straw.

"We had a good deal of conversation upon husbandry. The Deacon has about seventy bushels of potatoes this year on about one quarter of an acre of ground." (D. 22 October 1762: <u>WJA</u>, II, pp. 136-137)

(22)   "Hoc enim ratio naturalis, junctâ necessitate publicâ, exigit ut militibus potissimum praedia, ab hostibus occupata, pro bene meritis concederentur sub conditione tamen fidelitatis, quo eo securior esset respublica et ad patriam defendendam magis allicerentur." (D. 21 February 1765: <u>WJA</u>, II, p. 149) This quotation from Strykius came up at a meeting of the "sodality," a group of lawyer friends informally organized by Gridley for the purpose of improving their familiarity with the law. John Adams hosted, at Blodget's in Boston, the meeting referred to here. The Latin words <u>sub conditione fidelitates</u> mean "under condition of faith; on trust." (<u>Index</u>, p. 207)

(23-31) "Is it known that he ever advised the ministry to lay internal taxes upon us? that he ever solicited the office of distributer of stamps? or that he has ever done any thing to injure the people or to incur their displeasure, besides

p. 355 (cont.)

barely accepting of that office? . . . To be placed, only in pageantry, in the most conspicuous part of the town, with such ignominious devices around him, would be thought severity enough by any man of common sensibility. But to be carried through the town in such insolent triumph, and burned on a hill, to have his garden torn in pieces, his house broken open, his furniture destroyed, and his whole family thrown into confusion and terror, is a very atrocious violation of the peace, and of dangerous tendency and consequence.

"But, on the other hand, let us ask a few questions. Has not his Honor the Lieutenant-Governor discovered to the people, in innumerable instances, a very ambitious and avaricious disposition? Has he not grasped four of the most important offices in the Province into his own hands? Has not his brother-in-law, Oliver, another of the greatest places in government? Is not a brother of the Secretary, a judge of the superior court? Has not that brother a son in the House? . . . Has not the Lieutenant-Governor a near relation who is register of his own court of probate, and deputy secretary? Has he not another near relation who is Clerk of the House of Representatives? Is not this amazing ascendency of one family foundation sufficient on which to erect a tyranny? Is it not enough to excite jealousies among the people?" (D. 15 August 1765: WJA, II, pp. 150-151)

p. 355 (cont.)

(32) "This year, 1765, was the epoch of the Stamp Act. I drew up a petition to the selectmen of Braintree, and procured it to be signed by a number of respectable inhabitants, to call a meeting of the town to instruct their representative in relation to the stamps. . . . I prepared a draught of instructions at home, and carried them with me. . . . We retired to Mr. Niles's house, my draught was produced, and unanimously adopted without a dissenting voice. These were published in Draper's paper, as that printer first applied to me for a copy. They were decided and spirited enough. They rang through the State and were adopted in so many words, as I was informed by the representatives of that year, by forty towns, as instructions to their representatives. . . .

p. 356
(1-2)

". . . He [Samuel Adams] told me the town of Boston had employed him to draw instructions for their representatives; that he felt an ambition which was very apt to mislead a man, --that of doing something extraordinary; and he wanted to consult a friend who might suggest some thoughts to his mind. I read his instructions, and showed him a copy of mine. I told him I thought his very well as far as they went, but he had not gone far enough. Upon reading mine, he said he was of my opinion, and accordingly took into his some paragraphs from mine." (Autobiography, WJA, II, pp. 152-154)

p. 356 (cont.)

(3-12) "The year 1765 has been the most remarkable year of my life. That enormous engine, fabricated by the British Parliament, for battering down all the rights and liberties of America, I mean the Stamp Act, has raised and spread through the whole continent a spirit that will be recorded to our honor with all future generations. In every colony, from Georgia to New Hampshire inclusively, the stamp distributers and inspectors have been compelled by the unconquerable rage of the people to renounce their offices. . . .

"The people, even to the lowest ranks, have become more attentive to their liberties, more inquisitive about them, and more determined to defend them, than they were ever before known or had occasion to be; innumerable have been the monuments of wit, humor, sense, learning, spirit, patriotism, and heroism, erected in the several colonies and provinces in the course of this year. . . .

". . . The Governor has no authority to distribute or even to unpack the bales; the Act has never been proclaimed nor read in the Province; yet the probate office is shut, the custom-house is shut, the courts of justice are shut, and all business seems at a stand. Yesterday and the day before, the two last days of service for January Term, only one man asked me for a writ, and he was soon determined to wave his request. I have not drawn a writ since the first of November. . . .

". . . And if this authority is once acknowledged and

p. 356 (cont.)

established, the ruin of America will become inevitable. . . . But I must endeavor, in some degree, to compensate the disadvantage, by posting my books, reducing my accounts into better order, and by diminishing my expenses,--but, above all, by improving the leisure of this winter in a diligent application to my studies. . . .

". . . Thirty years of my life are passed in preparation for business; I have had poverty to struggle with, envy and jealousy and malice of enemies to encounter, no friends, or but few, to assist me; so that I have groped in dark obscurity, till of late, and had but just become known and gained a small degree of reputation, when this execrable project was set on foot for my ruin as well as that of America in general, and of Great Britain." (D. 18 December 1765: WJA, II, pp. 154-156)

(13-16) "About twelve o'clock came in Messrs. Crafts and Chase, and gave me a particular account of the proceedings of the Sons of Liberty, on Tuesday last, in prevailing on Mr. Oliver to renounce his office of distributer of stamps, by a declaration under his hand and under his oath, taken before Justice Dana in Hanover Square, under the very tree of liberty, nay, under the very limb where he had been hanged in effigy, August 14th, 1765. . . .

"About one o'clock came in Mr. Clark, one of the con-

p. 356 (cont.)

stables of the town of Boston, with a letter from Mr. William Cooper, their town-clerk, in these words:

> 'Sir:--I am directed by the town to acquaint you, that they have this day voted unanimously that Jeremiah Gridley, James Otis, and John Adams, Esquires, be applied to as counsel to appear before his Excellency the Governor in council, in support of their memorial praying that the courts of law in this Province may be opened. . . . Boston, December 18th, 1765.'"

(D. 19 December 1765: WJA, II, pp. 156-157)

(17)   "The original of this is preserved." (WJA, II, p. 157n)

(18-23) "But when I recollect my own reflections and speculations yesterday, a part of which were committed to writing last night, and may be seen under December 18th, and compare them with the proceedings of Boston yesterday, of which the foregoing letter informed me, I cannot but wonder, and call to mind my Lord Bacon's observation about secret, invisible laws of nature, and communications and influences between places that are not discoverable by sense.

". . . Shall we contend that the Stamp Act is void--that the Parliament have no legal authority to impose internal taxes upon us, because we are not represented in it--and, therefore, that the Stamp Act ought to be waved by the judges as against natural equity and the constitution?"
(D. 19 December 1765: WJA, II, p. 157)

p. 356 (cont.)

(24-30) "Among the papers of Mr. Adams, the following abstract remains of the authorities on which he relied upon this occasion:-- . . .

"'Common law is common right. 1 Inst. 142 a. Coke's Proem to 2 Inst.

"'The law is the subject's best birthright. 2 Inst. 56.

"'Want of right and want of remedy is all one; for where there is no remedy there is no right. 1 Inst. 95b. . . .

"'A statute must be construed that no innocent man may, by a literal construction, receive damage. Wood, p. 9. . . .

"'Actus Dei nemini facit injuriam; actus legis nulli facit injuriam.'" (WJA, II, pp. 158, n. 3-159n) The Latin words Pound uses, actus/ legis nulli facit injuriam, mean "an act of law does harm to none." (Index, p. 2)

(31)   "My advice to the town will be, to take the board at their word, and to choose a committee immediately; in the first place, to wait on the Governor in council, as the supreme court of probate, and request of them a determination of the point,--whether the officers of the probate courts in the Province can be justified in proceeding with business without stamps; in the next place, to wait on the honorable the judges of the superior court, to request their determination of the same question; and, in the third place, to wait on the judges of the inferior court for the county of Suffolk

p. 356 (cont.)

with the same request, in pursuance of the recommendation of the honorable board; and, unless a speedy determination of the question is obtained in all these courts in this way, to request of the Governor a convention of the two houses, and, if that is refused, to endeavor to call one themselves." (D. 21 December 1765: <u>WJA</u>, II, p. 162)

(32-34) "But there is another sort of seekers worse than the other two,--such as seek to be Governors, Lieutenant-Governors, Secretaries, Custom-house officers of all sorts, Stamp-officers of all sorts,--in fine, such as seek appointments from the crown. These seekers are actuated by a more ravenous sort of ambition and avarice, and they merit a more aggravated condemnation. These ought to be avoided and dreaded as the plague, as the destroying angels; and the evil spirits are as good objects of your trust as they." (D. 25 December 1765: <u>WJA</u>, II, p. 166)

(35) "If there is any one who cannot see the tendency of that Act to reduce the body of the people to

p. 357 ignorance, poverty, dependence, his want of eye-
(1) sight is a disqualification for public employment."
D. 27 December 1765: <u>WJA</u>, II, p. 167)

(2-3) "Etter is another of the poisonous talkers, but

p. 357 (cont.)

not equally so. Cleverly and Veasey [clergymen with Loyalist sympathies] are slaves in principle; they are devout, religious slaves, and a religious bigot is the worst of men."
(D. 29 December 1765: WJA, II, p. 169)

(3-4)   "The national attention is fixed upon the colonies; the religion, administration of justice, geography, numbers, &c., of the colonies, are a fashionable study. But what wretched blunders do they make in attempting to regulate them. They know not the character of Americans." (D. 31 December 1765: WJA, II, p. 170)

(4-10)   "This year brings ruin or salvation to the British Colonies. The eyes of all America are fixed on the British Parliament. In short, Britain and America are staring at each other; and they will probably stare more and more for some time.

". . . In his examination of the last question, he [Mr. Deberdt, colonial agent to Lord Dartmouth] goes upon the principle of the Ipswich instructions; namely, that the first settlers of America were driven by oppression from the realm, and so dismembered from the dominions, till at last they offered to make a contract with the nation, or the Crown, and to become subject to the Crown upon certain conditions, which contract, subordination, and conditions, were wrought into

p. 357 (cont.)

their charters, which gave them a right to tax themselves.
. . . And, indeed, it appears from Hutchinson's History
and the Massachusetts Records, that the Colonies were considered formerly, both here and at home, as allies rather than
subjects. The first settlement, certainly, was not a national
act; that is, not an act of the people nor the Parliament.
Nor was it a national expense; neither the people of England
nor their representatives contributed any thing towards it.
Nor was the settlement made on a territory belonging to the
people nor the Crown of England." (D. 1 January 1766: WJA,
II, pp. 170-172)

(11)   "A great storm of snow last night; weather
tempestuous all day. Waddled through the snow driving my
cattle to water at Doctor Savil's;--a fine piece of glowing
exercise." (D. 2 January 1766: WJA, II, p. 173)

(12)   "Hampden [pseudonym of James Otis for his controversial papers] has given us, in yesterday's Gazette, a long
letter to Pym [pseudonym of writer in England supporting the
Crown] upon shutting up the courts; in which he proves, from
Holt's and Pollexfen's argument at the revolution conference,
from Grotius De Jure Belli, (book 1, ch. 3, s. 2,) that
shutting up the courts is an abdication of the throne, a discharge of the subjects from their allegiance, and a total

140

p. 357 (cont.)

dissolution of government, and reduction of all men to a state of nature; and he proves, from Bracton, that partial tumults, &c., are not a <u>tempus guerrium</u>, (<u>bellorum</u>,) a time of war." (D. 7 January 1766: <u>WJA</u>, II, p. 174)

(13-16) "One Thompson came to me at Cunningham's, in the evening, and engaged me in a cause of Sampson vs. Buttar, which is for entering a vessel at Louisburg and taking away ten barrels of rum." (D. 13 January 1766: <u>WJA</u>, II, pp. 176-177) This was the day that the inferior court of common pleas opened at Boston.

(17-19) "The January packet arrived at New York has brought the King's speech, the addresses of Lords and Commons, 14th of January, and many private letters, which inform that Mr. Pitt was in the House of Commons, and declared himself against Grenville and for a repeal of the Stamp Act, upon principle; called it the most impolitic, arbitrary, oppressive, and unconstitutional Act that ever was passed; denied that we were represented in the House of Commons, (Q. Whether the House of Commons or the Parliament?) and asserted that the House granted taxes in their representative capacity, not in their legislative, and, therefore, that the Parliament had not the right to tax the colonies." (D. 28 March 1766: <u>WJA</u>, II, pp. 190-191)

p. 357 (cont.)

(20-24) "This Eaton, Goffe set up, as Pynchon tells me, to be a justice, but Thacher got him indicted in the county of Essex for a barrator, which defeated the scheme of Goffe, and he came near conviction. Goffe grew warm, and said that Eaton's character was as good as any man's at the bar.

"Spent the evening at Mr. Pynchon's, with Farnham, Sewall, Sargeant, Colonel Saltonstall, &c. very agreeably. Punch, wine, bread and cheese, apples, pipes and tobacco." (D. 5 November 1766: WJA, II, p. 201)

(25-28) "A fine morning; oated at Martin's, where we saw five boxes of dollars, containing, as we were told, about eighteen thousand of them, going in a horse-cart from Salem custom-house to Boston, in order to be shipped for England." (D. 6 November 1766: WJA, II, p. 201)

(29-32) "Went up to my common pasture to give directions about trimming the trees, that is, lopping and trimming the walnuts and oaks, and felling the pines and savins and hemlocks. An irregular, misshapen pine will darken the whole scene in some places. These I fell without mercy, to open the prospect and let in the sun and air, that the other wood may grow the faster, and that the grass may get in for feed." (D. 7 November 1766: WJA, II, p. 201)

p. 357 (cont.)

(33)   I have been unable to identify a reference to a "case between negro and owner" at this point in the text. A second mention of the phrase occurs in line 9, p. 358, of this canto (LXIV), and is fully identified there. The two references may be to the same case.

(33-34) "This observation, of his being envied, I have heard made by Nat Thayer before now. 'He [Lieutenant-Governor Hutchinson] was capable and greatly promoted, and therefore envied; at the same time a craving man.'" (D. 11 November 1766: <u>WJA</u>, II, pp. 202-203)

p. 358

(1-2)   "Arrived at Dr. Tufts's, where I found a fine wild goose on the spit, and cranberries stewing in the skillet for dinner." (D. 8 April 1767: <u>WJA</u>, II, p. 206)

(3)   "I was afraid of my health; but they urged so many reasons, and insisted on it so much, that, being determined at last to hazard the experiment, I wrote a letter to the town of Braintree, declining an election as one of their selectmen, and removed in a week or two with my family into the White House, as it was called, in Brattle Square, which several of the old people told me was a good omen, as Mr. Bollan had lived formerly in the same house for many years." (Autobiography: <u>WJA</u>, II, p. 210)

p. 358 (cont.)

(4-5)   "Although this offer was unexpected to me, I was in an instant prepared for an answer. The office [of Advocate-General in the Court of Admiralty] was lucrative in itself, and a sure introduction to the most profitable business in the Province; and what was of more consequence still, it was a first step in the ladder of royal favor and promotion. But I had long weighed this subject in my own mind. . . . But I had always rejected these proposals, on account of the unsettled state of the country and my scruples about laying myself under any restraints or obligations of gratitude to the government for any of their favors. The new statutes had been passed in Parliament, laying duties on glass, paint, &c. and a board of commissioners of the revenue was expected, which must excite a great fermentation in the country, of the consequence of which I could see no end.

"My answer to Mr. Sewall was very prompt, 'That I was sensible of the honor done me by the Governor; but must be excused from accepting his offer.'" (Autobiography: WJA, II, p. 211)

(6)   "The year before this, that is, in 1767, my son John Quincy Adams was born, on the eleventh day of July, at Braintree; and, at the request of his grandmother Smith, christened by the name of John Quincy, on the day of the death of his great grandfather, John Quincy of Mount Wollas-

p. 358 (cont.)

ton." (Autobiography: WJA, II, p. 210)

(7-8)   "He [Jonathan Sewall] also knew that the British government, including the King, his Ministers, and Parliament, apparently supported by a great majority of the nation, were persevering in a system wholly inconsistent with all my ideas of right, justice, and policy, and therefore I could not place myself in a situation in which my duty and my inclination would be so much at variance." (Autobiography: WJA, II, p. 212)

(9)   "This year, 1768, I attended the Superior Court at Worcester, and the next week proceeded to Springfield, in the county of Hampshire, where I was accidentally engaged in a cause between a negro and his master, which was argued by me, I know not how; but it seems it was in such a manner as engaged the attention of Major Hawley, and introduced an acquaintance which was soon after strengthened into a friendship that continued till his death." (Autobiography: WJA, II, p. 213)

(10)   "This convention was proposed in a regular town meeting of the citizens of Boston, held on the 12th and continued on the 13th of September. A circular letter was addressed on the 14th, by the selectmen, to the selectmen

p. 358 (cont.)

of the other towns, proposing the 22d as the day of meeting for the convention. In this paper the error was committed of assigning among the really good reasons for the call, the obviously false one of 'an apprehension of an approaching war with France.' The consequence was, that an advantage was given to the loyalists, of which they availed themselves effectively to weaken the moral force of the measure, although more than a hundred towns were represented under only a week's notice." (WJA, II, p. 213, n. 1)

(11-17) "'About one o'clock at noon, October the first, the troops began landing, under cover of the ship's cannon, without molestation; and, having effected it, marched into the Common with muskets charged, bayonets fixed, drums beating, fifes playing, &c. making, with the train of artillery, upward of seven hundred men.' Gordon, i, 247.

"The population of Boston, at this period, did not exceed sixteen thousand souls. It had been retrograde during the preceding twenty-five years." (WJA, II, p. 213, n. 2)

(18-22) "During my absence on this circuit, a convention sat in Boston, the commissioners of the customs had arrived, and an army landed. On my return, I found the town full of troops, and, as Dr. Byles, of punning memory, expressed it, our grievances red-dressed. Through the whole succeeding

p. 358 (cont.)

Fall and Winter, a regiment was exercised by Major Small, in Brattle Square, directly in front of my house. The spirit-stirring drum and the ear-piercing fife aroused me and my family early enough every morning, and the indignation they excited, though somewhat soothed, was not allayed by the sweet songs, violins and flutes, of the serenading Sons of Liberty under my windows in the evening." (Autobiography: WJA, II, p. 213)

(23-25) "On the other hand, I had read enough in history to be well aware of the errors to which the public opinions of the people were liable in times of great heat and danger, as well as of the extravagances of which the populace of cities were capable when artfully excited to passion, and even when justly provoked by oppression. In ecclesiastical controversies to which I had been a witness, in the contest at Woburn and on Martha's Vineyard, and especially in the trial of Hopkins and Ward, which I had heard at Worcester, I had learned enough to show me, in all their dismal colors, the deceptions to which the people in their passions are liable, and the total suppression of equity and humanity in the human breast, when thoroughly heated and hardened by party spirit." (Autobiography: WJA, II, p. 214)

(26-27) "They [the Instructions to representatives for 1768

p. 358 (cont.)

and 1769] will be found in the Boston Gazette for those years, and, although there is nothing extraordinary in them of matter or style, they will sufficiently show the sense of the public at that time." (Autobiography: WJA, II, p. 215)

(28-31) "In the fall of the year 1768, a great uproar was raised in Boston on account of the unlading in the night of a cargo of wines from the sloop Liberty, from Madeira, belonging to Mr. Hancock, without paying the customs. Mr. Hancock was prosecuted upon a great number of libels, for penalties upon acts of Parliament, amounting to ninety or an hundred thousand pounds sterling. He thought fit to engage me as his counsel and advocate, and a painful drudgery I had of his cause." (Autobiography: WJA, II, p. 215)

(32-35) "My client, Mr. Hancock, never consented to it; he never voted for it himself, and he never voted

p. 359 for any man to make such a law for him. . . .

(1-4) Constructions and arbitrary distinctions made, in short, only for so many by-words, so many cries to deceive a mob, have always been the instruments of arbitrary power, the means of lulling and ensnaring men into their own servitude; for whenever we leave principles and clear, positive laws, and wander after constructions, one construction or consequence is piled upon another, until we get at an immense

p. 359 (cont.)

distance from fact and truth and nature, lost in the wild regions of imagination and possibility, where arbitrary power sits upon her brazen throne, and governs with an iron sceptre. It is a hardship, therefore, scarcely to be endured, that such a penal statute should be made to govern a man and his property without his actual consent, and only upon such a wild chimera as a virtual and constructive consent." (<u>WJA</u>, II, p. 215, n. 2)

(5-6) "I was thoroughly weary and disgusted with the court, the officers of the Crown, the cause, and even with the tyrannical bell that dangled me out of my house every morning; and this odious cause [of defending John Hancock] was suspended at last only by the battle of Lexington, which put an end, forever, to all such prosecutions." (Autobiography: <u>WJA</u>, II, p. 216)

(7-9) "At Mr. [Norton] Quincy's. Here is solitude and retirement. Still, calm, and serene, cool, tranquil, and peaceful,--the cell of the hermit; out at one window you see Mount Wollaston, the first seat of our ancestors, and beyond that, Stony Field Hill, covered over with corn and fruits; out at the other window, an orchard, and, beyond that, the large marsh called the broad meadows; from the east window of the opposite chamber, you see a fine plain covered with

p. 359 (cont.)

corn, and beyond that the whole harbor and all the islands; from the end window of the east chamber, you may see with a prospect-glass every ship, sloop, schooner, and brigantine, that comes in or goes out." (D. 14 August 1769: <u>WJA</u>, II, pp. 216-217) John Adams may have misdated this entry 14 August instead of 13 August (a Sunday). The next entry, for a Monday, is also dated 14 August.

(10-11) "Dined with three hundred and fifty Sons of Liberty, at Robinson's, the sign of Liberty Tree, in Dorchester. We had two tables laid in the open field, by the barn, with between three and four hundred plates, and an awning of sailcloth over head, and should have spent a most agreeable day, had not the rain made some abatement in our pleasures." (D. 14 August 1769: <u>WJA</u>, II, p. 218) The entry for this day does not identify the Liberty tree as a buttonwood, and, for the record, Catherine Drinker Bowen, in her biography <u>John Adams and the American Revolution</u> (New York: Universal-Grosset, 1950), writes that the Liberty Tree was an elm (p. 270).

(12-13) "The evening spent in preparing for the next day's newspaper,--a curious employment, cooking up paragraphs, articles, occurrences, &c., working the political engine!" (D. 3 September 1769: <u>WJA</u>, II, p. 219)

p. 359 (cont.)

(14)   "The morning at Bracket's, upon the case of the whale. The afternoon, at the office, posting books." (D. 19 October 1769: <u>WJA</u>, II, p. 221)

(15-23) "But there is a secret behind, that has never been hinted in public, and that Hutchinson dreaded should be produced before the public. <u>You</u> know, Mr. Tudor, that I had imported from London, and then possessed, the only complete set of the British Statutes at Large, that then existed in Boston, and, as I believe, in all the Colonies. In that work is a statute which expressly prohibits impressments in America; almost the only statute in which the word or idea of impressment is admitted. The volume which contains that statute, doubled down in dog's ears, I had before me, on the table, with a heap of other books. I was determined that if the law of God, of nature, of nations, of the common law of England, and our American prescriptions and charters, could not preserve the lives of my clients, that statute should, if it could. The conclave dreaded the publication of that statute, which they intended to get repealed, and which they and their successors have since procured to be repealed." (L. John Adams to Judge William Tudor, dated 30 December 1816: <u>WJA</u>, II, p. 226n) John Adams here refers to the case of four sailors he defended in 1769 who murdered a Lieutenant Panton of the frigate Rose while resisting impressment. See <u>WJA</u>,

p. 359 (cont.)

II, pp. 224n-226n for the entire account of the trial related by John Adams.

(24) "About nine o'clock we were alarmed with the ringing of bells, and, supposing it to be the signal of fire, we snatched our hats and cloaks, broke up the club, and went out to assist in quenching the fire, or aiding our friends who might be in danger. In the street we were informed that the British soldiers had fired on the inhabitants, killed some and wounded others, near the town-house." (Autobiography: WJA, II, p. 229)

(25) Pound's comment. See Canto LXII, p. 342, line 13.

(26-35) "The next morning, I think it was, sitting in my office, near the steps of the town-house stairs,
p. 360 Mr. Forrest came in, who was then called the Irish
(1-2) Infant. I had some acquaintance with him. With tears streaming from his eyes, he said, 'I am come with a very solemn message from a very unfortunate man, Captain Preston, in prison. He wishes for counsel, and can get none. I have waited on Mr. Quincy, who says he will engage, if you will give him your assistance; without it, he positively will not. Even Mr. Auchmuty declines, unless you will engage.' I had no hesitation in answering, that counsel ought to be

p. 360 (cont.)

the very last thing that an accused person should want in a free country; that the bar ought, in my opinion, to be independent and impartial, at all times and in every circumstance, and that persons whose lives were at stake ought to have the counsel they preferred. But he must be sensible this would be as important a cause as was ever tried in any court or country of the world; and that every lawyer must hold himself responsible not only to his country, but to the highest and most infallible of all tribunals, for the part he should act. He must, therefore, expect from me no art or address, no sophistry or prevarication, in such a cause, nor any thing more than fact, evidence, and law would justify.
. . .
"Upon this, Forrest offered me a single guinea as a retaining fee, and I readily accepted it. From first to last I never said a word about fees, in any of those cases, and I should have said nothing about them here, if calumnies and insinuations had not been propagated that I was tempted by great fees and enormous sums of money." (Autobiography: WJA, II, pp. 230-231)

(3-5)   Pound refers here to the following editor's note: "Hutchinson, who in his third volume has done much to embody, in a permanent form, these floating insinuations of the day against the leading men of the patriotic party, alludes to

p. 360 (cont.)

this affair in the following insidious manner:

"'Captain Preston had been well advised to retain two gentlemen of the law, who were strongly attached to the cause of liberty, <u>and to stick at no reasonable fees for that purpose</u>; and this measure proved of great service to him.'" (WJA, II, p. 231, n. 1) The Latin words <u>ego scriptor cantilenae</u> mean "I, the writer of the canto." (<u>Index</u>, p. 57)

(6-7)   "Before or after the trial, Preston sent me ten guineas, and at the trial of the soldiers afterwards, eight guineas more, which were all the fees I ever received or were offered to me, and I should not have said any thing on the subject to my clients if they had never offered me any thing." (Autobiography: <u>WJA</u>, II, p. 231)

(8)   "Among other things will be found a labored controversy, between the House and the Governor, concerning these words: 'In General Court assembled, and by authority of the same.' I mention this merely on account of an anecdote, which the friends of government circulated with diligence, of Governor Shirley, who then lived in retirement at his seat in Roxbury. Having read this dispute, in the public prints, he asked, 'Who has revived those old words? They were expunged during my administration.' He was answered, 'The Boston seat.' 'And who are the Boston seat?' 'Mr.

154

p. 360 (cont.)

Cushing, Mr. Hancock, Mr. Samuel Adams, and Mr. John Adams.' 'Mr. Cushing I knew, and Mr. Hancock I knew,' replied the old Governor, 'but where the devil this brace of Adamses came from, I know not.'" (Autobiography: WJA, II, p. 233)

(9)   "It had been customary for years to rely upon some one person as a guide in the legal and constitutional questions that might come up in the controversies with the Executive. Thus, although Samuel Adams was now the master mover, John Adams seems to have this year succeeded to the post of legal adviser, which had been filled by Oxenbridge Thacher and James Otis." (WJA, II, p. 233n)

(9-10) "The juries in both cases [of Captain Preston and of the soldiers], in my opinion, gave correct verdicts. It appeared to me, that the greatest service which could be rendered to the people of the town, was to lay before them the law as it stood, that they might be fully apprized of the dangers of various kinds which must arise from intemperate heats and irregular commotions. Although the clamor was very loud among some sorts of people, it has been a great consolation to me, through life, that I acted in this business with steady impartiality, and conducted it to so happy an issue." (Autobiography: WJA, II, p. 236)

p. 360 (cont.)

(11-14) "Stephens says, that the whole colony of Connecticut has given more implicit observance to a letter from the selectmen of Boston than to their Bibles for some years; and that, in consequence of it, the country is vastly happier than it was; for every family has become a little manufactory-house, and they raise and make within themselves many things for which they used to run in debt to the merchants and traders. So that nobody is hurt but Boston and the maritime towns." (D. 26 June 1770: <u>WJA</u>, II, p. 237)

(15)   "This passage was used in the December following with much force in the introduction of the argument in defence of Captain Preston and the soldiers. His son, John Quincy Adams, said of it:--

"'The writer has often heard from individuals, who had been present among the crowd of spectators at the trial, the electrical effect produced upon the jury and upon the immense and excited auditory, by the first sentence with which he opened his defence, which was the following citation from the then recently published work of Beccaria [<u>Essay on Crimes and Punishments</u>].'" (<u>WJA</u>, II, pp. 238n-239n)

Here is the citation: "'If, by supporting the rights of mankind, and of invincible truth, I shall contribute to save from the agonies of death one unfortunate victim of tyranny, or of ignorance equally fatal, his blessing and

p. 360 (cont.)

tears of transport will be a sufficient consolation to me for the contempt of all mankind.'" (D. 28 June 1770: <u>WJA</u>, II, p. 238)

(16-18) "Journeying to Plymouth, at a tavern, I found a man who either knew me before, or by inquiring of some person then present, discovered who I was. He went out and saddled my horse and bridled him, and held the stirrup while I mounted. 'Mr. Adams,' says he, 'as a man of liberty, I respect you; God bless you! I'll stand by you while I live, and from hence to Cape Cod you wont find ten men amiss.'" (D. 28 June 1770: <u>WJA</u>, II, p. 239)

(19)   "A few years ago, a person arraigned for a rape at Worcester, named me to the court for his counsel. I was appointed, and the man was acquitted, but remanded in order to be tried on another indictment for an assault with intention to ravish. When he had returned to prison, he broke out, of his own accord, 'God bless Mr. Adams; God bless his soul. I am not to be hanged, and I don't care what else they do to me.' Here was his blessing and his transport, which gave me more pleasure when I first heard the relation, and when I have recollected it since, than any fee would have done.

"This was a worthless fellow; but <u>nihil</u> <u>humanum</u>, <u>alienum</u>.

p. 360 (cont.)

His joy, which I had in some sense been instrumental in procuring, and his blessings and good wishes, occasioned very agreeable emotions in the heart." (D. 28 June 1770: WJA, II, p. 239) The Latin words nihil humanum alienum mean "nothing human is foreign." (Index, p. 155)

(20-23) "This same landlord, I find, is a high son; he has upon his sign-board, 'Entertainment for the Sons of Liberty,' under the portrait of Mr. Pitt. Thus the spirit of liberty circulates through every minute artery of the Province. . . .

"Drank coffee at home with Mr. Farnham, who came in to see me; and then went to D. Sewall's, where I spent an hour with Farnham, Winthrop, Sewall, and when I came away, took a view of the comet, which was then near the north star; a large bright nucleus in the centre of a nebulous circle." (D. 1 July 1770: WJA, II, p. 243)

(24-32) "Rode to Patten's, of Arundel, and Mr. Winthrop and I turned our horses into a little close, to roll and cool themselves, and feed upon white honeysuckle. . . .

". . . After dinner, Farnham, Winthrop, Sewall, Sullivan, and I, walked a quarter of a mile down the river to see one Poke, a woman at least one hundred and ten years of age, some say one hundred and fifteen. When we came to the house,

158

p. 360 (cont.)

nobody was at home but the old woman, and she lay in bed asleep under the window. We looked in at the window and saw an object of horror;--strong muscles withered and wrinkled to a degree that I never saw before. After some time her daughter came from a neighbor's house, and we went in. The old woman roused herself, and looked round very composedly upon us, without saying a word. The daughter told her, 'here is a number of gentlemen come to see you.' 'Gentlemen,' says the old antediluvian, 'I am glad to see them; I want them to pray for me; my prayers, I fear, are not answered; I used to think my prayers were answered, but of late I think they are not; I have been praying so long for deliverance;--Oh, living God, come in mercy! Lord Jesus, come in mercy! Sweet Christ, come in mercy! I used to have comfort in God, and set a good example; but I fear, &c.'" (D. 2 July 1770: <u>WJA</u>, II, pp. 244-245) The Latin words <u>SUBILLAM/</u> <u>Cumis ego occulis meis</u> (lines 26-27) mean "Sybil/ at Cumae I with my own eyes." The Greek <u>tu theleis</u> (line 29) means "what do you want?" The Latin <u>respondebat illa</u> (line 29) means "she replied." The Greek <u>apothanein</u> (line 30) means "to die." (<u>Index</u>, p. 207)

(33)   "Mr. Winthrop, Mr. Adams, and myself, endeavored to recollect the old distich,--

'Gutta cavat lapidem non vi, sed saepe cadendo.'

p. 360 (cont.)

So far we got, but neither of these gentlemen had ever heard the other part; I, who had some years ago been very familiar with it, could not recollect it; but it is,—

'Sic homo fit doctus, non vi, sed saepe legendo.'

"Mr. Mason led us a jaunt over sharp rocks to the point of the island opposite to Nantasket, where, in a hideous cavern formed by a great prominent rock, he showed us the animal plant or flower, a small, spongy, muscular substance, growing fast to the rock, in figure and feeling resembling a young girl's breast, shooting out at the top of it a flower, which shrinks in and disappears upon touching the substance."
(D. 19 August 1770: <u>WJA</u>, II, p. 248) The Latin words quoted by Pound, <u>non vi sed saepe legendo</u>, mean "not by violence but by frequent reading." (<u>Index</u>, p. 156)

(34-35) "Rode to Cambridge, in company with Colonel Severn Ayers and Mr. Hewitt, from Virginia, Mr. Bull and Mr. Trapier, from South Carolina, Messrs. Cushing, Hancock, Adams, Tom Brattle, Dr. Cooper, and William Cooper. . . .

". . . Ayers informed me, that in the reign of Charles II. an act was sent over from England, with an instruction to the Governor, and he procured the Assembly to pass it, granting a duty of two shillings a hogshead upon all tobacco exported from the Colony, to his Majesty forever. This duty amounts now to a revenue of five thousand pounds sterling a

p. 360 (cont.)

year, which is given, part to the Governor, part to the Judges, &c. to the amount of about four thousand pounds, and what becomes of the other one thousand is unknown. The consequence of this is, that the Governor calls an Assembly when he pleases, and that is only once in two years." (D. 22 August 1770: <u>WJA</u>, II, pp. 249-250) The reference to "Carolina" in line 35 appears to be a misprint for "Virginia," the home colony of Colonel Severn Ayers.

p. 361

(1-2)   "Met a committee of the House, at the representatives' room, to consider of a plan for a society for encouraging arts, agriculture, manufactures, and commerce, with the Province. . . .

". . . Hemp, silk, and many other commodities, might be introduced here and cultivated for exportation. The mulberry tree succeeds as well in our climate and soil as in any." (D. 7 February 1771: <u>WJA</u>, II, p. 252)

(3-5)   "While the people of all the other great kingdoms in Europe have been insidiously deprived of their liberties, it is not unnatural to expect that such as are interested to introduce arbitrary government, should see with envy, detestation, and malice, the people of the British empire, by their sagacity and valor, defending theirs to the present

p. 361 (cont.)

times. . . .

"The British empire has been much alarmed, of late years, with doctrines concerning juries, their powers and duties, which have been said, in printed papers and pamphlets, to have been delivered from the highest tribunals of justice. Whether these accusations are just or not, it is certain that many persons are misguided and deluded by them to such a degree, that we often hear in conversation doctrines advanced for law, which, if true, would render juries a mere ostentation and pageantry, and the Court absolute judges of law and fact." (D. 12 February 1771: <u>WJA</u>, II, pp. 252-253)

(6) "Dined at Mr. Hancock's, with the members, Warren, Church, Cooper, &c. and Mr. Harrison, and spent the whole afternoon, and drank green tea, from Holland, I hope, but don't know." (D. 14 February 1771: <u>WJA</u>, II, p. 255)

(7-8) "Saturday I rode from Martin's in Northborough to Boston on horseback, and from thence to Braintree in a chaise; and when I arrived at my little retreat, I was quite overcome with fatigue. Next morning felt better, and arose early, and walked up Penn's Hill, and then round by the meadow home. . . . The young trees, walnuts and oaks, which were pruned and trimmed by me, are grown remarkably. Nay,

p. 361 (cont.)

the pines have grown the better for lopping." (D. 1 May 1771: WJA, II, p. 258)

(9-10) "I have very cheerfully sacrificed my interest, and my health, and ease and pleasure, in the service of the people. I have stood by their friends longer than they would stand by them. I have stood by the people much longer than they would stand by themselves." (D. 2 May 1771: WJA, II, p. 260)

(11-12) "The people in this part of Connecticut make potash, and raise a great number of colts, which they send to the West Indies and barter away for rum, &c." (D. 7 June 1771: WJA, II, p. 271)

(13) "The town of Hartford is not very compact; there are some very handsome and large houses, some of brick. . . .

". . . Middletown, I think, is the most beautiful town of all." (D. 8 June 1771: WJA, II, pp. 272-273) The Diary entry for 8 June 1771 contains a detailed account of John Adams's impression of the two towns.

(14-15) "Took my departure from Middletown homewards the same way I went down; very hot; oated at Hartford, and

p. 361 (cont.)

reached Bissell's of Windsor, twenty-three miles, before dinner, just as they had got their Indian pudding and their pork and greens upon the table, one quarter after twelve."
(D. 10 June 1771: <u>WJA</u>, II, p. 276)

(16-22) "Posterity will scarcely find it possible to form a just idea of this gentleman's character; but if this wretched journal should ever be read by my own family, let them know that there was upon the scene of action, with Mr. Hutchinson, one determined enemy [John Adams] to those principles and that political system to which alone he owes his own and his family's late advancement; one who thinks that his character and conduct have been the cause of laying a foundation for perpetual discontent and uneasiness between Britain and the colonies; of perpetual struggles of one party for wealth and power at the expense of the liberties of this country, and of perpetual contention and opposition in the other party to preserve them, and that this contention will never be fully terminated, but by wars and confusions and carnage. Caesar, by destroying the Roman republic, made himself perpetual dictator. Hutchinson, by countenancing and supporting a system of corruption and all tyranny, has made himself Governor, and by the mad idolatry of the people, always the surest instruments of their own servitude, laid prostrate at the feet of both. With great anxiety and hazard,

p. 361 (cont.)

with continual application to business, with loss of health, reputation, profit, and as fair prospects and opportunities of advancement as others who have greedily embraced them, I have, for ten years together, invariably opposed this system and its fautors. . . .

"Read this day's paper. The melodious harmony, the perfect concords, the entire confidence and affection that seem to be restored [between Governor Hutchinson and colonists], greatly surprise me. Will it be lasting? I believe there is no man in so curious a situation as I am;--I am, for what I can see, quite left alone in the world." (D. 13 June 1771: WJA, II, pp. 278-279)

(23-24) "Boarded at Treadwell's; have had no time to write. Landlord and landlady are some of the grandest people alive; landlady is the great granddaughter of Governor Endicott, and has all the great notions of high family that you find in Winslows, Hutchinsons, Quincys, Salttonstalls, Chandlers, Leonards, Otises, and as you might find with more propriety in the Winthrops. Yet she is cautious and modest about discovering it. She is a new light; continually canting and whining in a religious strain." (D. 22 June 1771: WJA, II, p. 281)

(25-26) "The indian preacher cried, Good God! that ever

p. 361 (cont.)

Adam and Eve should eat that apple, when they knew in their own souls it would make good cider." (D. 23 July 1771: WJA, II, p. 289)

(27-30) "Dined this day, spent the afternoon, and drank tea, at Judge Rope's, with Judges Lynde, Oliver and Hutchinson, Sewall, Putnam and Winthrop. Mrs. Ropes is a fine woman, very pretty and genteel. . . . Drank tea at Judge Rope's, spent the evening at Colonel Pickman's. He is very sprightly, sensible, and entertaining, talks a great deal, tells old stories in abundance about the witchcraft, paper money, Governor Belcher's administration, &c." (D. 9 November 1771: WJA, II, pp. 291-292)

(31-34) "The malice of the court and its writers seems to be principally directed against these two gentlemen [John and Samuel Adams]. They have been steadfast and immovable in the cause of their country from the year 1761, and one of them, Mr. Samuel Adams, for full twenty years before. They have always, since they were acquainted with each other, concurred in sentiment that the liberties of this country had more to fear from one man, the present Governor Hutchinson, than from any other man, nay, than from all other men in the world. This sentiment was founded in their knowledge of his character, his unbounded ambition, and his unbounded

p. 361 (cont.)

popularity. This sentiment they have always freely, though decently, expressed in their conversation and writings, which the Governor well knows, and which will be remembered as long as his character and administration." (D. 9 February 1772: <u>WJA</u>, II, p. 295)

(35)   "But there is not one of all these [the wealthy colonists with whom John Adams has associated] who derives more pleasure from his property than I do from mine; my little farm, and stock, and cash afford me as much satisfaction as all their immense tracts, extensive navigation, sumptuous buildings, their vast sums at interest, and stocks in trade yield to them. . . . The rich are seldom remarkable for modesty, ingenuity, or humanity. Their wealth has rather a tendency to make them penurious and selfish." (D. 30 June 1772: <u>WJA</u>, II, pp. 296-297)

p. 362

(1)   "'I want to know [said James Otis to John Adams], if I was to come into court and ask the court if they were at leisure to hear a motion, and they should say, yes, and I should say,--"May it please your Honors, I have heard a report and read an account that your Honors are to be paid your salaries, for the future, by the Crown out of a revenue raised from us without our consent; as an individual of the

p. 362 (cont.)

community, as a citizen of the town, as an attorney and barrister of this court, I beg your Honors would inform me whether that report is true, and if it is, whether your Honors determine to accept of such an appointment;" or suppose the substance of this should be reduced to a written petition, would this be a contempt? Is mere impertinence a contempt?'" (D. 27 October 1772: <u>WJA</u>, II, pp. 299-300)

(2)   "I said [to an English gentleman] there was no more justice left in Britain than there was in hell; that I wished for war, and that the whole Bourbon family was upon the back of Great Britain; avowed a thorough disaffection to that country; wished that any thing might happen to them, and, as the clergy prayed of our enemies in time of war, that they might be brought to reason or to ruin." (D. 31 December 1772: <u>WJA</u>, II, p. 308)

(3-6)   "Governor Hutchinson, in the plenitude of his vanity and self-sufficiency, thought he could convince all America and all Europe that the Parliament of Great Britain had an authority supreme, sovereign, absolute, and uncontrollable over the Colonies, in all cases whatsoever. In full confidence of his own influence, at the opening of a session of the legislature, he made a speech to both Houses, in which he demonstrated, as he thought, those mighty truths beyond

p. 362 (cont.)

all contradiction, doubt, or question. . . .

"I had quoted [in answering Governor Hutchinson's legal and constitutional arguments] largely from a law authority which no man in Massachusetts, at that time, had ever read. Hutchinson and all his law counsels were in fault; they could catch no scent. They dared not deny it, lest the book should be produced to their confusion. It was humorous enough to see how Hutchinson wriggled to evade it. He found nothing better to say than that it was 'the artificial reasoning of Lord Coke.' The book was Moore's Reports. The owner of it, for, alas! master, it was borrowed, was a buyer, but not a reader, of books. It had been Mr. Gridley's." (L. John Adams to Judge William Tudor dated 8 March 1817: WJA, II, p. 311 and p. 313)

(7)   "It was of great importance that the people should form a correct opinion on this subject [of the independence of Judges]; and therefore I sent to the press a letter in answer, which drew me on to the number of eight letters, which may be seen in the Boston Gazette for this year [1773]. . . . These papers accordingly contributed to spread correct opinions concerning the importance of the independence of the Judges to liberty and safety, and enabled the Convention of Massachusetts, in 1779, to adopt them into the constitution of the Commonwealth, as the State of New York

p. 362 (cont.)

had done before partially, and as the constitution of the United States did afterwards, in 1787." (Autobiography: WJA, II, p. 317)

(8-12) "Monday. This afternoon received a collection of seventeen letters written from this Province, Rhode Island, Connecticut, and New York, by Hutchinson, Oliver, Moffat, Paxton, and Rome, in the years 1767, 1768, 1769. . . .

"These curious projectors and speculators in politics, will ruin this country. Cool, thinking, deliberate villain, malicious and vindictive, as well as ambitious and avaricious." (D. 22 March 1773: WJA, II, p. 318)

(13) "These are the celebrated letters transmitted by Dr. Franklin from London to Mr. Thomas Cushing at Boston, then Speaker of the House, the publication of which caused a duel between Messrs. Temple and Whately, in England." (WJA, II, p. 318n)

(14-15) "I have communicated to Mr. Norton Quincy and to Mr. Wibird the important secret. They are as much affected by it as any others. Bone of our bone, born and educated among us! Mr. Hancock is deeply affected; is determined, in conjunction with Major Hawley, to watch the vile serpent, and his deputy serpent, Brattle." (D. 24 April 1773: WJA, II, p. 318)

p. 362 (cont.)

(16-17) "In the letter to Dr. Hosack, already mentioned, Mr. Adams distinctly states that Sir John Temple told him, in Holland, that he had furnished these letters to Dr. Franklin. . . . If, in addition to this evidence, any credence at all be given to the rumor mentioned in the text, scarcely a doubt can remain that Sir John Temple was the man who procured them, although the way he did it remains hidden as ever." (WJA, II, p. 319, n. 1)

(18) "Fine, gentle rain, last night and this morning, which will lay a foundation for a crop of grass." (D. 24 April 1773: WJA, II, p. 319)

(19) This appears to be Pound's comment.

(20) "Mr. Dana says the falsehoods and misrepresentations in Rome's letters are innumerable and very flagrant." (D. 16 July 1773: WJA, II, p. 322)

(21-23) "Colonel Howarth attracted no attention, until he discovered his antipathy to a cat." (D. 30 August 1773: WJA, II, p. 323)

(24-26) "Last night, three cargoes of Bohea tea were emptied into the sea. . . . This destruction of the tea is so

p. 362 (cont.)

bold, so daring, so firm, intrepid and inflexible, and it must have so important consequences, and so lasting, that I cannot but consider it as an epocha in history. This, however, is but an attack upon property. Another similar exertion of popular power may produce the destruction of lives. . . .

"The question is, Whether the destruction of this tea was necessary? I apprehend it was absolutely and indispensably so. They could not send it back. The Governor, Admiral, and Collector and Comptroller would not suffer it. It was in their power to have saved it, but in no other. It could not get by the castle, the men-of-war, &c. Then there was no other alternative but to destroy it or let it be landed. To let it be landed, would be giving up the principle of taxation by parliamentary authority, against which the continent has struggled for ten years." (D. 17 December 1773: <u>WJA</u>, II, pp. 323-324) John Adams here speaks of the "Boston Tea Party."

(27-31) "I had a real respect for the judges; three of them, Trowbridge, Cushing, and Brown, I could call my friends. [Peter] Oliver and Ropes, abstracted from their politics, were amiable men, and all of them were very respectable and virtuous characters. I dreaded the effect upon the morals and tempers of the people, which must be produced by any

p. 362 (cont.)

violence offered to the persons of those who wore the robes and bore the sacred characters of judges; and moreover, I felt a strong aversion to such partial, and irregular recurrences to original power. The poor people themselves, who by secret manoeuvres are excited to insurrection, are seldom aware of the purposes for which they are set in motion, or of the consequences which may happen to themselves; and, when once heated and in full career, they can neither manage themselves nor be regulated by others. . . .

". . . I answered that I knew not whether any one would approve of my opinion, yet I believed there was one constitutional resource; but I knew not whether it would be possible to persuade the proper authority to have recourse to it. Several voices at once cried out, 'A constitutional resource! what can it be?' I said it was nothing more nor less than an impeachment of the Judges, by the House of Representatives, before the Council. . . .

". . . The first time I saw Judge Trowbridge he said to me, 'I see, Mr. Adams, you are determined to explore the constitution, and bring to life all its dormant and latent powers, in defence of your liberties as you understand them.' I answered, 'I should be very happy if the constitution could carry us safely through all our difficulties without having recourse to higher powers not written.' The members of the House becoming soon convinced that there was something for

p. 362 (cont.)

them to do, appointed a committee to draw up articles of impeachment against the Chief Justice Oliver. Major Hawley, who was one of this committee, would do nothing without me, and insisted on bringing them to my house to examine and discuss the articles, paragraph by paragraph, which was readily consented to by the committee. Several evenings were spent in my office upon this business until very late at night. One morning, meeting Ben Gridley, he said to me, 'Brother Adams, you keep late hours at your house; as I passed it last night long after midnight, I saw your street door vomit forth a crowd of senators.'" (Autobiography: WJA, II, pp. 328-329 and p. 331)

(32) Pound's comment.

CANTO LXV

p. 363

(1-3) "When the Superior Court came to sit in Boston the grand jurors and petit jurors, as their names were called over, refused to take the oaths. When examined and demanded their reasons for this extraordinary conduct, they answered to a man that the Chief Justice [Peter Oliver] of that court stood impeached of high crimes and misdemeanors before his Majesty's Council, and they would not sit as jurors while that accusation was depending." (Autobiography: WJA, II, p. 332)

(4) "Last evening Justice Pemberton spent with me. He says that Moses Gill has made many justices by lending money." (D. 13 March 1774: WJA, II, p. 336)

(5-14) "Between the fort and the city [New York] is a beautiful ellipsis of land, railed in with solid iron, in the centre of which is a statue of his majesty on horseback, very large, of solid lead gilded with gold, standing on a pedestal of marble, very high. We then walked up the Broad Way, a fine street, very wide, and in a right line from one end to the other of the city. In this route we saw the old church and the new church. The new is a very magnificent building, cost

p. 363 (cont.)

twenty thousand pounds, York currency. . . . We then walked down to a ship-yard, where a Dutch East India ship is building of eight hundred tons burthen." (D. 20 August 1774: <u>WJA</u>, II, p. 346)

(14-15) "Another party [among the various political factions in the colony of New York], he [Mr. McDougall of New York] says, are intimidated lest the levelling spirit of the New England Colonies should propagate itself into New York." (D. 22 August 1774: <u>WJA</u>, II, p. 350)

(16-21) "The city [of New York] cannot tax itself; the constables, assessors, &c., are chosen annually; they petition the assembly every year to be empowered by law to assess the city for a certain sum. The whole charge of the Province is annually between five and six thousand pounds, York money. Mr. Cushing says the charge of the Massachusetts is about twelve thousand, lawful money, which is sixteen thousand, York currency. The support of Harvard College, and of forts and garrisons and other things, makes the difference. . . . Mr. Ebenezer Hazard waited on me with a letter, requesting my assistance in making his collection of American State papers. I recommended him to Mr. S. Adams, and Dr. Samuel Mather. I advised him to publish from Hackluyt, the Voyage of Sebastian Cabot, in this collection. He thought

p. 363 (cont.)

it good advice. (D. 23 August 1774: <u>WJA</u>, II, p. 352)

(22-26) "This whole Colony of New Jersey is a champaign. About twelve o'clock we arrived at the tavern in Princeton, which holds out the sign of Hudibras, near Nassau Hall College. . . . By this time the bell rang for prayers; we went into the chapel; the President soon came in, and we attended. The scholars sing as badly as the Presbyterians at New York. . . . We went into the Presidents's house, and drank a glass of wine. He [the President of Princeton] is as high a son of liberty as any man in America. He says it is necessary that the Congress should raise money and employ a number of writers in the newspapers in England, to explain to the public the American plea, and remove the prejudices of Britons." (D. 27 August 1774: <u>WJA</u>, II, pp. 355-356)

(27-29) "He [Mr. Lynch of South Carolina] told us that Colonel Washington made the most eloquent speech at the Virginia Convention that ever was made. Says he, 'I will raise one thousand men, subsist them at my own expense, and march myself at their head for the relief of Boston.'" (D. 31 August 1774: <u>WJA</u>, II, p. 360)

(30-31) "'The distinctions [said Patrick Henry] between

p. 363 (cont.)

Virginians, Pennsylvanians, New Yorkers, and New Englanders, are no more. I am not a Virginian, but an American.'" (from John Adams's notes of discussions of first meetings of Congress at Philadelphia: <u>WJA</u>, II, p. 367)

(32)   "'Before the reign of Henry IV. [said Joseph Galloway] an attempt was made to give the tenants
p. 364   <u>in</u> <u>capite</u> a right to vote. Magna Charta--arch-
(1-3)   bishops, bishops, abbots, earls, and barons, and tenants <u>in</u> <u>capite</u> held all the lands in England.

"'It is of the essence of the English constitution that no laws shall be binding, but such as are made by the consent of the proprietors in England.

"'How then, did it stand with our ancestors when they came over here? They could not be bound by any laws made by the British Parliament, excepting those made before. I never could see any reason to allow that we are bound to any law made since, nor could I ever make any distinction between the sorts of law.

"'I have ever thought we might reduce our rights to one--an exemption from all laws made by British Parliament since the emigration of our ancestors. . . .

"'I am well aware that my arguments tend to an independency of the Colonies, and militate against the maxims that there must be some absolute power to draw together all

p. 364 (cont.)

the wills and strength of the empire.'" (from John Adams's notes on debates at the first Congress: <u>WJA</u>, II, pp. 372-373) The phrase <u>in capite</u> refers "to the holding of land under direct grant of the lord or king; lit.: in chief." (<u>Index</u>, p. 99)

(4-10) "The first committee was instructed to prepare a bill of rights, as it was called, or a declaration of the rights of the Colonies; the second, a list of infringements or violations of those rights. Congress was pleased to appoint me on the first committee, as the member for Massachusetts.

". . . It was, indeed, very much against my judgment that the committee was so soon appointed, as I wished to hear all the great topics handled in Congress at large in the first place. They were very deliberately considered and debated in the committee, however. The two points which labored the most were: 1. Whether we should recur to the law of nature, as well as to the British constitution, and our American charters and grants. Mr. Galloway and Mr. Duane were for excluding the law of nature. I was very strenuous for retaining and insisting on it, as a resource to which we might be driven by Parliament much sooner than we were aware. 2. The other great question was, what authority we should concede to Parliament; whether we should deny the authority

p. 364 (cont.)

of Parliament in all cases; whether we should allow any authority to it in our internal affairs; or whether we should allow it to regulate the trade of the empire with or without any restrictions. . . . After a multitude of motions had been made, discussed, negatived, it seemed as if we should never agree upon any thing. Mr. John Rutledge of South Carolina, one of the committee, addressing himself to me, was pleased to say, 'Adams, we must agree upon something; you appear to be as familiar with the subject as any of us, and I like your expressions,--"<u>the necessity of the case</u>," and "<u>excluding all ideas of taxation, external and internal</u>;" I have a great opinion of that same idea of the necessity of the case, and I am determined against all taxation for revenue. Come, take the pen and see if you can't produce something that will unite us.' Some others of the committee seconding Mr. Rutledge, I took a sheet of paper and drew up an article. When it was read, I believe not one of the committee was fully satisfied with it; but they all soon acknowledged that there was no hope of hitting on any thing in which we could all agree with more satisfaction. All therefore agreed to this, and upon this depended the union of the Colonies." (Autobiography: <u>WJA</u>, II, pp. 373-375)

(11-12) "Dined at Mr. Willing's, who is a judge of the supreme court here, with the gentlemen from Virginia, Mary-

p. 364 (cont.)

land, and New York. A most splendid feast again,--turtle and everything else. . . . We drank coffee, and then Reed, Cushing, and I strolled to the Moravian evening lecture, where we heard soft, sweet music, and a Dutchified English prayer and preachment." (D. 11 September 1774: WJA, II, pp. 378-379)

(13-14) "This was one of the happiest days of my life. In Congress we had generous, noble sentiments, and manly eloquence. This day convinced me that America will support the Massachusetts or perish with her." (D. 17 September 1774: WJA, II, p. 380) "On this day the celebrated resolutions of Suffolk County, in Massachusetts, had been laid before Congress, and resolutions were adopted by the Congress expressive of sympathy and support." (WJA, II, p. 380n)

(15-17) "'We [said Patrick Henry of the Galloway Plan which proposed an American legislature subservient to the British government] shall liberate our constituents from a corrupt House of Commons, but throw them into the arms of an American Legislature, that may be bribed by that nation which avows, in the face of the world, that bribery is a part of her system of government.'" (from John Adams's notes on debates at the first Congress: WJA, II, p. 390)

p. 364 (cont.)

(18-19) "The probability is that it [the discussion of an non-importation agreement] took place on or before the 6th of October, when the committee appointed to consider and report upon the subject were finally instructed to insert the following clause:--

"'That from and after the first day of December next, no molasses, coffee, or pimento, from the British plantations or from Dominica, or wines from Madeira and the Western Islands, or foreign indigo, be imported into these Colonies.'" (Editor's headnote: WJA, II, p. 393)

(20) "Dined at the Library Tavern, with Messrs. Markoe and a dozen gentlemen from the West Indies and North Carolina. A fine bowling-green here; fine turtle, and admirable wine." (D. 21 October 1774: WJA, II, p. 400)

(21) "In Congress, nibbling and quibbling as usual. There is no greater mortification than to sit with half a dozen wits, deliberating upon a petition, address, or memorial." (D. 24 October 1774: WJA, II, p. 401)

(22-24) "Took our departure, in a very great rain, from the happy, the peaceful, the elegant, the hospitable, and polite city of Philadelphia. It is not very likely that I shall ever see this part of the world again, but I shall ever

p. 364 (cont.)

retain a most grateful, pleasing sense of the many civilities I have received in it, and shall think myself happy to have an opportunity of returning them." (D. 28 October 1774: <u>WJA</u>, II, p. 402)

(25)   "Breakfasted at Colonel Henshaw's, of Leicester; dined at Woodburn's, of Worcester. Furnival made the two young ladies come in and sing us the new Liberty Song." (D. 8 November 1774: <u>WJA</u>, II, p. 404)

(26)   I have been unable to identify the source of this line; it may be Pound's comment.

(27)   "These papers [written under the signature of Massachusettensis] were well written, abounded with wit, discovered good information, and were conducted with a subtlety of art and address wonderfully calculated to keep up the spirits of their [the Loyalist] party, to depress ours, to spread intimidation, and to make proselytes among those whose principles and judgment give way to their fears; and these compose at least one third of mankind." (Autobiography: <u>WJA</u>, II, p. 405)

(28)   "This measure of imbecility, the second petition to the King [sponsored by John Dickinson of Pennsylvania as

p. 364 (cont.)

a proposal of reconciliation], embarrassed every exertion of Congress; it occasioned motions and debates without end for appointing committees to draw up a declaration of the causes, motives, and objects of taking arms, with a view to obtain decisive declarations against independence, &c." (Autobiography: WJA, II, p. 415)

(28-33) "I was daily urging all these things, but we were embarrassed with more than one difficulty, not only with the party in favor of the petition to the King, and the party who were jealous of independence, but a third party, which was a Southern party against a Northern, and a jealousy against a New England army under the command of a New England General. Whether this jealousy was sincere, or whether it was mere pride and a haughty ambition of furnishing a southern General to command a northern army, (I cannot say); but the intention was very visible to me that Colonel [George] Washington was their object, and so many of our staunchest men were in the plan, that we could carry nothing without conceding to it. . . . Mr. [John] Hancock himself had an ambition to be appointed commander-in-chief. . . . 'I am determined [said John Adams to Samuel Adams] this morning to make a direct motion that Congress should adopt the army before Boston, and appoint Colonel Washington commander of it.' Mr. Adams seemed to think very seriously of it, but said

p. 364 (cont.)
nothing.

". . . Mr. Washington, who happened to sit near the door, as soon as he heard me allude to him [in making the motion that Washington be made commander], from his usual modesty, darted into the library-room. Mr. Hancock,--who was our President [presiding at Congress], which gave me an opportunity to observe his countenance while I was speaking on the state of the Colonies, the army at Cambridge, and the enemy, --heard me with visible pleasure; but when I came to describe Washington for the commander, I never remarked a more sudden and striking change of countenance. Mortification and resentment were expressed as forcibly as his face could exhibit them. Mr. Samuel Adams seconded the motion, and that did not soften the President's physiognomy at all." (Autobiography: WJA, II, pp. 415-417)

(34)   "He [Dr. Benjamin Rush] mentions many particular instances in which [John] Dickinson has blundered;
p. 365   he thinks him warped by the Quaker interest and
(1)   the church interest too; thinks his reputation past the meridian, and that avarice is growing upon him." (D. 24 September 1775: WJA, II, pp. 427-428)

(2)   "Mr. Upham informs that this town of Brookfield abounds with a stone, out of which alum, copperas, and

p. 365 (cont.)

sulphur are made. Out of one bushel of this stone, he made five pounds of copperas;--he put the stone into a tub, poured water on it, let it stand two or three days, then drew it off, and boiled the liquor away; let it stand and it shot into a kind of crystals; adding chamber-lye and alkaline salts to the copperas, and that makes alum." (D. 28 January 1776: <u>WJA</u>, II, p. 432)

(3)   "I suppose your ladyship has been in the twitters, for some time, because you have not received a letter by every post, as you used to do. But I am coming to make my apology in person. I yesterday asked and obtained leave of absence." (L. John Adams to his wife, 11 October 1776: <u>WJA</u>, II, p. 433n)

(4-5)   "Set out from Philadelphia towards Boston. Oated at the Red Lion; dined at Bristol; crossed Trenton Ferry long before sunset; drank coffee at the ferry-house on the east side of the Delaware, where I put up, partly to avoid riding in the evening air, and partly because thirty miles is enough for the first day, as my tendons are delicate, not having been once on horseback since the eighth day of last February." (D. 13 October 1776: <u>WJA</u>, II, p. 433)

(6-9)   "Mrs. Langley showed us the Society of Single

p. 365 (cont.)

Women [in the German community at Bethlehem, Pennsylvania]; then Mr. Edwine showed us the waterworks and the manufactures;--there are six sets of works in one building; a hemp-mill, an oil-mill, a mill to grind bark for the tanners; then the fullers-mill, both of cloth and leather, the dyer's house, and the shearer's house. They raise a great deal of madder." (D. 23 September 1777: WJA, II, p. 440)

(10-11) "The following resolution appears upon the Journal of Congress, for the 23d of September, 1775:--

"'Resolved, That a committee be appointed to purchase a quantity of woollen goods, for the use of the army, to the amount of five thousand pounds sterling.'" (Editor's head-note: WJA, II, p. 445)

(12)   "Extract from the [Secret] Journals [of Congress], 25 September [1775]:--

"'The delegates, from Pennsylvania, produced an account of the powder imported, and how it has been disposed of.'" (WJA, II, p. 448, n. 2)

(13)   "Johnson. A hundred tons of powder was wanted. Ross. In case of its arrival, Congress was to pay fourteen pounds; if men-of-war or custom-house officers should get it, Congress was to pay first cost only, as I understood it.

p. 365 (cont.)

Zubly. We are highly favored; fourteen pounds we are to give, if we get the powder, and fourteen pounds, if we don't get it. I understand, persons enough will contract to supply powder at fifteen pounds and run all risks." (Notes/Debates, 25 September 1775: WJA, II, p. 449)

(14-15) "Cushing. I move that we take into consideration a method of keeping up an army in the winter." (Notes/Debates, 25 September 1775: WJA, II, p. 450)

(16-23) "R. R. Livingston. . . . Ammunition cannot be had, unless we open our ports. I am for doing away our non-exportation agreement entirely. I see many advantages in leaving open the ports, none in shutting them up. . . .

"Chase. . . . We can't support the war and our taxes without trade. Emissions of paper cannot continue. I dread an emission for another campaign. We can't stand it without trade. . . .

"We must trade with foreign nations, at the risk indeed, but we may export our tobacco to France, Spain, or any other foreign nation. If we treat with foreign nations, we should send to them as well as they to us. . . .

"E. Rutledge differs with all who think the non-exportation should be broke, or that any trade at all should be carried on. . . . Our people will go into manufactures, which

p. 365 (cont.)

is a source of riches to a country. We can take our men from agriculture and employ them in manufactures. Agriculture and manufactures cannot be lost; trade is precarious.

"R. R. Livingston . . . . The Americans are their own carriers now, chiefly; a few British ships will be out of employ." (Notes/Debates, 4 October 1775: WJA, II, pp. 453-455)

(24) "Zubly. . . . The navy can stop our harbors and distress our trade; therefore it is impracticable to open our ports. . . . I am clearly against any proposition to open our ports to all the world; it is not prudent to threaten; the people of England will take it we design to break off, to separate." (Notes/Debates, 5 October 1775: WJA, II, p. 457)

(25-27) "Lee. Suppose provisions should be sold in Spain for money, and cash sent to England for powder. . . .

"R. R. Livingston. We are between hawk and buzzard; we puzzle ourselves between the commercial and warlike opposition." (Notes/Debates, 6 October? 1775: WJA, II, p. 461)

(28-30) "October 10. On the preceding day, the Congress had adopted a resolution, in the following words:—

"'That it be recommended to the Convention of New Jersey,

p. 365 (cont.)

that they immediately raise, at the expense of the continent, two battalions, consisting of eight companies each, and each company of sixty-eight privates, officered with one captain, one lieutenant, one ensign, four sergeants, and four corporals.'" (Editor's headnote: <u>WJA</u>, II, p. 467)

(31-33) "Who shall have the appointment of the officers, in the two battalions to be raised in New Jersey [writes John Adams]? . . .

"<u>Chase</u>. In my Province, we want officers. Gentlemen have recommended persons, from personal friendships, who were not suitable; such friendships will have more weight in the Colonies. . . .

"<u>Ward</u>. I would rather take the opinion of General Washington [about the appointment of officers] than of any convention. . . .

"<u>E</u>. <u>Rutledge</u>. The appointment, hitherto, has been as if the money belonged to particular Provinces, not to the Continent. We can't reward merit; the Governor appointed officers with us." (Notes/Debates, 10 October 1775: <u>WJA</u>, II, pp. 467-468)

(34-35) Pound's comment: a recapitulation of the subjects of the debates he has thus far referred to. Here
p. 366 are the line correspondences, with the line on

p. 366 (cont.)

(1-4)   which the subject is first mentioned, each found on p. 365, in parentheses. Line 34 (16); line 35 (12); line 35 (31). Page 366, line 1 (23); line 1 (21); lines 2-3 (31).

(5-22)   "<u>Lee</u>. It has been moved to bring the debate to one point by putting the question, whether the custom-houses shall be shut up, and the officers discharged from their several functions. This would put New York, North Carolina, the lower Counties, and Georgia, upon the same footing with the other Colonies. I, therefore, move you, that the customhouses be shut, and the officers discharged; this will remove jealousies and divisions.

"<u>Zubly</u>. The measure we are now to consider is extremely interesting. I shall offer my thoughts. . . .

". . . Every thing we want for the war is powder and shot. Second thing necessary, that we have arms and ammunition. Third, we must have money; the continental credit must be supported; we must keep up a notion that this paper is good for something; it has not yet a general circulation. The Mississippi scheme, in France, and the South Sea scheme, in England, were written for our learning; a hundred millions fell in one day. Twenty men-of-war may block up the harbor of New York, Delaware River, Chesapeake Bay, the Carolinas, and Georgia. Whether we can raise a navy, is an important question. We may have a navy, and, to carry on the war, we

p. 366 (cont.)

must have a navy. Can we do this without trade? Can we gain intelligence without trade? Can we get powder without trade? . . . My resolution was, that I would do and suffer any thing, rather than not be free; but I am resolved not to do impossible things; if we must trade, we must trade with somebody, and with somebody that will trade with us; either with foreigners or Great Britain; if with foreigners, we must either go to them or they must come to us; we can't go to them, if our harbors are shut up. I look upon the trade with foreigners as impracticable. . . . Spaniards are too lazy to come to us. If we can't trade with foreigners, we must trade with Great Britain. Is it practicable? will it quit cost? will it do more hurt than good? This is breaking our association. Our people will think we are giving way, and giving all up; they will say, one mischievous man has overset the whole navigation. I speak from principle; it has been said here that the association was made in terrorem." (Notes/Debates, 12 October 1775: WJA, II, pp. 469-470) The Italian word commerciabili in line 11 means "for trade." (Index, p. 42) The Latin phrase in terrorem in line 22 means "in terror; for the purpose of terror (?)." (Index, p. 100)

(23)   Pound's comment.

(24-33) "Deane. I would have traders prohibited from im-

p. 366 (cont.)

porting unnecessary articles, and from exporting live stock, except horses. . . .

"Chase. We have letters from Guadaloupe, Martinique, and the Havana, that they will supply us with powder for tobacco. . . .

"Chase. The proposition is for exporting for a special purpose,--importing powder. . . . Each colony should carry on this trade, no individuals. . . .

"Jay. We have more to expect from the enterprise, activity and industry of private adventurers, than from the lukewarmness of assemblies. We want French woollens, Dutch worsteds, duck for tents, German steel, &c. Public virtue is not so active as private love of gain. Shall we shut the door against private enterprise? . . .

"Wythe. Can't see the least reason for restraining our trade, as little can be carried on. My opinion is, we had better open our trade altogether. It has long been my opinion, and I have heard no arguments against it." (Notes/Debates, 20 October 1775: WJA, II, pp. 474-476)

(34-35) "Wythe. Why should not America have a navy? No maritime power near the sea-coast can be safe without it. It is no chimera. The Romans suddenly built one in their Carthaginian war. Why may not we lay a foundation for it? We abound with firs, iron ore,

p. 367

(1)

p. 367 (cont.)

tar, pitch, turpentine; we have all the materials for construction of a navy." (Notes/Debates, 21 October 1775: <u>WJA</u>, II, p. 479)

(2)   "<u>Extract from the Journals</u>:--

"'The Committee appointed to prepare an estimate, and to fit out the vessels, brought in their report, which being taken into consideration, &c.

"'<u>Resolved</u>, That two more vessels be fitted out with all expedition, &c.'"   (<u>WJA</u>, II, p. 484n)

(3)   "<u>Extract from the Journals</u>.
                    1776. February 16. Friday.
"'Agreeable to the order of the day, the Congress resolved itself into a committee of the whole, to take into consideration the propriety of opening the ports, and the restrictions and regulations of the trade of these Colonies after the first of March next.'

"(This discussion was continued from time to time until the sixth of April, when the Congress came in to sundry resolutions taking off the restrictions on trade.)" (Editor's headnote: <u>WJA</u>, II, p. 485)

(4-11)   "'Can't we [writes John Adams] oblige Britain to keep a navy on foot, the expense of which will be double to

p. 367 (cont.)

what they will take from us? I have heard of bullion Spanish flotas being stopped, lest they should be taken, but perishable commodities never were stopped. Open your ports to foreigners; your trade will become of so much consequence that foreigners will protect you.' . . .

"<u>Wythe</u>. The ports will be open the 1st March. The question is whether we shall shut them up. <u>Faece Romuli non Republica Platonis</u>. Americans will hardly live without trade. . . .

"We might get some of our produce to market, by authorizing adventurers to arm themselves, and giving letters of marque, make reprisals. 2d. By inviting foreign powers to make treaties of commerce with us.

"But other things are to be considered, before such a measure is adopted; in what character shall we treat?--as subjects of Great Britain,--as rebels? Why should we be so fond of calling ourselves dutiful subjects? If we should offer our trade to the Court of France, would they take notice of it any more than if Bristol or Liverpool should offer theirs, while we profess to be subjects? No. We must declare ourselves a free people." (Notes/Debates, n.d.: <u>WJA</u>, II, pp. 485-486) The Latin <u>Faece Romuli non Republica Platonis</u> means "in the dregs of Romulus, not in Plato's republic." (<u>Index</u>, p. 66)

p. 367 (cont.)

(12) "<u>Resolved</u>, That [blank space] be a committee to prepare a draught of firm confederation, to be reported as soon as may be to this Congress, to be considered and digested and recommended to the several Assemblies and Conventions of these United Colonies, to be by them adopted, ratified, and confirmed." (Notes/Debates, n.d.: <u>WJA</u>, II, pp. 486-487)

(13-18) "<u>Resolved</u>, That it be recommended to the several Assemblies, Conventions, Councils of Safety, and Committees of Correspondence and Inspection, that they use their utmost endeavors, by all reasonable means, to promote the culture of flax, hemp, and cotton, and the growth of wool, in these United Colonies.

"<u>Resolved</u>, That it be recommended to the Assemblies, Conventions, and Councils of Safety, that they take the earliest measures for erecting, in each and every Colony, a society for the encouragement of agriculture, arts, manufactures, and commerce; and that a correspondence be maintained between such societies, that the numerous natural advantages of this country, for supporting its inhabitants, may not be neglected.

"<u>Resolved</u>, That it be recommended to the said Assemblies, Conventions, and Councils of Safety, that they consider of ways and means of introducing the manufactures of duck and

p. 367 (cont.)

sail-cloth into such Colonies where they are not now understood, and of increasing and promoting them where they are." (Extract from the Journals, 21 March 1776: <u>WJA</u>, II, p. 487)

(19)   "Is it the interest of France to stand neuter, to join with Britain, or to join with the Colonies? Is it not her interest to dismember the British empire?" (from John Adams's notes for a speech in Congress, 1 March 1776: <u>WJA</u>, II, p. 488; see also p. 487, n. 3)

(20-21) "Resentment is a passion implanted by nature for the preservation of the individual. . . . A man may have the faculty of concealing his resentment, or suppressing it, but he must and ought to feel it; nay, he ought to indulge it, to cultivate it; it is a duty. His person, his property, his liberty, his reputation, are not safe without it." (from John Adams's notes for a speech in Congress, 4 March? 1776: <u>WJA</u>, II, p. 488; see also p. 487, n. 3)

(22-23) "<u>Hooper</u>. I wish to see the day that slaves are not necessary. Whites and negroes cannot work together. Negroes are goods and chattels, are property. A negro works under the impulse of fear, has no care of his master's interest." (Notes/Debates, 1 August 1776: <u>WJA</u>, II, p. 498)

p. 367 (cont.)

(24)   "Mr. Richard Henry Lee, of Virginia, Mr. Sherman, of Connecticut, and Mr. Gadsden, of South Carolina, were always on my side [in debates in Congress], and Mr. Chase, of Maryland, when he did speak at all, was always powerful, and generally with us." (Autobiography: <u>WJA</u>, II, p. 506)

(25-35)   "Cushing, two Adamses, and Paine, all destitute of fortune, four poor pilgrims, proceeded in one coach, were escorted through Massachusetts, Connecticut, New York, and New Jersey, into Pennsylvania. We were met at Frankfort by Dr. Rush, Mr. Mifflin, Mr. Bayard, and several others of the most active sons of liberty in Philadelphia, who desired a conference with us. . . . They represented to us that the friends of government in Boston and in the Eastern States, in their correspondence with their friends in Pennsylvania and all the Southern States, had represented us as four desperate adventurers. 'Mr. Cushing was a harmless kind of man, but poor, and wholly dependent on his popularity for his subsistence. Mr. Samuel Adams was a very artful, designing man, but desperately poor, and wholly dependent on his popularity with the lowest vulgar for his living. John Adams and Mr. Paine were two young lawyers, of no great talents, reputation, or weight, who had no other means of raising themselves into consequence, than by courting popularity.'* [*"Compare this with the language of the Rev. Jacob Duche, in his letter to

p. 367 (cont.)

General Washington: 'Bankrupts, attorneys, and men of desperate fortunes are the colleagues of Mr. Hancock.'" Editor's note.] . . .

". . . Writings of his [Thomas Jefferson's] were handed about, remarkable for the peculiar felicity of expression. Though a silent member in Congress, he was so prompt, frank, explicit, and decisive upon committees and in conversation, not even Samuel Adams was more so, that he soon seized upon my heart; and upon this occasion I gave him my vote, and did all in my power to procure the votes of others. I think he had one more vote than any other, and that placed him at the head of the committee [to prepare a Declaration of Independence]. I had the next highest number, and that placed me the second. The committee met, discussed the subject, and then appointed Mr. Jefferson and me to make the draught, I suppose because we were the two first on the list.

"The sub-committee met. Jefferson proposed to me to make the draught. I said, 'I will not.' 'You should do it.' 'Oh! no.' 'Why will you not? You ought to do it.' 'I will not.' 'Why?' 'Reasons enough.' 'What can be your reasons?' 'Reason first--You are a Virginian, and a Virginian ought to appear at the head of this business. Reason second--I am obnoxious, suspected, and unpopular. You are very much otherwise. Reason third--You can write ten times better than I can.' 'Well,' said Jefferson, 'if you are decided, I will

p. 367 (cont.)

do as well as I can.' 'Very well. When you have drawn it up, we will have a meeting.' . . .

". . . Congress was impatient, and the instrument was reported, as I believe, in Jefferson's handwriting, as he first drew it. Congress cut off about a quarter of it, as I expected they would; but they obliterated some of the best of it, and left all that was exceptionable, if any thing in it was. I have long wondered that the original draught has not been published. I suppose the reason is, the vehement philippic against negro slavery." (L. John Adams to Timothy Pickering, 6 August 1822, in reply to a letter from Pickering inquiring about the origin of the Declaration of Independence: <u>WJA</u>, II, p. 512n and p. 514n; the complete account may be found on pp. 512n-515n)

p. 368

(1)   Pound's comment.

(2-5)   "I have omitted some things in 1775, which must be inserted. On the eighteenth of September, it was resolved in Congress,--

"'That a secret committee be appointed to contract for the importation and delivery of a quantity of gunpowder, not exceeding five hundred tons.

"'That in case such a quantity of gunpowder cannot be

p. 368 (cont.)

procured, to contract for the importation of so much saltpetre, with a proportionable quantity of sulphur, as with the powder procured will make five hundred tons.

"'That the committee be empowered to contract for the importation of forty brass field pieces, six pounders, for ten thousand stand of arms, and twenty thousand good plain double-bridled musket locks.'" (Autobiography: <u>WJA</u>, III, p. 3)

(6-7)   "On the 13th, Congress having proceeded to the election of a committee to form the board of war and ordnance, the following members were chosen. Mr. John Adams, Mr. Sherman, Mr. Harrison, Mr. Wilson, and Mr. E. Rutledge; and Richard Peters, Esq. was elected secretary. The duties of this board kept me in continual employment, not to say drudgery, from the 12th of June, 1776, till the 11th of November, 1777, when I left Congress forever." (Autobiography: <u>WJA</u>, III, p. 6)

(8-12)   "As a considerable part of my time, in the course of my profession, had been spent upon the sea-coast of Massachusetts, in attending the courts and lawsuits at Plymouth, Barnstable, Martha's Vineyard, to the southward, and in the counties of Essex, York, and Cumberland to the eastward, I had conversed much with the gentlemen who conducted our cod

p. 368 (cont.)

and whale fisheries, as well as the other navigation of the country, and had heard much of the activity, enterprise, patience, perseverance, and daring intrepidity of our seamen. I had formed a confident opinion that, if they were once let loose upon the ocean, they would contribute greatly to the relief of our wants, as well as to the distress of the enemy. I became therefore at once an ardent advocate for this motion, which we carried, not without great difficulty. The opposition to it was very loud and vehement. Some of my own colleagues appeared greatly alarmed at it, and Mr. Edward Rutledge never displayed so much eloquence as against it. . . . It was an infant, taking a mad bull by his horns; and what was more profound and remote, it was said it would ruin the character, and corrupt the morals of all our seamen. It would make them selfish, piratical, mercenary, bent wholly upon plunder, &c. &c." (Autobiography: WJA, III, p. 7)

(13-15) "When his lordship [Lord Howe] observed to us, that he could not confer with us as members of Congress, or public characters, but only as private persons and British subjects, Mr. John Adams answered somewhat quickly, 'Your lordship may consider me in what light you please, and, indeed, I should be willing to consider myself, for a few moments, in any character which would be agreeable to your lordship, except that of a British subject.'" (Autobiog-

p. 368 (cont.)

raphy: WJA, II, pp. 79-80; the account of the entire visit to Lord Howe may be found on pp. 73-81)

(16)   "The resolutions, which may be seen in the Journal, contain the whole plan of an army of eighty-eight battalions, to be enlisted as soon as possible, to serve during the war." (Editor's note: WJA, III, p. 82n: see asterisk)

(17-23) "It should have been observed before, that in announcing to me the intelligence of my appointment [to go to France], Langdon neither expressed congratulation nor regret, but I soon afterwards had evidence enough that he lamented Mr. Deane's recall, for he had already formed lucrative connections in France, by Mr. Deane's recommendation, particularly with Mr. Le Ray de Chaumont, who had shipped merchandises to him to sell upon commission, an account of which, rendered to Chaumont by Langdon, was shown to me by the former, at Passy, in 1779, in which almost the whole capital was sunk by the depreciation of paper money.

". . . I had every reason to expect that ships would be ordered from Rhode Island and from Halifax to intercept the Boston [the frigate on which John Adams sailed to France], and that intelligence would be secretly sent them, as accurately as possible, of the time when she was to sail. For there always have been and still are spies in America, as

p. 368 (cont.)

well as in France, England, and other countries. . . .

". . . My practice as a barrister, in the counties of Essex, Plymouth, and Barnstable, had introduced me to more knowledge, both of the cod and whale fisheries, and of their importance, both to the commerce and naval power of this country, than any other man possessed who would be sent abroad if I refused; and this consideration had no small weight in producing my determination." (Autobiography: <u>WJA</u>, III, pp. 91-92) The date <u>1804</u> mentioned in line 21 is the year John Adams wrote the "Autobiography."

(24-30) "TO SAMUEL TUCKER. <u>Navy Board--Eastern Department</u>, <u>Boston</u>, February, 1778. SIR:--Notwithstanding the general instructions given you, you are now to consider the Hon. John Adams, Esq. (who takes passage in the Boston) as one of the commissioners with the Hon. Benjamin Franklin and Arthur Lee, Esquires; and therefore, any applications or orders received from him, as valid as if received from either of the other two. You are to afford him, on his passage, every accomodation in your power, and to consult him, on all occasions, with respect to your passage and general conduct, and the port you shall endeavor to get into, and on all occasions have great regard to the importance of his security and safe arrival. We are your humble servants, WILLIAM VERNON, JAMES WARREN. (Editor's note: <u>WJA</u>, III, p. 94n)

p. 368 (cont.)

Line 25 refers to the following passage: "The wind was very high, and the sea very rough; but, by means of a quantity of hay in the bottom of the boat, and good watch-coats, with which we were covered, we arrived on board the Boston, about five o'clock, tolerably warm and dry." (D. 13 February 1778: <u>WJA</u>, III, p. 94)

(31)   "Sunday. This morning, weighed the last anchor, and came under sail, before breakfast." (D. 15 February 1778: <u>WJA</u>, III, p. 95)

(32-34) "'At 6, A. M., saw three large ships bearing east, standing to the northward. I mistrusted they were cruising for me. I hauled my wind to the southward; found they did chase me.'" (Log Book, 19 February 1778: <u>WJA</u>, III, p. 98n)

(35)   "'Ship still in chase, but being poorly manned, dare not attack her. . . . The next morning saw

p. 369   the same ship ahead, standing to the southward

(1-3)   and westward. I could not weather her on that tack. After running three hours to the westward, the wind favoring me, I then hove in stays, and came to windward of the ship, about four miles. Was satisfied it was the same ship; she tacked, and continued chasing me all day, but I rather gain upon her.'" (Log Book, 20 February 1778: <u>WJA</u>,

p. 369 (cont.)
III, p. 99, n. 1)

(4-5) "The <u>mal de mer</u> seems to be merely the effect of agitation. The smoke, and smell of sea-coal, the smell of stagnant, putrid water, the smell of the ship where the sailors lie, or any other offensive smell, will increase the qualminess, but do not occasion it." (D. 19 February 1778: <u>WJA</u>, III, p. 98)

(6-9) "When the night approached, the wind died away, and we were left rolling and pitching in a calm, with our guns all out, our courses all drawn up, and every way prepared for battle; the officers and men appeared in good spirits, and Captain Tucker said his orders were to carry me to France, and to take any prizes that might fall in his way; he thought it his duty, therefore, to avoid fighting, especially with an unequal force, if he could, but if he could not avoid an engagement, he would give them something that should make them remember him. . . . We lost sight of our enemy [see lines 1-3 this page], who did not appear to me very ardent to overtake us. But the wind increased to a hurricane." (Travels/Negotiations: <u>WJA</u>, III, p. 99)

(10-16) "We lost sight of our enemy, it is true, but we found ourselves in the Gulf stream, in the midst of an

p. 369 (cont.)

épouvantable orage; the wind north-east, then north, and then north-west.

"It would be fruitless to attempt a description of what I saw, heard, and felt, during these three days and nights. To describe the ocean, the waves, the winds; the ship, her motions, rollings, wringings, and agonies; the sailors, their countenances, language, and behavior, is impossible. No man could keep upon his legs, and nothing could be kept in its place; an universal wreck of every thing in all parts of the ship, chests, casks, bottles, &c. No place or person was dry." (D. 21, 22, 23 February 1778: WJA, III, pp. 99-100)

(17-20) "'Heavy thunder and sharp lightning. At midnight the ship was struck by lightning at the mainmast and topmast, and wounded twenty-three men, and struck down three. Although we were in the greatest danger, received but little damage.'" (Log Book, 21 February 1778: WJA, III, p. 100n)

(21-26) "'Heavy gales and head sea. One thing and another continually giving way on board the ship. Lay by under mainsail. Down top gallant yards; at 4 P. M. carried away slings and chains of mizzen yards; at 4 A. M. somewhat moderate; made sail, and began to repair the rigging.'" (Log Book, 22 February 1778: WJA, III, p. 100n)

p. 369 (cont.)

(27-28) "Mr. Johnny's [John Quincy Adams's] behavior gave me a satisfaction that I cannot express; fully sensible of our danger, he was constantly endeavoring to bear it with a manly patience, very attentive to me, and his thoughts constantly running in a serious strain." (D. 24, 25 February 1778: <u>WJA</u>, III, p. 101)

(29-35) "A few [observations] I will set down. 1st. I have seen the inexpressible inconvenience of
p. 370 having so small a space between decks, as there
(1) is in the Boston. . . . 3d. The ship is furnished with no pistols, which she ought to be, with at least as many as there are officers, because there is nothing but the dread of a pistol will keep many of the men to their quarters in time of action. 4th. This ship is not furnished with good glasses, which appear to me of very great consequence. Our ships ought to be furnished with the best glasses that art affords; their expense would be saved a thousand ways. 5th. There is the same general inattention, I find, to economy, in the navy, that there is in the army. 6th. There is the same general relaxation of order and discipline. 7th. There is the same inattention to the cleanliness of the ship, and the persons and health of the sailors, as there is at land to the cleanliness of the camp, and the health, and cleanliness of the soldiers. 8th. The practice of profane cursing

p. 370 (cont.)

and swearing, so silly as well as detestable, prevails in a most abominable degree. It is indulged and connived at by officers, and practised, too, in such a manner, that there is no kind of check against it. And I take upon me to say, that order of every kind will be lax as long as this is so much the case." (D. 26 February 1778: WJA, III, pp. 101-102)

(2)   "Discovered that our mainmast was sprung in two places; one beneath the main deck, where if the mast had wholly failed in the late storm, it must have torn up the main deck, and the ship must have foundered. This is one among many instances, in which it has already appeared that our safety has not depended on ourselves." (D. 1 March 1778: WJA, III, p. 104)

(3-4)   "Our little world is all wet and damp. There is nothing I can eat or drink without nauseating. We have no spirits for conversation, nor any thing to converse about. We see nothing but sky, clouds, and sea, and then sea, clouds, and sky." (D. 3 March 1778: WJA, III, p. 105)

(4-5)   "This morning we have the pleasantest prospect we have yet seen; a fine easy breeze from the southward, which gives us an opportunity of keeping our true course, a soft, clear, warm air, a fair sun, no sea. We have a great number

p. 370 (cont.)

of sails spread, and we go at the rate of nine knots, yet the ship has no perceptible motion, and makes no noise. . . .

"Whenever I arrive at any port in Europe, whether in Spain or France, my first inquiry should be concerning the designs of the enemy. What force they mean to send to America? where they are to obtain men? what is the state of the British nation? what the state of parties? what the state of finances and of stocks? Then the state of Europe, particularly France and Spain. What the real designs of those courts? What the condition of their finances? what the state of their armies, but especially, of their fleets? what number of ships they have fitted for the sea? what their names, number of men and guns, weight of metal, &c., where they lie, &c." (D. 5 March 1778: WJA, III, pp. 105-106)

(5-6) "I happened to be upon the quarter deck, and in the direction from the ship to the yard, so that the ball went directly over my head." (D. 14 March 1778: WJA, III, p. 109)

(6-10) "It must be to this occasion [lines 5-6], being the only one upon which a shot was fired by an enemy, that Mr. Sprague, in his Eulogy of Adams and Jefferson, refers, in the following anecdote. He doubtless had it from Tucker in his latest days, when a sailor's stories commonly lose

p. 370 (cont.)

nothing in the telling.

"'Discovering an enemy's ship, neither Commodore Tucker nor Mr. Adams could resist the temptation to engage, although against the dictates of prudent duty. Tucker, however, stipulated that Mr. Adams should remain in the lower part of the ship, as a place of safety. But no sooner had the battle commenced, than he was seen on deck, with a musket in his hands, fighting as a common marine. The Commodore peremptorily ordered him below; but called instantly away, it was not until considerable time had elapsed, that he discovered this public minister still at his post, intently engaged in firing upon the enemy. Advancing, he exclaimed, "Why are you here, sir? I am commanded by the Continental Congress to carry you in safety to Europe, **and I will do it;**" and, seizing him in his arms, forcibly carried him from the scene of danger.'" (Editor's note: <u>WJA</u>, III, p. 109, n. 1)

(11-15) "She was a letter of marque, with fourteen guns, eight nines, and six sixes. She fired upon us, and one of her shot went through our mizzen yard. . . . We, upon this, turned our broadside, which the instant she saw, she struck. Captain Tucker very prudently ordered his officers not to fire.

"The prize is the ship Martha, Captain McIntosh, from London to New York, loaded with a cargo of great value. The

p. 370 (cont.)

captain told me that seventy thousand pounds sterling was insured upon her at Lloyd's, and that she was worth eighty thousand. The captain is very much a gentleman." (D. 14 March 1778: WJA, III, p. 109)

(16)   "Five weeks yesterday since my embarkation. This morning, a heavy wind and high sea. We go east, south-east." (D. 21 March 1778: WJA, III, p. 111)

(17-22) "Mr. McIntosh is of North Britain, and appears to be very decided against America in this contest; and his passions are so engaged that they easily enkindle. . . .

". . . Numbers of small birds, from the shore, came along today; some of them, fatigued, alighted on our rigging, yards, &c., and one of them we caught, a little lark he was called. These birds lose the shore, and get lost, and then they fly until they are so fatigued that the instant they alight upon a ship they drop to sleep." (D. 28 March 1778: WJA, III, pp. 112-113)

(23-24) "We have been becalmed all day in sight of Oléron. . . . I feel a curiosity to visit this Island of Oléron, so famous in antiquity for her sea laws; at least, I take this to be the place." (D. 29 March 1778: WJA, III, p. 115)

p. 370 (cont.)

(25-35)   "This forenoon a fisherman came alongside, with hakes, skates, and gurnards; we bought a few and

p. 371   had a high regale.

(1)   "This river is very beautiful on both sides; the plantations are very pleasant, on the south side especially; we saw, all along, horses, oxen, cows, and great flocks of sheep grazing, the husbandmen ploughing, &c., and the women, half a dozen in a drove, with their hoes. The churches, convents, gentlemen's seats, and the villages appear very magnificent.

"This river seldom swells with freshes; for the rural improvements, and even the fishermen's houses, are brought quite down to the water's edge. The water in the river is very foul to all appearance, looking all the way like a mud puddle. . . . The buildings, public and private, are of stone; and a great number of beautiful groves appear between the grand seats and best plantations; a great number of vessels lay in the river.

"The pleasure resulting from the sight of land, cattle, houses, &c., after so long, so tedious and dangerous a voyage, is very great." (D. 30 March 1778: <u>WJA</u>, III, p. 116)

(2-10)   "My first inquiry should be, who is Agent for the United States of America at Bordeaux, at Blaye, &c.; who are the principal merchants on this river concerned in the Ameri-

p. 371 (cont.)
can trade? . . .

"This morning the captain and a passenger came on board the Boston, from the Julie, a large ship bound to St. Domingue, to make us a visit. They invited us on board to dine. . . . The first dish was a fine French soup, which I confess I liked very much. Then a dish of boiled meat. Then the lights of a calf, dressed one way and the liver another. Then roasted mutton, then fricasseed mutton, a fine salad, and something very like asparagus, but not it. The bread was very fine, and it was baked on board. We had prunes, almonds, and the most delicate raisins I ever saw. . . . None of us understood French, none of them English; so that Doctor Noel stood interpreter. . . . On the quarter deck I was struck with the hens, capons and cocks, in their coops, the largest I ever saw." (D. 31 March 1778: <u>WJA</u>, III, pp. 116-117) The Provençal phrase <u>de lonh</u>, quoted by Pound in line 3, means "far-off." (<u>Index</u>, p. 50)

(11-13) "'At 2 P. M. came to sail up the river to town. Saluted a small town called Blaye, with the Independent salute.'" (Log Book: <u>WJA</u>, III, p. 117, n. 2)

(14-16) "All the gentlemen we have seen to-day agree that Doctor Franklin has been received by the King in great pomp, and that a treaty is concluded, and they all expect war

p. 371 (cont.)

every moment." (D. 31 March 1778: WJA, III, p. 117)

(17-22) "This morning Mr. J. C. Champagne, négociant et courtier de marine, at Blaye, came on board to make a visit and pay his compliments. He says, that of the first growths of wines in the Province of Guienne there are four sorts, Chateau-Margaux, Haut-brion, Lafitte, and Latour.

". . . Mr. McCreery came on board our boat, and conducted us up to his lodgings. Mr. Pringle was there. We dined there in the fashion of the country; we had fish and beans, and salad, and claret, champagne, and mountain wine. After dinner, Mr. Bondfield, who is agent here, invited me to take a walk, which we did, to his lodgings, where we drank tea; then we walked about the town, and to see the new comedie; after this we went to the opera, where the scenery, the dancing, the music, afforded to me a very cheerful, sprightly amusement, having never seen any thing of the kind before. [Our American theatres had not then existed even in contemplation.] (D. 1 April 1778: WJA, III, p. 118) The brackets are in the original text.

(23) "Visited the custom-house, the post-office; visited the commandant of the chateau Trompette, a work of Vauban's. Visited the Premier President of the Parliament of Bordeaux." (D. 2 April 1778: WJA, III, p. 118)

p. 371 (cont.)

(24-26) "He [the Premier President of the Parliament of Bordeaux] knew that I had gone through many dangers and sufferings in the cause of liberty, and he had felt for me in them all. 'He had reason,' he said, 'to feel for the sufferers in the cause of Liberty, because he had suffered many years in that cause himself. He had been banished for cooperating with Mr. Malesherbes, and the other courts and parliaments of the kingdom, in the time of Louis XV. in their remonstrances against the arbitrary conduct and pernicious edicts of the court, &c. &c.' Mr. Bondfield had to interpret all this effusion of compliments; and I thought it never would come to an end. But it did; and I concluded, upon the whole, there was a form of sincerity in it, decorated and almost suffocated with French compliments." (Travels/Negotiations: WJA, III, p. 119)

(27) "Went to the coffee-house; went to the comedie, saw Les deux Avares." (D. 2 April 1778: WJA, III, p. 119)

(28-29) "The log-book continues to the 9th of September, 1779; and at the end is a list of prizes captured in the latest voyage. Captain Tucker, though not a polished, was an energetic and successful commander." (Editor's note: WJA, III, p. 120n)

p. 371 (cont.)

(30-31) "The garden [where the French honored John Adams at a party before his departure from Bordeaux] was beautifully illuminated with an inscription, God save the Congress, Liberty and Adams." (D. 3 April 1778: <u>WJA</u>, III, pp. 119-120)

p. 372

(1-4) "Afternoon, passed through Chatellerault, another city nearly as large as Poitiers, and as old, and the streets as narrow. When we stopped at the post to change our horses, about twenty young women came about the chaise with their elegant knives, scissors, tooth-picks, &c., to sell. The scene was new to me, and highly diverting. Their eagerness to sell a knife was as great as that of some persons I have seen in other countries to get offices. We arrived in the evening at Les Ormes, the magnificent seat of the Marquis D'Argenson. It is needless to make particular remarks upon this country. Every part of it is cultivated. The fields of grain, the vineyards, the castles, the cities, the parks, the gardens, every thing is beautiful, yet every place swarms with beggars." (D. 6 April 1778: <u>WJA</u>, III, p. 121)

(5) "L'hotel de Valois, Rue de Richelieu, is the name of the house and street [in Paris, which John Adams reached on 8 April 1778] where I now am." (D. 9 April 1778: <u>WJA</u>, III, p. 122)

p. 372 (cont.)

(6)   "Although Mr. Deane, in addition to these [apartments and furniture], had a house, furniture, and equipage, in Paris, I determined to put my country to no further expense on my account, but to take my lodgings under the same roof with Dr. Franklin, and to use no other equipage than his, if I could avoid it. This house was called the Basse cour de Monsieur Le Ray de Chaumont, which was, to be sure, not a title of great dignity for the mansion of ambassadors, though they were no more than American ambassadors. Nevertheless, it had been nothing less than the famous Hotel de Valentinois, with a motto on the door, 'Se sta bene, non si muove,' which I thought a good rule for my conduct."
(Travels/Negotiations: WJA, III, p. 123)

(7-13) "TO JOHN ROSS. Passy, 13 April, 1778. SIR,--
. . . We do not think it within our province to make an entire settlement with you. The money in Mr. Schweighauser's hands, which you say is under the direction and order of Mr. R. Morris, ought to be disposed of according to those orders.
. . . We are, sir, your most obedient servants, B. FRANKLIN, ARTHUR LEE, JOHN ADAMS.

"TO J. WILLIAMS. Passy, 13 April, 1778. SIR,--We are sorry to inform you that the state of our funds admits of no further expenditure, without danger of bringing us into great difficulties. It is, therefore, our desire, that you abstain

p. 372 (cont.)

from any further purchases, and close your accounts, for the present, with as little expense as possible. . . .

"We are, sir, your most obedient humble servants, BENJAMIN FRANKLIN, ARTHUR LEE, JOHN ADAMS." (Travels/Negotiations: WJA, III, p. 128)

(14)   "Mr. Beaumarchais was another of Mr. Deane's confidential friends. This man's character, as a writer of dramas and memoirs, is public enough. His intrigues, as developed by himself in some of his writings, are curious enough. There is one fact which came to my knowledge, which may be thought of more importance. The confidential friend of Mr. Beaumarchais at court, was the queen's treasurer." (Travels/Negotiations: WJA, III, p. 131)

(15)   "Dined this day with Madame Helvetius. One gentleman, one lady, Dr. F., his grandson, and myself, made the company; an elegant dinner." (D. 15 April 1778: WJA, III, p. 132)

(16)   "After dinner went to the Long-champ, where all the carriages in Paris were paraded, which, it seems, is a custom on Good Friday." (D. 17 April 1778: WJA, III, p. 133)

p. 372 (cont.)

(17-18) "Mr. Ferdinand Grand was a Protestant, from Switzerland, who had a house in Paris, and a small country house near us in Passy. Himself, his lady, neice, and sons, composed as decent, modest, and regular a family, as I ever knew in France. It was, however, by M. Chaumont's influence with the Count de Vergennes and M. de Sartine, that he obtained the reputation and emolument of being the banker to the American ministers." (Travels/Negotiations: WJA, III, p. 136)

(19-20) "Dined with the Duchess d'Enville, at her house, with her daughter and grand-daughter, dukes, abbots, &c. &c. &c." (D. 20 April 1778: WJA, III, p. 137) "Among whom was M. Condorcet, a philosopher, with a face as pale, or rather as white, as a sheet of paper, I suppose from hard study." (Travels/Negotiations: WJA, III, p. 137)

(21-30) "It is with much grief and concern that I have learned, from my first landing in France, the disputes between the Americans in this kingdom; the animosities between Mr. Deane and Mr. Lee; between Dr. Franklin and Mr. Lee; between Mr. Izard and Dr. Franklin; between Dr. Bancroft and Mr. Lee; between Mr. Carmichael and all. . . . Dr. Franklin, Mr. Deane, and Dr. Bancroft, are friends. The Lees and Mr. Izard are friends. . . .

"The public business has never been methodically con-

p. 372 (cont.)

ducted. There never was, before I came, a minute book, a letter book, or an account book; and it is not possible to obtain a clear idea of our affairs.

"Mr. Deane lived expensively, and seems not to have had much order in his business, public or private; but he was active, diligent, subtle, and successful, having accomplished the great purpose of his mission to advantage. . . .

"Dr. Franklin, one of my colleagues, is so generally known that I shall not attempt a sketch of his character at present. That he was a great genius, a great wit, a great humorist, a great satirist, and a great politician, is certain. That he was a great philosopher, a great moralist, and a great statesman, is more questionable.

"Mr. Arthur Lee, my other colleague, was a native of Virginia. . . . Their [Arthur's and his brothers'] father had given them all excellent classical educations, and they were all virtuous men. . . .

"I may have said before, that public business had never been methodically conducted. There never was, before I came, a minute-book, a letter-book, or an account-book; or, if there had been, Mr. Deane and Dr. Franklin had concealed them from Mr. Lee, and they were now nowhere to be found." (D. 21 April 1778: WJA, III, pp. 138-139; p. 143)

(31)   "In the evening went to the French comedy, and

p. 372 (cont.)

happened to be placed in the first box, very near to the celebrated Voltaire, who attended the performance of his own Alzire." (D. 27 April 1778: WJA, III, p. 144)

(32-33) "Madame la Duchess d'Ayen a cinq or six enfans, contre la coutume de ce pays çi." (D. 1 May 1778: WJA, III, p. 149) The French here means "Madame the Duchess d'Ayen has five or six children/contrary to the custom of the country." (Index, p. 146)

(34) "When I began to attempt a little conversation in French, I was very inquisitive concerning this great family of Noailles, and I was told by some of the most intelligent men in France, ecclesiastics, as well as others, that there were no less than six marshals of France of this family; that they held so many offices, under the King, that they received eighteen millions of livres annually from the crown; that the family had been remarkable, for ages, for their harmony with one another, and for doing nothing, of any consequence, without a previous council and concert; that, when the American Revolution commenced, a family council had been called to deliberate upon that great event, and determine what part they should take in it, or what conduct they should hold towards it. After they had sufficiently considered, they all agreed, in opinion, that it was a crisis of the highest

p. 372 (cont.)

importance in the affairs of Europe, and of the world; that it must affect France in so essential a manner, that the King could not, and ought not, to avoid taking a capital interest and part in it; that it would, therefore, be the best policy of the family to give their countenance to it as early as possible; and that it was expedient to send one of their sons over to America to serve in her army, under General Washington. The Prince de Poix, as the heir apparent of the Duke of Mouchy, they thought of too much importance to their views and expectations, to be risked in so hazardous a voyage, and so extraordinary a service, and, therefore, it was concluded to offer the enterprise to the Viscount de Noailles, and if he should decline it, to the Marquis de la Fayette. The Viscount, after due consideration, thought it most prudent to remain at home for the present. The Marquis, who was represented as a youth of the finest accomplishments, and most amiable disposition, panting for glory, and ardent to distinguish himself in military service, most joyfully consented to embark in the enterprise. All France pronounced it to be the first page in the history of a great man."
(Travels/Negotiations: WJA, III, p. 149)

(35)   "I shall insert these letters, because they will serve, among many others, to show the number of persons who had their eyes fixed upon our little treasury, and under what

p. 372 (cont.)

a variety of pretences and pretended authorities they set up their claims upon us for money. Dr. Franklin, after he found that Mr. Lee and I agreed in opinion, and were determined to sign and send them, did not choose to let them go without his name." (Travels/Negotiations: <u>WJA</u>, III, p. 151)

p. 373

(1-2)   "TO MR. ROSS, AT NANTES. Passy, 3 May, 1778. SIR,--In a former letter, you wrote us that you would send us the invoices, &c., of the goods shipped on the public account, if we thought it necessary. We wrote for those which would answer for the money we had advanced to you. The reason given in yours of the 18th, for refusing them, does not appear to us at all sufficient." (Travels/Negotiations: <u>WJA</u>, III, p. 152)

(3-4)   "This morning, Dr. Franklin, Mr. Lee, and Mr. Adams, went to Versailles, in order that Mr. Adams might be presented to the King. Waited on the Count de Vergennes, at his office, and, at the hour of eleven, the Count conducted us into the King's bed chamber, where he was dressing, one officer putting on his sword, another his coat, &c." (D. 8 May 1778: <u>WJA</u>, III, p. 155)

(5-12) "I accordingly wrote to Mr. Samuel Adams [in a

p. 373 (cont.)

letter dated 21 May 1778], as follows:--

"'Our affairs in this kingdom I find in a state of confusion and darkness, that surprises me. Prodigious sums of money have been expended, and large sums are yet due; but there are no books of account, nor any documents from whence I have been able to learn what the United States have received as an equivalent. . . .

"'The truth is, in my humble opinion, our system is wrong in many particulars.

"'1. In having three commissioners at this Court. One in the character of envoy is enough. At present, each of the three is considered in the character of a public minister plenipotentiary, which lays him under an absolute necessity of living up to this character, whereas one alone would be obliged to incur no greater expense, and would be quite sufficient for all the business of a public minister.

"'2. In leaving the salaries of these ministers at an uncertainty. You will never be able to obtain a satisfactory account of the public moneys while this system continues; it is a temptation to live at too great an expense, and gentlemen will feel an aversion to demanding a rigorous account.

"'3. In blending the business of a public minister with that of a commercial agent.'" (Travels/Negotiations: WJA, III, pp. 159-160)

p. 373 (cont.)

(13-14) "Mr. Deane never succeeded in throwing much light upon his mode of doing business in France." (Editor's note: <u>WJA</u>, III, p. 161n)

(15) "There was a sort of morality [exhibited by the people of France]. There was a great deal of humanity, and what appeared to me real benevolence. Even their politeness was benevolence. There was a great deal of charity and tenderness for the poor. There were many other qualities that I could not distinguish from virtues." (Travels/Negotiations: <u>WJA</u>, III, p. 171)

(16-17) "The king was the royal carver for himself and all his family [at the supper John Adams attended at Versailles]. His majesty ate like a king, and made a royal supper of solid beef, and other things in proportion." (Travels/Negotiations: <u>WJA</u>, III, p. 174)

(18) "There are reasons to believe that it [a long letter proposing agreement with America] came with the privity of the King [George III]. You may possibly see it some time. Full of flattery, and proposing that America should be governed by a Congress of American peers, to be created and appointed by the King; and of bribery, proposing that a number, not exceeding two hundred American peers, should be

p. 373 (cont.)

made, and that such as had stood foremost, and suffered most, and made most enemies in this contest, as Franklin, Washington, Adams, and Hancock, by name, should be of the number." (L. John Adams to Elbridge Gerry, 9 July 1778: <u>WJA</u>, III, pp. 177-178)

(19-20) "We walked up the mountain to the pavilion and dwelling-house of Madame du Barry. The situation is one of the most extensive and beautiful about Paris. . . . Madame du Barry was walking in the garden; she sent us word she should be glad to see us, but we answered it was too late, we had so far to go." (D. 17 July 1778: <u>WJA</u>, III, pp. 181-182)

(21)   "Dined with the Abbés Chalut and Arnoux. Returned at night and found M. Turgot, Abbe Condillac, Madame Helvetius, and the Abbé, &c." (D. 26 November 1778: <u>WJA</u>, III, p. 186)

(22)   "Called on M. Genet. M. Genet's son went with me and my son to see the Menagerie." (D. 3 March 1779: <u>WJA</u>, III, p. 192)

(23-24) "I dined on Monday with Mr. Schweighauser; Tuesday with Mr. Johnson; last evening at the Comedie, where we had

p. 373 (cont.)

the Barbier de Seville and L'Epreuve nouvelle. The stage here [at Nantes, where John Adams had stopped on his journey home to the United States] is not like that of Paris; a poor building, the company on the stage, great part of it, and not very clean nor sweet. The actors indifferent." (D. 14 April 1779: WJA, III, p. 193)

(25-26) "At dinner, much conversation about the electrical eel, which gives a shock to a ring of persons, like the touch of a bottle or conductor." (D. 9 May 1779: WJA, III, p. 199)

(27-28) "Eccentricities and irregularities are to be expected from him [John Paul Jones]. They are in his character, they are visible in his eyes. His voice is soft and still and small; his eye has keenness and wildness and softness in it." (D. 13 May 1779: WJA, III, p. 202)

[The French frigate, the Sensible, on which John Adams had sailed, arrived at Boston on 2 August 1779. On 9 August John Adams was chosen to represent Braintree at the Convention called to frame a constitution for Massachusetts. Having served at the Convention, he sailed, again on the Sensible, for Europe on 13 November. The ship reached Ferrol, Spain (near Corunna), on 8 December 1779. See WJA, III, headnote p. 229; p. 229; p. 231.]

p. 373 (cont.)

(29)   "He [the French Consul from Corunna] told me that the office of consul was regulated by an ordinance of the King; but that some nations had entered into particular stipulations with the King; that the consuls of different nations were differently treated by the same nation; that as Consul of France he had always claimed the privileges of the most favored nation; that he inquired what privileges were enjoyed by the consuls of England, Italy, Germany, &c. &c.; that there is for the province of Galice a sovereign court of justice, which has both civil and criminal jurisdiction; that it is without appeal in all criminal cases, but in some civil cases an appeal lies to the Council; that there is not time for an application for pardon, for they execute forthwith; that hanging is the capital punishment; they burn sometimes, but it is after death; that there was lately a sentence for parricide; the law required that the criminal should be headed up in a hogshead with an adder, a toad, a dog, a cat, &c. and cast into the sea; that he looked at it, and found that they had printed those animals on the hogshead, and that the dead body was put into the cask; that the ancient law of the Visigoths is still in use, with the institutes, codes, no-velles, &c. of Justinian, the currant law and ordonnances of the King; that he will procure for me a passport from the General or Governor of the Province, who resides at Corunna, which will secure me all sorts of facilities as I ride the

p. 373 (cont.)

country; but whether through the kingdom, or only through the province of Galice, I don't know. (D. 14 December 1779: WJA, III, pp. 232-233)

(30) "This morning we arose at five or six o'clock. Went over in a boat, and mounted our mules, thirteen of them in number, and two muleteers; one of whom went before for a guide, and the other followed after to pick up stragglers." (D. 15 December 1779: WJA, III, p. 235)

(31-35) "I have found the pork of this country to-day and often before, the most excellent and delicious, as
p. 374 also the bacon, which occasioned my inquiry into
(1-5) the manner of raising it. The Chief Justice [at Corunna, where John Adams was visiting] informed me, that much of it was fatted upon chestnuts, and much more upon Indian corn, which was much better; but that in some provinces of Spain they had a peculiar kind of acorns, growing upon old pasture oaks, which were very sweet, and produced better pork than either chestnuts or Indian corn; that there were parts of Spain where they fatted hogs upon vipers; they cut off their heads, and gave the bodies to their swine, and they produced better pork than chestnuts, Indian corn, or acorns.

"These gentlemen told us that all kinds of grain would come to a good market in this country, even Indian corn, for

p. 374 (cont.)

they never raised more than their bread, and very seldom enough; pitch, tar, turpentine, timber, masts, &c. would do; salt-fish, spermaceti candles, &c. rice, &c. Indigo and tobacco come from their own colonies. The Administrator of the King's Tobacco told me that ten million weight was annually consumed in Spain in smoking." (D. 19 December 1779: WJA, III, pp. 238-239)

(6)   "Drank tea at Signor Lagoanere's. Saw the ladies drink chocolate in the Spanish fashion." (D. 22 December 1779: WJA, III, p. 240)

(7)   "Dined on board the Belle Poule with the officers of the Galatea and the Belle Poule." (D. 24 December 1779: WJA, III, p. 240)

(8-17)   "Travelled from Betanzos to Castillano. The roads still mountainous and rocky. We broke one of our axle-trees, early in the day, which prevented us from going more than four leagues in the whole.

"The house where we lodge is of stone, two stories high. We entered into the kitchen,--no floor but the ground, and no carpet but straw, trodden into mire by men, hogs, horses, mules, &c. In the middle of the kitchen was a mound, a little raised with earth and stone, upon which was a fire, with

p. 374 (cont.)

pots, kettles, skillets, &c. of the fashion of the country, about it. There was no chimney. The smoke ascended, and found no other passage than through two holes drilled through the tiles of the roof, not perpendicularly over the fire, but at angles of about forty-five degrees. . . .

". . . There was a flight of steps of stone, from the kitchen floor up into a chamber, covered with mud and straw; on the left hand, as you ascended the stairs, was a stage built up about half way from the kitchen floor to the chamber floor; on this stage was a bed of straw on which lay a fatting hog. . . . The chamber had a large quantity of Indian corn in ears, hanging over head upon sticks and pieces of slit work--perhaps an hundred bushels; in one corner was a large bin full of rape seed or colza; on the other side, another bin full of oats. . . . Yet, amidst all these horrors, I slept better than I have done before since my arrival in Spain." (D. 27 December 1779: WJA, III, pp. 241-242)

(18-19) "Went from Castillan to Baamonde. . . . There is here and there a valley, and here and there a farm that looks beautifully cultivated; but in general the mountains are covered with furze, and are not well cultivated. I am astonished to see so few trees; scarce an elm, oak, or any other tree to be seen; a very few walnut trees, and a very few fruit trees." (D. 28 December 1779: WJA, III, p. 242)

p. 374 (cont.)

(20-23) "At Lugo, where we arrived yesterday. . . . We went to see the Cathedral at Lugo, which is very rich. . . . Two Irish gentlemen came to pay their respects to me,-- Michael Meagher O'Reilly and Lewis O'Brien. O'Brien afterwards sent me a meat-pie and a minced-pie and two bottles of Frontenac wine, which gave us a fine supper.

"Arrived at Gallego in very good season, having made six leagues and a half from Lugo. . . .

"I see nothing but signs of poverty and misery among the people. . . . Nothing appears rich but the churches; nobody fat but the clergy. The roads, the worst without exception that ever were passed, in a country where it would be easy to make them very good. No symptoms of commerce, or even of internal traffic; no appearance of manufactures or industry." (D. 30 December 1779: WJA, III, p. 244) John Adams gives an account of "St James Campostella" (line 21) in his diary entry for 28 December 1779 (WJA, III, pp. 243-244). Pound appears to have combined that account with the visit to Lugo.

(24-25) "We are now on the highest ground of all, and within gun-shot of the line between Galice and Leon. . . . The people wear broad-brimmed hats or caps made of woollen cloth, like their coats, jackets, and breeches, which are all of a color, made of black sheep's wool, without dyeing."

p. 374 (cont.)

(D. 31 December 1779: WJA, III, p. 245) As the year 1780 arrived (line 24), John Adams's journey to France across Spain was not yet complete.

(26-27) "The river Valcarce flows between two rows of mountains, rising on each hand to a vast height—the most grand, sublime, awful objects; yet they are cultivated up to their highest summits. . . . The houses are uniformly the same through the whole country, hitherto,—common habitations for men and beasts; the same smoky, filthy holes; not one decent house have I seen from Corunna." (D. 1 January 1780: WJA, III, p. 246)

(28-35) "Tuesday. Found clean beds and no fleas for the first time in Spain [at Astorga, where John Adams
p. 375 arrived on 3 January 1780]. . . . Saw the market
(1-4) of vegetables, onions, and turnips—the largest I ever saw—cabbages, carrots, &c.; saw the market of fuel, wood, coal, turf, and brush. Saw numbers of the Mauregato women, as fine as squaws, and a great deal more nasty; crucifixes, beads and chains, ear-rings and finger-rings, in silver, brass, glass, &c. about their necks, &c. . . .

"This day was brought me the Gazette de Madrid of the 24th of December, in which is this article:

"'Coruña, 15 de Diciembre. Hoy mismo han llegado á

p. 375 (cont.)

esta Plaza el Caballero Juan Adams, miembro del Congreso Americano y su Ministro Plenipotenciario a la Corte de Paris, y Mr. Deane, Secretario de Embaxada, quienes salieron de Boston, el 15 de Noviembre ultimo, á bordo de la Fregata Francesa de Guerra la Sensible, que entró en el Ferrol el dia 8 del corriente. Trahe la noticia de que habiendo los Ingleses evacuado a Rhode Island y retirado todas sus tropas a Nueva Yorck, los Americanos tomaron posesion de todos los puestos evacuados.'" (D. 4 January 1780: WJA, III, p. 247) The Spanish words quoted by Pound, Hoy mismo han llegado/ a esta plaza el Caballero/ Juan Adams miembro/ etc/ los Ingleses/ evacuando Rhode Island/ los Americanos tomaron..., mean "Today have arrived at this square the knight/ John Adams member/ etc/ the Englishmen evacuating Rhode Island/ the Americans took over." (Index, p. 96)

(5-6) "Rode from Astorga to Leon, eight leagues. This is one great plain; the road very fine; great flocks of sheep and cattle. . . . The vast range of Asturias Mountains covered with snow on our left; the weather as pleasant as could be, though cold; some frost and ice on the roads." (D. 5 January 1780: WJA, III, p. 248)

(7-8) "The river which comes down from the mountains of Asturias is not now very large; but in the spring, when the

p. 375 (cont.)

snows melt upon the mountains, it is swelled by the freshes to a very great size. This river runs also down into the kingdom of Portugal. . . . We passed through several very little villages, in every one of which we saw the young people, men and women, dancing a dance that they call fandango." (D. 6 January 1780: WJA, III, p. 249)

(9-12) "Tuesday. Arrived at Burgos. . . . Every individual person in company has a great cold. We go along sneezing and coughing, as if we were fitter for an hospital than for travellers on the road. My servant and all the other servants in company behave worse than ever I knew servants behave; they are dull, inactive, unskilful. The children are sick, and in short my patience was never so near being exhausted as at present. . . .

". . . Upon my inquiry after the religious houses in Burgos, our guide went out and procured me the following information: [here appears a list, by name, of the thirty-three religious houses in Burgos]." (D. 11 January 1780: WJA, III, pp. 251-252)

(13-14) "In the last house in Spain we found one chimney, which was the only one we saw since we left that in the house of M. Destournelles, the French Consul in Corunna." (Travels/Negotiations, concerning the events of 20 January 1780: WJA, III, p. 257)

p. 375 (cont.)

(15)   "We passed by Angoulême yesterday morning, and encircled almost the whole town. It stands upon a high hill, and is walled all round; a fine, airy, healthy situation, with several streams of water below it, and fine interval lands. The river Charente runs by it." (D. 5 February 1780: <u>WJA</u>, III, p. 258)

(16-17)   "The Count [de Vergennes] might imagine that I was so little read in the law of nations and the negotiations of ambassadors, and had so little experience in the world, or, to use one of his own expressions on another occasion, so much <u>bonhomie</u>, that, upon the intimation in his letter, I would, in all simplicity and <u>naiveté</u>, send him a copy of my instructions." (Travels/Negotiations: <u>WJA</u>, III, p. 262)

(18)   "The nature of my instructions I was not at all satisfied with, and was consequently more determined to keep them from the French, as well as English and other courts. The articles relative to the boundaries of the United States and to the fisheries were by no means agreeable to me; and I had already reasons enough to suspect, and, indeed, to believe, that the French Court, at least the Count de Vergennes, would wish me to go to the utmost extent of them in relinquishing the fisheries, and in contracting the boundaries of the United States; whereas, on the contrary, it was my un-

p. 375 (cont.)

alterable determination to insist on the fisheries, and on an ample extension of our boundaries, as long as my instructions would justify me." (Travels/Negotiations: **WJA**, III, p. 263)

(19)   Pound's comment.

(20-27) "The Count [de Vergennes] evades ingeniously enough his improper attempt to draw out my instructions from their concealment. But his anxiety to have my commission to negotiate a treaty of commerce with Great Britain concealed, excited some surprise and some perplexity. I was not clear that I suspected his true motives. The United States were clearly at as full liberty to negotiate concerning commerce as concerning peace. In both they must be governed by their treaties with France, but not in one more than the other. However, time brought to light what I but imperfectly suspected. The Count meditated at that time, no doubt, what he soon carried into execution with too much success,--his intrigues with Congress, at Philadelphia, to get my commission to negotiate a treaty of commerce annulled, without renewing it to the five commissioners whom they afterwards appointed to negotiate peace. It was intended to keep us embroiled with England as much, and as long as possible, even after a peace. It had that effect for eleven years. The United States never had spirit, decision, and independence, to

p. 375 (cont.)

remove this obstacle to a friendly understanding with England, till 1794, when Mr. Jay sacrificed, and Mr. Washington diminished his popularity, by a treaty which excited the insolent rage of France without a color of justice. The members of Congress who suffered themselves to become the instruments of the Count and of his minister, the Chevalier de la Luzerne, and his secretary, M. Marbois, in this humiliating and pernicious measure of annihilating the power of negotiating on commerce, I am not able to enumerate very exactly. Those who are disposed to investigate the subject are at liberty to to it." (Travels/Negotiations: <u>WJA</u>, III, pp. 265-266)

(28)   Pound's comment.

(29-34) "Setting off on a journey with my two sons [Charles and John Quincy] to Amsterdam. Lodged at Compiegne. Friday night, lodged at Valenciennes. Saturday, arrived at Brussels.

"This road is through the finest country I have anywhere seen. The wheat, rye, barley, oats, peas, beans, and several other grains, the hemp, flax, grass, clover, lucern, sainfoin, &c. The pavements and roads are good. The rows of trees on each side the road, and around many squares of land. The vines, the cattle, the sheep, in short every thing upon this road is beautiful and plentiful. Such immense fields

p. 375 (cont.)

and heavy crops of wheat I never saw anywhere." (D. 27 July 1780: **WJA**, III, p. 267)

(35)   "The church music here [at the cathedral in Brussels] is in the Italian style. A picture in tapestry was hung up, of a number of Jews stabbing the wafer, the <u>bon</u> <u>Dieu</u>, and blood gushing in streams from the bread. This insufferable piece of pious villany shocked me beyond measure; but thousands were before it, on their knees, adoring. . . .

p. 376 (1-4)

"In this town is a great plenty of stone, which I think is the same with our Braintree north-common stone. It is equally hard, equally fine grain, capable of a fine polish. I think the color is a little darker than the Braintree stone. . . . The late Prince Charles was a brother of the Empress Queen,--<u>l'Imperatrice</u> <u>Reine</u>--Uncle of the Emperor and the Queen of France. He was extremely beloved by the people, and has left an excellent character. The Emperor did not like him, it is said. In the late war the Emperor called upon this Prince for money. The Prince wrote to dissuade him from it. The Emperor sent again. The Prince wrote back, that he saw they were determined, and they must appoint another governor of this province, for he could not execute their orders. Upon this the imperial court desisted." (D. 30 July 1780: **WJA**, III, p. 268)

p. 376 (cont.)

(5-6)   "We rode round the environs of the town [Rotterdam]; then to his [Mr. Dubbledemuts's] country seat, where we supped. The meadows are very fine; the horses and cattle large; the intermixture of houses, trees, ships, and canals, throughout this town, is very striking; the neatness here is remarkable." (D. 5 August 1780: WJA, III, p. 269)

(7)   "John Derk, Baron Van der Capellen tot de Pol, of Overyssel, was a man of marked character, and one whose services, rendered to the cause of America during the struggle for recognition in Holland, deserves to be remembered." (Editor's note: WJA, III, p. 270, n. 1)

(8)   "He [Baron Van der Capellen] fears that the Prince, and the proprietors of English funds, will unite in endeavors to make it up by a dishonorable peace." (D. 14 January 1781: WJA, III, p. 270)

(9-10)   "Not long afterwards, though himself [Baron Van der Capellen] a nobleman, he distinguished himself by an endeavor to put an end to certain feudal burdens that weighed upon the people of his neighborhood, the confirmation of which had been eagerly sought by many of his own class. This drew upon him their indignation, which showed itself in the States of Overyssel, by the adoption of a decree censuring

p. 376 (cont.)

him for sedition and slander, and demanding of him a humble apology, and promise of amendment, on penalty of exclusion from the position in the States to which his rank entitled him, in case of refusal. He declined the condition, and remained excluded four years, and until the popular voice demanded his restoration in a manner it was not deemed safe to neglect. His triumph was complete, and it took place at the same time with that of the United States over the resistance of Great Britain in Holland." (Editor's note: <u>WJA</u>, III, p. 270, n. 1)

(11) "Engelbert Francis Van Berckel, Pensionary of the City of Amsterdam, was another prominent friend of America, in Holland. Under his auspices, a plan of a commercial treaty was secretly in train of negotiation, until the moment when the capture of Henry Laurens and of his papers, disclosed the whole proceeding to the British ministry. They immediately demanded, through their minister, Sir Joseph Yorke, the exemplary punishment of M. Van Berckel, which not having been promptly decided upon, was the principal cause assigned in the declaration of Great Britain for the war that ensued." (Editor's note: <u>WJA</u>, III, pp. 270, n. 2-271n)

(12-16) "Fell into conversation naturally with Don Joas Theolomico de Almeida, Envoy extraordinary of Portugal. He

p. 376 (cont.)

said to me, 'The peace is yet a good way off; there will be no peace this winter; there will be another campaign, and no peace until the winter following. . . . As to the independence of America, that is decided.' . . .

"The Comte Montagnini de Mirabel, minister plenipotentiary of the King of Sardinia, asked what was the principle of the indecision of Great Britain. 'Why don't they acknowledge your independence? They must have some intelligence that is not public.' I answered, 'I don't believe there is any principle or system in it. It is merely owing to their confusion.' . . .

"M. Boreel, the Baron de Lynden de Hemmen, and the President of the Grand Committee, all members of the Assembly of their H. M., told me that five copies of the treaties would be made out according to my desire, the English and Dutch side by side upon every page, and the treaty would be signed next week." (D. 14 September 1782: WJA, III, pp. 272-273)

(17)   John Adams was 46 years of age in 1782 when the treaties with the Dutch were prepared for signature. See WJA, III, p. 273, top, at left-hand margin.

(18-19) "They showed me this evening the lady who holds at her house an assembly, every evening, where the whole

p. 376 (cont.)

<u>corps</u> <u>diplomatique</u> assist; the lady who used to preside at Sir Joseph Yorke's table, and see that all was in order there.

"The Comte de Welderen came as usual and made his compliments to me. The Rhinegrave de Salm, Colonel Bentinck, Mr. Van der Dussen, and other officers; in short, I never spent so social an evening at Court." (D. 14 September 1782: <u>WJA</u>, III, p. 273)

(20-21) "'The Minister from Prussia, M. de Thulemeyer, is very civil, attacks me, (as he expresses it,) in English, and wishes to meet me on horseback, being both great riders; will converse freely with me upon astronomy, or natural history, or any mere common affairs; will talk of news, battles, sieges, &c.; but these personages are very reserved in politics and negotiations; they must wait for instructions.' Letter of J. A. in <u>Dipl</u>. <u>Corresp</u>. vol. vi. p. 390." (<u>WJA</u>, III, p. 273n)

(22-25) "There is in the Rotterdamsche Courant of to-day, the following article from Philadelphia, of the 7th of August:

"'Het is opmerkelyk dat de Staaten-General, de onafhankelijkheit der Vereenigde Staaten, juist op den 19 April, dezes Jaars erkend hebben, zynde die dag de zevende verjaring van den veldslag by Lexington, en dat deze zaak nog opmer-

p. 376 (cont.)

kelyker maakt is, dat de Eerste Memoire van den Heer Adams, die zulk een grooten indruk op de Hollandsche Natie gemaakt heeft, gedagteekend is den 19 April, 1781.'" (D. 5 October 1782: WJA, III, p. 279) The Dutch words Pound quotes, VERJARING/ van den veldslag by Lexington/ Eerste Memoire dan den Heer Adams/ INDRUK of de Hollandsche Natie, mean "Concerning/ the battle of Lexington/ First memoir by Mr. Adams/ Impression of the Dutch Navy." (Index, p. 237)

(26-29) "At twelve, went to the State House; was received as usual at the head of the stairs by M. de Santheuvel, and M. de Lynden, Deputies from Holland and Zealand, and conducted into the Truce Chamber, where we signed and sealed the treaty of commerce and the convention concerning recaptures.

". . . The Duke [de la Vauguyon] was pleased to say, and with a warmth that proved him sincere, that he rejoiced to hear it [that John Adams would go to Paris for peace negotiations with England], for it seemed by it that Mr. Jay and I were cordial, and he thought further, it was absolutely necessary I should be there, for that the immovable firmness that heaven had given me would be useful and necessary upon this occasion." (D. 8 October 1782: WJA, III, pp. 280-281)

(30-34) "As the commerce of Bruges and Ostend have grown out of the American Revolution and the Neutral Confederation,

p. 376 (cont.)

it may be worth while to make the following extract:

"Extract from the Journal of Count Sarsfield.

"'5 June, 1782. J'ai trouvé Bruges dans un grand mouvement, par le commerce qui y arrive. J'ai compté de vingt à vingt-cinq navires dans le Bassin; it en peut tenir beaucoup plus, et on va l'agrandir. On abat les fortifications; tous les magazins de la ville sont remplis; on en construit de nouveaux, qui seront fort grands. La journée d'un homme qui n'a que ses bras est de 16s. et nourri.'" (D. 10 October 1782: WJA, III, p. 283) The French quoted by Pound, vingt a vingtcinq navires dans le bassin/ . . ./ magazins de la ville sont remplis,/ journee d'un homme 15 [sic] s/ et nourri, means "twenty to twenty-five ships in the basin/ . . ./ warehouses (or armories) of the city are filled/ a man's day (is worth) 15 sous,/ including food." (Index, p. 239)

(35)   "Extract from the Journal of Count Sarsfield.

"'1 July, at the Hague. Tout ce qui vient de se passer en Hollande, la révolution qui s'y est faite dans les esprits en faveur de la France, la maniere dont M. le Duc Louis de Brunswick a été écarté des affaires, au moins en apparence; enfin, cet ouvrage de M. le Duc de la Vauguyon mérite que j'en parle un peu.'" (D. 10 October 1782: WJA, III, pp. 284-285) The French quoted by Pound, OEuvre [see ouvrage] de M. le Duc de Vauguyon, means "the work of the Duke of

p. 376 (cont.)

Vauguyon." (Index, p. 158)

p. 377

(1)   "Spent most of the day in signing obligations for the United States. It is hard work to sign one's name sixteen hundred times after dinner." (D. 11 October 1782: WJA, III, pp. 288-289)

(2-4)   "This morning, at ten, made my visit to the President Van Randwyck, of Guelderland, to take leave of their High Mightinesses, and presented Mr. Dumas as chargé des affaires in my absence. Went next to the Hotel de Dordrecht, to take leave of Mr. Gyzelaer, and next, to that of Amsterdam, to take leave of Mr. Visscher, who was more bold and open than ever I knew him. Said, it was the Stadholder, who was the greatest--'le plus g. t. de ce pays-ci, entete comme une mule,' &c." (D. 15 October 1782: WJA, III, p. 291)
The French quoted by Pound, le plus grand t....de ce pays-ci/ entete comme une, means "the biggest t. . . of this country/ stubborn as a." (Index, p. 122)

(5)   "Rode to Mons, in a great rain. Dined at the Couronne de l'Empereur; very well and very cheap. Rode to Valenciennes, and found our axletree broken again. Put up at the Post House." (D. 23 October 1782: WJA, III, p. 296)

p. 377 (cont.)

(6-15) "Parted from Pont Saint Maxence for Chantilly. . . . Walked round the gardens, fish-ponds, grottos, and water-spouts, and looked at the carps and swans that came up to us for bread. Nothing is more curious than this. Whistle, or throw a bit of bread into the water, and hundreds of carps, large and fat as butter, will be seen swimming near the top of the water towards you, and will assemble all in a huddle before you. Some of them will thrust up their mouths to the surface, and gape at you, like young birds in a nest to their parents for food. While we were viewing the statue of Montmorency, Mademoiselle de Bourbon came out into the round house at the corner of the castle, dressed in beautiful white, her hair uncombed, hanging and flowing about her shoulders, with a book in her hand, and leaned over the bar of iron; but soon perceiving that she had caught my eye, and that I viewed her more attentively than she fancied, she rose up with that majesty and grace which persons of her birth affect, if they are not taught, turned her hair off both her shoulders with her hands, in a manner that I could not comprehend, and decently stepped back into the chamber, and was seen no more. . . .

"The first thing to be done in Paris, is always to send for a tailor, peruke-maker, and shoemaker, for this nation has established such a domination over the fashion, that neither clothes, wigs, nor shoes, made in any other place,

p. 377 (cont.)

will do in Paris. This is one of the ways in which France taxes all Europe, and will tax America. It is a great branch of the policy of the Court to preserve and increase this national influence over the mode, because it occasions an immense commerce between France and all the other parts of Europe. . . .

"Mr. Jay, [lodges at] Rue des petits Augustins, Hôtel d'Orléans." (D. 26 October 1782: WJA, III, pp. 297-298)

(16-17) "Between two as subtle spirits as any in this world [Benjamin Franklin and John Jay], the one malicious, the other, I think, honest, I shall have a delicate, a nice, a critical part to act. Franklin's cunning will be to divide us; to this end he will provoke, he will insinuate, he will intrigue, he will manoeuvre. My curiosity will at least be employed in observing his invention and his artifice. Jay declares roundly, that he will never set his hand to a bad peace. Congress may appoint another, but he will make a good peace or none." (D. 27 October 1782: WJA, III, p. 300)

(18-22) "Called on Jay, and went to Oswald's, and spent with him and Strachey, from eleven to three, in drawing up the articles respecting debts, and tories, and fishery. I drew up the article anew in this form.

p. 377 (cont.)

"'That the subjects of His Britannic Majesty, and the people of the said United States, shall continue to enjoy unmolested, the right to take fish of every kind, on all the Banks of Newfoundland, in the Gulf of Saint Lawrence, and all other places, where the inhabitants of both countries used, at any time heretofore, to fish; and also to dry and cure their fish on the shores of Nova Scotia, Cape Sable, the Isle of Sable, and on the shores of any of the unsettled bays, harbors, or creeks of Nova Scotia and the Magdalen Islands; and His Britannic Majesty, and the said United States, will extend equal privileges and hospitality to each other's fishermen as to his own.'" (D. 4 November 1782: WJA, III, p. 302)

(23) "The compliments that have been made me since my arrival in France, upon my success in Holland, would be considered as a curiosity if committed to writing. . . . Compliments are the study of this people [the French], and there is no other so ingenious at them." (D. 10 November 1782: WJA, III, p. 306)

(23-28) "He [Mr. Whitefoord, the Secretary to the British negotiator, Mr. Oswald] sat down, and we fell into conversation about the weather, and the vapors and exhalations from Tartary, which had been brought here last spring by the winds,

p. 377 (cont.)

and given us all the influenza; thence, to French fashions, and the punctuality with which they insist upon people's wearing thin clothes in spring and fall, though the weather is ever so cold, &c. . . .

"For my own part, I thought America had been long enough involved in the wars of Europe. She had been a foot-ball between contending nations from the beginning, and it was easy to foresee that France and England both would endeavor to involve us in their future wars. I thought it our interest and duty to avoid as much as possible, and to be completely independent, and have nothing to do, but in commerce, with either of them." (D. 11 November 1782: <u>WJA</u>, III, pp. 307-308)

(28-31) "'You are afraid,' says Mr. Oswald to-day, 'of being made the tools of the powers of Europe.' 'Indeed I am,' says I. 'What powers?' said he. 'All of them,' said I. 'It is obvious that all the powers of Europe will be continually manoeuvring with us, to work us into their real or imaginary balances of power.'" (D. 18 November 1782: <u>WJA</u>, III, p. 316)

(31-32) "I said I was the more surprised at this [news that Marbois also wished the United States to give up its interests in the fisheries], as Mr. Marbois, on our passage

p. 377 (cont.)

to America, had often said to me, that he thought the fishery our natural right and our essential interest, and that we ought to maintain it, and be supported in it; yet that he appeared now to be manoeuvring against it; I told him [Franklin] that I always considered their extraordinary attack upon me, not as arising from any offence or any thing personal, but as an attack upon the fishery; there had been great debates in Congress upon issuing the first commission for peace, and in settling my instructions; that I was instructed not to make any treaty of commerce with Britain without an express clause acknowledging our right to the fishery; this [French] Court knew that this would be, when communicated to the English, a strong motive with them to acknowledge our right; and, to take away this, they [the French ministers] had directed their intrigues against me, to get my commission annulled, and had succeeded. . . ." (D. 20 November 1782: WJA, III, pp. 319-320)

(32-33) "Bancroft said to-day, that it was often said among the French people, that Mons. de Vergennes loved Spain too well, and was too complaisant to the Spanish Court; that he was ambitious of being made a grandee of Spain, in order to cover his want of birth, for that he was not nobly born. This, I fancy, is a mistake; but such are the objects which men pursue,--titles, ribbons, stars, garters, crosses, keys,

p. 377 (cont.)

are the important springs that move the ambition of men in high life." (D. 22 November 1782: <u>WJA</u>, III, p. 326)

    (34-35)   "At Newfoundland it was the same; the fish, in March or April, were in shore in all the creeks,
p. 378   bays, and harbors, that is, within three leagues
(1-2)   of the coasts or shores of Newfoundland and Nova Scotia; that neither French nor English could go from Europe and arrive early enough for the first fare; that our vessels could, being so much nearer, an advantage which God and nature had put into our hands; but that this advantage of ours had ever been an advantage to England, because our fish had been sold in Spain and Portugal for gold and silver, and that gold and silver sent to London for manufactures; that this would be the course again; that France foresaw it, and wished to deprive England of it, by persuading her to deprive us of it; that it would be a master stroke of policy if she could succeed, but England must be completely the dupe before she could succeed.

". . . As a source of profit, had England rather France should supply the markets of Lisbon and Cadiz with fish, and take the gold and silver, than we? France would never spend any of that money in London; we should spend it all very nearly." (D. 25 November 1782: <u>WJA</u>, III, pp. 328-329)

p. 378 (cont.)

(2-3)   Pound here refers to the same passage from which he took lines 31-32 of Canto LXV (p. 377).

(4-11)   "'Give me leave to tell you [Mr. Oswald] sir,' said I, 'you are mistaken [in believing that France wishes all the world to acknowledge American independence]. If I have not been mistaken in the policy of France, from my first observation of it to this hour, they have been as averse to other powers acknowledging our independence as you have been.' Mr. Jay joined me in the same declaration. 'God!' says he, 'I understand it now; there is a gentleman going to London this day,--I will go home and write upon the subject by him.'"   (D. 9 December 1782: <u>WJA</u>, III, p. 347)

(12-14)   "I went first to Mr. Jay, and made some additions to the joint letter, which I carried first to Mr. Laurens, who made some corrections and additions, and then to Passy, to Dr. Franklin, who proposed a few other corrections; and showed me an article he has drawn up for the definitive treaty, to exempt fishermen, husbandmen, and merchants, as much as possible, from the evils of future wars. This is a good lesson to mankind at least."   (D. 13 December 1782: <u>WJA</u>, III, p. 349)

(15-16)   "The Count de Lynden showed me his gold snuff-box,

254

p. 378 (cont.)

set with diamonds, with the miniature of the King of Sweden, presented to him on taking leave of that Court. The King is like Mr. Hancock." (D. 21 December 1782: <u>WJA</u>, III, p. 350)

(17-18)   "Wednesday. Christmas.

"<u>Lady</u> <u>Lucan's</u> <u>Verses</u> <u>on</u> <u>Ireland</u>.

> "'Hear this, ye great, as from the feast ye rise,
> Which every plundered element supplies!
> Hear, when fatigued, not nourished, ye have dined;
> The food of thousands is to roots confined.
>
> Eternal fasts that know no taste of bread,
> Nor where who sows the corn by corn is fed;
> Throughout the year, no feast o'er crowns his board--
> Four pence a day, ah! what can that afford?
>
> Open our ports at once, with generous minds,
> Let commerce be as free as waves and winds;
> Seize quick the time, for now, consider well,
> Whole quarters of the world at once rebel.'"

(D. 25 December 1782: <u>WJA</u>, III, p. 351)

(19-24) "The Duke de la Rochefoucauld made me a visit to-day, and desired me to explain to him some passages in the Connecticut Constitution which were obscure to him, which I did." (D. 26 December 1782: <u>WJA</u>, III, p. 352) In line 21 Pound repeats line 18, p. 378.

(25)   See <u>Index</u>, p. 58, which suggests that the Mr. Eliot referred to in this line may perhaps be T. S. Eliot.

(26-29) "One of these first days of January, I had a con-

p. 378 (cont.)

versation with Mr. Benjamin Vaughan upon the liberty of navigation, as claimed by the confederated neutral powers and the Dutch. I showed him the necessity England was in of acceding to it, and the importance of doing it soon, that they might have it to say that they had arranged their affairs with the Dutch was well as with the United States. He said he saw the importance of pulling at the hairs, one by one, when you could not pull out the whole tail at once. That he had written, and would write again, to my Lord Shelburne upon the subject; 'But,' says he, 'you cannot blame us for endeavoring to carry this point to market, and get something by it. We cannot prevent the French from getting some territory in the East Indies more than they had, and perhaps we may buy this of the Dutch for this point.'" (D. 1 January 1783: WJA, III, p. 353)

(30) Pound's comment.

(31-32) "He [Mr. W. T. Franklin, grandson of Benjamin Franklin] showed me an extract of a letter of Dr. Franklin to Congress concerning him, containing a studied and long eulogium,--sagacity beyond his years, diligence, activity, fidelity, genteel address, facility in speaking French; recommends him to be secretary of some mission; thinks he would make an excellent minister, but does not propose him

p. 378 (cont.)
for it as yet.

"This letter and other circumstances convince me that the plan is laid between the Count de Vergennes and the Doctor, to get Billy made minister to this Court, and, not improbably, the Doctor to London. Time will show." (D. 11 January 1783: <u>WJA</u>, III, p. 355)

(33)   "Went to Versailles, to pay my respects to the King and royal family, upon the event of yesterday. Dined with the foreign ambassadors at the Count de Vergennes'. The King appeared in high health and in gay spirits; so did the Queen. Madame Elizabeth is grown very fat." (D. 21 January 1783: <u>WJA</u>, III, p. 359)

(33-34) "Mr. Whitefoord made me a visit. He said it was the fatal policy of the Earl of Chatham, in supporting the King of Prussia against the House of Austria, that had given an Austrian Queen to France; that the French had contrived to marry the King's two brothers to princesses of Savoy, by which they had damped the zeal of another of the allies of England, the King of Sardinia." (D. 23 January 1783: <u>WJA</u>, III, p. 359)

(35)   "I have been injured, and my country has joined in the injury; it has basely prostituted its own

p. 379

(1-2) honor by sacrificing mine. But the sacrifice of me was not so servile and intolerable as putting us all under guardianship. Congress surrendered their own sovereignty into the hands of a French minister. Blush! blush! ye guilty records! blush and perish! It is glory to have broken such infamous orders. Infamous, I say, for so they will be to all posterity. How can such a stain be washed out? Can we cast a veil over it and forget it?" (D. 18 February 1783: <u>WJA</u>, III, p. 359)

The following two references should be noted concerning the "infamous orders" mentioned by John Adams. First: "R. [Mr. Ridley] is still full of Jay's firmness and independence; has taken upon himself to act without asking advice, or even communicating with the Count de Vergennes, and this even in opposition to an instruction. This instruction, which is alluded to in a letter I received at the Hague, a few days before I left it, has never yet been communicated to me. It seems to have been concealed designedly from me." (D. 27 October 1782: <u>WJA</u>, III, pp. 299-300) Second: "This is probably the instruction to the commissioners, 'ultimately to govern themselves by the advice and opinion of the French ministry,' carried through Congress on an amendment, and after a severe struggle." (Editor's note: <u>WJA</u>, III, p. 300n)

(2-3) "Dined in company with M. Malesherbes, the famous

p. 379 (cont.)

first president of the Court of Aids, uncle of the Chevalier de la Luzerne, and son of the Chancelier de Lamoignon." (D. 24 February 1783: <u>WJA</u>, III, p. 360)

(4)   "De Mably says, there are in France three orders of citizens,--the first order is of the clergy; 2. the second of the nobility; 3. and the third is called <u>Le Tiers État</u>. There are several classes in the order of the clergy; seven or eight classes in the order of nobles; and thirty classes in the <u>Tiers État</u>." (D. 27 February 1783: <u>WJA</u>, III, p. 360) The French phrase <u>tiers etat</u> means "third estate; the people, commons." (<u>Index</u>, p. 223)

(5)   "Dined at Passy; the Spanish ambassador, the Count de Rochambeau, the Chevalier de Chastellux, Mr. Jay, &c., present. Chastellux said to the Abbe Morlaix, that I was the author of the Massachusetts Constitution, and that it was the best of them all, and that the people were very contented with it." (D. 9 March 1783: <u>WJA</u>, III, p. 361)

(5)   "Mercure de France, 1 February, 1783, page 26, Academie Royale de Musique:-- . . .

"'Il est vrai, qu'un artiste qui se présente après vingt-cinq ans de gloire et de succès, ne devroit pas éprouver les mêmes dégoûts; son nom fameux dans l'empire

p. 379 (cont.)

des arts, paroitroit fait pour en imposer à ses détracteurs.
Mais si dans le nouveau pays ou il arrive, son art est encore
ignoré; s'il y regne un faux savoir, pire que l'ignorance;
si l'on y a la manie des préférences, des <u>préférences exclusives</u>, et que l'on ait déjà choisi l'objet de ces préférences,
son nom lui devient inutile, ou même dangereux; et la réputation qui le précéde, en éveillant l'envie, n'est pour lui
qu'un obstacle de plus.'" (D. 10 March 1783: <u>WJA</u>, III, pp.
361-362) The French quoted by Pound, <u>S'il regne un faux
savoir</u>, means "if a false knowledge reigns." (<u>Index</u>, p. 199)

(6-10) "I told him [Mr. Hartley], that I was so convinced
that Great Britain and America would soon feel the necessity
and convenience of a right plan of commerce, that I was not
anxious about it; that it was simply from a pure regard to
Great Britain, and to give them an opportunity of alluring
to themselves as much of our commerce as, in the present
state of things, would be possible, that I should give myself
any trouble about it; that I had never had but one principle
and one system concerning this subject, before, during, or
since the war, and that had generally been the system of
Congress, namely, that it was not our interest to hurt Great
Britain, any further than was necessary to support our independence and our alliances; that the French Court had sometimes endeavored to warp us from this system, in some degrees

p. 379 (cont.)

and particulars; that they had sometimes succeeded with some American ministers and agents, Mr. Deane particularly, and I must add, that Dr. Franklin had not adhered to it at all times with so much firmness as I could have wished; and indeed Congress itself, from the fluctuations of its members, or some other cause, had sometimes appeared to lose sight of it; that I had constantly endeavored to adhere to it, but this inflexibility had been called stubborness, obstinacy, vanity, &c., and had exposed me to many attacks and disagreeable circumstances; that it had been to damp the ardor of returning friendship, as I supposed, which had induced the French minister to use his influence to get the commission to make a treaty of commerce with Great Britain revoked without appointing another; that I did not care a farthing for a commission to Great Britain, and wished that the one to me had never existed; but that I was very sorry it was revoked without appointing another; that the policy of this [French] Court he might well think would be to lay every stumbling block between Great Britain and America; they wished to deprive us of the fisheries and western lands for this reason; they espoused the cause of the tories for this reason.

"I told him the Comte de Vergennes and I were pursuing different objects; he was endeavoring to make my countrymen meek and humble, and I was laboring to make them proud. . . .

p. 379 (cont.)

"I am not fond of talking; but I wanted to convey into his mind a few things for him to think upon. None of the English gentlemen have come here apprized of the place where their danger lay." (D. 29 April 1783: <u>WJA</u>, III, pp. 364-365)

(11-15) "When we met Mr. Hartley, on Tuesday last, at Mr. Laurens's, I first saw and first heard of Mr. Livingston's letter to Dr. Franklin upon the subject of peace, dated January 7, 1782. The peace is made, and the negotiations all passed, before I knew of this letter, and at last by accident. Such is Dr. Franklin. . . .

"Between five and six I made my visit to the Duke of Manchester, the British ambassador, upon his arrival. Not at home. Left my card. The next day, or next but one, the Duke returned my visit, came up to my apartment, and spent a half hour in familiar conversation. He is between fifty and sixty, a composed man, plain Englishman." (D. 3 May 1783: <u>WJA</u>, III, pp. 367-368)

(16-21) "Visited Mr. Hartley. He said he thought the Dutch negotiations in a bad way, and that there would be a civil contest in Holland; a struggle between the Stadtholder and the States.

"Mr. Hartley said, that some Dutch friends he had in

p. 379 (cont.)

London had told him there would be a civil dissension in Holland, and he was now more convinced of it. He said the King of Prussia and the King of England would take the part of the Stadtholder. I answered, they would do well to consider, whether, in that case, France and the Emperor would not assist the republicans, and thus throw all Europe into a flame.

"I told him I thought the English policy towards the republic all wrong; they were wrong to make themselves partisans of the Stadtholder against the Republicans; that they ought to be impartial; that they were interested in the conservation of the liberties of that country; if that spot should be annexed to the Empire or to France, it would be fatal to Great Britain; . . . I had always been ready to acknowledge that I could not distinctly foresee what would be the consequence of our independence in Europe; it might depress England too much, and elevate the House of Bourbon too high; if this should be the case, neither England nor America could depend upon the moderation of such absolute monarchies and such ambitious nations; . . . both might find it necessary to their safety to join, and, in such a case, it would be of great importance to both to have Holland join them; whereas the policy of the British Court, if pursued, would drive the Dutch into the arms of France, and fix them there; that I hoped the case put would never

p. 379 (cont.)

happen; but England would have a stronger reason than ever, now, to cultivate the friendship of Holland. . . ." (D. 20 May 1783: <u>WJA</u>, III, pp. 369-370)

(22-23) "'Whereas, it is expedient that an intercourse and commerce should be opened between the people and territories subject to the Crown of Great Britain, and those of the United States of America; and that this intercourse and commerce should be established on the most enlarged principles of reciprocal benefit to both countries. . . .'" (from the proposed statement, drafted by John Adams, that a treaty of commerce be negotiated between England and the United States, D. 22 May 1783: <u>WJA</u>, III, p. 374)

(23-26) "It was observed last evening, that all the laws of Great Britain for the regulation of the plantation trade, were contrived solely for the benefit of Great Britain. . . .

"He [Baron de Waltersdorf, chamberlain of the King of Denmark] said, that some Danish vessels had gone to America, loaded with linens, duck, sail-cloth, &c." (D. 22 May 1783: <u>WJA</u>, III, p. 374; p. 376)

(27) "Mr. Laurens says, the English are convinced that the method of coppering ships is hurtful. The copper corrodes all the iron, all the bolts, spikes, and nails, which it

p. 379 (cont.)

touches. The vessel falls to pieces all at once. They attribute the late losses of so many ships to this." (D. 23 May 1783: WJA, III, p. 377)

(28-33) "Went to Versailles; had a conference with the Count de Vergennes; made my court, with the Corps diplomatique, to the King, Queen, Monsieur, Madame, the Comte d'Artois, Madame Elizabeth, Mesdames Victoire and Adelaide. Dined with the ambassadors. Had much conversation with the ambassadors of Spain, Sardinia, M. Markow, from Russia, the Dutch ambassadors, &c. It was to me, notwithstanding the cold and rain--the equinoctial storm at the time of the solstice, when all the rooms had fires like winter--the most agreeable day I ever saw at Versailles. . . .

"The Sardinian Ambassador said to me, 'It was curious to remark the progress of commerce; the furs which the Hudson Bay Company sent to London, from the most northern regions of America, were sent to Siberia, within one hundred and fifty leagues of the places where they were hunted.'" (D. 17 June 1783: WJA, III, pp. 379-380)

CANTO LXVI

p. 380

(1-3) "The Duke [de la Vauguyon] said, it would be very difficult to regulate this matter. They could not let us bring their sugars to Europe, neither to France nor any other port. This would lessen the number of French ships and seamen." (D. 18 June 1783: WJA, III, p. 381)

(4-5) "At first, I rode twice a day in my carriage, in the Bois de Boulogne; but, afterwards, I borrowed Mr. Jay's horse, and have generally ridden twice a day, until I have made myself master of this curious forest." (D. 14 September 1783: WJA, III, p. 383)

(6-7) "From the windows in my chamber, and more distinctly from those of the chambers one story higher, you have a view of the village of Issy, of the castle royal of Meudon, of the palace of Bellevue, of the castle of the Duke of Orleans at St. Cloud, and of Mont Calvaire. . . .

"In riding over this forest [the Bois de Boulogne], you see some neat cattle, some horses, a few sheep, and a few deers, bucks, does, and fawns, now and then a hare, and sometimes a few partridges; but game is not plenty in this wood." (D. 7 October 1783: WJA, III, pp. 383-384)

p. 380 (cont.)

(7-8)   "Dined at Amiens [on a journey to London], and put up at night at Abbeville." (D. 21 October 1783: <u>WJA</u>, III, p. 385)

(8)   "I went into the ploughed ground to examine its composition, and found it full of flint stones, such as the road from Chantilly to Calais is made of, and all the fields on that road are full of. In short, the white stones of the cliffs, and the flint stone of the fields, convince me that the lands here are the same with those on the other side the channel, and but a continuation of the same soil. From this mountain we saw the whole channel, the whole town and harbor of Dover." (D. 24 October 1783: <u>WJA</u>, III, p. 386)

(8-12)   "Went to see Mr. Jay, who is lodged with Mr. Bingham in Harley Street, Cavendish Square, No. 30; and, in the afternoon, went to see Mr. Johnson, Great Tower Hill, who informed me that a vessel with one thousand hogsheads of tobacco is passed by, in the channel, from Congress to Messrs. Willinks." (D. 27 October 1783: <u>WJA</u>, III, p. 387)

(13)   "The Hague, June 22. Tuesday." (D. 22 June 1784: <u>WJA</u>, III, p. 387)

(14-15)   "One of the foreign ambassadors said to me,

p. 380 (cont.)

'You have been often in England.' 'Never, but once in November and December, 1783.' 'You have relations in England, no doubt.' 'None at all.' 'None, how can that be? you are of English extraction?' 'Neither my father or mother, grandfather or grandmother, great grandfather or great grandmother, nor any other relation that I know of, or care a farthing for, has been in England these one hundred and fifty years; so that you see I have not one drop of blood in my veins but what is American.' 'Ay, we have seen,' said he, 'proof enough of that.' This flattered me, no doubt, and I was vain enough to be pleased with it." (D. 3 May 1785: WJA, III, p. 392)

(16-17) "He [Comte de Vergennes] said that the King of France never sent them [Morocco] any naval stores; he sent them glaces and other things of rich value, but never any military stores." (D. 20 March 1785: WJA, III, p. 391)

(18-19) "He [Duke of Dorset] said that Lord Carmarthen was their minister of foreign affairs; that I must first wait upon him, and he would introduce me to his Majesty; but that I should do business with Mr. Pitt very often. I asked him Lord Carmarthen's age. He said, thirty-three. He said I should be stared at a great deal." (D. 3 May 1785: WJA, III, p. 392)

p. 380 (cont.)

(20-22) "The posts within the limits of the United States not yet surrendered by the English are,--

"Oswegatchy, in the River St. Lawrence. Oswego, Lake Ontario. Niagara and its dependencies. Presqu' Isle, east side of Lake Erie. Sandusky, ditto. Detroit. Michilimakinac. St. Mary's, south side of the strait between Lakes Superior and Huron, bottom of the Bay des Puantz. St. Joseph, bottom of Lake Michigan." (D. n.d. May 1785: WJA, III, p. 393)

(23-24) "Dined in Bolton street, Picadilly, at the Bishop of Saint Asaph's. . . .

"Mrs. Shipley, at table, asked many questions about the expense of living in Philadelphia and Boston. Said she had a daughter who had married less prudently than they wished, and they thought of sending them to America." (D. 26 March 1786: WJA, III, p. 393)

(25-26) "Presented Mr. Hamilton to the Queen at the drawing-room." (D. 30 March 1786: WJA, III, p. 393)

(27-33) "London, April. Mr. Jefferson and myself went in a post-chaise to Woburn farm, Caversham,
p. 381 Wotton, Stowe, Edgehill, Stratford upon Avon,
(1-6) Birmingham, the Leasowes, Hagley, Stourbridge,

p. 381 (cont.)

Worcester, Woodstock, Blenheim, Oxford, High Wycombe, and back to Grosvenor Square. . . .

". . . Architecture, painting, statuary, poetry, are all employed in the embellishment of these residences of greatness and luxury. A national debt of two hundred and seventy-four millions sterling, accumulated by jobs, contracts, salaries, and pensions, in the course of a century might easily produce all this magnificence. . . .

"Pope's pavilion and Thomson's seat made the excursion poetical. Shenstone's Leasowes is the simplest and plainest, but the most rural of all. I saw no spot so small that exhibited such a variety of beauties." (D. n.d. April 1786: WJA, III, pp. 394-395)

(7-9) "Wednesday. This is the anniversary of the battle of Lexington, and of my reception at the Hague by their High Mightinesses.

"This last event is considered by the historians and other writers and politicians of England and France as of no consequence; and Congress and the citizens of the United States in general concur with them in sentiment." (D. 19 April 1786: WJA, III, p. 396)

(10-13) "Went with Mr. Jefferson and my family to Osterly, to view the seat of the late banker, Child. The house is

p. 381 (cont.)

very large; it is three houses, fronting as many ways; between two is a double row of six pillars, to which you rise by a flight of steps; within, is a square, a court, a terrace paved with large slate. The green-house and hot-house were curious. Blowing roses, ripe strawberries, cherries, plums, &c., in the hot-house.

"The pleasure grounds were only an undulating gravel walk, between two borders of trees and shrubs; all the evergreens, trees, and shrubs, were here. There is a water for fish ponds and for farm uses, collected from the springs and wet places in the farm and neighborhood. Fine flocks of deer and sheep, wood doves, guinea hens, peacocks, &c." (D. 20 April 1786: WJA, III, pp. 396-397)

(14) "Viewed the British Museum. Dr. Grey, who attended us, spoke very slightly of Buffon. Said 'he was full of mauvaise foi; no dependence upon him; three out of four of his quotations not to be found; that he had been obliged to make it his business to examine the quotations; that he had not found a quarter of them.'" (D. 24 April 1786: WJA, III, p. 397)

(15-19) "We breakfasted at Rumford, and turned out of the way to see the seat of Lord Petre, at Thorndon. Mr. Hollis prefers the architecture of this house to that at

p. 381 (cont.)

Stow, because it is more conformable to Palladio,--his Bible for this kind of knowledge. There are in the back front six noble Corinthian pillars. . . .

". . . The library is semicircular, with windows and mahogany colonnades, very elegant, but contrived more as an ornamental passage to the chapel then for study. There are two stoves; but at neither of them could a student be comfortable in cold weather." (D. 24 July 1786: WJA, III, p. 401)

(20)   "Quincy, July 12. Tuesday. Yesterday mowed all the grass on Stony-field Hill." (D. 12 July 1796: WJA, III, p. 416)

(21)   "This day my new barn was raised, near the spot where the old barn stood, which was taken down by my father when he raised his new barn in 1737." (D. 13 July 1796: WJA, III, p. 416)

(22-25) "I arose by four o'clock, and enjoyed 'the charm of earliest birds;' their songs were never more various, universal, animating, or delightful.

"My corn this year has been injured by two species of worms,--one of the size and shape of a caterpillar, but of a mouse color, lies at the root, eats off the stalk, and

p. 381 (cont.)

then proceeds to all the other plants in the hill, till he frequently kills them all; the other is long and slender as a needle, of a bright yellow color; he is found in the center of the stalk near the ground, where he eats it off, as the Hessian fly eats the wheat. My brother taught me the method of finding these vermin and destroying them. They lie commonly near the surface.

"I have been to see my barn, which looks very stately and strong. Rode up to Braintree, and saw where T. has been trimming red cedars. He has not much more to do." (D. 14 July 1796: WJA, III, pp. 416-417)

(26) "Went with three hands to Braintree, and cut between forty and fifty red cedars, and with a team of five cattle brought home twenty-two of them at a load." (D. 15 July 1796: WJA, III, p. 417)

(27) "Yesterday, Dr. Tufts and Mr. Otis and family dined with me. Otis was very full of elections, and had many things to say about Pinckney and Henry, Jefferson and Burr. He says there was a caucus at Philadelphia; that they agreed to run Jefferson and Burr; that Butler was offended and left them. Otis takes it for granted the President [Washington] will retire." (D. 17 July 1796: WJA, III, p. 417) The Otis mentioned here is

p. 381 (cont.)

Samuel Allyne Otis, Secretary of the Senate. (WJA, III, p. 417n)

(28) "T. is mowing the bushes, cutting the trees, and leaves only the white oaks, which he trims and prunes as high as he can reach." (D. 20 July 1796: WJA, III, p. 419)

(29) "Rode down to the barley and black-grass at the beach. The barley is better than I hoped. The clover has taken pretty well in general; parts where the tide has flowed are killed." (D. 23 July 1796: WJA, III, p. 420)

(30-33) "Mr. Howell lodged with us, and spent the whole morning in conversation concerning the affairs of his mission. He said, by way of episode, that the President would resign, and that there was one thing which would make Rhode Island unanimous in his successor, and that was, the funding system. He said they wanted Hamilton for Vice-President. I was wholly silent." (D. 11 August 1796: WJA, III, p. 423)

(34-35) "Are you not representing every member of parliament as renouncing the transactions at Runing

p. 382 Mede, (the meadow, near Windsor, where Magna

(1-5) Charta was signed;) and as repealing in effect the bill of rights, when the Lords and Commons asserted

p. 382 (cont.)

and vindicated the rights of the people and their own rights, and insisted on the king's assent to that assertion and vindication? Do you not represent them as forgetting that the prince of Orange was created King William, by the people, on purpose that their rights might be eternal and inviolable? . . .

". . . Let us take it for granted, that the same great spirit which once gave Caesar so warm a reception, which denounced hostilities against John till Magna Charta was signed, which severed the head of Charles the First from his body, and drove James the Second from his kingdom, the same great spirit (may heaven preserve it till the earth shall be no more) which first seated the great grandfather of his present most gracious majesty on the throne of Britain,--is still alive and active and warm in England; and that the same spirit in America, instead of provoking the inhabitants of that country, will endear us to them for ever, and secure their good-will. . . .

". . . The prospect now before us in America, ought in the same manner to engage the attention of every man of learning, to matters of power and of right, that we may be neither led nor driven blindfolded to irretrievable destruction. Nothing less than this seems to have been meditated for us, by somebody or other in Great Britain. There seems to be a direct and formal design on foot, to

p. 382 (cont.)

enslave all America." (Dissertation: <u>WJA</u>, III, pp. 460-464)

(6-7) "It [the Dissertation] was printed in the month of August of the year 1765, in the Boston Gazette, there divided into four numbers, and without any title whatever. It attracted much attention in Massachusetts and in England, where it was attributed to Jeremy Gridley, then well known as at the head of the bar in the Colony. Thomas Hollis immediately procured it to be reprinted in the London Chronicle, and three years later, in 1768, caused it to be published by Almon, at the end of a small octavo volume, entitled 'The True Sentiments of America,' with the caption by which it has ever since been known." (Editor's headnote to Dissertation: <u>WJA</u>, III, p. 447)

(8-10) "Considering the present scarcity of money, we have reason to think, the execution of that act [The Stamp Act] for a short space of time would drain the country of its cash, strip multitudes of all their property, and reduce them to absolute beggary. And what the consequence would be as to the peace of the province, from so sudden a shock and such a convulsive change in the whole course of our business and subsistence, we tremble to consider. We further apprehend this tax to be unconstitutional. We

p. 382 (cont.)

have always understood it to be a grand and fundamental principle of the constitution, that no freeman should be subject to any tax to which he has not given his own consent, in person or by proxy." (Instructions: <u>WJA</u>, III, pp. 465-466) The Latin phrase <u>OB PECUNIAE SCARSITATEM</u>, which also appears in Cantos 42 and 43, means "on account of scarcity of money." (<u>Index</u>, p. 158) The Latin approximates the opening phrase of this quotation.

(11-12) "Sir,--The revolution which one century has produced in your opinions and principles is not quite so surprising to me as it seems to be to many others. You know very well, I had always a jealousy that your humanity was counterfeited, your ardor for liberty cankered with simulation, and your integrity problematical at least." (Clarendon: <u>WJA</u>, III, p. 469)

(13)   "THE EARL OF CLARENDON TO WILLIAM PYM." (Clarendon: See title, <u>WJA</u>, III, p. 469)

(13-14) "From the Supplement to the Boston Gazette, Monday, 13 January, 1766." (Clarendon: <u>WJA</u>, III, p. 469n)

(15)   "You, of all mankind, should have been the last to be hired by a minister to defend or excuse such taxes

p. 382 (cont.)

and such courts,--taxes [like the Stamp Act] more injurious and ruinous than Danegeld of old, which our countryman Speed says, 'emptied the land of all the coin, the kingdom of her glory, the commons of their content, and the sovereign of his wonted respects and observance;'--courts which seem to have been framed in imitation of an ancient jurisdiction, at the bare mention of which I have often seen your eyes lighten, I mean the court of the masters of the king's forfeitures." (Clarendon: WJA, III, p. 470)

(16-22) "Give me leave, now, to ask you, Mr. Pym, what are the powers of the new courts of admiralty in America? Are the trials in these courts per pares or per legem terrae? Is there any grand jury there to find presentments or indictments? Is there any petit jury to try the fact, guilty or not? Is the trial per legem terrae, or by the institutes, digests, and codes and novels of the Roman law?" (Clarendon: WJA, III, pp. 471-472) The Latin per pares et legem terrae means "by peers and the law of the land"; the Latin petit means "seeks"; the Latin per legem terrae means "by the law of the land." (Index, p. 170 and p. 171)

(23-24) "The people, even to the lowest ranks, have become more attentive to their liberties, more inquisitive

p. 382 (cont.)

about them, and more determined to defend them, than they were ever before known or had occasion to be; innumerable have been the monuments of wit, humor, sense, learning, spirit, patriotism, and heroism, erected in the several provinces in the course of this year. Their counties, towns, and even private clubs and sodalities have voted and determined; their merchants have agreed to sacrifice even their bread to the cause of liberty; their legislatures have resolved; the united colonies have remonstrated; the presses have everywhere groaned; and the pulpits have thundered; and such of the crown officers as have wished to see them enslaved, have everywhere trembled, and all their little tools and creatures been afraid to speak and ashamed to be seen." (Clarendon: WJA, III, p. 476)

(25-32) "The people in America have discovered the most accurate judgment about the real constitution, I say, by their whole behavior, excepting the excesses of a few, who took advantage of the general enthusiasm to perpetrate their ill designs; though there has been great inquiry and some apparent puzzle among them about a formal, logical, technical definition of it. Some have defined it to be the practice of parliament; others, the judgments and precedents of the king's courts; but either of these definitions would make it a constitution of wind and

p. 382 (cont.)

weather, because the parliaments have sometimes voted the king absolute, and the judges have sometimes adjudged him to be so. Some have called it custom, but this is as fluctuating and variable as the other. Some have called it the most perfect combination of human powers in society which finite wisdom has yet contrived and reduced to practice for the preservation of liberty and the production of happiness. This is rather a character of the constitution and a just observation concerning it, than a regular definition of it, and leaves us still to dispute what it is." (Clarendon: WJA, III, p. 477) The Chinese ideogram in line 31, "ching ming," a part of which previously appeared in Canto 63 (p. 352), means "a true definition." (Index, p. 269)

p. 383

(1-2) "The judges answer to questions of fact as well as law; being few, they might be easily corrupted; being commonly rich and great, they might learn to despise the common people, and forget the feelings of humanity, and then the subject's liberty and security would be lost. But by the British constitution, ad quaestionem facti respondent juratores,--the jurors answer to the question of fact. In this manner, the subject is guarded in the execution of the laws. The people choose a grand jury, to make inquiry and presentment of crimes. Twelve of these must agree in finding

p. 383 (cont.)

the bill. And the petit jury must try the same fact over again, and find the person guilty, before he can be punished. Innocence, therefore, is so well protected in this wise constitution, that no man can be punished till twenty-four of his neighbors have said upon oath that he is guilty." (Clarendon: WJA, III, p. 481)

(3-5) "True religion, my friend Bradford, was the grand motive, with you and me, to undertake our arduous and hazardous enterprise, and to plant a religion in the world, on the large and generous principles of the Bible, without teaching for doctrines the commandments of men, or any mixture of those pompous rituals, and theatrical ceremonies, which had been so successfully employed to delude and terrify men out of all their knowledge, virtue, liberty, piety, and happiness." (Winthrop: WJA, III, p. 487)

(6) "If we go back so far as the reign of Elizabeth, we find her, on one occasion, infringing on this privilege of the commons, of judging solely of their own elections and returns. This attempt was, however, so warmly resented by the commons that they instantly voted,--'That it was a most perilous precedent, when two knights of a county were duly elected, if any new writ should issue out, for a second election, without order of the house itself.'" (Winthrop:

p. 383 (cont.)
WJA, III, p. 491)

(6-12) "After this vote, which had in it something of the spirit of liberty and independency, we hear of no more disputes upon that subject till we come to the reign of James the First, whose whole life was employed in endeavoring to demolish every popular power in the constitution, and to establish the awful and absolute sovereignty of kingship, that, as he expressed himself to the convocation, Jack and Tom and Dick and Will might not meet and censure him and his council. . . . Outlaws, whether for misdemeanors or debts, had been declared by the judges, in the reign of Henry the Sixth, incapable by law of a seat in the house, where they themselves must be lawgivers. Sir Francis Goodwin was now chosen for the county of Bucks; and his return was made as usual into chancery. The chancellor decreed him an outlaw, vacated his seat, and issued writs for a new election. Sir John Fortescue was chosen in his room. But the first act of the house was to reverse the decree of the chancellor, and restore Goodwin to his seat. At James's instigation, the lords desired a conference on this subject, but were absolutely refused by the commons, as the question regarded entirely their own privileges. . . . 'By this course,' said one member, 'the free election of the counties is taken away; and none shall be chosen but

p. 383 (cont.)

such as shall please the king and council. Let us therefore with fortitude, understanding, and sincerity, seek to maintain our privileges. This cannot be misconstrued any contempt in us, but merely a maintenance of our common rights, which our ancestors have left us, and which is just and fit for us to transmit to our posterity.' . . . 'A chancellor,' added a third, 'by this course may call a parliament consisting of what persons he pleases. Any suggestion, by any person, may be the cause of sending a new writ. It is come to this plain question, whether the chancery or parliament ought to have authority.'" (Winthrop: __WJA__, III, pp. 491-492)

(13-24) "GENTLEMEN,--After the repeal of the late American Stamp Act, we were happy in the pleasing prospect of a restoration of that tranquillity and unanimity among ourselves, and that harmony and affection between our parent country and us, which had generally subsisted before that detestable act. But with the utmost grief and concern, we find that we flattered ourselves too soon, and that the root of bitterness is yet alive. The principle on which that act was founded continues in full force, and a revenue is still demanded from America.

"We have the mortification to observe one act of parliament after another passed for the express purpose of

p. 383 (cont.)

raising a revenue from us; to see our money continually collecting from us, without our consent, by an authority in the constitution of which we have no share, and over which we have no kind of influence or control; to see the little circulating cash that remained among us for the support of our trade, from time to time transmitted to a distant country, never to return, or, what in our estimation is worse, if possible, appropriated to the maintenance of swarms of officers and pensioners in idleness and luxury, whose example has a tendency to corrupt our morals, and whose arbitrary dispositions will trample on our rights.

"Under all these misfortunes and afflictions, however, it is our fixed resolution to maintain our loyalty and duty to our most gracious Sovereign, a reverence and due subordination to the British parliament, as the supreme legislative in all cases of necessity, for the preservation of the whole empire, and our cordial and sincere affection for our parent country; and to use our utmost endeavors for the preservation of peace and order among ourselves; waiting with anxious expectation, for a favorable answer to the petitions and solicitations of this continent for relief." (Boston Instructions: WJA, III, pp. 501-502)

(25-26) "INSTRUCTIONS OF THE TOWN OF BOSTON TO THEIR REPRESENTATIVES, 17 JUNE, 1768." (See title, WJA, III,

p. 383 (cont.)

p. 501) These Instructions had been preceded by the event of the seizure of John Hancock's sloop Liberty for violation of revenue laws (see headnote: WJA, III, p. 501)

(27-33) "There is an Act of Parliament in being which has never been repealed, for the encouragement of the trade to America. We mean by the 6th Anne chap. xxxvii sect. 9, it is enacted, 'That no mariner or other person who shall serve on board, or be retained to serve on board any privateer or trading ship or vessel that shall be employed in any part of America, nor any mariner, or other person, being on shore in any part thereof, shall be liable to be impressed or taken away by any officer or officers, of or belonging to any of her majesty's ships-of-war, impowered by the lord high admiral or any other person whatsoever, unless such mariner shall have before deserted from such ship-of-war belonging to her majesty, at any time after the fourteenth day of February, 1707, upon pain that any officer or officers so impressing or taking away, or causing to be impressed or taken away, any mariner or other person, contrary to the tenor and true meaning of this act, shall forfeit to the master or owner or owners of any such ship or vessel, twenty pounds for every man he or they shall so impress or take, to be recovered with full costs of suit, in any court within any part of her majesty's dominions.'

p. 383 (cont.)

So that any impresses of any mariner from any vessel whatever, appear to be in direct violation of an act of parliament." (Boston Instructions, 17 June 1768: <u>WJA</u>, III, pp. 503-504)

(34-35) "In the spring of 1769, an unusual number of British troops were stationed in Boston. The main guard, '<u>unluckily</u>,' as Hutchinson expresses it, and 'without any design to give offence, had been stationed in a house which was before unoccupied, opposite to the door of the court house; and, as is usual, some small field pieces were placed before the door of the guard-house, and thus <u>happened</u> to point to the door of the court house.' However usual this may have been elsewhere, it was so unprecedented an event in Boston as to give rise to a reasonable suspicion of some design to overawe the legislature about to assemble there. At the annual town meeting, it was decided to appoint a committee to draw up instructions to their representatives, suitable for the emergency. Mr. Adams was placed at the head of this committee, and reported the following paper." (Editor's headnote for Boston Instructions, 15 May 1769: <u>WJA</u>, III, p. 505)

p. 384

(1-4)   "TO THE HONORABLE JAMES OTIS, AND THOMAS CUSHING,

p. 384 (cont.)
ESQUIRES; MR. SAMUEL ADAMS, AND JOHN HANCOCK, ESQUIRE.

"GENTLEMEN,--You have once more received the highest testimony of the confidence and affection of your constituents, which the constitution has empowered them to exhibit,--the trust of representing them in the great and general court, or assembly of this province. This important trust is committed to you at a time when your country demands the exertion of all your wisdom, fortitude, and virtue, and therefore, it is presumed, a free communication of our sentiments cannot but be agreeable to you.

"The first object of your attention is the privilege of that assembly of which you are now chosen to be members. The debates there must be free. You will therefore exert yourselves to remove every thing that may carry the least appearance of an attempt to awe or intimidate." (Boston Instructions, 15 May 1769: <u>WJA</u>, III, pp. 505-506)

(5-8)   "Another object of great importance, and which requires your earliest attention, is a late flagrant and formal attack upon the constitution itself,--an attempt not only to deprive us of our liberties, privileges, and immunities of our charter, but the rights of British subjects. . . .

"It is unnecessary for us, at this time, to repeat our well-known sentiments concerning the revenue which is

p. 384 (cont.)

continually levied upon us, to our great distress, and for no other end than to support a great number of very unnecessary placemen and pensioners." (Boston Instructions, 15 May 1769: <u>WJA</u>, III, p. 507)

(9)   "Next to the revenue itself, the late extensions of the jurisdiction of the admiralty are our greatest grievance. The American courts of admiralty seem to be forming by degrees into a system that is to overturn our constitution and to deprive us entirely of our best inheritance, the laws of the land. . . .

". . . In the forty-first section of the statute of the fourth of George III. chap. xv. we find that 'all the forfeitures and penalties inflicted by this or any other act of parliament, relating to the trade and revenues of the British colonies or plantations in America, which shall be incurred there, may be prosecuted, sued for, and recovered in any court of admiralty in the said colonies.' Thus these extraordinary penalties and forfeitures are to be heard and tried, not by a jury, nor by the law of the land, but by the civil law of a single judge!" (Boston Instructions, 15 May 1769: <u>WJA</u>, III, pp. 507-508)

(9-16)   "And this hardship is the more severe, as we see in the same page of the statute, and the section immediately

p. 384 (cont.)

preceding,—'That all penalties and forfeitures which shall be incurred in Great Britain shall be prosecuted, sued for, and recovered in any of his majesty's courts of record in Westminster, or in the court of exchequer in Scotland respectively.' Here is a contrast that stares us in the face! A partial distinction that is made between the subject in Great Britain and the subject in America! The parliament in one section guarding the people of the realm and securing to them the benefit of a trial by jury and the law of the land, and by the next section depriving Americans of those important rights. Is not this distinction a brand of disgrace upon every American—a degradation below the rank of Englishman? Is it not with respect to us a repeal of the twenty-ninth chapter of Magna Charta? 'No freeman shall be taken or imprisoned or disseised of his freehold or liberties or free customs or outlawed or exiled or any otherwise destroyed, nor will we pass upon him nor condemn him, but by lawful judgment of his peers or the law of the land.' Englishmen are inviolably attached to the important right expressed in this clause, which for many centuries has been the noblest monument and firmest bulwark of their liberties. One proof of this attachment, given us by a great sage of the law, we think proper to mention, not for your information, but as the best expression of the sense of your constituents. 'Against this ancient

p. 384 (cont.)

and fundamental law, and in the face thereof,' says Lord Coke, 'I find an act of parliament made, that as well justices of assize as justices of peace, without any finding or presentment of twelve men, upon a bare information for the king before them made, should have full power and authority by their discretions to hear and try men for penalties and forfeitures.' His lordship, after mentioning the repeal of this statute, and the fate of Empson and Dudley, who received the full weight of the national vengeance for acting under it, concludes with a reflection, which, if well considered, might be sufficient to discourage such attacks upon fundamental principles: 'The ill-success of this statute, and the fearful end of these two oppressors, should deter other from committing the like, and should admonish parliaments, that instead of this ordinary and precious trial by the law of the land, they bring not in absolute and partial trials by discretion.' Such are the feelings and reflections of an Englishman upon a statute not unlike the statute now under consideration, and upon courts and judges not unlike the courts and judges of admiralty in America!" (Boston Instructions, 15 May 1769: WJA, III, pp. 508-509)

(17)   "We, therefore, earnestly recommend to you, by every legal measure, to endeavor that the power of these

p. 384 (cont.)

courts may be confined to their proper element, according to the ancient English statutes; and that you petition and remonstrate against the late extensions of their jurisdiction; and, we doubt not, the other colonies and provinces who suffer with us under them will cheerfully harmonize with this in any justifiable measures that may be taken for redress." (Boston Instructions, 15 May 1769: WJA, III, p. 510)

(18)   "The assumption of the payment of the judges' salaries by the king, in conjunction with the natural and general tendency, in all ages and countries, of the legal profession to side with authority, threatened to put the administration of the law completely under the control of government. The people of Massachusetts, greatly alarmed at this state of things, which was not relieved by the signs of temporizing visible in some leading quarters, first resorted, at this moment, to the expedient, which afterwards proved so effective, of a regular organization of committees of correspondence in the towns. Among those who had given signs of a disposition to change his course, was General William Brattle, of Cambridge, senior member of the council, who seized the opportunity of a town meeting, called to remonstrate against the measure, to make a speech designed to reconcile the popular sentiment to it. Relying

p. 384 (cont.)

upon the silence of the bar, it would seem that he ventured so far as to challenge the patriotic party, and even Mr. Adams, by name as the most prominent lawyer attached to it, to dispute his positions. The following papers were the result." (Judiciary, Editor's headnote: <u>WJA</u>, III, p. 513)

(19-26) "CAMBRIDGE, 21 December, 1772.

"At a legal meeting of the freeholders, and other inhabitants of the town of Cambridge, on Monday the 14th instant, the following vote passed, namely,--

"<u>Voted</u>, That a committee be appointed to write to the committee appointed by the town of Boston, and acknowledge the vigilance and care, discovered by the metropolis, of the public rights and liberties; acquainting them that this town will heartily concur in all salutary, proper, and constitutional measures for the redress of those intolerable grievances which threaten, and, if continued, must overthrow the happy civil constitution of this province; and that said committee take under consideration the rights, as stated by the committee of correspondence of the town of Boston, and the infringements and violations of the same, and make report at the adjournment of this meeting.

"After which the town voted the following instructions to their representative, Captain Thomas Gardner, namely,--

p. 384 (cont.)

"Sir,--We, his majesty's most dutiful and loyal subjects, freeholders and other inhabitants of the town of Cambridge, in town meeting legally assembled this fourteenth day of December, 1772, to consult upon such measures as may be thought most proper to be taken at this alarming crisis, and most conducive to the public weal,--do, therefore, with true patriotic spirit declare, that we are and ever have been ready to risk our lives and fortunes in defence of his majesty, King George the Third, his crown and dignity, and in the support of constitutional government. . . . We have been sighing and groaning under oppression for a number of years; our natural and charter rights are violated in too many instances here to enumerate; our money extorted from us, and appropriated to augment our burdens; we have repeatedly presented our most decent, dutiful, and loyal petitions to our most gracious sovereign for a redress of our grievances, but no redress has as yet been obtained; whereby we have been almost driven to despair; and in the midst of our distress, we are still further alarmed with seeing the governor of the province made independent of the people, and the shocking report that the judges of the superior court of judicature, and other officers, have salaries affixed to their offices, dependent on the crown and ministry, independent of the grants of the commons of this province. By this establishment, our lives and

p. 384 (cont.)

properties will be rendered very precarious; as there is the utmost danger that through an undue influence the streams of public justice will be poisoned. . . .

"A true copy,

Attest, ANDREW BOARDMAN, Town Clerk."
(Judiciary: WJA, III, pp. 513-515)

(27-34) "I observed that no man in the province could say whether the salaries granted to the judges
p. 385 were *durante bene placito*, or *quamdiu bene se*
(1-2) *gesserint*, as the judges of England have their salaries granted them. I supposed the latter, though these words are not expressed, but necessarily implied; and that there was an essential difference between the one and the other; that I always thought the judges' salaries should be independent both upon the king and the people; that there was great danger to a commission arising from their dependency upon either; but their grant was only during the king's pleasure. There was no one living could be more offended at it than myself, or that would exert himself in a constitutional way more heartily, openly, and perseveringly to prevent the grants taking place. . . . Their commission is only declarative of their nomination and appointment. A civil commission by the common law can give no new powers. This is what I am persuaded the

p. 385 (cont.)

governor and council disclaim; it would be most dangerous to suppose and allow it, and tyranny in them to assume it. The great and general court of this province, and they only, have determined what powers and authorities unto the judges do appertain. What right, what estate vests in them, in consequence of their nomination and appointment, the common law of England, the birthright of every man here as well as at home, determines, and that is, an estate for life, provided they behave well. . . .

". . . I thought they [standing laws of the province] ought rather to be attended to and complied with, than to view ourselves in a state of nature, and be governed by any law now existing, because there was not one equal in authority and right to the statute law of this province, touching the point in controversy, and that I, in the most public manner, protested against their proceedings. That, for my own part, I did not look upon myself in a state of nature, and that it was a pity anybody should in this case, where (upon their own principles) they could have so easily removed all these difficulties without placing themselves in so bad a situation as to be in a state of nature, and to be governed by the laws of nature in direct repugnancy and opposition to the well known standing law of the province, founded upon the eternal reason and nature of things, the safety of every town in the government; but, notwithstanding, the votes

p. 385 (cont)

passed, as mentioned in your paper. . . . W. BRATTLE."
(Judiciary, Massachusetts Gazette, 4 January 1773: <u>WJA</u>,
III, pp. 517-519)

(3-7)   "The General proceeds,--'I was very far from
thinking there was any necessity of having <u>quamdiu bene se
gesserint</u> in their commissions; for they have their commissions now by that tenure as truly as if said words were in.'

"It is the wish of almost all good men that this was
good law. . . .

"The common law of England is so far from determining
that the judges have an estate for life in their offices,
that it has determined the direct contrary; the proofs of
this are innumerable and irresistible. My Lord Coke, in
his fourth Institute, 74, says, 'Before the reign of Edward
I. the chief justice of this court was created by letters-
patent, and the form thereof (taking one example for all)
was in these words:--

"'Rex, &c., archiepiscopis, episcopis, abbatibus,
prioribus, comitibus, baronibus, vice-comitibus, forestariis,
et omnibus aliis fidelibus regni Angliae, salutem. Cum pro
conservatione nostra, et tranquillitatis regni nostri, et
ad justitiam universis et singulis de regno nostro exhi-
bendam constituerimus dilectum et fidelem nostrum Philippum
Basset justiciarium Angliae <u>quamdiu nobis placuerit</u> capitalem,

p. 385 (cont.)

&c.' And my Lord Coke says afterwards in the same page, --'King Edward I. being a wise and prudent prince, knowing that, cui plus licet quam par est, plus vult quam licet, (as most of these summi justiciarii did) made three alterations. 1. By limitation of his authority. 2. By changing summus justiciarius to capitalis justiciarius. 3. By a new kind of creation, namely, by writ, lest, if he had continued his former manner of creation, he might have had a desire of his former authority; which three do expressly appear by the writ yet in use, namely,--Rex, &c. E. C. militi salutem. Sciatis quod constituimus vos justiciarium nostrum capitalem ad placita coram nobis teneda, <u>durante beneplacito nostro</u>. Teste, &c.'" (Judiciary, Boston Gazette, 11 January 1773: <u>WJA</u>, III, pp. 520-521) The Latin quoted by Pound, <u>sic</u>: <u>beneplacitu nostro</u>, means "thus: in accordance with our (royal) good pleasure." (<u>Index</u>, p. 198)

(8-10) "I have quoted a translation in this place, as I choose to do whenever I can obtain one; but I do not venture to translate passages myself, lest I should be charged with doing it unfairly. The original words of [Chancellor] Fortescue are unusual and emphatical: 'Ad regis nutum duratura.'" (Judiciary, Boston Gazette, 18 January 1773: <u>WJA</u>, III, p. 524) The Latin quoted by Pound, <u>Ad regis nutum duratura</u>, means "to endure at King's command." (<u>Index</u>, p. 198)

p. 385 (cont.)

(11-12) "Will it be said that this law, giving our judges cognizance of all matters of which the court of exchequer has cognizance, gives them the same estate in their offices which the barons of exchequer had? or will it be said that by 'the judges,' General Brattle meant the barons of the exchequer?" (Judiciary, Boston Gazette, 18 January 1773: WJA, III, p. 525)

(13-14) "The judges, indeed, did not expressly deny any of those sayings of Sir Thomas Powis, or of Sergeant Levinz, who spoke after him on the same side; but the reason of this is plain; because it was quite unnecessary, in that case, to determine what was common law; for both the office of custos rotulorum, and that of clerk of the peace, were created by statute, not erected by common law, as was clearly agreed both on the bench and at the bar." (Judiciary, Boston Gazette, 18 January 1773: WJA, III, p. 527) The Latin quoted by Pound, custos rotolorum, means "Keeper of the rolls (of peace)." (Index, p. 47)

(15-17) "The oracle himself was silenced by this power in the crown. 'Upon the 18th November, this term, Sir Henry Montague was made chief justice of the king's bench, in the place of Sir Edward Coke, the late chief justice, who, being in the king's displeasure, was removed from his

p. 385 (cont.)

place by a writ from the king, reciting that whereas he had appointed him by writ to that place, that he had now amoved him, and appointed him to desist from the further execution thereof." (Judiciary, Boston Gazette, 18 January 1773: <u>WJA</u>, III, p. 528)

(18-19) "'While so many terrors hung over the people, no jury durst have acquitted a man when the court was resolved to have him condemned. And, indeed, there scarcely occurs an instance during all these reigns, that the sovereign or the ministers were ever disappointed in the issue of a prosecution. Timid juries, and judges who held their offices during pleasure, never failed to second all the views of the crown.'" (John Adams quoting from Hume's History of England, Judiciary, Boston Gazette, 18 January 1773: <u>WJA</u>, III, pp. 528-529)

(20-26) "Mr. Hume, in the reign of James the Second, says,--'The people had entertained such violent prepossessions against the use which James here made of his prerogative, that he was obliged, before he brought on Hales's cause, to displace four of the judges, Jones, Montague, Charlton, and Nevil.'

". . . By concert between King James and Sir Edward [Hales], his coachman was employed to bring an action against

p. 385 (cont.)

him upon that statute, for the penalty. Sir Edward appears, and pleads a dispensation under the broad seal, to act <u>non obstante</u> that statute. To this the plaintiff demurs. When this action was to be brought to trial, the judges were secretly closeted by the king, and asked their opinions. Such as had scruples about judging as the court directed, were plainly told by the king himself, that he would have twelve judges of his own opinion, and turned them out of their offices. The judges mentioned by Hume were thus displaced, to their lasting honor; and one of them, Jones, had the fortitude and integrity to tell the king to his face, that he might possibly make twelve judges, but <u>he would scarcely find twelve lawyers of his opinion</u>." (Judiciary, Boston Gazette, 18 January 1773: <u>WJA</u>, III, p. 529-530)

(27-28) "I also fear the proofs that the common law of England has not determined the judges to have estates for life in their offices, appear to be very numerous, and quite irresistible. I very heartily wish General Brattle success in his researches after evidence of the contrary position; and while he is thus engaged, if I should find neither business more profitable nor amusement more inviting, I shall be preparing for your press a few other observations on his first publication. JOHN ADAMS." (Judiciary, Boston Gazette, 18 January 1773: <u>WJA</u>, III, p. 530)

p. 385 (cont.)

(29-35) "For the judges, whom the governor with the advice of council is empowered to nominate and

p. 386 appoint, are not vested with any powers at all

(1-2) by the charter; but by another clause in it, the great and general court or assembly 'shall forever have full power and authority to erect and constitute judicatories and courts of record, or other courts, to be held in the name of us, our heirs and successors, for the hearing, trying, and determining of all manner of crimes, offences, pleas, processes, plaints, actions, matters, causes, and things, whatsoever, arising or happening within our said province or territory, or between persons inhabiting and residing there, whether the same be criminal or civil, and whether the said crimes be capital or not capital, and whether the said pleas be real, personal, or mixt, and for the awarding and making out execution thereupon.'

"In pursuance of this authority, our legislature, in 1699, by a law, 2 William III. c. 3, have established 'a superior court of judicature, court of assize, and general jail delivery within this province, to be held by one chief justice and four other justices, to be appointed and commissionated for the same,' &c. Is not General Brattle, then, greatly mistaken when he says, that 'a nomination and appointment recorded is enough?' . . . And he [Lord Coke] there mentions the case of a letter-patent granted by Edward IV.

p. 386 (cont.)

in these words: 'We will and ordain that Richard Beauchampe, &c., should have it (that is, the office of the chancellor of the garter) for his life, and after his decease, that his successors should have it forever'; and 'it was resolved unanimously that this grant was void; for that a new office was erected, and it was not defined what jurisdiction or authority the officer should have; and, therefore, for the uncertainty, it was void.'" (Judiciary, Boston Gazette, 25 January 1773: WJA, III, pp. 537-538)

(3-5) "Thus it seems to be very clear that, by the common law of England, a commission was absolutely necessary for all the judges known at common law; and as to others, erected by statute, let the statute speak. By 27 H. 8, c. 24, it is enacted: 'That no person or persons, of what estate, degree, or condition soever they be, shall have any power or authority to make any justices of eyre, justices of assize, justices of peace, or justices of jail delivery; but that all such officers and ministers shall be made by letter-patent, under the king's great seal, in the name and by the authority of the king's highness, in all shires, counties palatine, Wales, &c., or any other his dominions, &c., any grants, usages, allowance, or act of parliament to the contrary notwithstanding.'" (Judiciary, Boston Gazette, 25 January 1773: WJA, III, p. 539)

CANTO LXVII

p. 387

(1-20) "This collection [of laws brought together by Edward the Confessor] is of higher antiquity than memory or history can reach; they have been used time out of mind, or for a time whereof the memory of man runneth not to the contrary. . . .

". . . King Alfred, who began his reign in 871, <u>magnus juris Anglicani conditor</u>, the great founder of the laws of England, with the advice of his wise men, collected out of the laws of Ina, Offa, and AEthelbert, such as were the best, and made them to extend equally to the whole nation, and therefore very properly called them the common law of England, because those laws were now first of all made common to the whole English nation. This <u>jus commune</u>, <u>jus publicum</u>, or folcright, that is, the people's right, set down in one code, was probably the same with the Doom-Book, or <u>liber judicialis</u>, which is referred to in all the subsequent laws of the Saxon kings, and was the book that they determined causes by. And in the next reign, that of Edward the elder, the king commands all his judges to give judgment to all the people of England according to the Doom-Book. And it is from this origin that our common law judges fetch that excellent usage of determining

p. 387 (cont.)

causes, according to the settled and established rules of law, and that they have acted up to this rule for above eight hundred years together, and continue to do so to this very day. . . .

". . . And I must add, it appears to me extraordinary, that a gentleman educated under that great Gamaliel, Mr. Read, should ever adduce the simple dictum of a counsel at the bar, uttered arguendo, and as an ornament to his discourse too, rather than any pertinent branch of his reasoning, as evidence of a point 'settled and determined by the greatest sages of the law formerly and more lately.' Does Sir Thomas Powis produce the Dome-Book itself in support of his doctrine [that judges of the king's bench and common pleas have estates for life in their offices]? That was irrecoverably lost for ages before he had a being. Does he produce any judicial decision, ancient or modern, to prove this opinion? No such thing pretended. Does he produce any legal authority, a Hengham, Britton, Fleta, Fortescue, Coke; or any antiquarian, Matthew Paris, Dugdale, Lambard, or any other? or even the single opinion of one historian to give a color to his doctrine? No such matter. . . .

". . . Towards the latter end of the Norman period, the power of the justiciar was broken, so that the aula regis, which was before one great court, only distinguished

p. 387 (cont.)

by several offices, and all ambulatory with the king before Magna Charta, was divided into four distinct courts,--chancery, exchequer, king's bench, and common pleas. The justiciary was laid aside, lest he should get into the throne, as Capet and Pepin, who were justiciars in France, had done there. . . .

". . . They [the Saxons] retained a vast variety of the regalia principis of the feudal system, from whence most branches of the present prerogatives of our kings are derived; and, among other regalia, the creation and annihilation of judges was an important branch. For evidence of this, we must look into the feudal law. It was in consequence of this prerogative that the courts were usually held in the aula regis, and often in the king's presence, who often heard and determined causes in person; and in those ages the justiciary was only a substitute or deputy to the king, whose authority ceased entirely in the king's presence. . . .

". . . 'Item cum delegans revocaverit jurisdictionem,' &c. Bracton, chap. 10, lib. 3." (Judiciary, Boston Gazette, 1 February 1773: WJA, III, pp. 540-546) The Italian arguendo (line 7) means "accusing." (Index, p. 11) Aula regum (line 12), or aula regis, refers to "the chief court of England during early Norman times." (Index, p. 13) The Latin summus justiciarius, mentioned

p. 387 (cont.)

in WJA, III, p. 544, and by Pound in line 13, means "chief justice." (Index, p. 207) The Latin Regalia principis (line 14) means "the rights royal of a prince." (Index, p. 182) The Latin cum delegans revocarit (line 19) means "when one who sends a delegate calls him back." (Index, p. 47)

(21-29) "General Brattle declares his opinion in very strong terms, 'that the governor and council cannot legally or constitutionally remove a justice of the superior court, as the commissions now are, unless there is a fair hearing and trial, and then a judgment that he hath behaved ill.'

"This I am content to make a question, after premising that we ought, in such inquiries, always to obtain precise ideas, and to give exact definitions of the terms we use, in order to arrive at truth. The question, then, appears to me to be different from what it would be, if we were to ask whether a justice of that court can be constitutionally removed, without a trial and judgment. Many people receive different ideas from the words legally and constitutionally. . . .

"General Brattle took the right way of establishing the independency of our judges, by affirming that they had estates for life by their nomination and appointment, and by common law, whether their commissions expressed

p. 387 (cont.)

<u>quamdiu</u> <u>se</u> <u>bene</u> <u>gesserint</u> or not, or whether they had any commissions at all or not; and if he could have proved these allegations, he would have got his cause. But he has been extremely unfortunate in having Bracton, Fortescue, Coke, Foster, Hume, Rapin, and Rushworth directly against him, and nothing in his favor but the say of a lawyer in arguing a cause for his client, and that say by no means so extensive as the General's assertions; for Powis himself does not say that judges at common law were in for their lives, without the clause <u>quamdiu</u> <u>se</u> <u>bene</u> <u>gesserint</u> in their commissions. The questions that have been considered are liberal, and of much importance. I have done little more than labor in the mines of ore and the quarries of stones. The materials are at the service of the public; and I leave them to the jeweller and lapidary, to refine, fabricate, and polish them." (Judiciary, Boston Gazette, 8 February 1773: <u>WJA</u>, III, p. 556; p. 558) The Chinese ideogram used at the side of lines 21-23 has previously appeared in Canto 63 (p. 352) and in Canto 66 (p. 382), and means "a true definition." (<u>Index</u>, p. 269)

(30) "It may, therefore, be safely affirmed, that there is no record of any justiciary or chief justice of king's bench or common pleas whose writ or patent was not <u>durante</u> <u>beneplacito</u>, quite down to the year

p. 387 (cont.)

1640, in the reign of Charles I. I say there is no record of any, because the story of Hubert de Burgh has no record extant to prove it, and rests upon no better evidence than Matthew Paris, which, in our present view of the matter, is no evidence at all, because he is no legal authority." (Judiciary, Boston Gazette, 15 February 1773: WJA, III, p. 565)

"Lord Campbell, in his late work, speaks of this case as an exception, thus: 'In vain hope of perpetuating his power, he [Hubert de Burgh] obtained a grant for life of chief justiciar, which hitherto had always been held during pleasure.'" (WJA, III, pp. 565n-566n)

(31-32) "Dr. Franklin, who was known to be an active and very able man, and to have great influence
p. 388 in the province of Pennsylvania, was in Boston
(1-4) in the year 1754, and Mr. Shirley communicated to him the profound secret,--the great design of taxing the colonies by act of parliament. This sagacious gentleman, this eminent philosopher and distinguished patriot, to his lasting honor, sent the Governor an answer in writing, with the following remarks upon his scheme, remarks which would have discouraged any honest man from the pursuit. The remarks are these:--

"'That the people always bear the burden best, when

p. 388 (cont.)

they have, or think they have, some share in the direction.

"'That when public measures are generally distasteful to the people, the wheels of government must move more heavily. . . .

"'That natives of America would be as likely to consult wisely and faithfully for the safety of their native country, as the governors sent from Britain, whose object is generally to make fortunes, and then return home, and who might therefore be expected to carry on the war against France, rather in a way by which themselves were likely to be gainers, than for the greatest advantage of the cause. . . .'" (Novanglus: WJA, IV, p. 19)

(5-6)   "Whether the ministry at home, or the junto here, were discouraged by these masterly remarks, or by any other cause, the project of taxing the colonies was laid aside; Mr. Shirley was removed from this government, and Mr. Pownall was placed in his stead.

"Mr. Pownall seems to have been a friend to liberty and to our constitution, and to have had an aversion to all plots against either; and, consequently, to have given his confidence to other persons than Hutchinson and Oliver, who, stung with envy against Mr. Pratt and others, who had the lead in affairs, set themselves, by propagating slanders against the Governor among the people, and especially

p. 388 (cont.)

among the clergy, to raise discontents, and make him uneasy in his seat. Pownall, averse to wrangling, and fond of the delights of England, solicited to be recalled, and after some time Mr. Bernard was removed from New Jersey to the chair of this province.

"Bernard was the man for the purpose of the junto. Educated in the highest principles of monarchy; naturally daring and courageous; skilled enough in law and policy to do mischief, and avaricious to a most infamous degree; needy, at the same time, and having a numerous family to provide for, he was an instrument suitable in every respect, excepting one, for this junto to employ. The exception I mean was blunt frankness, very opposite to that cautious cunning, that deep dissimulation, to which they had, by long practice, disciplined themselves." (Novanglus: <u>WJA</u>, IV, p. 21)

(7-11) "The intention of the junto was, to procure a revenue to be raised in America by act of parliament. Nothing was further from their designs and wishes, than the drawing or sending this revenue into the exchequer in England, to be spent there in discharging the national debt, and lessening the burdens of the poor people there. They were more selfish. They chose to have the fingering of the money themselves. Their design was, that the money

p. 388 (cont.)

should be applied, first, in a large salary to the governor. This would gratify Bernard's avarice; and then, it would render him and all other governors, not only independent of the people, but still more absolutely a slave to the will of the minister. They intended likewise a salary for the lieutenant-governor. This would appease in some degree the gnawings of Hutchinson's avidity, in which he was not a whit behind Bernard himself. In the next place, they intended a salary to the judges of the common law, as well as admiralty. And thus, the whole government, executive and judicial, was to be rendered wholly independent of the people, (and their representatives rendered useless, insignificant, and even burthensome,) and absolutely dependent upon, and under the direction of the will of the minister of state." (Novanglus: WJA, IV, pp. 23-24)

(12-13) "He [the British financier] chose to get the revenue into the exchequer, because he had hungry cormorants enough about him in England, whose cawings were more troublesome to his ears than the croaking of the ravens in America. And he thought, if America could afford any revenue at all, and he could get it by authority of parliament, he might have it himself, to give to his friends, as well as raise it for the junto here, to spend themselves, or give to theirs. This unfortunate, preposterous

p. 388 (cont.)

improvement, of Mr. Grenville, upon the plan of the junto, had wellnigh ruined the whole." (Novanglus: <u>WJA</u>, IV, pp. 24-25)

(14)   Pound's interpolation. The Latin <u>OBSTA PRINCIPIIS</u> means "resist the beginnings." (<u>Index</u>, p. 158)

(15)   "Besides, every farthing of expense which has been incurred, on pretence of protecting, defending, and securing America, since the last war, has been worse than thrown away; it has been applied to do mischief. Keeping an army in America has been nothing but a public nuisance." (Novanglus: <u>WJA</u>, IV, p. 47)

(16-18) "Let me ask this sincere writer [<u>Massachusettensis</u>] a simple question,--does he seriously believe that the designs of imposing other taxes [other than those recently applied on glass, paper, etc.], and of new-modelling our governments, would have been laid aside by the ministry or by the servants of the crown here?" (Novanglus: <u>WJA</u>, IV, p. 50)

(19-20) "They [the tories] had now got the governor's salary out of the revenue, a number of pensions and places; they knew they could at any time get the judges' salaries

p. 388 (cont.)

from the same fountain; and they wanted to get the people reconciled and familiarized to this, before they went upon any new projects." (Novanglus: WJA, IV, p. 51)

(20-21) "We are then told, that the whigs erected a provincial democracy, or republic, in the province. I wish Massachusettensis knew what a democracy or a republic is. But this subject must be considered another time." (Novanglus: WJA, IV, p. 57)

(22) Pound's interpolation. The Latin Irritat mulcet et falsis terroribus implet means "annoys, soothes, and fills with false fears." (Index, p. 101)

(23-24) "It has often been observed by me, and it cannot be too often repeated, that colonization is casus omissus at common law. There is no such title known in that law." (Novanglus: WJA, IV, p. 121)

(25-28) "When a subject left the kingdom by the king's permission, and if the nation did not remonstrate against it, by the nation's permission too, at least connivance, he carried with him, as a man, all the rights of nature. His allegiance bound him to the king, and entitled him to protection. But how? Not in France; the King of England

p. 388 (cont.)

was not bound to protect him in France. Nor in America. Nor in the dominions of Louis. Nor of Sassacus, or Massachusetts. He had a right to protection and the liberties of England, upon his return there, not otherwise. How, then, do we New Englandmen derive our laws? I say, not from parliament, not from common law, but from the law of nature, and the compact made with the king in our charters. Our ancestors were entitled to the common law of England when they emigrated, that is, to just so much of it as they pleased to adopt, and no more. They were not bound or obliged to submit to it, unless they chose it. By a positive principle of the common law they were bound, let them be in what part of the world they would, to do nothing against the allegiance of the king. But no kind of provision was ever made by common law for punishing or trying any man, even for treason committed out of the realm. He must be tried in some country of the realm by that law, the country where the overt act was done, or he could not be tried at all. Nor was any provision ever made, until the reign of Henry VIII., for trying treasons committed abroad, and the acts of that reign were made on purpose to catch Cardinal Pole." (Novanglus: <u>WJA</u>, IV, p. 122)

(29-34) "When King Henry VIII, and his parliament threw

p. 388 (cont.)

off the authority of the pope, stripped his holiness of his supremacy, and invested it in himself by an act of parliament, he and his courtiers seemed to think that all the rights of the holy see were transferred to him; and it was a union of these two, (the most impertinent and fantastical ideas that ever got into a human pericranium, namely,--that, as feudal sovereign and supreme head of the church together, a king of England had a right to all the land his subjects could find, not possessed by any Christian state or prince, though possessed by heathen or infidel nations,) which seems to have deluded the nation about the time of the settlement of the colonies. But none of these ideas gave or inferred any right in parliament, over the new countries conquered or discovered; and, therefore, denying that the colonies are a part of the realm, and that as such they are subject to parliament, by no means deprives us of English liberties. Nor does it 'build up absolute monarchy in the colonies.' For, admitting these notions of the common and feudal law to have been in full force, and that the king was absolute in America, when it was settled; yet he had a right to enter into a contract with his subjects, and stipulate that they should enjoy all rights and liberties of Englishmen forever, in consideration of their undertaking to clear the wilderness, propagate Christianity, pay a fifth part of ore, &c. . . .

p. 388 (cont.)

". . . His [Dudley's] meaning was, that English liberties were confined to the realm, and, out of that, the king was absolute. But this was not true; for an English king had no right to be absolute over Englishmen out of the realm, any more than in it; and they were released from their allegiance, as soon as he deprived them of their liberties." (Novanglus: WJA, IV, pp. 125-126)

(35) Pound's comment, summarizing the denial by John Adams of the following statements of
p. 389 Massachusettensis: "'. . . our charters sup-
(1) pose regal authority in the grantor. . . . If that authority be derived from the British (he should have said English) crown, it presupposes this territory to have been a part of the British (he should have said English) dominion, and as such subject to the imperial sovereign. . . .

"'. . . if that authority was vested in the person of the king in a different capacity, the British constitution and laws are out of the question, and the king must be absolute as to us, as his prerogatives have never been limited.'" (Novanglus: WJA, IV, pp. 126-127)

(2-4) "There is no fundamental or other law that makes

p. 389 (cont.)

a king of England absolute anywhere, except in conquered countries; and an attempt to assume such a power, by the fundamental laws, forfeits the prince's right even to the limited crown." (Novanglus: WJA, IV, p. 127)

(5-7)   "The patriots of this province desire nothing new; they wish only to keep their old privileges. They were, for one hundred and fifty years, allowed to tax themselves, and govern their internal concerns as they thought best. Parliament governed their trade as they thought fit. This plan they wish may continue forever. But it is honestly confessed, rather than become subject to the absolute authority of parliament in all cases of taxation and internal polity, they will be driven to throw off that of regulating trade." (Novanglus: WJA, IV, p. 131)

(8)   "There are so many particulars in the case of Wales analogous to the case of America, that I must beg leave to enlarge upon it." (Novanglus: WJA, IV, p. 132)

(9)   "Now Wales was always part of the dominions of England. 'Wales was always feudatory to the kingdom of England.' It was always held of the crown of England, or the kingdom of England; that is, whoever was King of

p. 389 (cont.)

England had a right to homage, &c. from the Prince of Wales. But yet Wales was not parcel of the realm or kingdom, nor bound by the laws of England. I mention and insist upon this, because it shows that, although the colonies are bound to the crown of England; or, in other words, owe allegiance to whosoever is King of England; yet it does not follow that the colonies are a parcel of the realm or kingdom, and bound by its laws." (Novanglus: WJA, IV, p. 133)

(10-12) "It [the Statutum Walliae] begins, not in the style of an act of parliament: 'Edwardus Dei gratia Rex Angliae, Dominus Hyberniae, et Dux Aquitaniae, omnibus fidelibus suis, &c. in Wallia. Divina Providentia, quae in sui dispositione, says he, non fallitur, inter alia dispensationis suae munera, quibus nos et Regnum nostrum Angliae decorare dignata est, terram Walliae, cum incolis suis prius nobis jure feudali subjectam, jam sui gratia, in proprietatis nostrae dominium, obstaculis quibuscumque cessantibus, totaliter et cum integritate convertit, et coronae regni praedicti, tanquam partem corporis ejusdem annexuit et univit.'" (Novanglus: WJA, IV, p. 134)
The Latin quoted by Pound, Edwardus Deo Gratia Angliae/ Dom. Hib. et Dux Aquitaniae terram Walliae cum incolis suis/ in nostrae proprietatis dominium, means "Edward

318

p. 389 (cont.)

by the Grace of God (King) of England,/ Lord of Ireland, and Duke of Aquitaine (holding) the land of Wales together with its inhabitants/ in possession of our private ownership." (<u>Index</u>, p. 57)

(13-24) "Henry had long cast a wishful eye upon Ireland; and now, partly to divert his subjects from the thoughts of Becket's murder, partly to appease the wrath of the pope for the same event, and partly to gratify his own ambition, he [Henry II] lays hold of a pretence, that the Irish had taken some natives of England and sold them for slaves, and applies to the pope for license to invade that island. Adrian III., an Englishman by birth, who was then pontiff, and very clearly convinced in his own mind of his right to dispose of kingdoms and empires, was easily persuaded, by the prospect of Peter's pence, to act as emperor of the world, and make an addition to his ghostly jurisdiction of an island which, though converted to Christianity, had never acknowledged any subjection to the see of Rome. He issued a bull, premising that Henry had ever shown an anxious care to enlarge the church, and increase the saints on earth and in heaven; that his design upon Ireland proceeded from the same pious motives; that his application to the holy see was a sure earnest of success; that it was a point incontestable, that all Christian kingdoms belonged to the

p. 389 (cont.)

patrimony of St. Peter; that it was his duty to show among them the seeds of the gospel, which might fructify to their eternal salvation. He exhorts Henry to invade Ireland, exterminate the vices of the natives, and oblige them to pay yearly, from every house, a penny to the see of Rome; gives him full right and entire authority over the whole island; and commands all to obey him as their sovereign.

"Macmorrogh, a licentious scoundrel, who was king of Leinster, and had been driven from his kingdom for his tyranny by his own subjects, in conjunction with Ororic, king of Meath, who made war upon him for committing a rape upon his queen, applied to Henry for assistance to restore him, and promised to hold his kingdom in vassalage of the crown of England. Henry accepted the offer, and engaged in the enterprise. It is unnecessary to recapitulate all the intrigues of Henry, to divide the Irish kingdoms among themselves, and set one against another, which are as curious as those of Edward I. to divide the kingdom of Wales, and play Lewellyn's brothers against him, or as those of the ministry, and our junto, to divide the American colonies, who have more sense than to be divided. It is sufficient to say, that Henry's expeditions terminated, altogether by means of those divisions among the Irish, in the total conquest of Ireland, and its annexation forever to the English crown." (Novanglus: **WJA**, IV, pp. 151-152)

p. 389 (cont.)

(25-27) "The 1 Henry V. c. 8: 'All Irishmen and Irish clerks, beggars, shall depart this realm before the first day of November, except graduates, sergeants, &c.' is explained by 1 Henry VI. c. 3, which shows 'what sort of Irishmen only may come to dwell in England.' It enacts, that all persons born in Ireland shall depart out of the realm of England, except a few; and that Irishmen shall not be principals of any hall, and that Irishmen shall bring testimonials from the lieutenant or justice of Ireland, that they are of the king's obeisance. By the 2d Henry VI. c. 8, 'Irishmen resorting into the realm of England, shall put in surety for their good abearing.'" (Novanglus: WJA, IV, p. 155)

(28-30) "The contract I here alluded to, is what is called Poyning's law, the history of which is briefly thus. . . .

"While Poyning resided in Ireland [c. 1495], he called a parliament, which is famous in history for the acts which it passed in favor of England and Englishmen, settled in Ireland. By these, which are still called Poyning's laws, all the former laws of England were made to be of force in Ireland, and no bill can be introduced into the Irish parliament unless it previously receive the sanction of the English privy council; and by a

p. 389 (cont.)

construction, if not by the express words, of these laws, Ireland is still said to be bound by English statutes in which it is specially named. Here, then, let Massachusettensis pause, and observe the original of the notion, that countries might be bound by acts of parliament, if 'specially named,' though without the realm. Let him observe, too, that this notion is grounded entirely on the voluntary act, the free consent of the Irish nation, and an act of an Irish parliament, called Poyning's law. Let me ask him, has any colony in America ever made a Poyning's act? Have they ever consented to be bound by acts of parliament, if specially named?" (Novanglus: WJA, IV, pp. 156-157)

(30-35) "And this appears fully in Lord Coke himself: 'Ireland originally came to the kings of England by conquest; but who was the first conqueror thereof hath been a question. I have seen a charter made by King Edgar, in these words: Ego Edgarus Anglorum Basileus, omniumque insularum oceani, quae Britanniam circumjacent, imperator et dominus, gratias ago ipsi Deo omnipotenti regi meo, qui meum imperium sic ampliavit et exaltavit super regnum patrum meorum, &c. Mihi concessit propitia divinitas, cum anglorum imperio omnia regna insularum oceani, &c., cum suis ferocissimis rebibus usque Norvegiam, maximamque partem Hiberniae, cum sua nobilissima civitate de Dublina,

p. 389 (cont.)

Anglorum regno subjugare, quapropter et ego Christi gloriam et laudem in regno meo exaltare, et ejus servitium amplificare devotus disposui, &c. Yet for that it was wholly conquered in the reign of Henry II., the honor of the conquest of Ireland is attributed to him. That Ireland is a dominion separate and divided from England it is evident from our books, 20 H. VI. 8; Sir John Pilkington's case, 32 H. VI. 25; 20 Eliz.; Dyer, 360; Plow. Com. 360, and 2 R. 3, 12: Hibernia habet parliamentum, et faciunt leges, et statuta nostra non ligant eos quia non mittunt milites ad parliamentum, (which is to be understood, unless they be specially named,) sed personae eorum sunt subjecti regis, sicut inhabitantes in Calesia, Gasconia, et Guyan.'" (Novanglus: WJA, IV, p. 161) The Latin quoted by Pound, EDGARDUS ANGLORUM BASILEUS/ insularum oceani imperator et dominus gratiam ago/ Deo omnip. qui meum imperium/ sic ampliavit et explicavit super regnum patrum meorum/ concessit propitia devinitatis . . ./ Hibernia habet parliamentum, means "EDGAR, KING OF THE ENGLISH,/ emperor and ruler of the isles of the ocean, I thank/ almighty God who so enlarged and extended my kingdom beyond the kingdom of my fathers,/ granted the good offices of divinity . . ./ Ireland has a parliament." (Index, pp. 56-57)

p. 390

(1-4)   "Methinks I hear his lordship [Lord Mansfield? or Lord North?], upon this occasion, in a soliloquy somewhat like this: 'We are now in the midst of a war, which has been conducted with unexampled success and glory. We have conquered a great part, and shall soon complete the conquest of the French power in America. His majesty is near seventy years of age, and must soon yield to nature. The amiable, virtuous, and promising successor, educated under the care of my nearest friends, will be influenced by our advice. We must bring the war to a conclusion; for we have not the martial spirit and abilities of the great commoner [the elder Pitt]; but we shall be obliged to leave upon the nation an immense debt. How shall we manage that? Why, I have seen letters from America, proposing that parliament should bring America to a closer dependence upon it, and representing that if it does not, she will fall a prey to some foreign power, or set up for herself. These hints may be improved, and a vast revenue drawn from that country and the East Indies, or at least the people here may be flattered and quieted with the hopes of it.'" (Novanglus: WJA, IV, p. 167)

(4-6)   "In conformity to the system contained in these words, my Lord Mansfield and my Lord North, together with their little friends, Bernard and Hutchinson, have 'conceived

p. 390 (cont.)

the great design of annexing' all North America 'to the realm of England;' and 'the better to effectuate this idea, they all maintain that North America is holden of the crown.'" (Novanglus: WJA, IV, p. 166)

(7-8) "But American governments and constitutions were never erected by parliament; their regalia and jurisdiction were not given by parliament, and, therefore, parliament have no authority to take them away." (Novanglus: WJA, IV, p. 169) The Latin regalia means "the rights royal." (Index, p. 182; see Regalia principis)

(9) "We now come to Jersey and Guernsey, which Massachusettensis says, 'are no part of the realm of England, nor are they represented in parliament, but are subject to its authority.' A little knowledge of this subject will do us no harm; and, as soon as we shall acquire it, we shall be satisfied how these islands came to be subject to the authority of parliament." (Novanglus: WJA, IV, p. 169)

(10-15) "The cases of Chester and Durham, counties palatine within the realm, shall conclude the fatiguing ramble. Chester was an earldom and a county; and in the 21st year of King Richard II. A.D. 1397, it was, by an

p. 390 (cont.)

act of parliament, erected into a principality, and several castles and towns were annexed to it, saving to the king the rights of his crown. This was a county palatine, and had *jura regalia* before this erection of it into a principality. . . .

"Considering the great seal of England and the process of the king's courts did not run into Chester, it was natural that malefactors should take refuge there, and escape punishment, and, therefore, a statute like this was of indispensable necessity; and, afterwards, in 1535, another statute was made, 27 Henry VIII. c. 5, for the making of justices of the peace within Chester, &c. . . .

". . . It [a statute from the time of Henry VIII] recites a part of the petition to the king, from the inhabitants of Chester, stating, 'that the county palatine had been excluded from parliament, to have any knights and burgesses there; by reason whereof, the said inhabitants have hitherto sustained manifold disherisons, losses, and damages, as well in their lands, good, and bodies, as in the good civil and politic governance and maintenance of the commonwealth of their said country. . . .' For remedy whereof, two knights of the shire and two burgesses for the city are established.

"I have before recited all the acts of parliament which were ever made to meddle with Chester, except the

p. 390 (cont.)

51 Henry III. stat. 5, in 1266, which only provides that the justices of Chester and other bailiffs shall be answerable in the exchequer, for wards, escheats, and other bailiwicks; yet Chester was never severed from the crown or realm of England, nor ever expressly exempted from the authority of parliament; yet, as they had generally enjoyed an exemption from the exercise of the authority of parliament, we see how soon they complain of it as grievous, and claim a representation as a right; and we see how readily it was granted. America, on the contrary, is not in the realm; never was subject to the authority of parliament by any principle of law; is so far from Great Britain that she never can be represented; yet, she is to be bound in all cases whatsoever!" (Novanglus: *WJA*, IV, pp. 170-172) The Latin *jure regalia* (line 10) means "royal rights." (*Index*, p. 107)

(16-17) "The next [statute naming Durham] is 31 Elizabeth, c. 9, and recites, that 'Durham is, and of long time hath been, an ancient county palatine, in which the Queen's writ hath not, nor yet doth run.' . . .

"And after this, we find no other mention of that bishopric in any statute until 25 Charles II. C. 9. This statute recites, 'whereas, the inhabitants of the county palatine of Durham have not hitherto had the liberty and

p. 390 (cont.)

privilege of electing and sending any knights and burgesses to the high court of parliament, although the inhabitants of the said county palatine are liable to all payments, rates, and subsidies granted by parliament, equally with the inhabitants of other counties, cities, and boroughs, in this kingdom, who have their knights and burgesses in the parliament, and are therefore concerned equally with others, the inhabitants of this kingdom, to have knights and burgesses in the said high court of parliament, of their own election, to represent the condition of their county, as the inhabitants of other counties, cities, and boroughs of this kingdom have.' It enacts two knights for the county, and two burgesses for the city." (Novanglus: WJA, IV, p. 173)

(18-21) "Massachusettensis then comes to the first charter of this province; and he tells us, that in it we shall find irresistible evidence, that our being a part of the empire, subject to the supreme authority of the state, bound by its laws, and subject to its protection, were the very terms and conditions by which our ancestors held their lands and settled the province. This is roundly and warmly said, but there is more zeal in it then knowledge. As to our being part of the empire, it could not be the British empire, as it is called, because that was not then in being, but

p. 390 (cont.)

was created seventy or eighty years afterwards. It must be the English empire, then; but the nation was not then polite enough to have introduced into the language of the law, or common parlance, any such phrase or idea." (Novanglus: WJA, IV, p. 173)

(22-25) "As to being subject to its protection, we may guess what ideas king and parliament had of that, by the protection they actually afforded to our ancestors. Not one farthing was ever voted or given by the king or his parliament, or any one resolution taken about them. . . . But 'our charter is in the royal style.' What then? Is that the parliamentary style? The style is this: 'Charles, by the grace of God, King of England, Scotland, France, and Ireland, Defender of the Faith,' &c. Now, in which capacity did he grant that charter; as King of France, or Ireland, or Scotland, or England? He governed England by one parliament, Scotland by another. Which parliament were we to be governed by?" (Novanglus: WJA, IV, p. 174)

(26-29) "In Moore's Reports, in the case of the union of the realm of Scotland with England, it is resolved by the judges, that 'the seal is alterable by the king at his pleasure, and he might make one seal for both kingdoms (of England and Scotland); for seals, coin, and

p. 390 (cont.)

leagues, are of absolute prerogative to the king without parliament, not restrained to any assent of the people;' and in determining how far the great seal doth command out of England, they made this distinction: 'That the great seal was current for remedials, which groweth on complaint of the subject, and thereupon writs are addressed under the great seal of England; which writs are limited, their precinct to be within the places of the jurisdiction of the court that was to give the redress of the wrong.' (Novanglus: WJA, IV, pp. 174-175)

(30-31) "Lands are holden according to the original notices of feuds, of the natural person of the lord. Holding lands, in feudal language, means no more than the relation between lord and tenant. The reciprocal duties of these are all personal. Homage, fealty, &c., and all other services, are personal to the lord; protection, &c. is personal to the tenant. And therefore no homage, fealty, or other services, can ever be rendered to the body politic, the political capacity, which is not corporated, but only a frame in the mind, an idea." (Novanglus: WJA, IV, pp. 176-177)

(32) "Then the writer asks, 'whether this looks like a distinct state or independent empire?' I answer, no.

p. 390 (cont.)

And that it is plain and uncontroverted, that the first charter was intended only to erect a corporation within the realm; and the governor and company were to reside within the realm; and their general courts were to be held there. Their agents, deputies, and servants only were to come to America. And if this had taken place, nobody ever doubted but they would have been subject to parliament. But this intention was not regarded on either side; and the company came over to America, and brought their charter with them. And as soon as they arrived here, they got out of the English realm, dominions, state, empire, call it by what name you will, and out of the legal jurisdiction of parliament. The king might, by his writ or proclamation, have commanded them to return; but he did not."
(Novanglus: *WJA*, IV, p. 177)

(33-35) "Hostilities at Lexington, between Great Britain and her colonies, commenced on the nineteenth of
p. 391   April, two days succeeding the publication of
(1-2)   this last essay. Several others were written, and sent to the printers of the Boston Gazette, which were probably lost amidst the confusion occasioned by that event."
(Note to the Edition of 1819: *WJA*, IV, p. 177n)

(3)   "The following letter seems to have been an

p. 391 (cont.)

effort to embody the ideas then uppermost in the writer's mind, made at the request of Richard Henry Lee, of Virginia, to whom it was addressed.

". . . As the earliest trace of the author's plan of government, it seems proper to be inserted here." (Editor's headnote: <u>WJA</u>, IV, p. 185)

(4-7) "Philadelphia, 15 November, 1775.

"DEAR SIR,--The course of events naturally turns the thoughts of gentlemen to the subjects of legislation and jurisprudence; and it is a curious problem, what form of government is most readily and easily adopted by a colony upon a sudden emergency. . . .

"A legislative, an executive, and a judicial power comprehend the whole of what is meant and understood by government. It is by balancing each of these powers against the other two, that the efforts in human nature towards tyranny can alone be checked and restrained, and any degree of freedom preserved in the constitution." (L. John Adams to R. H. Lee, 15 November 1775: <u>WJA</u>, IV, pp. 185-186)

(7) John Dunlap printed John Adams's "Thoughts on Government: Applicable to the Present State of the American Colonies," in Philadelphia in the year 1776. See

p. 391 (cont.)

title page for this work: WJA, IV, p. 189.

(8)   "In January, 1776, Mr. George Wythe, of Virginia, passing an evening with me, asked me what plan I would advise a colony to pursue, in order to get out of the old government and into a new one. I sketched in words a scheme, which he requested me to give him in writing. Accordingly, the next day, I delivered to him the following letter [containing what became "Thoughts on Government]. He lent it to his colleague, Richard Henry Lee, who asked me to let him print it; to which I consented, provided he would suppress my name; for if that should appear, it would excite a continental clamor among the tories, that I was erecting a battering-ram to demolish the royal government and render independence indispensable." (John Adams's account of how "Thoughts on Government" came to be written, dated QUINCY, 21 July 1811: WJA, IV, "Preface," p. 191)

(8-11)   "Nothing is more certain, from the history of nations and nature of man, than that some forms of government are better fitted for being well administered than others.

"We ought to consider what is the end of government, before we determine which is the best form. Upon this

p. 391 (cont.)

point all speculative politicians will agree, that the happiness of society is the end of government, as all divines and moral philosophers will agree that the happiness of the individual is the end of man. . . .

"All sober inquirers after truth, ancient and modern, pagan and Christian, have declared that the happiness of man, as well as his dignity, consists in virtue. Confucius, Zoroaster, Socrates, Mahomet, not to mention authorities really sacred, have agreed in this." (Thoughts/Government: <u>WJA</u>, IV, p. 193)

(12-18) "Fear is the foundation of most governments; but it is so sordid and brutal a passion, and renders men in whose breasts it predominates so stupid and miserable, that Americans will not be likely to approve of any political institution which is founded on it.

"Honor is truly sacred, but holds a lower rank in the scale of moral excellence than virtue. Indeed, the former is but a part of the latter, and consequently has not equal pretensions to support a frame of government productive of human happiness.

"The foundation of every government is some principle or passion in the minds of the people. The noblest principles and most generous affections in our nature, then, have the fairest chance to support the noblest and most generous

p. 391 (cont.)

models of government.

"A man must be indifferent to the sneers of modern Englishmen, to mention in their company the names of Sidney, Harrington, Locke, Milton, Nedham, Neville, Burnet, and Hoadly. No small fortitude is necessary to confess that one has read them. The wretched condition of this country, however, for ten or fifteen years past, has frequently reminded me of their principles and reasonings. They will convince any candid mind, that there is no good government but what is republican. That the only valuable part of the British constitution is so; because the very definition of a republic is 'an empire of laws, and not of men.'" (Thoughts/Government: <u>WJA</u>, IV, p. 194) At line 16 Pound interpolates, from Cavalcanti's "Donna mi prega," the Italian <u>ma</u> <u>che</u> <u>si</u> <u>sente</u> <u>dicho</u>, which means "but that is felt, I say." (<u>Index</u>, p. 133)

(19-20) "The principal difficulty lies, and the greatest care should be employed, in constituting this representative assembly. It should be in miniature an exact portrait of the people at large. It should think, feel, reason, and act like them." (Thoughts/Government: <u>WJA</u>, IV, p. 195)

(21-24) "The dignity and stability of government in all its branches, the morals of the people, and every blessing of society depend so much upon an upright and skilful administration of justice, that the judicial power ought to be distinct from both the legislative and executive,

p. 391 (cont.)

and independent upon both, that so it may be a check upon both, as both should be checks upon that. The judges, therefore, should be always men of learning and experience in the laws, of exemplary morals, great patience, calmness, coolness, and attention. Their minds should not be distracted with jarring interests; they should not be dependent upon any man, or body of men." (Thoughts/ Government: <u>WJA</u>, IV, p. 198)

(24-26) "A representative assembly, although extremely well qualified, and absolutely necessary, as a branch of the legislative, is unfit to exercise the executive power, for want of two essential properties, secrecy and despatch." (Thoughts/Government: <u>WJA</u>, IV, p. 196)

(27-33) "These colonies, under such forms of government [with a system of checks and balances], and in such a union, would be unconquerable by all the monarchies of Europe.

"You and I, my dear friend, have been sent into life at a time when the greatest lawgivers of antiquity would have wished to live. How few of the human race have ever enjoyed an opportunity of making an election of government, more than of air, soil, or climate, for themselves or their children! When, before the present epocha, had

p. 391 (cont.)

three millions of people full power and a fair opportunity to form and establish the wisest and happiest government that human wisdom can contrive?" (Thoughts/Government: <u>WJA</u>, IV, p. 200)

(34-35) "Before this reaches you, the resolution for finally separating from Britain will be handed
p. 392 to Congress by Colonel Nelson. I put up with
(1-11) it in the present form for the sake of unanimity. 'Tis not quite so pointed as I could wish.

"Excuse me for telling you of what I think of immense importance; 'tis to anticipate the enemy at the French Court. The half of our Continent offered to France, may induce her to aid our destruction, which she certainly has the power to accomplish. . . .

"Excuse me again. The confederacy;--that must precede an open declaration of independency and foreign alliances. Would it not be sufficient to confine it, for the present, to the objects of offensive and defensive nature, and a guaranty of the respective colonial rights? If a minute arrangement of things is attempted, such as equal representation, &c., &c., you may split and divide; certainly will delay the French alliance, which with me is every thing. . . .

". . . A silly thing, published in Philadelphia by a

p. 392 (cont.)

native of Virginia [apparently in answer to John Adams's "Thoughts on Government"], has just made its appearance here [in Williamsburgh, Virginia, from where Patrick Henry was writing this letter], strongly recommended, 'tis said, by one of our delegates now with you,--Braxton. His reasonings upon and distinction between private and public virtue, are weak, shallow, evasive, and the whole performance an affront and disgrace to this country; and, by one expression, I suspect his whiggism.

". . . Would to God you and your Sam Adams were here! It shall be my incessant study, so to form our portrait of government, that a kindred with New England may be discerned in it; and if all your excellencies cannot be preserved, yet I hope to retain so much of the likeness, that posterity shall pronounce us descended from the same stock. . . .

"P.S.--Will you and S. A. now and then write? (L. Patrick Henry to John Adams, 20 May 1776: WJA, IV, pp. 201-202)

(12-13) "In the month of January, 1776, the delegates of North Carolina were authorized by the colonial legislature, to apply to Mr. Adams for his views of the nature of the government it would be proper to form, in case of a final dissolution of the authority of the Crown. The

p. 392 (cont.)

following letter, addressed to Mr. John Penn, one of the number, was the reply. . . .

"No copy of this letter was retained by Mr. Adams. It was not printed until 1814, when Mr. John Taylor, of Caroline County, Virginia, to whom it had come from the hands of Mr. Penn, inserted it in his work, entitled 'An Inquiry into the Principles and Policy of the Government of the United States,' from whence it is now taken." (Editor's headnote: <u>WJA</u>, IV, p. 203)

(14-19) "If I was possessed of abilities equal to the great task you have imposed upon me, which is to sketch out the outlines of a constitution for a colony, I should think myself the happiest of men in complying with your desire. Because, as politics is the art of securing human happiness, and the prosperity of societies depends upon the constitution of government under which they live, there cannot be a more agreeable employment to a benevolent mind than the study of the best kinds of government. . . .

"In order to determine which is the best form of government, it is necessary to determine what is the end of government. And I suppose, that in this enlightened age, there will be no dispute, in speculation, that the happiness of the people, the great end of man, is the end of government; and, therefore, that form of government

p. 392 (cont.)

which will produce the greatest quantity of happiness is the best. . . .

"<u>A single assembly is liable to all the vices, follies, and frailties of an individual</u>; subject to fits of humor, transports of passion, partialities of prejudice; and, from these and other causes, apt to make hasty results and absurd judgments; all which errors ought to be corrected, and inconveniences guarded against, by some controlling power. . . .

"Let the two houses, then, by joint ballot, choose a governor. <u>Let him be chosen annually. Divest him of most of those badges of slavery called prerogatives</u>, and give him a negative upon the legislature." (L. John Adams to John Penn, n.d., 1776: <u>WJA</u>, IV, pp. 203-204; p. 206)

(20-21) "A letter of the same description was addressed to Jonathan Dickinson Sergeant, of New Jersey, in answer to a similar application, made at the time of the formation of the constitution in that State; but no copy has been found." (Editor's note: <u>WJA</u>, IV, p. 209n)

(22)   "'Resolved, That it is of the essence of a free republic, that the people be governed by FIXED LAWS OF THEIR OWN MAKING.'" (<u>WJA</u>, IV, p. 215) This resolution, one of two passed by the Massachusetts convention on

p. 392 (cont.)

3 September 1779, led to the framing of a new constitution for Massachusetts.

(23-24) "It is the duty of the people, therefore, in framing a Constitution of Government, to provide for an equitable mode of making laws, as well as for an impartial interpretation and a faithful execution of them, that every man may, at all times, find his security in them." (Preamble to the "Report of a Constitution" for Massachusetts: WJA, IV, pp. 219-220)

(25-26) "'[An inhabitant] having a freehold estate within the commonwealth, of the annual income of three pounds, or any estate of the value of sixty pounds, shall have a right to give in his vote for the senators for the district of which he is an inhabitant.'" (from the Massachusetts constitution proposed in 1779: WJA, IV, p. 236n)

(27-30) "Wisdom and knowledge, as well as virtue, diffused generally among the body of the people, being necessary for the preservation of their rights and liberties, and as these depend on spreading the opportunities and advantages of education in the various parts of the country, and among the different orders of the people, it shall be the duty of legislators and magistrates, in

p. 392 (cont.)

all future periods of this commonwealth, to cherish the interests of literature and the sciences, and all seminaries of them; especially the university at Cambridge, public schools and grammar schools in the towns; to encourage private societies and public institutions, rewards and immunities for the promotion of agriculture, arts, sciences, commerce, trades, manufactures, and a natural history of the country; to countenance and inculcate the principles of humanity and general benevolence, public and private charity, industry and frugality, honesty and punctuality in their dealings, sincerity, good humor, and all social affections and generous sentiments among the people." (from the Massachusetts constitution proposed in 1779: WJA, IV, p. 259)

(31-34) "'I was somewhat apprehensive [wrote John Adams in 1809] that criticism and objections would be
p. 393   made to the section, and particularly that the
(1-2)   "natural history," and the "good humor," would be stricken out; but the whole was received very kindly, and passed the convention unanimously, without amendment.'"

"It is a singularity [wrote Charles Francis Adams in an editor's comment], perhaps worthy of note in connection with these injunctions, that the individuals who have since been elevated by the popular voice to the chief

p. 393 (cont.)

offices of the state, with a single exception, have not been noted among their fellow-citizens for any superior acquisitions of learning or intellectual culture." (WJA, IV, p. 261n; the entire footnote, pp. 259, n. 1-261n, concerning John Adams's inclusion of such a passage in the proposed Massachusetts constitution, is of great interest.)

(3-8)   "Speculations upon government have gone out of vogue in the United States; partly by reason of a general satisfaction with the existing form of constitution, and a disposition to do nothing to disturb it; partly for another and more singular cause. In few countries, even those most despotically governed, can greater unwillingness prevail among educated men, to publish opinions on this subject, conflicting with received ideas. The experience of the author of the Defence furnished a memorable lesson of the danger incurred by a public man through an unreserved expression of his convictions, however honestly entertained. . . . The author was met with a storm of pamphlets and newspaper assaults, which pursued him as long as he remained in public life. Whether owing to this cause or not, the fact is certain, that no leading political man, since his day, has been known to express a serious doubt of the immaculate nature of the government established by the majority." (Editor's Preface to A Defence

p. 393 (cont.)

of the Constitutions of Government of the United States of America: WJA, IV, pp. 276-277)

(9)   "While it would be rash to say, that nothing further can be done to bring a free government, in all parts, still nearer to perfection, the representations of the people are most obviously susceptible of improvement." (Preface, by John Adams, to the Defence: WJA, IV, p. 284)

(10)   Pound's comment.

(11-12) "It is impossible to read in Thucydides, his account of the factions and confusions throughout all Greece, which were introduced by this want of an equilibrium, without horror. 'During the few days that Eurymedon, with his troops, continued at Corcya, the people of that city extended the massacre to all whom they judged their enemies. . . .

"'Such things ever will be,' says Thucydides, 'so long as human nature continues the same.'. But if this nervous historian had known a balance of three powers, he would not have pronounced the distemper so incurable, but would have added—so long as parties in cities remain unbalanced. He adds,—'Words lost their signification;

p. 393 (cont.)

brutal rashness was fortitude; prudence, cowardice; modesty, effeminacy; and being wise in every thing, to be good for nothing: the hot temper was manly valor; calm deliberation, plausible knavery; he who boiled with indignation, was trustworthy; and he who presumed to contradict, was ever suspected." (Preface/Defence: WJA, IV, pp. 285-286)

(13-20) "Mr. Hume has collected, from Diodorus Siculus alone, a few massacres which happened in only sixty of the most polished years of Greece:--'From Sybaris, 500 nobles banished; of Chians, 600 citizens; at Ephesus, 340 killed, 1000 banished; of Cyrenians, 500 nobles killed, all the rest banished; the Corinthians killed 120, banished 500; Phaebidas banished 300 Boeotians. Upon the fall of the Lacedaemonians, democracies were restored in many cities, and severe vengeance taken of the nobles; the banished nobles returning, butchered their adversaries at Phialae, in Corinth, In Megara, In Phliasia, where they killed 300 of the people; but these again revolting, killed above 600 of the nobles, and banished the rest. . . . The inhabitants of AEgesta, to the number of 40,000, were killed, man, woman, and child, for the sake of their money; all the relations of the Libyan army, fathers, brothers, children, killed; 7000 exiles killed after

p. 393 (cont.)

capitulation.'" (Preface/ Defence: <u>WJA</u>, IV, pp. 286-287)

(21-23) "The kings are supported by their armies; the nobles support the crown, as it is in full possession of the gift of all employments; but they support it still more by checking its ministers, and preventing them from running into abuses of power and wanton despotism; otherwise the people would be pushed to extremities and insurrections. It is thus that the nobles reconcile the monarchical authority to the obedience of the subjects; but take away the standing armies, and leave the nobles to themselves, and in a few years, they would overturn every monarchy in Europe, and erect aristocracies." (Preface/ Defence: <u>WJA</u>, IV, p. 288)

(24) "Although the detail of the formation of the American governments is at present little known or regarded either in Europe or in America, it may hereafter become an object of curiosity. It will never be pretended that any persons employed in that service had interviews with the gods, or were in any degree under the inspiration of Heaven, more than those at work upon ships or houses, or laboring in merchandise or agriculture; it will forever be acknowledged that these governments were contrived merely by the use of reason and the senses, as Copley

p. 393 (cont.)

painted Chatham; West, Wolf; and Trumbull, Warren and Montgomery; as Dwight, Barlow, Trumbull, and Humphries composed their verse, and Belknap and Ramsay history; as Godfrey invented his quadrant, and Rittenhouse his planetarium; as Boylston practised inoculation, and Franklin electricity; as Paine exposed the mistakes of Raynal, and Jefferson those of Buffon, so unphilosophically borrowed from the despicable dreams of De Pau." (Preface/ Defence: WJA, IV, pp. 292-293)

(25)   John Adams dated his Preface to his Defence January 1, 1787, at Grosvenor Square, London, England. See WJA, IV, p. 298.

(26)   "Called wihtout expectation, and compelled without previous inclination, though undoubtedly at the best period of time, both for England and America, suddenly to erect new systems of laws for their future government, they [the American patriots] adopted the method of a wise architect, in erecting a new palace for the residence of his sovereign. They determined to consult Vitruvius, Palladio, and all other writers of reputation in the art; to examine the most celebrated buildings, whether they remain entire or in ruins; to compare these with the principles of writers; and to inquire how far both the theories

p. 393 (cont.)

and models were founded in nature, or created by fancy; and when this was done, so far as their circumstances would allow, to adopt the advantages and reject the inconveniences of all." (Preface/ Defence: <u>WJA</u>, IV, p. 293)

(27-28) "If the publication of these papers should contribute any thing to turn the attention of the younger gentlemen of letters in America to this kind of inquiry, it will produce an effect of some importance to their country. The subject is the most interesting that can engage the understanding or the heart; for whether the end of man, in this stage of his existence, be enjoyment, or improvement, or both, it can never be attained so well in a bad government as a good one." (Preface/ Defence: <u>WJA</u>, IV, p. 294)

(29-34) "The practicability or the duration of a republic, in which there is a governor, a senate, and a
p. 394 house of representatives, is doubted by Tacitus,
(1) though he admits the theory to be laudable: 'Cunctas nationes et urbes, populus, aut priores, aut singuli, regunt. Delecta ex his et constituta reipublicae forma, laudari facilius quam inveniri; vel, si evenit, haud diuturna esse potest.' Cicero asserts, 'Statuo esse optime constitutam rempublicam, quae ex tribus generibus illis,

p. 394 (cont.)

regali, optimo, et populari, modice confusa,' in such peremptory terms the superiority of such a government to all other forms, that the loss of his book upon republics is much to be regretted. . . .

"'Ut in fidibus aut tibiis, atque in cantu ipso, ac vocibus, concentus est quidam tenendus ex distinctis sonis, quem immutatum aut discrepantem aures eruditae ferre non possunt; isque concentus, <u>ex dissimillimarum vocum</u> <u>moderatione</u>, <u>concors tamen efficitur et congruens</u>; sic <u>ex summis et infimis et interjectis ordinibus</u>, ut sonis, moderata ratione, civitas consensu dissimillimorum concinit; et quae harmonia a musicis dicitur in cantu, ea est in civitate concordia arctissimum atque optimum omni in republica vinculum incolumitatis; eaque sine justitia nullo pacto esse potest.' As all the ages of the world have not produced a greater statesman and philosopher united than Cicero, his authority should have great weight. . . .

"'Ubi justitia vera non est, nec jus potest esse.'" (Preface/Defence: <u>WJA</u>, IV, pp. 294-296) The Latin quoted by Pound, <u>facilius laudari quam invenire/ vel haud diuturna/ optime modice confusa . . ./ concors tamen efficitur . . . civitas consensu/ ubi justitia non est, nec just potest esse</u>, means "it is more easily praised than discovered/ or not lasting/ excellently blended in moderation . . ./ is nevertheless brought about in unison . . . a state by

p. 394 (cont.)

agreement/ where there is no justice, there can be no law."
(Index, p. 66)

(2-3) "St. Marino was its [the republic of San Marino's] founder, a Dalmatian by birth, and by trade a mason. He was employed about thirteen hundred years ago in the reparation of Rimini, and after he had finished his work, retired to this solitary mountain, as very proper for the life of a hermit, which he led in the greatest austerities of religion."
(Defence: WJA, IV, p. 304)

(4-7) "The whole history of Geneva, since that period [the sixteenth century], follows of course. The people, by their own supineness, have given up all balance and betrayed their own privileges, as well as the prerogatives of their first magistrates, into the hands of a few families."
(Defence: WJA, IV, p. 345)

(8-9) "The nobility are allowed to trade in the wholesale way; to carry on velvet, silk, and cloth manufactures; and to have shares in merchant ships; and some of them, as the Palavicini, are actually the greatest merchants in Genoa." (Defence: WJA, IV, p. 347)

(10-11) "The republic of Venice has existed longer than

p. 394 (cont.)

that of Rome or Sparta, or any other that is known in history. It was at first democratical; and its magistrates, under the names of tribunes, were chosen by the people in a general assembly. . . .

"This magistrate must not be called king, but duke, and afterwards doge; he was to be for life, but at his death another was to be chosen; he was to have the nomination of all magistrates, and the power of peace and war. The unbounded popularity and great real merit of Paul Luc Anafeste added to the pressure of tribune tyranny and the danger of a foreign enemy, accomplished this revolution. The new doge was to consult only such citizens as he should judge proper; this, instead of giving him a constitutional council, made him the master; he, however, sent polite messages to those he liked best, praying that they would come and advise him." (Defence: WJA, IV, pp. 347-348)

(11-13) "Out of fifty successively exercising the powers of this office during this period [c. tenth century], five were massacred, nine deposed, five of whom were banished with deprivation of sight, five voluntarily abdicated, and one was killed in foreign war." (Defence: WJA, IV, p. 348, n. 2)

(14-15) "For a long course of years [c. tenth century]

p. 394 (cont.)

after this, the Venetian history discloses scenes of tyranny, revolt, cruelty, and assassination, which excite horror. Doges endeavoring to make their power hereditary, associating their eldest sons with them in office, and both together oppressing the people; these rising, and murdering them, or driving them into banishment, never once thinking of introducing a third order between them and their first magistrate, nor any other form of government, by which his power or theirs might be limited. . . . There was no assembly but that of the people, and another called the council of forty, for the administration of justice. This body, in the twelfth century, formed something like a plan of government." (Defence: <u>WJA</u>, IV, pp. 348-349)

(16-21) "There can be, in the nature of things, no balance without three powers. The aristocracy is always more sagacious than an assembly of the people collectively, or by representation, and sooner or later proves an overmatch in policy. It is always more cunning, too, than a first magistrate, and always makes of him a doge of Venice, a mere ceremony, unless he makes an alliance with the people, to support him against it. What is the whole history of the wars of the barons but one demonstration of this truth? What are all the standing armies in Europe but another? These were all given to kings by the people, to defend them

p. 394 (cont.)

against aristocracies. The people have been generally of M. Turgot's mind, that balances and different orders were unnecessary; and, harassed to death by the domination of noble famiies, they have generally surrounded the throne with troops to humble them. They have commonly succeeded so far as to make the nobles dependent on the crown; but, having given up the balance which they might have held in their own hands, they are still subject to as much aristocratical domination as the crowns think proper to permit." (Defence: WJA, IV, pp. 354-355)

(22)   "The whole [of the six classes of nobles in Venice] make about two thousand five hundred." (Defence: WJA, IV, p. 356)

(23)   "Here [in the Republic of the United Provinces of the Low Countries] were a stadtholder, an assembly of the states-general, a council of state; the stadtholder hereditary had the command of armies and navies, and appointment of all officers, &c." (Defence: WJA, IV, p. 356)

(24)   "Poland and England. The history of these countries, the last especially, would confirm the general principle contended for. But who can think of writing

p. 394 (cont.)

upon this subject after De Lolme, whose book is the best defence of the political balance of three powers that ever was written?" (Defence: <u>WJA</u>, IV, p. 358)

(25-26) "The philosophical King Stanislaus felt most severely this want of a people. In his observations on the government of Poland, he laments, in very pathetic terms, the miseries to which they were reduced. . . .

"'We have a recent instance, in the insurrection in the Ukraine, which was only occasioned by the vexations of those among us who had there purchased lands. We despised the courage of the poor inhabitants of that country; they found a resource in despair; and nothing is more terrible than the despair of those who have no courage.'" (Defence: <u>WJA</u>, IV, pp. 371-373)

(27-30) "The ancient constitution of Rhodes was probably much like this of Neuchatel, in three branches, and was accordingly celebrated as one of the best models of government in antiquity, and had effect equally happy upon the order, liberty, commerce, and population of that country. This happy mixture in three branches has ever been the never-failing means of reconciling law and liberty, in ancient and in modern times. 'Ita demum liberam civitatem fore, ita aequatas leges, si sua quisque jura ordo, suam

p. 394 (cont.)

majestatem teneat.' This is the only constitution in which the citizens can truly be said to be in that happy condition of freedom and discipline, sovereignty and subordination, which the Greeks express so concisely by their ἄρχειν καὶ ἄρχεσθαι." (Defence: WJA, IV, p. 377) The Latin quoted by Pound, jura ordo . . . aequitas leges, means "rights order . . . equity laws." (Index, p. 107) The Greek ἄρχειν καὶ ἄρχεσθαι means "to rule and to be ruled." (Index, p. 260)

(31-32) "Among every people, and in every species of republics, we have constantly found a first magistrate, a head, a chief, under various denominations, indeed, and with different degrees of authority, with the title of stadtholder, burgomaster, avoyer, doge, gonfaloniero, president, syndic, mayor, alcalde, capitaneo, governor, or king; in every nation we have met with a distinguished officer. If there is no example, then, in any free government, any more than in those which are not free, of a society without a principal personage, we may fairly conclude that the body politic cannot subsist, any more than the animal body, without a head. If M. Turgot had made any discovery which had escaped the penetration of all the legislators and philosophers who have lived before him, he ought at least to have communicated it to the world for

p. 394 (cont.)

their improvement; but as he has never hinted at any such invention, we may safely conclude that he had none; and, therefore, that the Americans are not justly liable to censure for instituting <u>governors</u>." (Defence: <u>WJA</u>, IV, p. 379)

(33) "In every country we have found a variety of <u>orders</u>, with very great distinctions. In America, there are different orders of <u>offices</u>, but none of <u>men</u>. Out of office, all men are of the same species, and of one blood; there is neither a greater nor a lesser nobility." (Defence: <u>WJA</u>, IV, p. 380)

(34-35) "We have seen no one in government in which is a distinct separation of the legislative from the executive power, and of the judicial from both, or in which any attempt has been made to balance these powers with one another, or to form an equilibrium between the one, the few, and the many, for the purpose of enacting and executing equal laws, by common consent, for the general interest, excepting in England." (Defence: <u>WJA</u>, IV, p. 381)

CANTO LXVIII

p. 395

(1-5) "'For, not to mention the several republics of this composition in Gaul and Germany, described by Caesar and Tacitus, Polybius tells us, the best government is that which consists of three forms, <u>regis</u>, <u>optimatium</u>, <u>et populi imperio</u>. Such was that of Sparta in its primitive instituion by Lycurgus, who, observing the corruptions and depravations to which every one of these was subject, compounded his scheme out of all; so that it was made up of <u>reges</u>, <u>seniores</u>, <u>et populus</u>. Such also was the state of Rome under its consuls; and such, at Carthage, was the power in the last resort; they had their kings, senate, and people.' A limited and divided power seems to have been the most ancient and inherent principle, both of the Greeks and Italians, in matters of government. 'The difference between the Grecian monarchies and Italian republics was not very great. The power of those Grecian princes, who came to the siege of Troy, was much of a size with that of the kings of Sparta, the archon of Athens, the suffetes at Carthage, and the consuls at Rome.'" (Defence: <u>WJA</u>, IV, pp. 383-384) The Latin <u>Regis optimatium populique</u> means "of the king, of the aristocrats, of the people too." The Latin <u>reges</u>, <u>seniores et populus</u> means "kings, elders, and

p. 395 (cont.)
people." (Index, p. 183)

(6)   "'Ever since men have been united into governments, the hopes and endeavors after universal monarchy have been bandied among them. . . . The Athenians, the Spartans, the Thebans, and the Achaians, several times aimed at the universal monarchy of Greece; the commonwealths of Carthage and Rome affected the universal monarchy of the then known world.'" (Defence: WJA, IV, p. 387)

(7-9)   "'A usurping populace is its own dupe, a mere under-worker, and a purchaser in trust for some single tyrant, whose state and power they advance to their own ruin, with as blind an instinct as those worms that die with weaving magnificent habits for beings of a superior order to their own.

"'The people are much more dexterous at pulling down and setting up, than at preserving what is fixed; and they are not fonder of seizing more than their own, than they are of delivering it up again to the worst bidder, with their own into the bargain.'" (Defence: WJA, IV, p. 388)

(9-11)   "M. Turgot might have perceived in these writers that a government of laws and not of men was intended by them as a description of a commonwealth, not a definition of

p. 395 (cont.)

liberty." (Defence: WJA, IV, p. 405)

(12)   I have been unable to identify a passage containing these exact words, but the following statement is close to the Poundian idea: "Ambition strengthens at every advance, and at last takes possession of the whole soul so absolutely, that a man sees nothing in the world of importance to others to himself, but in his object." (Defence: WJA, IV, p. 406)

(13)   "'Let states take heed,' says Lord Bacon, 'how their nobility and gentlemen multiply too fast, for that makes the common subject grow to be a peasant and base swain driven out of heart, and, in effect, but a gentleman's laborer. How shall the plough, then, be kept in the hands of the owners, and not mere hirelings? how shall the country attain to the character which Virgil gives of ancient Italy, Terra potens armis, atque ubere gleba? how, but by the balance of dominion or property?'" (Defence: WJA, IV, p. 428)

(14-15) "'The vice of kingly government is monarchy; that of aristocracy, oligarchy; and of democracy, rage and violence; into which all of them, in process of time, must necessarily degenerate. To avoid which, Lycurgus united in one all the advantages of the best governments, to the end

p. 395 (cont.)

that no branch of it, by swelling beyond its bounds, might degenerate into the vice that is congenial to it, and that, while each was mutually acted upon by opposite powers, no one part might outweigh the rest. The Romans arrived at the same end by the same means.'" (Defence: WJA, IV, p. 443. See a more elaborate version of this statement on pp. 435-436)

(16-17) "Chimerical systems of legislation are neither new nor uncommon, even among men of the most resplendent genius and extensive learning. It would not be too bold to say, that some parts of Plato and Sir Thomas More are as wild as the ravings of Bedlam." (Defence: WJA, IV, p. 463)

(18-19) "A man may be a greater poet than Homer, and one of the most learned men in the world; he may spend his life in defence of liberty, and be at the same time one of the most irreproachable moral characters; and yet, when called upon to frame a constitution of government, he may demonstrate to the world that he has reflected very little on the subject. There is a great hazard in saying all this of John Milton; but truth and the rights of mankind demand it. In his 'Ready and Easy Way to Establish a Free Commonwealth,' this great author says, 'I doubt not but all ingenuous and knowing men will easily agree with me, that

p. 395 (cont.)

a free commonwealth, without single person or house of lords, is by far the best government, if it can be had; . . .'

. . .

". . . Had Milton's scheme been adopted, England would have been a scene of revolutions, carnage, and horror, from that time to this, or its liberties would have been at this hour the liberties of Poland, or the island would have been a province of France. What! a single assembly to govern England? an assembly of senators for life too? What! did Milton's ideas of liberty and free government extend no further than exchanging one house of lords for another, and making it supreme and perpetual? . . . John Milton was as honest a man as his nation ever bred, and as great a friend of liberty; but his greatness most certainly did not consist in the knowledge of the nature of man and of government, if we are to judge from this performance, or from 'The Present Means and Brief Delineation of a Free Commonwealth,' in his letter to General Monk." (Defence: WJA, IV, pp. 464-466)

(20)   "Solon's reputation for wisdom and integrity was universal; and, as he had friends in all parties, they procured the place of archon, with power to reform the constitution. His first object was to reconcile the rich with the poor; this he accomplished by lowering the interest

p. 395 (cont.)

without annulling the debt, and by taking from the creditor the exorbitant powers over the person and family of the debtor." (Defence: <u>WJA</u>, IV, p. 477)

(21-23) "Alcinous [in the <u>Odyssey</u>, Book VIII] is afterwards represented as describing the form of government to Ulysses:--

> 'Twelve princes in our realm dominion share
> O'er whom supreme imperial power I bear.'

"Mr. Pope, indeed, in this translation, has given him the air of a sovereign; but there is nothing like it in the original. There, Alcinous, with all possible simplicity and modesty, only says,--'Twelve illustrious kings, or archons, rule over the people, and I myself am the thirteenth.' . . .

". . . Mr. Pope has disguised this sentiment, and made it conformable to the notions of Englishmen and Americans; but has departed from the sense of Homer and from the fact." (Defence: <u>WJA</u>, IV, pp. 568-569)

(24) "Through the whole of Tacitus and Homer, the three orders are visible both in Germany and Greece; and the continual fluctuations of law, the uncertainty of life, liberty, and property, and the contradictory claims and continual revolutions, arose entirely from the want of having the prerogatives and privileges of those orders

p. 395 (cont.)

defined, from the want of independence in each of them, and a balance between them." (Defence: WJA, IV, p. 578)

(25-26) "But, if such a work [on the history of all governments whose records have survived] should be sufficiently encouraged by the public, (which is not probable, for mankind, in general, dare not as yet read or think upon CONSTITUTIONS,) it is too extensive for my forces, and ought not to be done in so much haste. The preceding has been produced upon the spur of a particular occasion, which made it necessary to write and publish with precipitation, or it might have been useless to have published at all. (Defence: WJA, VI, p. 217)

(27-28) "This dull, heavy volume, still excites the wonder of its author,--first, that he could find, amidst the constant scenes of business and dissipation in which he was enveloped, time to write it; secondly, that he had the courage to oppose and publish his own opinions to the universal opinion of America, and, indeed, of all mankind. Not one man in America then believed him. The work, however, powerfully operated to destroy his popularity. It was urged as full proof, that he was an advocate for monarchy, and laboring to introduce a hereditary president in America.   J. A. 1812" (See headnote, Davila: WJA, VI, p. 227)

p. 395 (cont.)

(29) "As each of them [the princes in Gaul], in default of direct heirs, may, according to his rank, be called to the crown, their interests are necessarily connected with those of the state. The people regard these privileges as inviolable. Neither length of time nor distance of degree has ever done them any injury. All these princes preserve the rank which nature has allotted them, to succeed to the throne. They have, indeed, in the course of time, taken different names, such as those of <u>Valois</u>, of <u>Bourbon</u>, of <u>Orléans</u>, of <u>Angoulême</u>, of <u>Vendôme</u>, of <u>Alençon</u>, of <u>Montpensier</u>; but they have not by these means lost the rights attached to the royal consanguinity, and that especially of succeeding to the crown." (Davila: <u>WJA</u>, VI, p. 230)

(30) "The reputation which is to be acquired by this kind of learning may be judged of by the language of Mr. Hume:--'Compositions the most despicable, both for style and matter, such as Rapin Thoyras, Locke, Sidney, Hoadley, &c., have been extolled and propagated and read, as if they had equalled the most celebrated remains of antiquity.' Such is the style in which this great writer speaks of writings which he most probably never read." (Defence: <u>WJA</u>, IV, p. 559)

p. 395 (cont.)

(31-32) "Their [the Franks'] great misfortune was, that, while it never was sufficiently ascertained, whether the sovereignty resided in the king or in the <u>national assembly</u>, it was equally uncertain whether the king had a negative on the assembly; whether the grandees had a negative on the king or the people; and whether the people had a negative on both or either." (Davila: <u>WJA</u>, VI, p. 228)

p. 396

(1-3)   "See the review of this work in the <u>Anthology</u>. The writer was 'a young man; a forward young man,'" (Davila: <u>WJA</u>, VI, p. 229, n. 2) This statement, made by John Adams in 1812, refers to a remark by a critic who reviewed "Discourses on Davila." See editor's note, <u>WJA</u>, VI, p. 225, for account of when "Discourses on Davila" was written.

(4)   "Pharamond was elected king by unanimous consent. . . . But as unlimited authority may easily degenerate into tyranny, the Franks, at the time of the election of their king, demanded the establishment of certain perpetual and irrevocable laws, which should regulate the order of succession to the throne, and prescribe in a few words the form of government. These laws, proposed by their priests, whom they named <u>Saliens</u>, and

p. 396 (cont.)

instituted in the fields, which take their name from the river <u>Sala</u>, were originally called <u>Salique</u> <u>laws</u>, and have been considered, from the establishment of the monarchy, as the primitive regulations and fundamental constitutions of the kingdom." (Davila: <u>WJA</u>, VI, p. 229)

(5-7)   "Here again is the French jargon of all authority in one centre, without one clear idea. 1812." (Davila: <u>WJA</u>, VI, p. 230, n. 1) See also the following passage: "Here again we meet with another inaccuracy, if not a contradiction in Davila; or rather with another proof of that confusion of law, and that uncertainty of the sovereignty, which for fifteen hundred years has been to France the fatal source of so many calamities. Here the sovereignty or whole power of the nation, is asserted to be in the <u>states</u> <u>general</u>; whereas only three pages before, he had asserted that the whole authority of the nation was united in the king." (Davila: <u>WJA</u>, VI, pp. 230-231)

(8)   "Misera Servitus est, ubi jus est vagum aut incognitum. 1804." (Davila: <u>WJA</u>, VI, p. 230, n. 2) The Latin <u>Miseria</u> <u>servitus</u>, <u>ubi</u> <u>jus</u> <u>vagum</u> means "Slavery is a misery, where rights are undefined." (<u>Index</u>, p. 145)

(9-11)   "Men, in their primitive conditions, however

p. 396 (cont.)

savage, were undoubtedly gregarious; and they continue to be social, not only in every stage of civilization, but in every possible situation in which they can be placed. As nature intended them for society, she has furnished them with passions, appetites, and propensities, as well as a variety of faculties, calculated both for their individual enjoyment, and to render them useful to each other in their social connections. There is none among them more essential or remarkable, than the <u>passion for distinction</u>. A desire to be observed, considered, esteemed, praised, beloved, and admired by his fellows, is one of the earliest, as well as keenest dispositions discovered in the heart of man." (Davila: <u>WJA</u>, VI, p. 232)

(12-16) "I shall leave these uncandid insinuations to those who delight in them; and take it for granted, that Mr. Hillhouse is sincere, that he honestly believes what he says, and proposes his amendments for the public good. . . .

"Would it not have been more conformable to the fact to have said, that those important features of our constitution were borrowed from our colonial constitutions? Every colony on the continent, except Pennsylvania, had a governor, a council or senate, and a house of representatives. The governors were not hereditary; the

p. 396 (cont.)

counsellors were not hereditary." (from a "Review" by John Adams of the "Propositions for Amending the Constitution," submitted by Mr. Hillhouse to the United States Senate in 1808: <u>WJA</u>, VI, p. 528)

(17)   "You cannot prevent them [caucuses in party politics] any more than you can prevent gentlemen from conversing at their lodgings.

". . . The communication by letters in the post offices, and by private hands, will be as easy as ever, and mercenary emissaries from the British and French courts may write, speak, and hold caususes, as well as federalists and republicans, when elections are annual, as well as at this time, when they are for two years, for six years, and for four years." (from the "Review" named in the preceding reference: <u>WJA</u>, VI, pp. 544-545)

(18-21) "Sir,--The 28th ultimo I had the honor of writing to you by the messenger, Frederick Weare, and of transmitting a vote of congress by which you are appointed a commissioner at the Court of France. Inclosed under this cover you will find a commission executed agreeable to the order of congress.

"You have no doubt heard, or will hear before this can reach you, of the little affair which happened last

p. 396 (cont.)

week in Jersey,--the attack by the Marquis de la Fayette, at the head of about four hundred militia and a detachment from Morgan's rifles, on a piquet of three hundred Hessians twice reinforced by British,--in which our troops were successful, killed about twenty, wounded more, took fourteen prisoners, and chased the enemy about half a mile." (L. Henry Laurens, President of Congress, to John Adams, 3 December 1777: WJA, VII, pp. 5-6)

(22-24) "Sir,--As you are going to France in a public character from the United States, will you give me leave to present you a letter of introduction for M. le Comte de Broglie, one for M. Moreau, the first Secretary to Count de Vergennes, Minister of State for Foreign Affairs, and two for my lady, who will be glad to see you, and to get news from me by your means?" (L. Baron de Kalb to John Adams, 27 December 1777: WJA, VII, p. 9)

(25-27) "Sir,--As General Knox will have the pleasure to see you before your going to France, I take the liberty of intrusting him with the inclosed letter for you, which you will find very importune, but I hope you will excuse, on account of my being very desirous to let my friends hear from me by every opportunity. Such a distance, so many enemies are between me and every relation, every

p. 396 (cont.)

acquaintance of mine, that I will not reproach myself with any neglect in my entertaining with them the best correspondence I can. . . .

". . . I hope you will hear good news from here, and send very good ones from there. Such is the desire of a friend to your country and the noble cause we are fighting for." (L. Marquis de la Fayette to John Adams, 9 January 1778: WJA, VII, pp. 10-11)

(28-30) "Gentlemen,--I find that the American affairs on this side of the Atlantic are in a state of disorder, very much resembling that which is so much to be regretted on the other, and arising, as I suppose, from the same general causes, the novelty of the scenes, the inexperience of the actors, and the rapidity with which great events have succeeded each other. . . .

"In order to correct some of these abuses, and to bring our affairs into a little better order, I have constantly given my voice against paying for things we never ordered, against paying persons who have never been authorized, and against throwing our affairs into a multiplicity of hands in the same place." (L. John Adams to the Committee of Commerce of the Congress, 24 May 1778: WJA, VII, pp. 14-15)

(31-33) "The difficulties which the privateers of the

p. 396 (cont.)

United States have experienced till now in the ports of France, either as to the sale of their prizes, or to secure their prisoners, must cease, from the change of circumstances. I make no doubt, on the other hand, but that the United States will grant the same facilities to French privateers." (L. M. De Sartine to the United States Commissioners to France, 29 July 1778: <u>WJA</u>, VII, p. 23)

    (34-35)   "At a time when the circumstances of the war may demand the attention of government, and, without
p. 397   doubt, call for so great expense, we are very
  (1-6)   sorry to be obliged to request your Excellency's advice respecting the subject of money; but the nature of the war in America, the vast extent of country to defend, and this defence having been made chiefly by militia engaged for short periods, which often obliged us to pay more men than could be brought into actual service, and, above all, this war having been conducted in the midst of thirteen revolutions of civil government against a nation very powerful both by sea and land, have occasioned a very great expense to a country so young, and to a government so unsettled. This has made emissions of paper money indispensable, in much larger sums than in the ordinary course of business is necessary, or than in any other circumstances would have been politic. In order to avoid the necessity

p. 397 (cont.)

of further emissions as much as possible, the congress have borrowed large sums of this paper money of the possessors, upon interest, and have promised the lenders payment of that interest in Europe, and we therefore expect that vessels from America will bring bills of exchange upon us for this interest, a large sum of which is now due." (L. United States Commissioners -- Benjamin Franklin, Arthur Lee, John Adams -- to Count de Vergennes, 28 August 1778: WJA, VII, p. 25)

(7-9) "We are at a loss to know how you claim the Theresa as your proper vessel, because M. Monthieu claims her as his, produces a written contract for the hire and demurrage of her, part of which we have paid, and the remainder he now demands of us." (L. United States Commissioners to M. de Beaumarchais, 10 September 1778: WJA, VII, p. 28)

(10-12) "In the letter of the Committee of Commerce to us, in which the foregoing resolution was inclosed, the Committee express themselves thus:--'This will be accompanied by a contract entered into between John Baptiste Lazarus de Theveneau de Francy, agent of Peter Augustin Caron de Beaumarchais, representative of the house of Roderique Hortalez & Co. and the Committee of Commerce.

p. 397 (cont.)

You will observe that their accounts are to be fairly stated, and what is justly due paid.'" (L. United States Commissioners to Count de Vergennes, 10 September 1778: WJA, VII, p. 29)

(13-17) "Sir,--I have received the letter which you did me the honor to write to me on the 15th instant, making inquiry as to the rent of my house, in which you live, for the past and the future. When I consecrated my house to Dr. Franklin and his associates, who might live with him, I made it fully understood that I should expect no compensation, because I perceived that you had need of all your means to send to the succor of your country, or to relieve your countrymen escaping from the chains of your enemies. I pray you, sir, to permit this arrangement to remain, which I made when the fate of your country was doubtful. When she shall enjoy all her splendor, such sacrifices on my part will be superfluous, and unworthy of her, but, at present, they may be useful, and I am most happy in offering them to you." (L. Le Ray de Chaumont to John Adams, 18 September 1778: WJA, VII, p. 32)

(18-28) "We have at length obtained a sight of M. Bersolle's accounts, and take this opportunity to communicate to you our observations upon them.

p. 397 (cont.)

"As by the resolutions of congress, the whole of all vessels of war taken by our frigates belong to the officers and men; nay, further, as they have even an additional encouragement of a bounty upon every man and every gun that is on board such prizes, it was never the intention of congress to be at any further expense on account of such prizes.

"Every article of these accounts, therefore, that relates to repairs of the Drake or furniture for the Drake, must be charged to Captain Jones, his officers, and men, and come out of the proceeds of the sale of the Drake, or be furnished upon her credit and that of the officers and men of the Ranger. It would certainly be a misapplication of the public interest, if we should pay any part of it.

"In the next place, all those articles of these accounts which consist in supplies of slops or other things furnished the officers and men of the Ranger must be paid for by them, not by us. Their shares of prize-money in the Drake, the Lord Chatham, and other prizes made by the Ranger will be abundantly sufficient to discharge these debts, and in no such cases can we justify advancing any thing to officers or men.

"As the Lord Chatham belongs, half to the public and half to the captors, all necessary expenses on her account

p. 397 (cont.)

should be paid; a moiety out of the captors' half, and the other moiety out of the half which belongs to the United States.

"All necessary supplies of munition and repairs to the Ranger, and of victuals to her company, we shall agree to pay at the expense of the United States." (L. United States Commissioners to M. Schweighauser, 4 November 1778: <u>WJA</u>, VII, p. 65)

(29-35) "Your Excellency will excuse our suggesting one reflection,--that whatever vessels of war are sent to America, they should be plentifully furnished with marine woollen cloths, especially blankets and gloves, or mittens, without which it is extremely difficult for the men to do their duty in the cold season upon that coast. We are, &c. &c. B. FRANKLIN, ARTHUR LEE, JOHN ADAMS." (L. United States Commissioners to M. de Sartine, 12 November 1778: <u>WJA</u>, VII, p. 69)

p. 398

(1)   "It is certain that a loan of money is very much wanted to redeem the redundancy of our paper bills; and without it, it is impossible to foresee what will be the consequence to their credit; and therefore every service that may be rendered in order to obtain it from this

p. 398 (cont.)

kingdom, from Spain or Holland, will be a most essential and acceptable service." (L. John Adams to the Marquis de La Fayette, 21 February 1779: <u>WJA</u>, VII, p. 84)

(2-4)   "Upon the whole I can assure you, that I do not think the good will of this Court to the good cause of America is at all diminished by the late little reverses in the fortune of war; and I hope Spain, who has now forty-nine ships of the line and thirty-one frigates ready for service, will soon, by declaring, turn the scale.
   "Remember me affectionately to master Johnny,
       "And believe me, with great esteem, sir, &c.
                       "B. FRANKLIN."   (L. Benjamin Franklin to John Adams, 3 April 1779: <u>WJA</u>, VII, p. 90)

(5)   "Italy, a country which declines every day from its ancient prosperity, offers few objects to our speculations. The privileges of the port of Leghorn, nevertheless, may render it useful to our ships when our independence shall be acknowledged by Great Britain, if, as we once flattered ourselves, the Court of Vienna might receive an American minister." (L. John Adams to the President of Congress, 4 August 1779: <u>WJA</u>, VII, p. 109)

p. 398 (cont.)

(6-8) "Sir,--I have the honor to transmit you herewith inclosed two commissions, wherein you are authorized and appointed minister plenipotentiary from these United States, to negotiate treaties of peace and commerce with Great Britain, accompanied with instructions in each case for your government in the execution of those several commissions. . . .

"Also two acts of congress of the 4th and 15th instants, ascertaining your salary, and making provision for your subsistence on your arrival in France." (L. Samuel Huntington, President of Congress, to John Adams, 20 October 1779: <u>WJA</u>, VII, p. 119)

(9-18) "My Dear General,--You know extremely well the skill of our enemies in forging false news, and their artifice in circulating it, not only through the various parts of Europe, but in the United States of America, to keep up the spirits of their friends and depress those of their adversaries. It is their annual custom in the winter to send abroad large cargoes of these lies, and they meet with a success in making them believed, that is really astonishing.

"Since my arrival here, I find they have been this winter at their old game again, and have circulated reports here, in Holland, and other parts of Europe, that they have

p. 398 (cont.)

made new contracts with other petty princes in Germany, by which, together with those made before, they will be able to draw seven thousand fresh troops from that country to serve in America; that, by appeasing the troubles in Ireland, they shall be able to avail themselves even of the military associations in that kingdom, by depending upon them for the defence of the country, and to draw near ten thousand men from thence for the service in America; that they have concluded a treaty with the Court of Petersburg, by which Russia is to furnish them with twelve ships of the line and twenty thousand men, which they say is of the more importance, on account of the intimate connection between Russia and Denmark, as the latter will be likely by this means to be drawn into the war with their numerous fleet of forty-five ships of the line." (L. John Adams to the Marquis de La Fayette, 18 February 1780: WJA, VII, p. 123)

(19)   See letter heads, WJA, VII, pp. 123-124.

(20)   "Whether it is that the art of political lying is better understood in England than in any other country, or whether it is more practised there than elsewhere, or whether it is accidental that they have more success in making their fictions gain credit in the world, I know not.

p. 398 (cont.)

But it is certain that every winter since the commencement of the present war with America, and indeed for some years before, they sent out large quantities of this manufacture over all Europe and throughout all America; and what is astonishing is, that they should still find numbers in every country ready to take them off their hands." (L. John Adams to M. Genet, 18 February 1780: WJA, VII, p. 124)

(21-22) "I am glad it is in my power generally to assure you that the many reports propagated by them [the British] and alluded to in your letter are not founded upon truth. New contracts with petty German princes have not, I believe, taken place; and if any such merchandise were sent to America, it would at most consist of a few recruits."
(L. Marquis de La Fayette to John Adams, 19 February 1780: WJA, VII, p. 125)

(23-24) "Mr. Burke's bill not being as yet public, we are not yet informed of the items of it. But as it already appears that it strikes at the department of secretary of state for America and at the board of trade, there seems to be little reason to doubt that it goes further, and strikes at the American board of commissioners, at all the American judges of admiralty, governors of provinces, secretaries, and custom-house officers of all denominations.

p. 398 (cont.)

". . . And from several late paragraphs in the papers, and from Mr. Fox's severe observations in the house of commons upon Governor Hutchinson, calling him in substance the 'firebrand that lighted up all the fire between the two countries,' it seems pretty clear that it is in contemplation to take away all these salaries and pensions." (L. John Adams to the President of Congress, 24 March 1780: WJA, VII, p. 136)

(25-28) "Do you think it worth while to work into your next article from London the following observations of Lord Bolingbroke?

"'The precise point at which the scales of power turn, like that of the solstice in either tropic, is imperceptible to common observation; and, in one case as in the other, some progress must be made in the new direction before the change is perceived. They who are in the sinking scale, for in the political balance of power, unlike to all others, the scale that is empty sinks, and that which is full rises; they who are in the sinking scale do not easily come off from the habitual prejudices of superior wealth, or power, or skill, or courage, nor from the confidence that these prejudices inspire.'" (L. John Adams to M. Genet, 29 April 1780: WJA, VII, pp. 155-156)

p. 398 (cont.)

(29-34) "The resolutions of congress for calling in and cancelling the two hundred millions of dollars emitted by them, have in general been well received. . . .

"Another benefit resulting from it is a supply of five millions of dollars of the new emission, every dollar of which is equal to forty dollars of the old emission. . . .

". . . The demands on the treasury are generally answered by warrants on the several States, which are careful, by some means or other, to discharge the drafts." (L. Elbridge Gerry to John Adams, 5 May 1780: <u>WJA</u>, VII, pp. 188-189)

(34-35) "According to the latter the assembly of Massachusetts has determined to adopt the resolution
p. 399   of congress, fixing the value of the paper money
(1-6)   at forty for one in specie. . . .

"But while I admit, sir, that that assembly could have recourse to the expedient above-mentioned, in order to lighten the load of its debt, I am far from agreeing that it is just and agreeable to the ordinary course of things to extend the effect to strangers as well as to citizens of the United States. . . .

"In order to make you sensible of this truth, I will not tell you, sir, that it is for the Americans alone to support the expense which may be caused by the defence of

p. 399 (cont.)

their liberty, and that they ought to consider the depreciation of their paper money purely as a tax which ought to be concentrated upon themselves, as the paper money was at first established only to relieve them from the necessity of paying one. I shall content myself to remark to you that the French, if they should be obliged to submit to the reduction proposed by congress, would find themselves victims of the zeal, and I may say of the rashness, with which they have exposed themselves in furnishing the Americans with arms, ammunition, and clothing; in a word, with all things of the first necessity, of which the Americans stood in the most urgent need. . . .

"These, sir, are the principal reflections occasioned by the resolution of congress of the 18th of March. . . .

"I shall not conceal from you that the Chevalier de la Luzerne has already received orders to make the strongest representations on the subject in question, and that the King is firmly persuaded that the United States will be eager to give to him on this occasion a mark of their attachment, by granting to his subjects the just satisfaction which they solicit, and which they expect from the wisdom and justice of the United States." (L. Count de Vergennes to John Adams, 21 June 1780: <u>WJA</u>, VII, pp. 190-192)

(7-10) "I thank your Excellency for the confidence which

p. 399 (cont.)

induced you to communicate this letter to me, and the continuance of which I shall ever study to deserve.

"When your Excellency says that his Majesty's minister at congress has already received orders to make representations against the resolutions of congress of the 18th of March, as far as they effect his subjects, I am at a loss to know with certainty whether your Excellency means only that such orders have lately passed and are sent off to go to America, or whether your Excellency means only that such orders were sent so long ago as to have reached the hand of the Chevalier de la Luzerne." (L. John Adams to Count de Vergennes, 22 June 1780: <u>WJA</u>, VII, p. 193)

(11-19) "It may not be amiss to state a few prices-current at Boston the last and the present year, in order to show the profits which have been made.

"Bohea tea, forty sous a pound at Lorient and Nantes, forty-five dollars. Salt, which costs very little in Europe, and used to be sold for a shilling a bushel, forty dollars a bushel, and in some of the other States two hundred dollars at times. . . .

"There are two other sources from which foreigners have made great profits,--the difference between bills of exchange and silver. During the whole of our history, when a man could readily get twenty-five paper dollars

p. 399 (cont.)

for one in silver, he could not get more than twelve paper dollars for one in a bill of exchange. Nearly this proportion was observed all along, as I have been informed. The agent of a foreign merchant had only to sell his goods for paper, or buy paper with silver at twenty-five for one, and immediately go and buy bills at twelve for one. So that he doubled his money in a moment.

"Another source was this,--the paper money was not alike depreciated in all places at the same time. It was forty for one at Philadelphia sometimes, when it was only twenty at Boston. The agent of a foreign merchant had only to sell his goods or send silver to Philadelphia and exchange it for paper, which he could lay out at Boston for twice what it cost him, and in this way again double his property. . . .

"Notwithstanding all, if any European merchant can show any good reason for excepting his particular case from the general rule, upon a representation of it to congress, I have no doubt they will do him justice." (L. John Adams to Count de Vergennes, 22 June 1780: <u>WJA</u>, VII, pp. 198-199; p. 201)

(20-23) "Mr. Mazzei called on me last evening to let me know he was this morning, at three, to set off on his journey to Italy. He desired me to write you that he has

p. 399 (cont.)

communicated to me the nature of his errand, but that his papers being lost, he waits for a commission and instructions from you; that being limited to five per cent., and more than that being given by the powers of Europe, and, indeed, having been offered by other States, and even by the ministers of congress, he has little hopes of succeeding at so low an interest; that he shall, however, endeavor to prepare the way in Italy for borrowing, and hopes to be useful to Virginia and the United States.

"I know nothing of this gentleman, but what I have learned of him here. His great affection for you, Mr. Wythe, Mr. Mason, and other choice spirits in Virginia, recommended him to me. I know not in what light he stands in your part; but here, as far as I have had opportunity to see and hear, he has been useful to us. He kept good company, and a good deal of it. He talks a great deal, and is a zealous defender of our affairs." (L. John Adams to Thomas Jefferson, 29 June 1780: WJA, VII, pp. 210-211)

(24-31) "His Majesty is by so much the more persuaded that congress will give their whole attention to this business [of results of depreciation of paper money], that that assembly, to judge by their reiterated assurances of the fact, value differently from yourself, sir, the union which subsists between France and the United States, and

p. 399 (cont.)

that they will assuredly feel that the French may deserve some preference over the other nations, who have no treaty with America, and who have not even as yet acknowledged her Independence. I have the honor to be &c.
DE VERGENNES." (L. Count de Vergennes to John Adams, 30 June 1780: <u>WJA</u>, VII, p. 213)

(32-33) "Our affairs wear their usual checkered aspect. Our governments are daily acquiring new strength. Our army, which I saw a few weeks ago at Morristown, has improved greatly in discipline since our former correspondence, in economy and healthiness." (L. Benjamin Rush to John Adams, 28 April 1780: <u>WJA</u>, VII, p. 214)

(34-35) "If a French fleet should constantly remain upon that coast, the number of these privateers would be doubled in a very few months. What havoc then must these armed vessels make, especially if a few French frigates should be also ordered to cruise for prizes among the provision vessels, merchant ships, and transports, passing and repassing to and from America and the West India Islands to Europe, and to and from America and the West Indies, and to and from Quebec, Nova Scotia, New York, Charleston, Savannah, and the Floridas. Such depredations have several times been made by our cruisers alone as to

p. 399 (cont.)
reduce the English at New York to very great distress; and it would be very easy in this way to reduce them to such misery as to oblige them to surrender at discretion." (L. John Adams to Count de Vergennes, 13 July 1780: WJA, VII, p. 224)

(36) "I should have been very happy if your Excellency had hinted at the reasons, which were then in
p. 400 your mind, because after reflecting upon this
(1-2) subject as maturely as I can, I am not able to collect any reasons, which appear to me sufficient for concealing the nature of my powers [to negotiate treaties of peace and commerce with England] in their full extent, from the Court of London. On the contrary, many arguments have occurred to me, which seem to show it to be both the policy of the United States, and my particular duty, to communicate them." (L. John Adams to Count de Vergennes, 17 July 1780: WJA, VII, p. 228) The reference to "February" is to when de Vergennes wrote John Adams (24 February 1780) asking him not to communicate to anyone his official powers to negotiate a treaty of commerce with the Court of London.

(3) "Three weeks ago I waited on the Count de Vergennes, at Versailles, to acquaint him that I had an

p. 400 (cont.)

intention of making a journey to Amsterdam for a few weeks, as I flattered myself I might form some acquaintances or correspondences there, and collect some intelligence, that might be useful to the United States." (L. John Adams to the President of Congress, 23 July 1780: WJA, VII, pp. 233-234)

(4)   "No facts are believed, but decisive military conquests; no arguments are seriously attended to in Europe, but force. It is to be hoped, our countrymen, instead of amusing themselves any longer with delusive dreams of peace, will bend the whole force of their minds to augment their navy, to find out their own strength and resources, and to depend upon themselves." (L. John Adams to Benjamin Franklin, 17 August 1780: WJA, VII, p. 248)

(5-6)   "The admirable models which have been transmitted through the world, and continued down to these days, so as to form an essential part of the education of mankind from generation to generation, by those two ancient towns, Athens and Rome, would be sufficient, without any other argument, to show the United States the importance to their liberty, prosperity, and glory, of an early attention to the subject of eloquence and language." (L. John Adams to the President of Congress, 5 September 1780: WJA, VII, p. 249)

p. 400 (cont.)

(7)   This Chinese ideogram means "a true definition." See Canto 63 (page 352, line 32); Canto 66 (page 382, line 31); and Canto 67 (page 387, lines 21-23).

(8-14)   "I consulted many; but the gentleman here intended was Mr. Bicker, a nephew of the two famous Bickers who defended Amsterdam more than a century before against a prince of Orange. . . . He advised me to inquire and consider what houses were too much connected with the British ministry. These must not be chosen. But he assured me I must ask other questions, such as,--what houses had other connections that would be equally likely to hinder or defeat the loan? He soon afterwards explained himself to mean, houses too much connected with the French ministry, and other houses whose solidity and credit were not sufficiently established; and he cautioned me, in confidence, particularly with regard to M. John de Neufville." (John Adams, Letters to the Boston Patriot, 1809: WJA, VII, p. 260n)

(15-19)   "When the loan is of three millions guilders, there is
The provision for negotiating the capital, . . .   2 per cent.
For the undertakers to furnish the capital, . .   2 per cent.
Brokerage, ... $\frac{1}{2}$ per cent.
Expenses of stamped paper for the bonds, print-
    ing, and proto collating the same, &c., . . $\frac{1}{2}$ per cent.
                                                     5 per cent.

p. 400 (cont.)

"And for the yearly paying off of 10 percent, as is stipulated, and which shall be prolonged or continued again for ten years,
For provision to the house of the loan, ... 1 per cent.
The undertakers, ... 1 per cent.
Brokerage, ... $\frac{1}{4}$ per cent.
$\overline{}$
$2\frac{1}{4}$ per cent.

"And in case there might be more negotiated than the prolongation of 10 per cent, then the expenses of that greater part are as above, 5 per cent." (L. M. Mylius to John Adams, 29 September 1780, explaining the terms of a loan to the United States: <u>WJA</u>, VII, p. 262)

(20-23) "'At dinner one day, with a large company, at the house of a great capitalist, I met the giant of the law in Amsterdam, Mr. Calkoen. . . . Interpreters were, therefore, necessary; but conversation that requires interpreters on both sides, is a very dull amusement. Though his questions were always ready, and my answers not less so, yet the interpretation was very slow and confused. After some time, one of the gentlemen asked me if I had any objection to answering Mr. Calkoen's questions in writing. I answered, none at all. It was soon agreed, that the questions and answers should be written. . . . This composition was read by him to a society of gentlemen of letters, about forty in number, who met at stated times in Amsterdam; and by that means, just sentiments of American affairs began to spread, and prevail over the continual misrepresentations of English and Stadtholderian gazettes, pamphlets, and

p. 400 (cont.)

newspapers.'" (John Adams's account of his writing of "Twenty-Six Letters upon Interesting Subjects respecting the Revolution of America': <u>WJA</u>, VII, headnote pp. 265-266)

(24-25) "That it would be unpleasant and burthensome to America to continue the war for eight or more years is certain. But will it not be unpleasant and burthensome to Great Britain too?" (Twenty-Six Letters: <u>WJA</u>, VII, p. 275)

(26-27) "I believe you will be pleased, when I tell you, that we are now come to the twenty-ninth, and last question, which is, 'What are the real damages sustained, or still to be suffered, by the loss of Charleston? And what influence has it had upon the minds of the people?' . . .

"The effect of the surrender of Charleston, and the defeat of Gates, has only been to awaken the people from their dreams of peace." (Twenty-Six Letters: <u>WJA</u>, VII, p. 312)

(28-32) "When England borrows, annually, a sum equal to all her exports, we ought not to be laughed at
p. 401   for wishing to borrow a sum, annually, equal to
(1)   a twelfth part of our annual exports. We may,

p. 401 (cont.)

and we shall, wade through, if we cannot obtain a loan; but we could certainly go forward with more ease, convenience, and safety by the help of one.

"I think we have not meanly solicited for friendship anywhere. But to send ministers to every great Court in Europe, especially the maritime courts, to propose an acknowledgement of the independence of America, and treaties of amity and of commerce, is no more than becomes us, and in my opinion is our duty to do." (L. John Adams to Benjamin Franklin, 14 October 1780: WJA, VII, pp. 316-317)

(2-7) "Ayant appris que le congrès vous a muni des memes pouvoirs qu'il avoit confié au Colonel Laurens dont la fâcheuse catastrophe me désole, et qu'entre autres votre mission a pour but une négociation pour l'Amérique Unie, jue prends la liberté de vous prier de m'en envoyer le plutôt possible les conditions; un parent m'ayant témoigné de l'inclination d'y placer 20,000 florins de Hollande.

". . . Le digne Tegelaar vous est connu, de même que mon intime Van der Kemp. Ce dernier peut à l'avenir être de grande utilité pour le congrès." (L. Baron Van Der Capellen to John Adams, 16 October 1780: WJA, VII, pp. 317-318) The French quoted by Pound, dont la fâcheuse catastrophe me désole . . . / un parent me témoigne de l'inclination d'y placer/ vingt mille florins d'Hollande/

p. 401 (cont.)

<u>Ven der Kemp peut être de grand utilité pour le Congrès</u>, means "whose regrettable catastrophe makes me most unhappy. . . / a relative indicates to me that he is inclined to invest/ twenty thousand Dutch florins in it/ Ven der Kemp can be very useful to the Congress." (<u>Index</u>, p. 53)

(8-16) "Understanding that in case of Mr. Laurens's absence you are charged with the affair of procuring a loan in Holland, I think it right to acquaint you, that by a letter from Mr. Jay of the 12th instant, from Madrid, we are informed that the King of Spain has been so good as to offer his guaranty for the payment of the interest and principal of a loan of money for the use of the United States. Mr. Grand thinks that no considerable use can be made here of that guaranty, on account of the considerable loan Mr. Necker is about to make; but that possibly it may have weight in Holland. . . .

"P. S. By a former letter from Mr. Jay, I find the sum to be one hundred and fifty thousand dollars, for which the King of Spain would be answerable, payable in the space of three years." (L. Benjamin Franklin to John Adams, 20 October 1780: <u>WJA</u>, VII, P. 318)

(17-18) "P. S. Si vous savez quelque chose de l'état de M. Laurens, depuis qu'il est enfermé a la Tour, je vous

p. 401 (cont.)

supplie de m'en faire part." (L. M. Dumas to John Adams, 1 November 1780: WJA, VII, p. 323) The French quoted by Pound, depuis qu'il . . . est enfermé a la Tour, means "since he . . . has been locked up in the Tower." (Index, p. 50)

(19) "A gentleman of great worth and skill advised me not to give more than four per cent interest. America is willing, however, to give a just interest, and all other reasonable terms, but she would not, like a young spendthrift heir, give any thing, to get money." (L. John Adams to M. Bicker, 6 November 1780: WJA, VII, p. 324)

(20-21) "I am very glad that you have had an interview with M. Bowens; but grieved that his broker Blomberg should be so ill that you find yourself constrained to have recourse to another. . . . Mortier and Meerkemaer are among the highest in repute, but they act under Messrs. Staphorst for Mr. A. G." (L. M. Bicker to John Adams, 7 November 1780: WJA, VII, p. 325)

(22-25) "The brokers Tenkate, when I was in business, had fee entry at my house. I think them capable; but I found them so liable to influence through their own interests, that I never could close with them. As to Mr. Van

p. 401 (cont.)

Vlooten, I think his residence is at Utrecht, and that he has fair opportunities of placing the money of citizens of that Province, who are not however capitalists to set agoing the negotiation in question." (L. M. Bicker to John Adams, 11 November 1780: <u>WJA</u>, VII, pp. 327-328)

(26-29) "I have left no measure unattempted that prudence could justify, but have neither procured any money, nor obtained the least hope of obtaining any. I have heretofore entertained hopes of obtaining something, but these hopes are all at an end." (L. John Adams to Commodore Gillon, 12 November 1780: <u>WJA</u>, VII, p. 328)

(30-34) "Whether Sir Joseph Yorke, after twenty years' residence in this republic, is ignorant of its constitution, or whether, knowing it, he treats it in this manner, on purpose the more palpably to insult it, I know not. The sovereignty resides in the states-general; but who are the states-general? Nor their High Mightinesses who assemble at the Hague to deliberate; these are only deputies of the states-general. The states-general are the regencies of the cities and the bodies of nobles in the several Provinces. The burgomasters of Amsterdam, therefore, who are called the regency, are one integral branch of the sovereignty of the seven United Provinces, and the most

p. 401 (cont.)

material branch of all, because the city of Amsterdam is one quarter of the whole republic, at least in taxes." (L. John Adams to the President of Congress, 16 November 1780: <u>WJA</u>, VII, p. 329)

(35) "And after my arrival here [in Holland], I had the opinion of persons who I had every reason to
p. 402 think knew best, that if proper powers should
(1-2) arrive from the thirteen United States, money might be had. But now all agree, that full powers have arrived, I do not find the same encouragement. This nation [the Dutch] has been so long in the habit of admiring the English, and disliking the French, so familiarized to call England the natural ally, and France the natural enemy of the republic, that it must be the work of time to eradicate these prejudices, although the circumstances are greatly altered. . . .

"The King of England demands a disavowal of the Amsterdam treaty, and the punishment of the regency. They will not be punished, nor their conduct disavowed. The King of England, therefore, must take such measures as he shall think his dignity and the essential interests of his people require. What these will be, time alone can discover. Many think he will declare war, but more are of a different opinion." (L. John Adams to the President of Congress,

p. 402 (cont.)

17 November 1780: <u>WJA</u>, VII, pp. 330-331)

(3-8)   "J'ai consulté sur cette affaire délicate mes meilleurs amis, et le résultat a été; qu'entamer ouvertement en mon nom une négociation en faveur des États Unis seroit donner de gaieté de coeur dans les embuches que mes ennemis ne cessent de dresser sous mes pas. Et sûrement, monsieur, la persécution entamée contre Monsieur Van Berckel et ses <u>complices</u>, c'est à dire contre tous ceux qui ont eu quelque correspondance avec les Américains, montre ce que j'aurois à attendre, si je me rendois coupable de ce que le roi d'Angleterre ne manqueroit pas de faire valoir comme un acte, par lequel j'aurois favorisé et soutenu la rebellion dans ses états. . . .

"Cependant, monsieur, je vous prie de ne pas trop presser votre départ. Les affaires de la république sont dans une violente crise. Le temps seul pourroit dans peu lever une grande partie des empechements susdits. . . .

"Quant à la conduite des Anglais, je crains que leur but (outre celui en général d'amuser la république par des négociations et des memoires de part et d'autre) ne soit de nous entrainer en <u>guerre</u> avant d'être admis à la neutralité armée, afin de donner occasion aux puissances conféderées de pouvoir nous refuser comme n'ayant pas la qualification requise, savoir, d'être une <u>puissance</u>

p. 402 (cont.)

<u>neutre</u>." (L. Van der Capellen to John Adams, 28 November 1780: <u>WJA</u>, VII, pp. 334-336) The French quoted by Pound, <u>la persecution contre M. Van Berckel/ et ses complices/ . . . de ne pas presser votre depart/ les affaires . . . crise . . . temps pourrait/ but des Anglais outre celui d'amuser la republique d'Holland</u>, means "the persecution against M. Van Berckel/ and his associates/ . . . not to rush your departure/ business . . . crisis . . . time could/ object of the English beyond that of amusing the Republic of Holland." (<u>Index</u>, p. 118)

(9-10) "Americans find here the politeness of the table, and a readiness to enter into their trade; but the public finds no disposition to afford any assistance, political or pecuniary. They impute this to a change in sentiments, to a loss of Charleston, the defeat of General Gates, to Arnold's desertion, to the inactivity of the French and Spaniards, &c. &c. &c. But I know better. It is not love of the English, although there is a great deal more of that than is deserved, but it is fear of the English and the Stadtholderian party. . . .

"The Dutch are now felicitating themselves upon the depth and the felicity of their politics. They have joined the neutrality, and have disavowed Amsterdam, and this has appeased the wrath of the English, the appearance of which, in Sir Joseph Yorke's Memorial, terrified them more than I ever saw any part of America intimidated in the worst crisis of her affairs." (L. John Adams to the President of Congress, 14 December 1780: WJA, VII, p. 342)

(11-15) "Tout crédit, soit d'un peuple, soit d'un particulier, dépend uniquement de deux choses, savoir, de l'opinion que l'on a de la bonne foi de l'emprunteur, et de la possibilité ou il se trouve de faire face à ses engagemens." (L. Baron Van der Capellen to John Adams, 24 December 1780: WJA, VII, p. 344) The French quoted by Pound, tout credit soit d'un peuple soit d'un particulier/ . . . de deux choses/ l'opinion de la bonne foi/ et de la possibilite/ ou il se trouve de faire face, means "all credit whether of a people or an individual/ . . . of two things/ the opinion as to the good faith/ and as to the chances/ of his meeting." (Index, p. 226)

(16-19) "Affairs are still in suspense. This day being Christmas, and yesterday Sunday, there was no public exchange held on either. But business, and especially stockjobbing, goes on without ceasing, being done at the coffee-houses on Sundays and holydays, when it cannot be held upon 'change." (L. John Adams to the President of Congress, 25 December 1780: WJA, VII, p. 346)

p. 402 (cont.)

(20-22) "There is nothing so instructive to aristocracy and democracy as the history of Holland, unless we except that of France for the last five-and-twenty years; nothing which ought so forcibly to admonish them to shake hands and mutually agree to choose an arbitrator between."
(John Adams, Letters to the Boston Patriot, 1809: WJA, VII, p. 348n)

CANTO LXIX

p. 403

(1-4)   "In this possible case [that Holland aligns itself with France, Spain, and America], a minister here from congress would be useful. In case the armed neutrality take it up, a minister authorized to represent the United States to all the neutral courts, might be of use." (L. John Adams, in Amsterdam, to the President of Congress, 31 December 1780: WJA, VII, p. 348)

(5-7)   "You will receive herewith inclosed a commission as minister plenipotentiary to the United Provinces of the low countries, with instructions for your government on that important mission, as also a plan of a treaty with those States, and likewise a resolve of congress relative to the declaration of the Empress of Russia, respecting the protection of neutral ships, &c." (L. Samuel Huntington, President of Congress, to John Adams, 1 January 1781: WJA, VII, p. 349)

(8-11) "As to a secret address, you may address under cover, à Madame la veuve de M. Henry Schorn, op de Agterburg wal, by de Hoogstraat, Amsterdam." (L. John Adams to Francis Dana, 18 January 1781: WJA, VII, p. 353) The

p. 403 (cont.)

French à Madame la veuve de M. Henry Schorn means "to Madame, the widow of M. Henry Schorn." The Dutch op de Agsterburg wal by de Hoogstraat means "up near the Agsterburg wall in the Hoogstraat." (Index, p. 7)

(12-29) "The depreciation of the money has been a real advantage, because it is a tax upon the people, paid as it advances, and therefore, prevents the public from being found in debt. It is true it is an unequal tax, and therefore causes what your friend, G. Livingston, justly calls perplexity, but by no means disables or weakens the people from carrying on the war. The body of the people lose nothing by it. The merchant, the farmer, the tradesman, the laborer loses nothing by it. They are the moneyed men, the capitalists, those who have money at interest and live upon fixed salaries,--that is, the officers of government,--who lose by it, and who have borne this tax. This you see is an ease and relief to the people at large. The consequence of this depreciation has been, that while England has increased her national debt sixty millions by this war, ours is not a tenth part of it, not six millions. Who then can hold out longest?

"This depreciation has no tendency to make the people submit to Great Britain, because that submission would not relieve, but increase the perplexity; for submission would

p. 403 (cont.)

not procure us peace. . . .

"As to the ability of America to pay. It depends upon a few words. America has between three and four millions of people. England and Scotland have between five and six. The lands in America produce as much as any other lands. The exports of America in 1774 were twelve millions, including too a great part of the commodities of the growth of America. England is two hundred millions in debt. America is six millions. England has spent sixty millions in this war. America six. Which people then are the ablest to pay? Yet England has credit, America not. Is this from reasoning or prejudice?" (L. John Adams to Baron Van Der Capellen, 21 January 1781: <u>WJA</u>, VII, pp. 357-359)

(30) "When will mankind cease to be the dupes of the insidious artifices of a British minister and stockjobber? Peace is a tub easily thrown out for the amusement of the whale, while the minister opens his budget, concerts his taxes, and contracts for his loan, and it never fails to be taken for a fish." (L. John Adams to M. Dumas, 17 March 1781: <u>WJA</u>, VII, p. 379)

(31-32) "I lived in daily and hourly hopes and expectations of an answer to some of my letters and communications,

p. 403 (cont.)

or of an invitation to some personal conference, in which I might be favored with some intimations of his Excellency's [Count de Vergennes's] sentiments of approbation or disapprobation, or his advice, criticims, or corrections of any thing he might think required any alteration. But nothing appeared. All was total silence and impenetrable mystery. Such a dead reserve, such a fixed determination not to commit himself to any thing, not even to an acknowledgement of the obligations of his own treaty with the United States, appeared to me to be poor encouragement to us to be over-communicative with the French ministry." (John Adams, Letters to the Boston Patriot, 1809: WJA, VII, p. 450n) This comment refers to communications from John Adams concerning the proposed congress at Vienna.

p. 404

(1)   "The answer to the articles relative to America, proposed by the two Imperial Courts, and the letters to the Count de Vergennes, I have the satisfaction to believe, defeated the profound and magnificent project of a congress at Vienna, for the purpose of chicaning the United States out of their independence." (John Adams, Letters to the Boston Patriot, 1809: WJA, VII, p. 452n)

(2-3)   "I have only time by Major Jackson, to inform

p. 404 (cont.)

congress, that upon information from the Count de Vergennes, that questions concerning peace, under the mediation of the two Imperial Courts, were in agitation, that required my presence here, I undertook the journey, and arrived here [in Paris from Amsterdam] last Friday night, the 6th of the month, and have twice waited on the Count de Vergennes at Versailles, who this day communicated to me the inclosed propositions.

"These propositions are made to all the belligerent powers, by the Courts of Petersburg and Vienna, in consequence of some wild propositions made to them by the Court of London, 'that they would undertake the office of mediators, upon condition that the league, as they call it, between France and their rebel subjects in America should be dissolved, and these left to make their terms with Great Britain, after having returned to their allegiance and obedience.'" (L. John Adams to the President of Congress, 11 July 1781: <u>WJA</u>, VII, pp. 433-434) References to the proposed congress at Vienna occur frequently in the correspondence found in <u>WJA</u>, VII, pp. 426-461.

(4-6) "La Cour de Londres, qui éludera autant, et aussi long-temps, qu'elle le pourra, l'aveu direct et indirect de l'indépendance des États Unis, s'autorisera des termes généraux dont on se sert en parlant d'eux, pour

p. 404 (cont.)

soutenir qu'elle ne s'est point obligée de traiter avec ses anciennes colonies comme avec une nation libre et indépendante, qu'elle n'est par conséquent point dans le cas d'admettre un plénipotentiaire de leur part, qu'elle est la maîtresse de ne voir dans leur réprésentant que le député d'une portion de ses sujets qui lui demandent grâce; d'ou il résulteroit, lorsque la médiation serait en activité, et qu'il serait question d'entamer les négociations, que l'on commencerait à contester sur le caractère que pourra déployer le plénipotentiaire Américain; que le Roi d'Angleterre ne voudra le regarder que comme son sujet, tandis que le congrès demandera qu'il soit admis comme représentant un peuple libre, au moyen de quoi la médiation se trouvera arrêtée dès le premier pas." (from the Answer of the Court of France to the Courts of Petersburg and of Vienna, concerning the proposed congress at Vienna: WJA, VII, p. 667)

See the following translation: "The Court of London, who will elude as much and as long as she can, any direct and indirect avowal of the independence of the United States, will take advantage of the general terms we employ in speaking of them, to maintain that she is not obliged to treat with her ancient Colonies, as with a free and independent nation; that she is not, consequently, in a situation to admit a plenipotentiary on their part; that

p. 404 (cont.)

she is the mistress, to see nothing in their representative but the deputy of a portion of her subjects, who appear to sue for pardon; from which it would result, when the mediation should be in activity, and the question should be to open and commence the negotiations, that they would begin to contest concerning the character which the American plenipotentiary may display; that the King of England will not regard him, but as his subject, while the congress shall demand that he be admitted as the representative of a free people; by which means the mediation will find itself arrested in its first step." (John Adams's translation of the above passage from the Answer of the French Court: WJA, VII, p. 671)

(7-8) "Cornwallis's fate, however, has somewhat emboldened them [the people of Holland], and I have received unexpected visits of congratulations from several persons of note; and there are appearances of a growing interest in favor of an alliance with France and America." (L. John Adams to the President of Congress, 4 December 1781: WJA, VII, p. 488)

(9) "Our country, by all accounts, is in great spirits. Paper money quite stopped; every thing conducted in silver. Trade flourishing, although many privateers

p. 404 (cont.)

and merchant vessels are taken. Crops the finest ever known." (L. John Adams to Francis Dana, 14 December 1781: <u>WJA</u>, VII, p. 495)

(10-11) "Votre Excellence saura de Monsieur de Neufville que j'ai l'intention de placer encore douze mille florins dans les fonds de l'Amérique. . . . J'ai honte d'être Hollandois, et je suis faché de le peine que j'ai si souvent prise, même avec cette chaleur qui fut l'effet de mon attachement pour les deux peuples, afin de prévenir que votre Excellence ne se formât une idée, que je croyois alors trop désavantageuse, du caractère de la nation." (L. Baron Van Der Capellen to John Adams, 6 January 1782: <u>WJA</u>, VII, p. 501) The French quoted by Pound, <u>J'ai honte d'etre Hollandais</u>, means "I am ashamed of being Dutch." (<u>Index</u>, p. 103)

(12) "I went next, at the hour agreed on, to the house of Haerlem, where I was received by the whole deputation, consisting of two burgomasters, two schepens, and a pensionary." (L. John Adams to the President of Congress, 14 January 1782: <u>WJA</u>, VII, p. 505)

(13-17) "I have been uniformly told that these four or five persons had such a despotic influence over loans; I

p. 404 (cont.)

have heretofore sounded them in various ways, and the result is, that I firmly believe they receive ample salaries, upon the express condition that they resist an American loan. There is a phalanx formed by British ministry, Dutch Court, proprietors of English stocks, and great mercantile houses in the interest of the British ministry, that support these undertakers and are supported by them." (L. John Adams to Benjamin Franklin, 25 January 1782: WJA, VII, p. 509)

(18-21) "The promise, which was made me by M. Bergsma, that I should have an answer from the Province of Friesland in three weeks, has been literally fulfilled. This gentleman, who, as well as his Province, deserves to be remembered in America, sent me a copy of the resolution in Dutch as soon as it passed. It is now public in all the gazettes, and is conceived in these terms.

"'The requisition of Mr. Adams, for presenting his letters of credence from the United States of North America to their High Mightinesses, having been brought into the assembly and put into deliberation, as also the ulterior address to the same purpose, with a demand of a categorical answer, made by him, as is more amply mentioned in the minutes of their High Mightinesses of the 4th of May, 1781, and the 9th of January, 1782; whereupon, it having been taken into consideration, that the said Mr. Adams would

p. 404 (cont.)

probably have some propositions to make to their High Mightinesses, and to present to them the principal articles and foundations upon which the congress, on their part, would enter into a treaty of commerce and friendship, or other affairs to propose, in regard to which despatch would be requisite;

"'It has been thought fit and resolved, to authorize the gentlemen, the deputies of this Province at the generality, and to instruct them, to direct things at the table of their High Mightinesses in such a manner, that the said Mr. Adams be admitted forthwith as minister of the congress of North America, with further order to the said deputies, that if there should be made, moreover, any similar propositions by the same, to inform immediately their Noble Mightinesses of them. . . .

"'Thus resolved at the Province House, the 26th of February, 1782.'" (L. John Adams to Secretary Livingston, 11 March 1782: WJA, VII, pp. 537-538)

(22)   "In answer to your inquiries, sir, I have only to say, that, at present, I have no powers from the United States of America to treat with the Hanseatic cities; but their situation is such, that there will be infallibly a considerable trade between them and America; and, therefore, I know of no objection against the congress entering into

p. 404 (cont.)

negotiations with them." (L. John Adams to J. U. Pauli, 11 April 1782: WJA, VII, p. 568)

(23-29) "I found the old gentleman [Henry Laurens, on parole from London, for his health, in Haerlem] perfectly sound in his system of politics. He has a very poor opinion both of the integrity and abilities of the new ministry, as well as the old. He thinks they know not what they are about; that they are spoiled by the same insincerity, duplicity, falsehood, and corruption with the former. Lord Shelburne still flatters the King with ideas of conciliation and a separate peace, &c,; yet the nation and the best men in it are for a universal peace and an express acknowledgment of American independence, and many of the best are for giving up Canada and Nova Scotia. . . .

"These are all but artifices to raise the stocks; and, if you think of any method to put a stop to them, I will cheerfully concur with you." (L. John Adams to Benjamin Franklin, 16 April 1782: WJA, VII, pp. 570-571)

(30-32) "Mr. Adams proposes,--
"1. If the houses of Fizeaux, Grand & Co., John Hodshon & Son, Messrs. Crommelins, Messrs. Van Staphorst, Messrs. De la Lande and Fynje, and Mr. John de Neufville & Son, will all join together in an American loan, Mr.

p. 404 (cont.)

Adams will open it, without demanding any stipulation for any certain sum.

"2. If the first proposition is not agreed to, Mr. Adams will open a loan with as many of those houses as will agree together, and enter into a stipulation with him to furnish the sum of five millions by the month of August." (John Adams's proposals for opening a loan in Holland, 30 April 1782: <u>WJA</u>, VII, p. 575)

(33-35) "Le Corps des négociants de cette ville souhaitant joindre leurs acclamations a ceux de toute la nation, au sujet de l'indépendance des États Unis de l'Amérique septentrionale publiquement reconnue par nos augustes souverains, m'a chargé de m'informer auprès de votre excellence, du jour, de l'heure, et du lieu, qu'il lui conviendra d'accorder audience à six députés du dit corps de nos négociants, chargés d'exprimer en leur nom, les vifs sentimens de joie et de satisfaction sincere, qu'ils ressentent de cet heureux événement, comme aussi de l'avantage de pouvoir vous présenter leurs respects en qualité de ministre des dits États." (L. Jocob Nolet to John Adams, 19 April 1782: <u>WJA</u>, VII, pp. 576-577) The French quoted by Pound, <u>Le corps des négociants de cette ville/ souhaitant joindre leurs acclamations a ceux de toute la nation</u>, means "the businessmen of this city/ wishing to

p. 404 (cont.)

add their acclamations to those of the whole nation." (<u>Index</u>, p. 120)

p. 405

(1-4)   "On m'a dit que ces Messieurs de Schiedam donneront un repas de cent couverts, et qu'il y aura beaucoup de personnes de Rotterdam." (L. M. Dumas to John Adams, 30 April 1782: <u>WJA</u>, VII, p. 576) The French used by Pound, <u>On</u> <u>m'a</u> <u>dit</u> <u>que</u> <u>ces</u> <u>Messieurs</u> <u>de</u> <u>Schiedam</u>/ <u>donnent</u> <u>ce</u> <u>repas</u> <u>de</u> <u>cent</u> <u>couverts</u>/ <u>et</u> <u>qu'il</u> <u>y</u> <u>aura</u> <u>beaucoup</u> <u>de</u> <u>personnes</u> <u>de</u> <u>Rotterdam</u>, means "I have been told that these gentlemen of Schiedam/ are giving this repast for a hundred people/ and that there will be many people from Rotterdam. (<u>Index</u>, p. 120)

(5-6)   "The affair of a loan gives me much anxiety and fatigue. It is true, I may open a loan for five millions, but I confess I have no hopes of obtaining so much. The money is not to be had. Cash is not infinite in this country." (L. John Adams to Benjamin Franklin, 2 May 1781 [John Adams, or perhaps the printer of the Charles Francis Adams edition of <u>WJA</u>, appears to have misdated this letter <u>1781</u> instead of <u>1782</u>]: <u>WJA</u>, VII, p. 580)

(7-11)   "We, therefore, to convince you of our

p. 405 (cont.)

inclination in this respect, do, without any hesitation, accept of the terms you proposed, of $4\frac{1}{4}$ per cent. for the remedium and other charges. . . .

"We have the honor to be, &c. WILHELM and JAN WILLINK, NIC. and JACOB VAN STAPHORST, DE LA LANDE AND FYNJE." (L. W. and J. Willink, Nic. and Jac. Van Staphorst, and De La Lande and Fynje to John Adams, 11 May 1782: <u>WJA</u>, VII, p. 583)

(12) "Once in my life the words <u>piddling</u>, &c., cost me very dear; but I shall never get them out of my head. I shall be plagued with piddling politicians as long as I live; at least, until I retire from the political career to the blue hills." (L. John Adams to Francis Dana, 13 May 1782: <u>WJA</u>, VII, p. 584)

(13-14) "As to the other point, if you will open the loan for three millions only at first, it would be, perhaps, better; but whether you open it for three or five, no other loan in behalf of the United States shall be opened by me, without your consent, or, at least, without the consent of two of the three houses, until it is full, except in one case, which is, that the loan in your hands should linger a long time without filling up, and I should obtain the warranty of the states-general, or of the states of Holland,

p. 405 (cont.)

or of the regency of Amsterdam, for opening a new loan, in which case I should submit the choice of a house to their High Mightinesses, to their Noble and Grand Mightinesses, or to the venerable magistrates of the city and; in either of these cases, your three houses will stand as fair to be employed, as any other. . . .

"You will please to inform Mr. Van Vlooten, that I have agreed with you, and that I shall be very glad if he will, forthwith, engage in the business with you, upon such terms as you and he shall agree on." (L. John Adams to Messrs. W. and J. Willink, N. and J. Van Staphorst, and De La Lande and Fynje, 13 May 1782: WJA, VII, p. 585)

(15-17) "Your Excellency shall authorize us to negotiate a sum of five millions of guilders, though we shall now only open a loan for three millions at the rate of five per cent. per annum for the time of ten years, and to be redeemed in the five following years, each year a fifth part, for which three thousand bonds of 1000 f. each shall be given, signed by your Excellency, and countersigned by us, as also paragraphed by a notary; and the coupons for the annual interest signed by your secretary, or anybody whom you will appoint for it." (L. Messrs. Willink and Others to John Adams, 16 May 1782: WJA, VII, p. 586)

(18-19) "The minister of the Emperor [Frederick II, the Great, of Prussia] is ninety years of age, and never appears at court, or anywhere else. I have never seen him or his secretary." (L. John Adams to Secretary

p. 405 (cont.)

Livingston, 4 September 1782: WJA, VII, p. 623)

(20-21) "Mr. Oswald [representing England] received yesterday a commission to treat of peace with the commissioners of the United States of America." (L. John Jay to John Adams, 28 September 1782: WJA, VII, p. 641)

(22) "I have the honor to inclose, for the information of congress, a copy of Mr. Fitzherbert's commission. The words quorumcunque statuum quorum interesse poterit include the United States, according to them, but not according to the King who uses them; so that there is still room to evade. How much nobler and more politic was Mr. Fox's idea, to insert the 'Ministers of the United States of America' expressly!" (L. John Adams to Secretary Livingston, 18 August 1782: WJA, VII, p. 613) The Latin statuum quorum means "of the condition of which." (Index, p. 206)

(23-25) "Amidst the innumerable crowd of loans which are open in this country, many of which have little success, I was much afraid that ours would have failed. I have, however, the pleasure to inform you, that I am at least one million and a half in cash,--about three millions of livres,--which will be a considerable aid to the operations of our financier at Philadelphia; and I hope your court,

p. 405 (cont.)

with their usual goodness, will make up the rest that may be wanting." (L. John Adams to Marquis de La Fayette, 29 September 1782: <u>WJA</u>, VII, p. 642)

(26-27) "On Friday last I was notified, by the messenger of their High Mightinesses, that the treaties would be ready for signature on Monday, this day. I am, accordingly, at noon, to go to the assembly, and finish the business." (L. John Adams to John Jay, 7 October 1782: <u>WJA</u>, VII, pp. 645-646)

(28-30) "Now, in order to induce Russia to grant this most advantageous privilege to France, France alleges that it will be for the interest of Russia to do it, because France will have a demand for greater quantities of the commodities of Russia, which she will, nevertheless, not be under a necessity of purchasing of Russia, <u>after the war</u>; for these reasons, that she can then obtain the same from America, and although, perhaps not at so cheap a rate, yet it will be for her interest, <u>if Russia shall refuse to grant this privilege</u>, to pay America from 15 to 20 percent. more for the same articles, as, by taking those articles from America, France would enable her to take off a greater quantity of the commodities of France, and the more easily to discharge the debts she may contract for them in France."

p. 405 (cont.)

(L. Francis Dana to John Adams, 15 October 1782: WJA, VII, p. 650)

(31-32) "There are great complaints of scarcity of money here [in Paris], and what there is is shut up. The King's loans do not fill. The war has lasted so long, and money has been scattered with so much profusion, that it is now very scarce in France, Spain, and England, as well as Holland." (L. John Adams to Robert Morris, 7 November 1782: WJA, VII, p. 664)

(33-34) "If Mr. Jay and I had yielded the punctilio of rank, and taken the advice of the Count de Vergennes and Dr. Franklin, by treating with the English or Spaniards, before we were put upon the equal footing that our rank demanded, we should have sunk in the minds of the English, French, Spaniards, Dutch, and all the neutral powers. The Count de Vergennes certainly knows this; if he does not, he is not even a European statesman; if he does know it, what inference can we draw, but that he means to keep us down if he can; to keep his hand under our chin to prevent us from drowning, but not to lift our heads out of the water?" (L. John Adams to Secretary Livingston, 8 November 1782: WJA, VIII, p. 4)

p. 406

(1-2)   "If there are in congress any of those gentlemen, with whom I had the honor to serve in the years 1775 and 1776, they may possibly remember, that in arguing in favor of sending ministers to Versailles, to propose a connection with that Court, I laid it down as a first principle, that we should calculate all our measures and foreign negotiations in such a manner, as to avoid a too great dependence upon any one power of Europe--to avoid all obligations and temptations to take any part in future European wars; that the business of America with Europe was commerce, not politics or war; and, above all, that it never could be our interest to ruin Great Britain, or injure or weaken her any further than should be necessary to support our independence, and our alliances, and that, as soon as Great Britain should be brought to a temper to acknowledge our sovereignty and our alliances, and consent that we should maintain the one, and fulfil the others, it would be our interest and duty to be her friends, as well as the friends of all the other powers of Europe, and enemies to none." (L. John Adams to Secretary Livingston, 5 February 1783: <u>WJA</u>, VIII, pp. 35-36)

(3-10)   "Nous sommes en attendant charmés de voir, que les États des autres provinces, et consequemment la république entière, ont, à l'exemple des États de Frise, reconnu la liberté et l'indépendance de l'Amérique;

p. 406 (cont.)

reconnoissance, qui, jointe aux bons offices que votre Excellence a employé, a déjà eu cette heureuse suite, qu'il a été conclu entre les deux états un traité d'amitié et de commerce, et qu'on a établi par là même, une base de bien-être et de prospérité réciproques. . . .

"LES MEMBRES DE LA SOCIÉTÉ BOURGEOISE "établie à Leeuwarde sous la devise, 'Par liberté et par zèle.' Et pour tous, W. WOPKENS. V. CATS." (L. the Society of Leeuwarden to John Adams, 29 April 1783: WJA, VIII, p. 56) The French quoted by Pound, Nous sommes en attendant charmés de voir/ que les états des autres provinces et conséquemment la/ république entière ont, à l'exemple des États de Frise/ reconnu . . ./ (signed) Les membres de la Société Bourgeoise, means "Meanwhile we are delighted to see/ that the states of the other provinces and consequently the/ entire republic have, following the example of the States of Friesland/ recognized . . ./ (signed) the members of the Société Bourgeoise." (Index, p. 157)

(11-12) A picture of the medal on which this inscription may be read is placed at the front of WJA, VIII. The Latin S.P.Q. Amst. faustissimo foedere juncta means "Senate and People of Amsterdam--in very fortunate union joined." (Index, p. 204)

p. 406 (cont.)

(13-15) "As to the loan in Holland, I have never troubled you nor any one else in America with details of the vexations of various kinds which I met with in the negotiation of it; indeed, I never thought it prudent or safe to do it. If I had told the whole truth, it could have done no good, and it might have done infinite mischief. In general, it is now sufficient to say, that private interest, party spirit, factions, cabals, and slanders have obstructed, perplexed, and tortured our loan in Holland, as well as all our other affairs, foreign and domestic. . . .

"A great many things are said to me, on purpose that they may be represented to you or to congress. Some of these I believe to be false, more of them I suspect, and some that are true would do no good. I think it necessary, therefore, to employ a little discretion in such cases." (L. John Adams to Robert Morris, 21 May 1783: WJA, VIII, p. 59)

(16-18) "I consulted his Lordship [Marquis of Carmarthen] about the etiquette of my letter of credence, and he gave me the same answers as the Comte de Vergennes gave you. His Lordship then said, that on Wednesday next, after the levee, I should be presented to his Majesty [King George III of England], in his closet, and there deliver my letter of

p. 406 (cont.)

credence; and that, on the next levee-day, Colonel Smith would be presented." (L. John Adams to Thomas Jefferson, 27 May 1785: <u>WJA</u>, VIII, pp. 251-252)

(18-20) "Can it be a secret understanding between St. James's and Versailles? The design of ruining, if they can, our carrying trade, and annihilating all our navigation and seamen, is too apparent." (L. John Adams to Thomas Jefferson, 18 July 1785: <u>WJA</u>, VIII, p. 279) At the top of this page is the following note by the editor: (<u>The rest in Cipher, and kept secret</u>.)

(21-23) "The provisions of the act of navigation, 12 Car. II. c. 18, would not be sufficient for our purpose. If the United States should agree in a law, that no goods should be suffered to be imported into the United States in any other than American bottoms (navigated by an American master, and three fourths of the seamen American), or in the ships of that European nation of which the merchandise imported was the genuine growth or manufacture, this would not accomplish our wish, because British and Irish ships would desire no other than to import into our States the manufactures of the British empire, and to export our produce in the same bottoms." (L. John Adams to John Jay, 8 August 1785: <u>WJA</u>, VIII, p. 297)

p. 406 (cont.)

(24-25) "We have hitherto been the bubbles of our own philosophical and equitable liberality; and, instead of meeting correspondent sentiments, both France and England have shown a constant disposition to take a selfish and partial advantage of us because of them, nay, to turn them to the diminution or destruction of our own means of trade and strength. I hope we shall be the dupes no longer than we must." (L. John Adams to John Jay, 10 August 1785: <u>WJA</u>, VIII, p. 299)

(26) "He [the emissary carrying the Barbary treaties] should be instructed further, to make diligent inquiry concerning the productions of those countries which would answer in America, and those of the United States which might find a market in Barbary, and to transmit all such information to congress as well as to us." (L. John Adams to Thomas Jefferson, 18 August 1785: <u>WJA</u>, VIII, p. 301)

(27-28) "Last night I received your favor of the 17th. If both governments [French and British] are possessed of the contents of my letter of the 7th, by opening it in the post-office, much good may those contents do them. They both know they have deserved them. I hope they will convince them of their error, and induce them to adopt more liberal principles towards us." (L. John Adams to

p. 406 (cont.)

Thomas Jefferson, 23 August 1785: <u>WJA</u>, VIII, p. 301)

(29-34) "I thought it was best there should be an explanation; for I was persuaded that an American jury would never give any interest for the time which ran during the war. Mr. Pitt said, that would surprise the people here [in England]; for that wars never interrupted the interest nor principal of debts, and that he did not see a difference between this war and any other, and the lawyers here made none. I begged his pardon here, and said, that the American lawyers made a wide difference; they contended that the late war was a total dissolution of all laws and government, and, consequently, of all contracts made under those laws; and that it was a maxim of law, that a personal right or obligation, once dissolved or suspended, was lost forever; that the intervention of the treaty and the new laws was necessary for the revival of those ancient rights and obligations; that these rights were in a state of non-existence during the war, and no interest during that period could grow out of them. . . .

". . . The fat of the spermaceti whale gives the clearest and most beautiful flame of any substance that is known in nature, and we are all surprised that you prefer darkness, and consequent robberies, burglaries, and murders in your streets, to the receiving, as a remittance, our

p. 406 (cont.)

spermaceti oil. The lamps around Grosvenor Square, I know, and in Downing Street, too, I suppose, are dim by midnight, and extinguished by two o'clock; whereas our oil would burn bright till nine o'clock in the morning, and chase away, before the watchmen, all the villains, and save you the trouble and danger of introducing a new police into the city." (L. John Adams to John Jay, 25 August 1785: <u>WJA</u>, VIII, p. 304; pp. 308-309)

p. 407

(1-7)   "This treaty, which the Irish call the Methuen treaty, from the name of the ambassador who signed it, and which they now claim the benefit of as Britons, although the Portuguese deny them to be Britons, and accordingly refuse their woollens, has had a vast effect both in Portugal and England. The consequence has been, that Portugal has now, for more than four-score years, clothed herself in British woollens, like an English colony, and has never been able to introduce woollen manufactures at home; and the British islands have drank no other wine than Port, Lisbon, and Madeira, although the wines of France are so much better." (L. John Adams to John Jay, 17 October 1785: <u>WJA</u>, VIII, p. 324)

(8)   "After the communication of those papers, I had

p. 407 (cont.)

the honor to observe to his Lordship, that, although they contained matters of some importance, I most sincerely wished there were nothing of greater difficulty and more danger between the two countries. His Lordship [Lord Carmarthen] wished so too." (L. John Adams to John Jay, 21 October 1785: <u>WJA</u>, VIII, p. 325)

(9) "Inclosed is a copy of the translation, from the Dutch into the English, of the contract entered into by me, in behalf of the United States, by virtue of their full power, for a million of guilders. This measure became absolutely necessary to prevent the total ruin of their credit, and the greatest injustice to their former creditors, who are possessed of their obligations: for the failure in payment of the interest, but for one day, would, in Holland, cause those obligations to depreciate in their value like paper money." (L. John Adams to John Jay, 16 June 1787: <u>WJA</u>, VIII, p. 441)

(10-13) "The affairs of this country, considered in a constitutional light, are mending fast. The minds of the nation have made a great progress. Opposition is not, of course, free from party spirit. Many things are done or said, which are not much to the purpose; but while desultory expeditions are rambling about, the main body moves slowly

p. 407 (cont.)

on the right road. This country will, within twelve or fifteen years, come to a pretty good constitution, the best perhaps that can be framed, but one. May <u>that</u> <u>one</u>, the only one truly consistent with the dignity of man, be forever the happy lot of the sons of America!" (L. Marquis De La Fayette, in Paris, to John Adams, 12 October 1787: <u>WJA</u>, VIII, p. 456)

(14-15) "You are afraid of the one, I, of the few. We agree perfectly that the many should have a full, fair, and perfect representation. You are apprehensive of monarchy, I, of aristocracy." (L. John Adams to Thomas Jefferson, 6 December 1787: <u>WJA</u>, VIII, p. 464)

(16-17) See the comment for page 408, lines 1-11, below.

(18-34) I have been unable to identify an exact source for these lines. The Latin <u>in</u> <u>margine</u> of line 18 means "in the margin" (<u>Index</u>, p. 99), and may suggest that there is no exact source in the <u>WJA</u>. Perhaps these lines express Pound's "editorial" judgment of Alexander Hamilton and his followers for their active antipathy toward John Adams as the leader of the Federalist party. John Adams published in the Boston Patriot in 1809 correspondence providing a detailed account of the relationship with Hamilton as he,

p. 407 (cont.)

Adams, saw it, and most of the names Pound mentions appear there at one time or another. This correspondence may be found in WJA, IX, pp. 239-310.

The Italian lines 25, 29, and 34 are all taken from Dante's Inferno: natural burella means "natural dungeon" (Index, p. 152); per l'argine sinistra dienno volta means "would turn to the left side" (Index, p. 170); quindi Cocito, Cassio membruto means "then Cocytus, Cassio with powerful limbs" (Index, p. 181)

p. 408

(1-11) The episode referred to here is introduced in lines 16-17 of page 407. I have been unable to locate the source of these lines in the WJA. An account of this episode of Mr. Madison's proposal, which grew out of Alexander Hamilton's plan to fund all foreign and domestic debts and was presented as an amendment to the Hamilton plan, can be found in the biography of John Adams by Page Smith, John Adams, II (Garden City, N. Y., 1963), pp. 787-788; p. 791.

CANTO LXX

p. 409

(1-4)   "For myself, I find the office I hold [of Vice-President], though laborious, so wholly insignificant, and, from the blind policy of that part of the world from whence I came, so stupidly pinched and betrayed, that I wish myself again at the bar, old as I am. My own situation is almost the only one in the world, in which firmness and patience are useless." (L. John Adams to John Trumbull, 23 January 1791: WJA, IX, p. 573)

(5)   I have been unable to locate in the sources a passage with these exact words. The following passage does refer to the same problem mentioned in the Poundian line:

"The President of the United States requests the Secretary of State to take into his consideration the following questions, and make report of his opinion in writing, viz.:

"1. Whether the refusal to receive Mr. Pinckney, and the rude orders to quit Paris and the territory of the republic, with such circumstances of indignity, insult, and hostility, as we have been informed of, are bars to all further measures of negotiation. Or, in other words, will a fresh mission to Paris be too great a humiliation of the American people in their own sense and that of the world?"

429

p. 409 (cont.)

(L. John Adams to the Heads of Department, 14 April 1797: WJA, VIII, p. 540)

(6) "General Forrest had communicated to Mr. Adams, from memory, having heard it read, the substance of one of the many letters circulated at this time by Mr. Jefferson, under the strongest injunctions that no copy should be allowed to be taken. It is worth while to contrast the opinion here expressed of Mr. J. with the uneasiness felt by Mr. Hamilton and his friends lest Mr. Adams should be led by that gentleman. Fortunate would it have been for all the parties, if the idea of leading Mr. Adams had not been always uppermost in their minds!" (Editor's note: WJA, VIII, p. 547n)

(7-8) "I wish you to get acquainted at Amsterdam with our bankers there, Messrs. Willink and Van Staphorst, and in France, if you are received there, to inquire into the conduct and character of our late and present consuls, and their inferior agents, and to find out what kind of speculations have been carried on there. You will see that Mr. Blount, the senator, has been speculating with the English, but some suspect this to be only a feint, and that the real design was upon France or Spain, or both. Swan, Hichborne, Edwards, &c., in connection with others in this country,

p. 409 (cont.)

have been speculating, and I fear these speculators have done this country no good. . . .

". . . Decorum must be observed. You will be surrounded with projectors and swindlers. You will not be deceived by them." (L. John Adams to Elbridge Gerry, 8 July 1797: WJA, VIII, p. 548)

(9-10)   "I sincerely wish peace and friendship with the French; but, while they countenance none but enemies of our Constitution and administration, and vilify every friend of either, self-defence, as well as fidelity to the public, will compel me to have a care what appointments I make.

"General Marshall took leave of me last night, and sails to-day in the Grace, Captain Willis, for Amsterdam. He is a plain man, very sensible, cautious, guarded, and learned in the law of nations." (L. John Adams to Elbridge Gerry, 17 July 1797: WJA, VIII, p. 549)

(11)   "'Recent intelligence of the wretched condition of numbers of our seamen, cast ashore, by French privateers, at St. Jago de Cuba (a place of no trade), who for want of means of returning, were constrained to enter on board the privateers, joined to the former accounts of the ill treatment of others and their imprisonment by Victor Hugues, determined me, with the concurrence of the Secretary of War,

p. 409 (cont.)
to send the Sophia on this voyage without more delay. She will sail this day.'" (L. Timothy Pickering to John Adams, 17 August 1797: WJA, VIII, pp. 550, n. 2-551n)

(12) "Santhonax's departure for France will be no relief to our commerce, nor will any negotiations going on, or treaties we can make, until our vessels arm in their own defence. This is my opinion." (L. John Adams to Timothy Pickering, 14 October 1797: WJA, VIII, pp. 553-554)

(12-13) "But the office of the secretary of the treasury is, in that bill, premeditatedly set up as a rival to that of the President; and that policy will be pursued, if we are not on our guard, till we have a quintuple or a centuple executive directory, with all the Babylonish dialect which modern pedants most affect." (L. John Adams to Oliver Wolcott, Secretary of the Treasury, 20 October 1797: WJA, VIII, p. 555)

(13-14) "This [reference to Timothy Pickering by John Adams in a letter to Pickering dated 26 October 1797] alludes to a passage in Mr. Pickering's letter touching the translation and publication of his despatch to General Pinckney of the 16th of January preceding. He says:
"'All the members of the legislature were furnished,

p. 409 (cont.)

and officers of government. M. Ségur and some others wish the case of gratitude had been touched more lightly. General Pinckney, however, thinks all that is said upon it was necessary. "The friends of Vergennes (says Mountflorence) do not like the facts laid to his charge. M. Marbois would have wished Colonel P. had not so deeply pressed that matter."'" (Editor's note: <u>WJA</u>, VIII, pp. 556n-557n)

(15-16) "I made the nomination according to the list presented to me by you, from General Washington, in hopes that rank might be settled among them by agreement or acquiescence, believing at the time, and expressing to you that belief, that the nomination and appointment would give Hamilton no command at all, nor any rank before any Major-General. This is my opinion still. I am willing to settle all decisively at present (and have no fear of the consequences), by dating the commissions, Knox on the first day, Pinckney on the second, and Hamilton on the third. . . .

"There has been too much intrigue in this business with General Washington and me; if I shall ultimately be the dupe of it, I am much mistaken in myself." (L. John Adams to J. McHenry, Secretary of War, 29 August 1798: <u>WJA</u>, VIII, pp. 587-588; see also 588n-590n)

(16) "Mr. McHenry's letter is dated the 25th of

p. 409 (cont.)

November. It urges the composition of such a message as would lead Congress to a declaration of war with France; it suggests the mention of the surrender by Spain of two posts on the east bank of the Mississippi, and a recommendation of the investment in the President of full power to take possession of Louisiana and the Floridas, on behalf of Spain, in case of danger of their being seized by the French." (Editor's note: WJA, VIII, p. 604n)

(17)   I have been unable to identify a passage containing these words.

(18-19) "One of them is, whether it will be expedient for the President to recommend to the consideration of Congress a declaration of war against France. This question supposes that France shall not have declared war against the United States. Otherwise, I suppose there will be no room for a question." (L. John Adams to Timothy Pickering, 20 October 1798: WJA, VIII, p. 609)

(20-25) "I have the honor to inform you, that there has lately been published, in the Boston gazettes, a letter signed 'Timothy Pickering,' addressed to P. Johnson, Esq., of Prince Edward county, Virginia, dated the 29th of September last, wherein Mr. Pickering, speaking of the despatches

p. 409 (cont.)
of the envoys, says that 'M. Talleyrand affects an utter ignorance of the persons, designated in the despatches by the letters W, X, Y, and Z; and in his letter of May 30th, with solemn grimace, requests Mr. Gerry immediately to communicate to him the names for which those letters stand. And Mr. Gerry, although he knew that Talleyrand was much better acquainted with X, Y, and Z, than he was himself, having complied with this insulting request, M. Talleyrand makes a formal record of their names,' &c." (L. Elbridge Gerry to John Adams, 20 October 1798: <u>WJA</u>, VIII, pp. 610-611)

(26-28) "He told me that if Daendels succeeded (he went the 17th at night) they meant to overturn the present men, whom he represented as peculators, and as men who exhausted every thing in enormous bribes, to arrange their internal affairs, and the first moment in their power to drive out the French [from Holland]; that opportunities would occur in the war, if it was renewed, and that they meant to embroil parties in France, if there was a chance of convulsion there, but that the great obstacle was the temper of England towards them; that this apprehension once settled by a secret understanding, they could join her and the United States against France; that this understanding ought to take place soon, because they would then work all their means to the grand

p. 409 (cont.)

object from the start of the new administration, which he hoped would be formed in a little time." (L. William Vans Murray to John Adams, 1 July 1798: <u>WJA</u>, VIII, p. 678) For the word "ciphered" in line 28, see <u>WJA</u>, VIII, p. 677n)

(29-31)   "I yesterday determined to nominate Mr. Murray to be minister plenipotentiary to the French republic.
p. 410   This I ventured to do upon the strength of a let-
(1-3)   ter from Talleyrand himself, giving declarations, in the name of his government, that any minister plenipotentiary from the United States shall be received according to the condition at the close of my message to Congress, of the 21st of June last. As there may be some reserves for chicane, however, Murray is not to remove from his station at the Hague until he shall have received formal assurances that he shall be received and treated in character. . . .

". . . There is not much sincerity in the cant about peace; those who snivel for it now, were hot for war against Britain a few months ago, and would be now, if they saw a chance. In elective governments, peace or war are alike embraced by parties, when they think they can employ either for electioneering purposes." (L. John Adams to George Washington, 19 February 1799: <u>WJA</u>, VIII, pp. 624-626)

(3-4)   "The nomination of Murray has had one good effect,

p. 410 (cont.)

at least. It has shown to every observing and thinking man the real strength or weakness of the Constitution, and where one part of that weakness resides. It has also produced a display of the real spirit of the parties in this country, and the objects they have in view. To me, it has laid open characters." (L. John Adams to Charles Lee, Attorney-General, 29 March 1799: WJA, VIII, p. 629)

(5-7) "Sir,--Divers causes and considerations, essential to the administration of the government, in my judgment, requiring a change in the department of State, you are hereby discharged from any further service as Secretary of State." (L. John Adams to Timothy Pickering, 12 May 1800: WJA, IX, p. 55)

(8-10) "I hereby authorize and request you to execute the office of Secretary of State so far as to affix the seal of the United States to the inclosed commission to the present Secretary of State, John Marshall, of Virginia, to be Chief Justice of the United States, and to certify in your own name on the commission as executing the office of the Secretary of State pro hâc vice." (L. John Adams to S. Dexter, Secretary of War, 31 January 1801: WJA, IX, pp. 95-96) The Latin pro hac vice means "in return." (Index, p. 178)

p. 410 (cont.)

(11-12) "Mr. Hamilton, in his pamphlet, speaking of Talleyrand's despatches, says, 'overtures so circuitous and informal, through a person who was not the regular organ of the French government for making them, to a person who was not the regular organ of the American government for receiving them, &c., were a very inadequate basis for the institution of a new mission.'

"Here again, Mr. Hamilton's total ignorance or oblivion of the practice of our own government, as well as the constant usage of other nations in diplomatic proceedings, appears in all its lustre. In 1784, the Congress of the United States, the then sovereign of our country, issued fifteen commissions, as I remember. If I mistake the number, Colonel Humphreys can correct me, for he was the secretary of legation to them all, and possesses, as I suppose, the original parchments, to John Adams, Benjamin Franklin, and Thomas Jefferson, to form commercial treaties with all the commercial powers of Europe and the Barbary States. Our instructions were to communicate these credentials to the ambassadors of these powers at Versailles, not to go to those courts. And we did communicate them in this informal and circuitous manner, and received very civil answers." (L. John Adams, to the Boston Patriot, 1809: WJA, IX, p. 273)

p. 410 (cont.)

(13) "The institution of an embassy to France, in 1799, was made upon principle, and in conformity to a system of foreign affairs, formed upon long deliberation, established in my mind, and amply opened, explained, and supported in Congress,--that is, a system of eternal neutrality, if possible, in all the wars of Europe,--at least eighteen years before President Washington's Proclamation of Neutrality, in 1794." (L. John Adams to the Boston Patriot, 1809: <u>WJA</u>, IX, p. 242)

(14-15) "Before this reaches you, the news will be familiar to you, that after the 3d of March I am to be a private citizen and your brother farmer. I shall leave the State with its coffers full, and the fair prospects of a peace with all the world smiling in its face, its commerce flourishing, its navy glorious, its agriculture uncommonly productive and lucrative." (L. John Adams to F. A. Van der Kemp, 28 December 1800: <u>WJA</u>, IX, p. 577)

(16-17) "Your anxiety for the issue of the election is, by this time, allayed. How mighty a power is the spirit of party! How decisive and unanimous it is! Seventy-three for Mr. Jefferson and seventy-three for Mr. Burr. May the peace and welfare of the country be promoted by this result! But I see not the way as yet. In the case of Mr. Jefferson,

p. 410 (cont.)

there is nothing wonderful; but Mr. Burr's good fortune surpasses all ordinary rules, and exceeds that of Bonaparte. All the old patriots, all the splendid talents, the long experience, both of federalists and antifederalists, must be subjected to the humiliation of seeing this dexterous gentleman rise, like a balloon, filled with inflammable air, over their heads." (L. John Adams to Elbridge Gerry, 30 December 1800: WJA, IX, pp. 577-578)

(18-19) "A group of foreign liars, encouraged by a few ambitious native gentlemen, have discomfited the education, the talents, the virtues, and the property of the country. The reason is, we have no Americans in America. The federalists have been no more Americans than the anties." (L. John Adams to Benjamin Stoddert, 31 March 1801: WJA, IX, p. 582)

(20)   Pound's comment. The Italian formato loc(h)o means "in a prepared place." The reference is to Cavalcanti's Donna mi prega. (Index, p. 71)

(21-24) "Make my compliments to Mrs. Warren, and tell her that I want a poetical genius to describe a late frolic among the sea-nymphs and goddesses. There being a scarcity of nectar and ambrosia among the celestials of the sea, Neptune

p. 410 (cont.)

has determined to substitute Hyson and Congo, and, for some of the inferior divinities, Bohea. Amphitrite, one of his wives, viz. the land, and Salaria, another of his wives, the sea, went to pulling caps upon the occasion, but Salaria prevailed. The Sirens should be introduced somehow, I cannot tell how, and Proteus, a son of Neptune, who could sometimes flow like water, and sometimes burn like fire, bark like a dog, howl like a wolf, whine like an ape, cry like a crocodile, or roar like a lion." (L. John Adams to James Warren, 22 December 1773: <u>WJA</u>, IX, p. 335) John Adams here is referring to telling in mythological dress the story of the Boston Tea Party of 16 December 1773.

(25-27) "The tories were never, since I was born, in such a state of humiliation as at this moment. Wherever I go, in the several counties, I perceive it more and more. They are now in absolute despair of obtaining a triumph without shedding an abundance of blood; and they are afraid of the consequences of this. Not that their humanity starts at it at all. The complaisance, the air of modesty and kindness to the Whigs, the show of moderation, the pains to be thought friends to liberty, and all that, is amazing. . . . To see them bowing, smiling, cringing, and seeming cordially friendly, to persons whom they openly avowed their malice against two years ago, and whom they would gladly butcher

p. 410 (cont.)

now, is provoking, yet diverting.

". . . For my own part, I am of the same opinion that I have been for many years, that there is not spirit enough on either side to bring the question to a complete decision, and that we shall oscillate like a pendulum, and fluctuate like the ocean, for many years to come, and never obtain a complete redress of American grievances, nor submit to an absolute establishment of parliamentary authority, but be trimming between both, as we have been for ten years past, for more years to come than you and I shall live." (L. John Adams to James Warren, 9 April 1774: WJA, IX, pp. 336-337)

(28) "Nero wished that the inhabitants of Rome had but one neck, that he might have the pleasure of cutting it off with his own hand at one blow. This, as it would have speedily terminated their misery, was humanity in comparison of the minister's project of turning famine into a populous city to devour its devoted inhabitants by slow torments and lingering degrees." (L. John Adams to William Woodfall, 14 May 1774: WJA, IX, p. 338)

(28-31) "The principal topic, however, was the enterprise to Philadelphia. I view the assembly, that is to be there, as I do the court of Areopagus, the council of the Amphictyons, a conclave, a sanhedrim, a divan, I know not what.

p. 410 (cont.)

I suppose you sent me there to school. I thank you for thinking me an apt scholar, or capable of learning. For my own part, I am at a loss, totally at a loss, what to do when we get there; but I hope to be there taught.

"It is to be a school of political prophets, I suppose, a nursery of American Statesmen. May it thrive and prosper and flourish, and from this fountain may there issue streams, which shall gladden all the cities and towns in North America, forever!" (L. John Adams to James Warren, 25 June 1774: <u>WJA</u>, IX, pp. 338-339)

(32)   "One thing I want that the southern gentlemen should be deeply impressed with; that is, that all acts of British legislation which influence and affect our internal polity, are as absolutely repugnant to liberty and the idea of our being a free people, as taxation or revenue acts. Witness the present regulation act for this province; and, if we shall not be subdued by what is done already, like acts will undoubtedly be made for other colonies. I expect nothing but new treasons, new felonies, new misprisions, new praemunires, and, not to say the Lord, the devil knows what." (L. Joseph Hawley to John Adams, 25 July 1774: <u>WJA</u>, IX, p. 345)

(33)   "Virginia has sown her wheat instead of tobacco;

p. 410 (cont.)

and so many of her planters have desisted from exporting the old crop, that the vessels cannot get freight. Their men are ready to march." (L. John Adams to James Warren, 15 March 1775: <u>WJA</u>, IX, p. 355)

(34)   I have been unable to identify a passage containing these words.

p. 411

(1)   "I have a great opinion of your knowledge and judgment, from long experience, concerning the channels and islands in Boston harbor; but I confess your opinion, that the harbor might be blocked up, and seamen and soldiers made prisoners at discretion, was too bold and enterprising for me, who am not very apt to startle at a daring proposal; but I believe I may safely promise you powder enough, in a little time, for any purpose whatever." (L. John Adams to Josiah Quincy, 29 July 1775: <u>WJA</u>, IX, p. 361)

(1)   "The Congress have voted, or rather a committee of the whole house have unanimously agreed, that the sum of two million dollars be issued in bills of credit, for the redemption of which, in a certain number of years, twelve colonies have unanimously pledged themselves." (L. John Adams to Elbridge Gerry, 18 June 1775: <u>WJA</u>, IX, p. 357)

p. 411 (cont.)

(2-4)   "It is certain, in theory, that the only moral foundation of government is, the consent of the people. But to what an extent shall we carry this principle? Shall we say that every individual of the community, old and young, male and female, as well as rich and poor, must consent, expressly, to every act of legislation? No, you will say, this is impossible. How, then, does the right arise in the majority to govern the minority, against their will? Whence arises the right of the men to govern the women, without their consent? Whence the right of the old to bind the young, without theirs? . . .

"But why exclude women?

"You will say, because their delicacy renders them unfit for practice and experience in the great businesses of life, and the hardy enterprises of war, as well as the arduous cares of state. Besides, their attention is so much engaged with the necessary nurture of their children, that nature has made them fittest for domestic cares. And children have not judgment or will of their own. True. But will not these reasons apply to others? Is it not equally true, that men in general, in every society, who are wholly destitute of property, are also too little acquainted with public affairs to form a right judgment, and too dependent upon other men to have a will of their own? . . .

"Harrington has shown that power always follows property.

p. 411 (cont.)

This I believe to be as infallible a maxim in politics, as that action and reaction are equal, is in mechanics. Nay, I believe we may advance one step farther, and affirm that the balance of power in a society, accompanies the balance of property in land. The only possible way, then, of preserving the balance of power on the side of equal liberty and public virtue, is to make the acquisition of land easy to every member of society; to make a division of the land into small quantities so that the multitude may be possessed of landed estates. If the multitude is possessed of the balance of real estate, the multitude will have the balance of power, and in that case the multitude will take care of the liberty, virtue, and interest of the multitude, in all acts of government." (L. John Adams to James Sullivan, 26 May 1776: WJA, IX, pp. 375-377)

(5)   "You kindly and politely express a concern for my health, and, if you have any regard for me, it is not without reason. I have been here four months, during which time I have never once been on horseback, and have found but little time to walk." (L. John Adams to Benjamin Hichborn, 29 May 1776: WJA, IX, p. 380)

(6-7)   "Horne, Bracton, Britton, Fleta, Thornton, Glanville, and Fortescue will exhibit to you this ancient face

p. 411 (cont.)

[of principles of law], and there you may contemplate all its beauties. . . .

"There is another science, my dear Sir, that I must recommend to your most attentive consideration, and that is the Civil Law. You will find it so interspersed with history, oratory, law, politics, and war and commerce, that you will find advantages in it every day. Wood, Domat, Ayliffe, Taylor, ought to be read. But these should not suffice. You should go to the fountain-head, and drink deep of the Pierian spring. Justinian's Institutes, and all the commentators upon them that you can find, you ought to read." (L. John Adams to Jonathan Mason, 21 August 1776: <u>WJA</u>, IX, p. 433)

(8-9) "I find the same perplexities here that we felt at Yorktown, a general inclination among the people to barter, and as general an aversion to dealing in paper money of any denomination; guineas, half joes, and milled dollars in as high estimation as in Pennsylvania. . . .

". . . The rapid translation of property from hand to hand, the robbing of Peter to pay Paul, alarms and distresses me beyond measure. The man who lent another a hundred pounds in gold four years ago, and is paid now in paper, cannot purchase with it one quarter part in pork, beef, or land, of what he could when he lent the gold." (L. John

p. 411 (cont.)

Adams to Elbridge Gerry, 6 December 1777: <u>WJA</u>, IX, pp. 469-470) I do not know what the "'61" in line 8 refers to. The letter from which this passage was taken was written in Braintree, but, as indicated above, dated 6 December 1777.

(10-11) "Your sentiments, that we are but half taught in the greatest national arts of government and war, are, I fear, too just. And I fear that the subject, which is at present most essentially connected with our government and warfare, I mean money, is least understood of any. I fear the regulation of prices will produce ruin sooner than safety. It will starve the army and the country, or I am ignorant of every principle of commerce, coin, and society. Barter will be the only trade." (L. John Adams to Benjamin Rush, 8 February 1778: <u>WJA</u>, IX, p. 472)

(12-18) "There is no news anywhere, excepting the innumerable reports circulated in every part of Europe by the emissaries of England, every one of which I know to be false. They still, however, find stockjobbers and other persons to believe them. These lies are calculated to make it believed, that there are great dissensions between the French and Americans, and between the Americans with one another. No extravagance is too great. Ten thousand of General Washington's army gone over to Clinton. Count D'Estaing making a

448

p. 411 (cont.)

procession through the streets of Boston with the Host, and seizing a meeting-house for a chapel, and the d---- knows what." (L. John Adams to James Lovell, 27 November 1788: <u>WJA</u>, IX, pp. 473-474)

(19)   I have been unable to identify a passage containing these words. In Canto 68 (p. 398, line 16) Pound referred to a letter written 18 February 1780 by John Adams, in which Adams mentioned British rumors about "20,000 russians" ready for war, but whether or not Pound was recalling that passage here, I do not know.

(20-23) "I am more solicitous about the means of procuring the salary you mention than the sum of it. I can make it do, if I can get it. But I wish I had power to borrow money, and also power to draw upon Dr. Franklin, or the American banker, in case of necessity. . . .

". . . My importance in that country will depend much upon the intelligence that shall be sent me by my friends, more than you can imagine. If you intend I shall do you any good, keep me constantly informed of every thing; the numbers and destinations of the army, the state of finance, the temper of the people, military operations; the state and the prospects of the harvests, the prices of goods, the price of bills of exchange, the rate between silver and paper.

p. 411 (cont.)

Nothing can come amiss. The growth or decline of the navy, the spirit and success of privateers, the number of prizes, the number, position, exertions, and designs of the enemy.

"Your election comes on this month, and it is sure. I wish I was as sure of getting safe to France." (L. John Adams to Elbridge Gerry, 4 November 1779: <u>WJA</u>, IX, pp. 506-507)

(24-33) These lines combine passages from two different letters of John Adams to two different people. Lines 24-26; 28; 30 all come from this quotation: "I love every tree and every rock upon all those mountains. Roving among these, and the quails, partridges, squirrels, &c., that inhabit them, shall be the amusement of my declining years. God willing, I will not go to Vermont [where his wife had bought some land]. I must be within the scent of the sea." (L. John Adams to James Warren, 17 June 1782: <u>WJA</u>, IX, pp. 512-513)

Lines 27; 29; 31-33--the lines in parentheses, the last of which would be closed after the word "Europe"--come from the following passage: "In substance it [French policy] has been this; in assistance afforded us in naval force and in money, to keep us from succumbing, and nothing more; to prevent us from ridding ourselves wholly of our enemies; to prevent us from growing powerful or rich; to prevent us from

p. 411 (cont.)

obtaining acknowledgments of our independence by other foreign powers, and to prevent us from obtaining consideration in Europe, or any advantage in the peace but what is expressly stipulated in the treaty; to deprive us of the grand fishery, the Mississippi River, the western lands, and to saddle us with the tories." (L. John Adams to Jonathan Jackson, 17 November 1782: <u>WJA</u>, IX, p. 515)

(33-34) "I have planted the American standard at the Hague. There let it wave and fly in triumph over Sir Joseph Yorke and British pride. I shall look down upon the flagstaff with pleasure from the other world.

"Not the declaration of American independence, not the Massachusetts Constitution, not the alliance with France, ever gave me more satisfaction or more pleasing prospects for our country than this event." (L. John Adams to James Warren, 6 September 1782: <u>WJA</u>, IX, pp. 513-514)

p. 412

(1-3) "They [the French] consider nobody but themselves. Their apparent respect and real contempt for all men and all nations but Frenchmen, are proverbial among themselves. They think it is in their power to give characters and destroy characters as they please, and they have no other rule but to give reputation to their tools, and to destroy the

p. 412 (cont.)

reputation of all who will not be their tools. Their efforts to 'populariser' Jefferson, and to 'dépopulariser' Washington, are all upon this principle. To a Frenchman the most important man in the world is himself, and the most important nation is France. He thinks that France ought to govern all nations, and that he ought to govern France. Every man and nation that agrees to this, he is willing to 'populariser'; every man or nation that disputes or doubts it, he will 'dépopulariser,' if he can." (L. John Adams to Henry Knox, 30 March 1797: <u>WJA</u>, VIII, p. 536)

(4-6) "I think, however, you cannot too soon send a minister to London to arrange finally a system of commerce, and to watch over all your interests in that country. French politics are now incessantly at work in England, and we may depend upon it they labor less for our good than their own. If our interests were the same with theirs, we might better trust them; yet not entirely, for they do not understand their own interests so well as we do ours." (L. John Adams to Arthur Lee, 12 April 1783: <u>WJA</u>, IX, p. 518)

(7-8) "I have hitherto paid the interest in Holland out of the principal; but this will by and by be impracticable, and then such a clamor and obloquy will succeed as will make us all ashamed of ourselves. How will it be pos-

p. 412 (cont.)

sible to vindicate the faith or the honor of our country?" (L. John Adams to Arthur Lee, 6 September 1785: <u>WJA</u>, IX, p. 537)

(9)   "Perhaps you will say that the air of a Court is as putrid as that of Amsterdam. In a moral and political sense, perhaps; but I am determined that the bad morals and false politics of other people shall no longer affect my repose of mind nor disturb my physical constitution. . . .

". . . It is a pretty amusement to play a game with nations as if they were fox and geese, or coins upon a checker-board, or the personages at chess, is it not? It is, however, the real employment of a statesman to play such a game sometimes; a sublime one, truly; enough to make a man serious, however addicted to sport. Politics are the divine science, after all. How is it possible that any man should ever think of making it subservient to his own little passions and mean private interests?" (L. John Adams to James Warren, 17 June 1782: <u>WJA</u>, IX, p. 512)

(10)   "I was appointed to that Assembly, but being a member of Congress, where the plan of Convention must be approved, there appeared an inconsistency for members of the former to have session in the latter, and so pass judgment at New York upon their opinion at Philadelphia. I therefore

p. 412 (cont.)

declined going to Convention, and came here, where we have lately contracted for the sale of six millions of acres, on the north-western side of Ohio, in the ceded territory, for lessening the domestic debt. And now, another offer is made for two millions more. I hope we shall at least be able to extinguish the domestic debt created by the late war, which is by far the greatest part of the debt." (L. R. H. Lee to John Adams, 3 September 1787: WJA, IX, p. 554)

(11-14) "There is a fine brook, through a meadow, by my house; shall I call it Hollis Brook? . . .

"I regret the loss of the book-shops, and the society of the few men of letters that I knew in London; in all other respects I am much better accommodated here. Shall I hope to hear from you as you have leisure? A letter left at the New England Coffee House will be brought me by some of our Boston captains." (L. John Adams to Thomas Brand-Hollis, 3 December 1788: WJA, IX, pp. 557-558)

(15-17) "But although I may flatter myself that under the favor of Heaven I have had as much success as could have been rationally expected, yet I find myself obliged with you to lament that your countrymen have not availed themselves of the advantages which Providence has placed in their power. After a generous contest for liberty, of twenty years' con-

p. 412 (cont.)

tinuance, Americans forgot wherein liberty consisted. After a bloody war in defence of property, they forgot that property was sacred. . . .

"Haec olim meminisse juvabit." (L. John Adams to Henry Marchant, 18 August 1789: WJA, IX, pp. 560-561) The Latin meminisse juvabit means "it will be pleasing to recall." (Index, p. 142)

(18-20) "No man, I believe, has influence with the President [Washington]. He seeks information from all quarters, and judges more independently than any man I ever knew. It is of so much importance to the public that he should preserve this superiority, that I hope I shall never see the time that any man will have influence with him beyond the powers of reason and argument." (L. John Adams to Silvanus Bourn, 30 August 1789: WJA, IX, p. 561)

(21-25) "The fisheries are so essential to the commerce and naval power of this nation, that it is astonishing that any one citizen should ever have been found indifferent about them. But it is certain that at a time when there were reasons to expect that more than one foreign nation would endeavor to deprive us of them, there were many Americans indifferent, and not a few even disposed to give them away. A knowledge of this was the first and strongest motive with me to embark for

p. 412 (cont.)

Europe a first and a second time. . . .

"The present of four boxes of fish has been received in my absence by my family; and is in every point of view very acceptable to me." (L. John Adams to Marston Watson, 7 November 1789: WJA, IX, pp. 562-563)

(26-32) "The Constitution [of France] is but an experiment, and must and will be altered. I know it to be impossible that France should be long governed by it. If the sovereignty is to reside in one assembly, the king, princes of the blood, and principal quality, will govern it at their pleasure as long as they can agree; when they differ, they will go to war, and act over again all the tragedies of Valois, Bourbons, Lorraines, Guises, and Colignis, two hundred years ago. . . .

"I thank you, Sir, for your kind compliment. As it has been the great aim of my life to be useful, if I had any reason to think I was so, as you seem to suppose, it would make me happy. . . . It is incredible how small is the number, in any nation, of those who comprehend any system of constitution or administration, and those few it is wholly impossible to unite." (L. John Adams to Richard Price, 19 April 1790: WJA, IX, p. 564)

(33-35) "I own that awful experience has concurred with

p. 413

(1)	reading and reflection, to convince me that Americans are more rapidly disposed to corruption in elections that [sic] I thought they were fourteen years ago [this would make it 1776 instead of the "'74" used by Pound].

"My friend Dr. Rush will excuse me, if I caution him against a fraudulent use of the words monarchy and republic. I am a mortal and irreconcilable enemy to monarchy. I am no friend to hereditary limited monarchy in America. . . . Do not, therefore, my friend, misunderstand me and misrepresent me to posterity. I am for a balance between the legislative and executive powers, and I am for enabling the executive to be at all times capable of maintaining the balance between the Senate and House, or in other words, between the aristocratical and democratical interests." (L. John Adams to Benjamin Rush, 18 April 1790: WJA, IX, p. 566) The Chinese ideogram on page 413 means "the middle, the axis, center, pivot: I am for balance; Confucius, 103: an axis round which something turns." (Index, p. 271)

(2-3)	"I know not how it is, but mankind have an aversion to the study of the science of government. Is it because the subject is dry? To me, no romance is more entertaining. Those who take the lead in revolutions are seldom well informed, and they commonly take more pains to inflame

p. 413 (cont.)

their own passions and those of society, than to discover truth; and very few of those who have just ideas have the courage to pursue them." (L. John Adams to Alexander Jardine, 1 June 1790: <u>WJA</u>, IX, pp. 567-567)

(4)   "I am situated on the majestic banks of the Hudson, in comparison of which your Thames is but a rivulet, and surrounded with all the beauties and sublimities of nature." (L. John Adams to Thomas Brand-Hollis, 1 June 1790: <u>WJA</u>, IX, p. 569)

(5)   See Canto 70, page 410, lines 16-17, above.

(6)   This line, and line 9 below, refer to the following statement: "My affectionate regards to Dr. Price, and all our good friends; and believe me yours <u>dum spiro</u>, &c." (L. John Adams to Thomas Brand-Hollis, 1 June 1790: <u>WJA</u>, IX, p. 569) The Latin <u>Dum Spiro</u>/ . . . <u>Dum Spiro Amo</u> means "while I breathe/ . . . while I breathe I love." (<u>Index</u>, p. 55)

(7)   "In this country the pendulum has vibrated too far to the popular side, driven by men without experience or judgment, and horrid ravages have been made upon property by arbitrary multitudes or majorities of multitudes. France has

p. 413 (cont.)

severe trials to endure from the same cause. Both have found, or will find, that to place property at the mercy of a majority who have no property, is 'committere agnum lupo.' My fundamental maxim of government is, never to trust the lamb to the custody of the wolf." (L. John Adams to Thomas Brand-Hollis, 11 June 1790: WJA, IX, p. 571) The Latin nec lupo committere agnum means "nor entrust a lamb to a wolf." (Index, p. 152)

(8)   "But, as you observe, the feelings of mankind are so much against any rational theory [of government], that I find my labor [in writing the Defence] has all been in vain, and it is not worth while to take any more pains upon the subject." (L. John Adams to John Trumbull, 23 January 1791: WJA, IX, p. 573)

(9)   See page 413, line 6, above.

CANTO LXXI

p. 414

(1-3) "A German ambassador once told me, 'he could not bear St. Paul, he was so severe against fornication.' On the same principle these philosophers cannot bear a God, because he is just." (L. John Adams to F. A. Vanderkemp, 3 March 1804: <u>WJA</u>, IX, p. 588)

(4) "From the year 1760 to the year 1800 I was swallowed up in cares, anxieties, and exertions for the public. At the close of the 18th century, I was dismissed, to the joy of both parties, to a retirement in which I was never more to see any thing but my plough between me and the grave." (L. John Adams to F. A. Vanderkemp, 5 February 1805: <u>WJA</u>, IX, pp. 589-590)

(4-5) "Now, Sir, to be serious, I do not curse the day when I was engaged in public affairs. I do not say when I became a politician, for that I never was. I cannot repent of any thing I ever did conscientiously and from a sense of duty." (L. John Adams to Benjamin Rush, 1 May 1807: <u>WJA</u>, IX, p. 593)

p. 414 (cont.)

(6-14) "Within the course of the year before the meeting of Congress, in 1774, on a journey to some of our circuit courts in Massachusetts, I stopped one night at a tavern in Shrewsbury, about forty miles from Boston, and as I was cold and wet, I sat down at a good fire in the bar-room to dry my great coat and saddle-bags till a fire could be made in my chamber. There presently came in, one after another, half a dozen, or half a score, substantial yeomen of the neighborhood, who, sitting down to the fire after lighting their pipes, began a lively conversation upon politics. As I believed I was unknown to all of them, I sat in total silence to hear them. One said, 'The people of Boston are distracted!' Another answered, 'No wonder the people of Boston are distracted. Oppression will make wise men mad.' A third said, 'What would you say, if a fellow should come to your house and tell you he was come to take a list of your cattle, that parliament might tax you for them at so much a head? and how should you feel, if he was to go and break open your barn, to take down your oxen, cows, horses, and sheep?' 'What should I say?' replied the first; 'I would knock him in the head.' 'Well,' said a fourth, 'if parliament can take away Mr. Hancock's wharf and Mr. Rowe's wharf, they can take away your barn and my house.' After much more reasoning in this style, a fifth, who had as yet

p. 414 (cont.)

been silent, broke out, 'Well, it is high time for us to rebel; we must rebel some time or other, and we had better rebel now than at any time to come. If we put it off for ten or twenty years, and let them go on as they have begun, they will get a strong party among us, and plague us a great deal more than they can now. As yet they have but a small party on their side.' I was disgusted with his word rebel, because I was determined never to rebel, as much as I was to resist rebellion against the fundamental privileges of the Constitution, whenever British generals or governors should begin it. I mention this anecdote to show that the idea of independence was familiar, even among the common people, much earlier than some persons pretend." (L. John Adams to Benjamin Rush, 21 May 1807: WJA, IX, pp. 597-598)

(15-20) "In the mean time apply all our resources to build frigates, some in every principal seaport. These frigates ought not to be assembled in any one port to become an object of a hostile expedition to destroy them. They should be separated and scattered as much as possible from New Orleans to Passamaquoddy. I never was fond of the plan of building line of battle ships. Our policy is not to fight squadrons at sea, but to have fast-sailing frigates to scour the seas and make impression on the

p. 414 (cont.)

enemy's commerce; and in this way we can do great things . . .

"I conclude with acknowledging that we have received greater injuries from England than from France, abominable as both have been. I conclude that whatever the government determines, I shall support as far as my small voice extends." (L. John Adams to J. B. Varnum, 26 December 1808: <u>WJA</u>, IX, pp. 607-608)

(21)   "If either of the belligerent powers [England or France] forces us all into a war, I am for fighting that power, whichever it may be." (L. John Adams to Daniel Wright and Erastus Lyman, 13 March 1809: <u>WJA</u>, IX, p. 615)

(22-24) "Our medium is depreciated by the multitude of swindling banks, which have emitted bank bills to an immense amount beyond the deposits of gold and silver in their vaults, by which means the price of labor and land and merchandise and produce is doubled, tripled, and quadrupled in many instances. Every dollar of a bank bill that is issued beyond the quantity of gold and silver in the vaults, represents nothing, and is therefore a cheat upon somebody." (L. John Adams to F. A. Vanderkemp, 16 February 1809: <u>WJA</u>, IX, p. 610)

(25-31) "From my earliest infancy I had listened with

p. 414 (cont.)

p. 415
(1-4)

eagerness to his [my father's] conversation with his friends during the whole expedition to Cape Breton, in 1745, and I had received very grievous impressions of the injustice and ingratitude of Great Britain towards New England in that whole transaction, as well as many others before and after it, during the years 1754, 1755, 1756, and 1757. The conduct of Generals Shirley, Braddock, Abercrombie, Webb, and above all Lord Loudon, which were daily discussed in Mr. Putnam's family, gave me such an opinion and such a disgust of the British government, that I heartily wished the two countries were separated for ever. I was convinced we could defend ourselves against the French, and manage our affairs better without, than with, the English. In 1758 and 1759, Mr. Pitt coming into Power, sent Wolfe, and Amherst, whom I saw with his army, as they passed through Worcester, and these conquered Cape Breton and Quebec. I then rejoiced that I was an Englishman, and gloried in the name of Briton. But, alas! how short was my triumph in British wisdom and justice! In February, 1761, I heard the argument in the council chamber in Boston upon writs of assistance, and there saw that Britain was determined to let nothing divert me from my fidelity to my country. . . .

". . . The 4th of March, 1801. The causes of my retirement are to be found in the writings of Freneau,

p. 415 (cont.)

Markoe, Ned Church, Andrew Brown, Paine, Callender, Hamilton, Cobbet, and John Ward Fenno and many others, but more especially in the circular letters of members of congress from the southern and middle States. Without a complete collection of all these libels, no faithful history of the last twenty years can ever be written, nor any adequate account given of the causes of my retirement from private life." (L. John Adams to Skelton Jones, 11 March 1809: WJA, IX, pp. 611-612)

(5-9)   "I am totis viribus against any division of the Union, by the North River, or by Delaware River, or by the Potomac, or any other river, or by any chain of mountains. I am for maintaining the independence of the nation at all events." (L. John Adams to Daniel Wright and Erastus Lyman, 13 March 1809: WJA, IX, p. 615) The Latin totis viribus means "with all my strength." (Index, p. 226)

(9-12)   "My invariable principle for five-and-thirty years has been, to promote, preserve, and secure the integrity of the Union, and the independence of the nation, against the policy of England as well as France. . . .

". . . The federal papers for the last year or two, assisted by English hirelings, have been employed in

p. 415 (cont.)

varnishing over the conduct of Great Britain, and in calumniating every impartial and disinterested man, till they appear to have obtained a temporary majority in New England. I greatly respect the public opinion of New England, when it is truly informed. In the present instance, with infinite grief I fear it is not." (L. John Adams to Joseph Lyman, 20 April 1809: <u>WJA</u>, IX, pp. 619-621)

(13-22) "A great minister of State, in the estimation of the world, the Comte de Vergennes, once said to me, "Mr. Adams, the newspapers govern the world!" Let me ask you, Mr. Perley, whether this apothegm has not been verified in our own country, sometimes to her profit, and sometimes to her loss. Let me ask you again, if the world is governed by ungovernable newspapers, whether it does not follow by necessary logical consequence that the world is ungovernable. . . .

"I have represented the British Constitution as the most perfect model that has as yet been discovered or invented by human genius and experience, for the government of the great nations of Europe. It is a masterpiece. It is the only system that has preserved or can preserve the shadow, the color, the semblance of liberty to the people in any of the great nations of Europe. . . . Our own Constitutions I have represented as the best for us in our

p. 415 (cont.)

peculiar situation, and while we preserve ourselves independent and unallied to any of the great powers of Europe. An alliance with either France or England would, in my humble opinion, put an end to our fine system of liberty. . . .

". . . A Convention in Pennsylvania had adopted a government in one representative assembly, and Dr. Franklin was the President of that Convention. The Doctor, when he went to France in 1776, carried with him the printed copy of that Constitution, and it was immediately propagated through France that this was the plan of government of Mr. Franklin. In truth, it was not Franklin, but Timothy Matlack, James Cannon, Thomas Young, and Thomas Paine, who were the authors of it. Mr. Turgot, the Duke de la Rochefoucauld, Mr. Condorcet, and many others, became enamored with the Constitution of Mr. Franklin. And in my opinion, the two last owed their final and fatal catastrophe to this blind love.

"In 1780, when I arrived in France, I carried a printed copy of the report of the Grand Committee of the Massachusetts Convention, which I had drawn up; and this became an object of speculation. Mr. Turgot, the Duke de la Rochefoucauld, and Mr. Condorcet and others, admired Mr. Franklin's Constitution and reprobated mine. Mr. Turgot, in a letter to Dr. Price, printed in London,

p. 415 (cont.)

censured the American Constitution as adopting three branches, in imitation of the Constitution of Great Britain. The intention was to celebrate Franklin's Constitution and condemn mine. I understood it, and undertook to defend my Constitution, and it cost me three volumes. . . .

"I was personally acquainted with Mr. Turgot, the Duke de la Rochefoucauld, and Mr. Condorcet. They were as amiable, as learned, and as honest men as any in France. But such was their inexperience in all that relates to free government, so superficial their reading in the science of government, and so obstinate their confidence in their own great characters for science and literature, that I should trust the most ignorant of our honest town meeting orators to make a Constitution sooner than any or all of them." (L. John Adams to Samuel Perley, 19 June 1809: <u>WJA</u>, IX, pp. 622-624)

(23)   "Your question, 'Through what means the military and commercial spirit can be most effectually entertained, and rendered permanently advantageous to a free nation, under a republican form of government,' is of great importance. But no man would discuss it. Nine tenths of our nation would say the militia, the other tenth a standing army. The merchants would all say, 'let commerce

p. 415 (cont.)

alone--merchants do as they please;' others would say, 'protect trade with a navy;' others, 'let commerce be annihilated.' Such questions would only make of our academies so many political caucuses.' (L. John Adams to F. A. Vanderkemp, 15 December 1809: WJA, IX, p. 625)

(24-28) "The Union appears to me to be the rock of our salvation, and every reasonable measure for its preservation is expedient. Upon this principle, I own, I was pleased with the purchase of Louisiana, because, without it, we could never have secured and commanded the navigation of the Mississippi. The western country would infallibly have revolted from the Union. Those States would have united with England, or Spain, or France, or set up an independence, or done any thing else to obtain the free use of that river. I wish the Constitution had been more explicit [about the acquisition of territory like Louisiana], or that the States had been consulted; but it seems Congress have not entertained any doubts of their authority, and I cannot say that they are destitute of plausible arguments to support their opinion. . . .

". . . The Constitution, it is true, must speak for itself, and be interpreted by its own phraseology; yet the history and state of things at the time may be consulted to elucidate the meaning of words, and determine the bona

p. 415 (cont.)

<u>fide</u> intention of the Convention." (L. John Adams to Josiah Quincy, 9 February 1811: <u>WJA</u>, IX, pp. 631-632)

(29) "This jealousy [of nobility] is often actuated by the purest spirit of patriotism, and the most perfect integrity, but if it is not checked and controlled, it never has ceased to encroach, until it has made the executive a mere head of wood, and drawn all the power and resources of the nation into the insatiable gulf, the irresistible vortex, of an aristocracy or an oligarchy." (L. John Adams to Josiah Quincy, 18 February 1811: <u>WJA</u>, IX, p. 634)

(30-32) "I agree with you in sentiment, that religion and virtue are the only foundations, not only of republicanism and of all free government, but of social felicity under all governments and in all the combinations of human society. But if I should inculcate this doctrine in my will, I should be charged with hypocrisy and a desire to conciliate the good will of the clergy towards my family, as I was charged by Dr. Priestley and his friend Cooper, and by Quakers, Baptists, and I know not how many other sects, for instituting a national fast, for even common civility to the clergy, and for being a church-going animal. . . .

p. 415 (cont.)

"If I should inculcate 'fidelity to the marriage bed,' it would be said that it proceeded from resentment to General Hamilton, and a malicious desire to hold up to posterity his libertinism." (L. John Adams to Benjamin Rush, 28 August 1811: <u>WJA</u>, IX, pp. 636-637; a second reference by John Adams to being "a church-going animal" occurs on p. 637)

(33-34) "Note. August 31, 1811. I had forgot the story of the four English girls whom General Pinckney was employed to hire in England, two for me and two for himself. <u>J. A.</u>" (See asterisk, <u>WJA</u>, IX, p. 637)

p. 416
(1)

(2-16) "Fifty-three years ago I was fired with a zeal, amounting to enthusiasm, against ardent spirits, the multiplication of taverns, retailers, and dram-shops, and tippling houses. Grieved to the heart to see the number of idlers, thieves, sots, and consumptive patients made for the physicians, in those infamous seminaries, I applied to the Court of Sessions, procured a committee of inspection and inquiry, reduced the number of licensed houses, &c. But I only acquired the reputation of a hypocrite and an ambitious demagogue by it. The number of licensed houses was soon reinstated; drams, grog, and sotting were not

p. 416 (cont.)

diminished, and remain to this day as deplorable as ever. You may as well preach to the Indians against rum as to our people. Little Turtle petitioned me to prohibit rum to be sold to his nation, for a very good reason; because he said I had lost three thousand of my Indian children in his nation in one year by it. Sermons, moral discourses, philosophical dissertations, medical advice, are all lost upon this subject. . . .

"Funds and banks I never approved, or was satisfied with our funding system; it was founded in no consistent principle; it was contrived to enrich particular individuals at the public expense. Our whole banking system I ever abhorred, I continue to abhor, and shall die abhorring.

"But I am not an enemy to funding systems. They are absolutely and indispensably necessary in the present state of the world. An attempt to annihilate or prevent them would be as romantic an adventure as any in Don Quixote or in Oberon. A national bank of deposit I believe to be wise, just, prudent, economical, and necessary. But every bank of discount, every bank by which interest is to be paid or profit of any kind made by the deponent, is downright corruption. It is taxing the public for the benefit and profit of individuals; it is worse than old tenor, continental currency, or any other paper money.

"Now, Sir, if I should talk in this strain, after I am

472

p. 416 (cont.)

dead, you know the people of America would pronounce that I had died mad." (L. John Adams to Benjamin Rush, 28 August 1811: <u>WJA</u>, IX, pp. 637-638)

(17-22) "There was a numerous family [of indians] in this town, whose wigwam was within a mile of this house. This family were frequently at my father's house, and I, in my boyish rambles, used to call at their wigwam, where I never failed to be treated with whortleberries, blackberries, strawberries, or apples, plums, peaches, &c., for they had planted a variety of fruit trees about them; but the girls went out to service and the boys to sea, till not a soul is left." (L. John Adams to Thomas Jefferson, 28 June 1812: <u>WJA</u>, X, p. 20)

(23-25) "When I was exerting every nerve to vindicate the honor, and demand a redress of the wrongs of the nation against the tyranny of France, the arm of the nation was palsied by one party. Now Mr. Madison is acting the same part, for the same ends, against Great Britain, the arm of the nation is palsied by the opposite party. And so it will always be while we feel like colonists, dependent for protection on France or England; while we have so little national public opinion, so little national principle, national feeling, national patriotism; while we have no

p. 416 (cont.)

sentiment of our own strength, power, and resources."
(L. John Adams to William Keteltas, 25 November 1812:
WJA, X, pp. 23-24)

(26-27) "At table, in the hearing of all the company, the Count [de Sade, admiral of a French squadron anchored at Ferrol, Spain] said to me, 'Your Congress will soon become one of the great maritime powers.' 'Not very soon, Monsieur le Comte; it must be a long time first.' 'Why a long time? No people have such advantages.' 'There are many causes in the way.' 'What difficulties? No nation has such nurseries for seamen so near it. You have the best timber for the hulks of ships, and best masts and spars; you have pitch, tar, and turpentine; you have iron plenty, and I am informed you grow hemp; you have skilful shipbuilders. What is wanting?' 'The will, Monsieur le Comte; the will may be wanting and nothing else.'" (L. John Adams to J. B. Varnum, 5 January 1813: WJA, X, p. 26)

(28-29) "The taxes must be laid, and the war supported."
(L. John Adams to William Plumer, 28 March 1813: WJA, X, p. 36)

(30) "I say, parties and factions will not suffer improvements to be made. As soon as one man hints at an

p. 416 (cont.)

improvement, his rival opposes it. No sooner has one party discovered or invented any amelioration of the condition of man, or the order of society than the opposite party belies it, misconstrues it, misrepresents it, ridicules it, insults it, and persecutes it. Records are destroyed. Histories are annihilated or interpolated or prohibited; sometimes by Popes, sometimes by Emperors, sometimes by aristocratical, and sometimes by democratical assemblies, and sometimes by mobs." (L. John Adams to Thomas Jefferson, 9 July 1813: WJA, X, p. 50)

(31-32) "I should render the Greek into English thus:

"'Nor does a woman disdain to be the wife of a bad rich man. But she prefers a man of property before a good man; for riches are honored, and a good man marries from a bad family, and a bad man from a good one. Wealth mingles races.'

"Now, please to tell me, whether my translation has not hit the sense of Theognis [in his poem] as exactly as that of Grotius?

"Tell me, also, whether poet, orator, historian, or philosopher, can paint the picture of every city, county, or State, in our pure, uncorrupted, unadulterated, uncontaminated federal republic, or, in France, England,

p. 416 (cont.)

Holland, and all the rest of Christendom or Mahometanism, in more precise lines or colors?" (L. John Adams to Thomas Jefferson, 2 September 1813: <u>WJA</u>, X, p. 64)

(33-34) "I have a faint recollection, that it [the Congress at Albany in 1754] was appointed by
p. 417 the British ministry for the ostensible purpose
(1-7) of ascertaining the boundaries of the several colonies to the eastward of Delaware; but in reality to propose the least offensive plan for raising a revenue in America. In 1739, Sir William Keith, a Scotch gentleman, who had been a lieutenant-governor of Pennsylvania, proposed such an assembly to the ministry. He also proposed the extension of the British stamp-duties to the colonies. He was then, I believe, in the Fleet prison. The hints he gave were embraced, the first in 1754, the second in 1764.

"It has been long a matter of surprise to me, that no gentleman of talents and character has undertaken to write a history of the former British colonies, now United States of America, at least from 1756 to 1806, a period of fifty very important years. Such a work would not only be a great benefit to posterity, but also to the author. It would sell well. . . .

"On reflection, I cannot refer to a single instance

p. 417 (cont.)

of disinterested or evident friendship of Great Britain towards this country during the period you mention. Every act which might bear such an aspect, has been performed for the interest of the administration alone, although coupled in some cases with that of their own island." (L. Thomas McKean to John Adams, 28 September 1813: <u>WJA</u>, X, pp. 73-75)

The dates mentioned by Pound in line 7 come from the following passage. "Were I a man of fortune, I would offer a gold medal to the man who should produce the most instances of the friendship of Great Britain toward this country from 1600 to 1813." (L. John Adams to Thomas McKean, 31 August 1813: <u>WJA</u>, X, p. 62)

(8) "<u>θέμις</u> was the goddess of honesty, justice, decency, and right; the wife of Jove, another name for Juno. She presided over all oracles, deliberations, and councils. She commanded all mortals to pray to Jupiter for all lawful benefits and blessings. Now, is not this (so far forth) the essence of Christian devotion? Is not this Christian piety? Is it not an acknowledgment of the existence of a Supreme Being, of his universal Providence, of a righteous administration of the government of the universe? And what can Jews, Christians, or Mahometans do more?" (L. John Adams to Thomas Jefferson, 4 October

p. 417 (cont.)

1813: <u>WJA</u>, X, pp. 75-76) The Latin <u>CONDITOR</u> means "the founder." (<u>Index</u>, p. 221) This word does not appear in this particular letter to Jefferson, and may perhaps be Pound's addition.

(9-13) "In the Congress of 1774, there was not one member, except Patrick Henry, who appeared to me sensible of the precipice, or, rather, the pinnacle on which he stood, and had candor and courage enough to acknowledge it. America is in total ignorance, or under infinite deception, concerning that assembly. To draw the characters of them all would require a volume, and would now be considered as a caricature-print; one third tories, another whigs, and the rest mongrels." (L. John Adams to Thomas Jefferson, 12 November 1813: <u>WJA</u>, X, pp. 78-79)

See also the following passage. "If I were called to calculate the divisions among the people of America, as Mr. Burke did those of the people of England, I should say that full one third were averse to the revolution. These, retaining that overweening fondness, in which they had been educated, for the English, could not cordially like the French; indeed, they most heartily detested them. An opposite third conceived a hatred of the English, and gave themselves up to an enthusiastic gratitude to France. The middle third, composed principally of the yeomanry,

478

p. 417 (cont.)

the soundest part of the nation, and always averse to war, were rather lukewarm both to England and France,; and sometimes stragglers from them, and sometimes the whole body, united with the first or the last third, according to circumstances." (L. John Adams to James Lloyd, n.d. January 1815: <u>WJA</u>, X, pp. 110-111) Pound appears to have combined details from these two passages.

(14-16) "The Society in London 'for propagating the gospel in foreign parts,' had about half a dozen missionaries, perhaps more, in the State of Delaware, to some of whom they gave a salary of 60±,. to others 50±. sterling a year. These ministers foresaw, that if America became an independent state or nation, their salaries would necessarily cease. It was their interest, therefore, to oppose the revolution, and they did oppose it, though with as much secrecy as practicable." (L. Thomas McKean to John Adams, 15 November 1813: <u>WJA</u>, X. p. 81)

(17-21) "Zaleucus, the legislator of Locris, and Charondas of Sybaris, were disciples of Pythagoras, and both celebrated to immortality for the wisdom of their laws, five hundred years before Christ. Why are those laws lost? I say, the spirit of party has destroyed them; civil, political, and ecclesiastical bigotry. Despotical, monarchical,

p. 417 (cont.)

aristocratical, and democratical fury, have all been employed in this work of destruction of every thing that could give us true light, and a clear insight of antiquity. For every one of these parties, when possessed of power, or when they have been undermost, and struggling to get uppermost, has been equally prone to every species of fraud and violence and usurpation." (L. John Adams to Thomas Jefferson, 25 December 1813: <u>WJA</u>, X, pp. 84-85)

(22-24) "In another place, p. 326, Priestley says, 'there is no circumstance of which M. Dupuis avails himself so much, or repeats so often, both with respect to the Jewish and Christian religions, as the history of the <u>fall of man</u>, in the beginning of the book of Genesis. I believe with him, and have maintained in my writings, that this history is either an allegory, or founded on uncertain tradition; that it is a hypothesis to account for the origin of evil, adopted by Moses, which, by no means, accounts for the facts.' [Adams writes, a few lines later, "I shall never be a disciple of Priestley."] . . .

"There is a work which I wish I possessed. It has never crossed the Atlantic. It is entitled <u>Acta Sanctorum</u>, in forty-seven volumes in folio. It contains the lives of the saints. It was compiled in the beginning of the sixteenth century by Bollandus, Henschenius, and Papebroch.

p. 417 (cont.)

What would I give to possess, in one immense map, one stupendous draught, all the legends, true, doubtful, and false? These Bollandists dared to discuss some of the facts, and to hint that some of them were doubtful. E. g. Papebroch doubted the antiquity of the Carmelites from Elias; and whether the face of Jesus Christ was painted on the handkerchief of St. Veronique; and whether the prepuce of the Savior of the world, which was shown in the church at Antwerp, could be proved to be genuine." (L. John Adams to Thomas Jefferson, begun in February and written in several parts at intervals, bears the date 14 March 1814 in the Charles Francis Adams edition: WJA, X, pp. 93-94)

(25-31) "That heroes come to bad ends, has been the experience of all ages. Alexander, Caesar, Charles XII., and Oliver Cromwell, and millions of others, as wild and delirious as they, have all come to a like catastrophe. Read the histories of our missionary societies. Is there not the same enthusiasm, the same heroism? I scarcely dare to say what I know, that many a kept mistress has dared for her lover as great hazards and sufferings, as any of these sublime heroes, temporal or spiritual. . . .

". . . The tories have 'intimated' to me in various secret, confidential, round-about ways, these mighty

p. 417 (cont.)

bugbears. 'Mr. Adams saved the fisheries once I hope his son will save them a second time. We have no confidence in Gallatin, Clay, Russell, or even Bayard; we believe they would all sacrifice the fisheries for Canada or even for peace.' My invariable answer has been, 'You deceive yourselves with imaginary fears. You know that the men Bayard, Russell, Clay, and even Gallatin would cede the fee simple of the United States, as soon as they would the fisheries.' . . .

"The lakes, the lakes, the lakes! shocking, indeed, that we have not the command of the lakes! But I could convince you that it is still more shocking that we have not the command of the ocean, or at least an independent power upon the ocean." (L. John Adams to Richard Rush, 30 May 1814: WJA, X, pp. 97-98)

(32) "France is humbled and Napoleon is banished; but the tyrant, the tyrant of tyrants is not fallen. John Bull still paws, and bellows terrible menaces and defiances." (L. John Adams to Mrs. Mercy Warren, 15 July 1814: WJA, X, p. 100)

(33-34) "Though France is humbled, Britain is not; though Bona[parte] is banished, a greater tyrant and wider usurper still domineers. John Bull is quite as

p. 417 (cont.)

unfeeling, as unprincipled, more powerful, has shed more blood than Bona. . . . He [Bonaparte] could no longer roar or struggle, growl or paw, he could only gasp his grin of death; I wish that France may not still regret him. But these are speculations in the clouds. I agree with you that the milk of human kindness in the Bourbons is safer for mankind than the fierce ambition of Napoleon." (L. John Adams to Thomas Jefferson, 16 July 1814: <u>WJA</u>, X, p. 102)

(34)   "All I can say is, that I would continue this war forever, rather than surrender one acre of our territory, one iota of the fisheries, as established by the third article of the treaty of 1783, or one sailor impressed from any merchant ship." (L. John Adams to James Madison, 28 November 1814: <u>WJA</u>, X, p. 106)

(35)   "There is not, Sir, in your masterly letter a more correct or important observation that that

p. 418   of 'the unhappy ignorance which exists among the

(1-4)   members of this great family, but resident in different sections of it, with regard to the objects and qualities of each other. This ignorance, the offspring of narrow prejudice and illiberality, is now presenting brimful the chalice of envy and hatred, where it should

p. 418 (cont.)

offer nothing but the cup of conciliation and confidence. It sprang from the little intercourse and less knowledge which the people of the then British Provinces possessed of each other antecedently to the American revolution, and instead of being dissipated by an event so honorable to them all, has been cherished and perpetuated for political party purposes, and for the promotion of the sinister views and ambitious projects of a few restless and unprincipled individuals, until the present period.' . . .

". . . In 1775, I labored day and night to lay the foundation of a navy, and in the four last years of the last century I hesitated at no expense to purchase navy yards, to collect timber to build ships, and spared no pains to select officers. And what was the effect? No part of my administration was so unpopular, not only in the western, the southern, and middle States, but in all New England, and, strange to tell, even in Marblehead, Salem, Newburyport, and Boston. . . .

"I wish not to fatigue you with too long a letter at once; but, Sir, I will defend my missions to France, as long as I have an eye to direct my hand, or a finger to hold my pen. They were the most disinterested and meritorious actions of my life. I reflect upon them with so much satisfaction, that I desire no other inscription

p. 418 (cont.)

over my gravestone than: 'Here lies John Adams, who took upon himself the responsibility of the peace with France in the year 1800.'" (L. John Adams to James Lloyd, n.d. January 1815: <u>WJA</u>, X, pp. 109-111; p. 113)

(5-9) "One party reads the newspapers and pamphlets of its own church, and interdicts all writings of the opposite complexion. The other party condemns all such as heresy, and will not read or suffer to be read, as far as its influence extends, any thing but its own libels. 'The avenue to the public ear is shut' in Massachusetts, as Mr. Randolph says it is in Virginia. With us, the press is under a virtual imprimatur, to such a degree, that I do not believe I could get these letters to you printed in a newspaper in Boston. Each party is deliberately and studiously kept in ignorance of the other. . . .

". . . I mean that stream of misrepresentations of the men and measures of the administration in circular letters from members of Congress to their constituents in the middle and especially in the southern States, which began as early as 1789, when Congress was held in New York, and continued through the eight years of Washington's administration, flowing all the time in peculiarly copious abundance against me, and which, in the electioneering parliamentary campaign of 1796, and from thence to 1801,

p. 418 (cont.)

swelled, raged, foamed in all the fury of tempest at sea against me. A collection of those circular letters would make many volumes, and contain more lies in proportion to the time than the <u>Acta Sanctorum</u>. Yet no measures were taken to raise dikes against this inundation!" (L. John Adams to James Lloyd, 11 February 1815: <u>WJA</u>, X, pp. 117-119)

(10-14) "The Irish, who are very numerous and powerful in Pennsylvania, had been, and still were enthusiasts for the French revolution, extremely exasperated against old England, bitterly prejudiced against New England, strongly inclined in favor of the southern interest and against the northern. . . . The English, Scotch, and Irish Presbyterians, the Methodists, Anabaptists, the Unitarians and Universalists, with Dr. Priestly at their head, and all the other sectaries, even many of the Episcopalians themselves, had been carried away with the French revolution, and firmly believed that Bonaparte was the instrument of Providence to destroy the Pope and introduce the millennium. . . .

". . . Mr. Jefferson knew them all. These parties had all been making their court to him for fifteen years." (L. John Adams to James Lloyd, 14 February 1815: <u>WJA</u>, X, p. 120) Concerning the word <u>Mihites</u> in line 10, the <u>Index</u>

p. 418 (cont.)

(p. 144) suggests that the word perhaps should be the Latin <u>milites</u>, meaning "soldiers." Some kind of error of transcription has occurred, but given the letter from which these lines are taken, I am not convinced that the <u>Index</u> has provided an appropriate correction.

(15-19) "'Hamilton has divided the federalists, and proposed to them to give you the go-by and bring in Pinckney. By this step he has divided the federalists, and given great offence to the honestest part of them. I am glad of it, for it will be the ruin of his faction.' My answer was, 'Colonel [Joseph] Lyman, it will be, as you say, the ruin of his faction; but it will also be the ruin of honester men than any of them.' And with these words I marched on, and left him to march the other way. I was soon afterwards informed by personal witnesses and private letters, that Hamilton had assembled a meeting of the citizens and made an elaborate harangue to them. He spoke of the President, John Adams, with respect! But with what respect, I leave you, Sir, to conjecture. Hamilton soon after called another more secret caucus to prepare a list of representatives for the city of New York, in their State legislature, who were to choose electors of President and Vice-President. He fixed upon a list of his own friends, people of little weight or consideration

p. 418 (cont.)

in the city or the country. Burr, who had friends in all circles, had a copy of this list brought to him immediately. He read it over, with great gravity folded it up, put it in his pocket, and, without uttering another word said, 'Now I have him all hollow;' but immediately went to Governor Clinton, General Gates, Chancellor Livingston, &c., &c., stirred them all up, and persuaded the Governor and the General to stand candidates, with a list of the most respectable citizens, to represent the city in the legislature. Burr's list was chosen, as common sense must have foreseen, by a great majority, went to Albany, and chose electors, who voted unanimously for Mr. Jefferson, though New York at all antecedent elections voted unanimously for Adams." (L. John Adams to James Lloyd, 17 February 1815: <u>WJA</u>, X, p. 125)

(20)   "Of course, consultation after consultation took place between me and my secretary of the treasury, Mr. Wolcott, concerning the terms of this loan [for revenue to support the army],--a loan that <u>now</u> appears but a trifle. Mr. Wolcott's opinion was, that the loan could not be obtained at a less interest than eight per cent. I objected to this interest. I thought it extravagant and unnecessary. I thought it might be had at six per cent. . . . At another interview, Mr. Wolcott

p. 418 (cont.)

persevered in his opinion that eight per cent. was the lowest interest at which the loan could be obtained. . . . Mr. Wolcott, however, at our next conference, persisted in his opinion, was afraid to publish proposals for the loan at a less interest than eight per cent. My patience, which had been put, by enemies and friends, to so many severe trials, was quite exhausted, and I broke out, 'This damned army will be the ruin of this country; if it must be so, it must; I cannot help it. <u>Issue your proposals as you please</u>.'" (L. John Adams to James Llyod, 21 February 1815: <u>WJA</u>, X, pp. 129-130)

(21-22) ". . . What was I to think of Mr. Pitt and the British cabinet? Was it possible that Miranda should be such a conjurer as to bewitch Mr. Pitt and his colleagues into a serious belief, that South America was to be revolutionized so easily by Miranda and his two Jesuits? Did they believe the South Americans capable of a free government, or a combination of free federative republics, according to Miranda's plan?" (L. John Adams to James Lloyd, 26 March 1815: <u>WJA</u>, X, p. 141)

(23) "Very fortunately for me and for this nation, the French Directory had a lucid interval, and gave me a fair opportunity to institute that mission to France,

p. 418 (cont.)

que vous fletrissez, that mission to France which you describe as the 'great shade in my Presidential escutcheon,' and which I wish to inscribe on my gravestone; and which, if we had escutcheons in this country, I would contrive to introduce into mine." (L. John Adams to James Lloyd, 29 March 1815: WJA, X, pp. 147-148)

(24-27) "The truth is, there is not one people of Europe that knows or cares any thing about constitutions. There is not one nation in Europe that understands or is capable of understanding any constitution whatever. . . . If there is a colorable exception, it is England." (L. John Adams to James Lloyd, 30 March 1815: WJA, X, pp. 149-150)

(28-30) "God forbid that American naval power should ever be such a scourge to the human race as that of Great Britain has been! I was engaged in the most earnest, sedulous, and, I must own, expensive exertions to preserve peace with the Indians, and prepare them for agriculture and civilization, through the whole of my administration. I had the inexpressible satisfaction of complete success. Not a hatchet was lifted in my time; and the single battle of Tippecanoe has since cost the United States a hundred times more money than it cost me to maintain universal and perpetual peace." (L. John Adams to James Lloyd, 31 March 1815: WJA, X, p. 153)

p. 419
(1-5) "Neither nature nor art has partitioned the sea into empires, kingdoms, republics, or states. There are no dukedoms, earldoms, baronies, or knight's fees, no freeholds, pleasure grounds, ornamented or unornamented farms,

p. 419 (cont.)

gardens, parks, groves, or forests there, appropriated to nations or individuals, as there are upon land. Let Mahomet, and the Pope, and Great Britain say what they will, mankind will act the part of slaves and cowards, if they suffer any nation to usurp dominion over the ocean or any portion of it. . . .

". . . We have a stronger and clearer right to all these fisheries in their largest extent than any Britons or Europeans ever had or could have, for they were all indebted to us and our ancestors for all these fisheries. We discovered them; we explored them; we settled the country, at our own expense, industry, and labor, without assistance from Britain or from Europe. . . .

". . . But we set up no claims but those asserted and acknowledged in the treaty of 1783. These we do assert, and these we will have and maintain.

". . . Former treaties, not formally repeated in a new treaty, are presumed to be received and acknowledged. The fisheries are therefore ours, and the navigation of the Mississippi theirs, that is the British, as much as ever." (L. John Adams to Richard Rush, 5 April 1815: WJA, X, pp. 160-161)

(6)   "Mr. Madison's administration has proved great points long disputed in Europe and America.

p. 419 (cont.)

"1. He has proved, that an administation under our present Constitution can declare war.

"2. That it can make peace.

"3. That money or no money, government or no government, Great Britain can never conquer this country or any considerable part of it.

"4. That our officers and men by land are equal to any from Spain and Portugal.

"5. That our trans-Alleghanian States, in patriotism, bravery, enterprise, and perseverance, are at least equal to any in the Union.

"6. That our navy is equal, <u>caeteris</u> <u>paribus</u>, to any that ever floated.

"In a few minutes I shall be elevated to your honorable rank of an octogenarian." (L. John Adams to Thomas McKean, 6 July 1815: <u>WJA</u>, X, pp. 167-168)

(7-11) "That our correspondence has been observed, is no wonder, for your hand is more universally known than your face. No printer has asked me for copies, but it is no surprise that you have been requested. These gentry will print whatever will sell; and our correspondence is thought such an oddity by both parties, that they imagine an edition would soon go off, and yield them profits. There has, however, been no tampering with your letters to

p. 419 (cont.)
me. They have all arrived in good order." (L. John Adams to Thomas Jefferson, 24 August 1815: <u>WJA</u>, X, p. 173)

(12-15) "I have received Memoirs of the life of Dr. Price, by William Morgan, F. R. S. . . . 'But some of his [Dr. Price's] correspondents were not quite so sanguine [about the beneficial prospects of the French revolution] in their expectations [as Dr. Price was] from the last of these revolutions, and among these the late American ambassador, Mr. John Adams. In a long letter, which he wrote to Dr. Price at this time, so far from congratulating him on the occasion, he expresses himself in terms of contempt in regard to the French revolution; and after asking rather too severely, what good was to be expected from a nation of atheists, he concludes with foretelling the destruction of a million of human beings, as the probable consequence of it. These harsh censures and gloomy predictions were particularly ungrateful to Dr. Price; nor can it be denied, that they must have then appeared as the effusions of a splenetic mind, rather than as the sober reflections of an unbiased understanding.' . . .

"Mr. Morgan has been more discreet and complaisant to you than to me. He has mentioned respectfully your letters from Paris to Dr. Price, but has given us none of

p. 419 (cont.)

them. As I would give more for those letters than for all the rest of the book, I am more angry with him for disappointing me than for all he says of me, and my letter, which, scambling as it is, contains nothing but sure words of prophecy." (L. John Adams to Thomas Jefferson, 13 November 1815: <u>WJA</u>, X, pp. 175-176)

(16)   "I do not recollect any <u>formal</u> speeches, such as are made in the British Parliament and our late Congresses, to have been made in the revolutionary Congress, though I was a member for eight years, from 1774 until the preliminaries of peace were signed. We had no time to hear such speeches; little for deliberation; action was the order of the day. . . .

"What changes in Europe have occurred since I had the pleasure of writing to you last! Louis XVIII. is again on the throne of France; the great Napoleon at the bottom of the wheel, never to rise more, a prisoner for life. The French nation miserable; Spain has reestablished the tribunal of the Inquisition, and restored the Jesuits." (L. Thomas McKean to John Adams, 20 November 1815: <u>WJA</u>, X, pp. 177-178)

(17)   "General Wilkinson may have written the military history of the war that followed the Revolution; that was

p. 419 (cont.)

an effect of it, and was supported by the American citizens in defence of it against an invasion of it by the government of Great Britain and Ireland, and all her allies, black, white, and pied; but this will by no means be a history of the American Revolution. The revolution was in the minds of the people, and in the union of the colonies, both of which were accomplished before hostilities commenced. This revolution and union were gradually forming from the year 1760 to 1775." (L. John Adams to Thomas McKean, 26 November 1815: <u>WJA</u>, X, p. 180)

(18)   "Another innovation was contrived, and a board of commissioners of the customs created; but the remonstrances and associations against the execution of the acts were so formidable, that the ministry thought it necessary to send a fleet and army to protect Temple, Hallowell, Paxton, Birch, and Robinson, their adherents and followers." (L. John Adams to Dr. J. Morse, 1 January 1816: <u>WJA</u>, X, p. 199)

(19-20) "When the cause came on, however, Mr. [James] Otis displayed so comprehensive a knowledge of the subject, showed not only the illegality of the writ, its insidious and mischievous tendency, but he laid open the views and designs of Great Britain, in taxing us, of destroying

p. 419 (cont.)

our charters and assuming the powers of our government, legislative, executive, and judicial, external and internal, civil and ecclesiastical, temporal and spiritual; and all this was performed with such a profusion of learning, such convincing argument, and such a torrent of sublime and pathetic eloquence, that a great crowd of spectators and auditors went away absolutely electrified. . . .

"Here, then, Sir, began the revolution in the principles, views, opinions, and feelings of the American people. Their eyes were opened to a clear sight of the danger that threatened them and their posterity, and the liberties of both in all future generations." (L. John Adams to Dr. J. Morse, 29 November 1815: <u>WJA</u>, X, pp. 183-184)

(21-22) "Had the door of a citizen been broken, to let in the soldiers, such was the inflammation of spirits that they would all have been made prisoners before morning; but the officers had too much sense. They put themselves and their men upon the compassionate list. 'The poor soldiers were innocent. They knew not why they were sent here. Can you see your fellow-creatures perish in your streets for want of shelter?' Humanity prevailed. . . . Wrangles and quarrels frequently occurred between the citizens and the soldiers; exasperation increased on both sides, till it broke out in the melancholy catastrophe of

p. 419 (cont.)

the 5th of March, 1771 [the Boston Massacre]. Now appeared the spirit of freemen; multitudes from Boston and the neighboring towns assembled spontaneously the next day, and from day to day. Strong guards were placed in the State House, and every man appeared to be ready at the toll of a bell or the sound of a gun to turn out with his arms. The assembly applied to the governor and council. Mr. Hutchinson was Lieutenant-Governor and commander-in-chief. Colonel Dalrymple was sent for. Samuel Adams appeared in his true character. His caution, his discretion, his ingenuity, his sagacity, his self-command, his presence of mind, and his intrepidity, commanded the admiration and loud applauses of both parties. The troops were ordered to the Castle, and Lord North called them from this time 'Sam Adams's two regiments.'" (L. John Adams to Dr. J. Morse, 1 January 1816: <u>WJA</u>, X, pp. 199-200)

(23-24) "I may return to it [the letter John Adams had received from William Tudor] hereafter, but at present, with your leave, I will continue a few hints on the judicial character of Chief Justice Hutchinson. I pass over that scenery, which he introduced, so showy and so shallow, so theatrical and so ecclesiastical, of scarlet and sable robes, of broad bands, and enormous tie wigs, more

p. 419 (cont.)

resembling fleeces of painted merino wool than any thing natural to man and that could breathe with him." (L. John Adams to William Tudor, 18 December 1816: <u>WJA</u>, X, pp. 232-233)

(24-25) These lines refer to the case John Adams argued for the trial of Michael Corbet and the three other sailors who killed Lieutenant Panton, of the Rose frigate, while resisting impressment. See <u>WJA</u>, X, p. 234n. See also Pound's first reference to this case in Canto 64, page 359, lines 15-23. This passage in Canto 64 is taken from a letter John Adams wrote to William Tudor on 30 December 1816, which Charles Francis Adams has inserted as a note in <u>WJA</u>, II, pp. 224-226.

(26-27) "This was a delicate and a dangerous crisis [following the Boston Massacre]. . . . The whole militia of the city was in requisition, and military watches and guards were everywhere placed. We were all upon a level; no man was exempted; our military officers were our only superiors. I had the honor to be summoned, in my turn, and attended at the State House with my musket and bayonet, my broadsword and cartridge-box, under the command of the famous Paddock. I know you will laugh at my military figure; but I believe there was not a more obedient soldier

p. 419 (cont.)

in the regiment, nor one more impartial between the people and the regulars." (L. John Adams to William Tudor, 15 April 1817: <u>WJA</u>, X, pp. 251-252)

(28-29) "So far from believing in the total and universal depravity of human nature, I believe there is no individual totally depraved. The most abandoned scoundrel that ever existed, never yet wholly extinguished his conscience, and, while conscience remains, there is some religion. Popes, Jesuists, and Sorbonnists, and Inquisitors, have some conscience and some religion. So had Marius and Sylla." (L. John Adams to Thomas Jefferson, 19 April 1817: <u>WJA</u>, X, p. 254)

(29-34) "You 'never profoundly admired Mr. Hancock. He had vanity and caprice.' I can say, with

p. 420 truth, that I profoundly admired him, and more
(1-2) profoundly loved him. If he had vanity and caprice, so had I. And if his vanity and caprice made me sometimes sputter, as you know they often did, mine, I well know, had often a similar effect upon him. . . . His father died when he was very young. His uncle, the most opulent merchant in Boston, who had no children, adopted him, placed him in Mr. Lovell's school, educated him at Harvard college, and then took him into his store.

p. 420 (cont.)

And what a school was this! Four large ships constantly plying between Boston and London, and other business in proportion. This was in 1755. He became an example to all the young men of the town. Wholly devoted to business, he was as regular and punctual at his store as the sun in his course. His uncle sent him to London, from whence, after a residence of about a year, he returned to his store, with the same habits of business, unaltered in manners or deportment, and pursued his employments with the same punctuality and assiduity, till the death of his uncle, who left him his business, his credit, his capital, and his fortune; who did more--he left him the protector of his widow. . . . No alterations appeared in Mr. Hancock, either from his travels in England, or from his accession to the fortune of his uncle. . . .

"What shall I say of his fortune, his ships? His commerce was a great one. Your honored father told me, at that time, that not less than a thousand families were, every day in the year, dependent on Mr. Hancock for their daily bread . . . .

"At the time of this prosperity, I was one day walking in the mall, and, accidentally, met Samuel Adams. In taking a few turns together, we came in full view of Mr. Hancock's house. Mr. Adams, pointing to the stone building, said, 'This town has done a wise thing to-day.' 'What?' 'They

500

p. 420 (cont.)

have made that young man's fortune their own.' His prophecy was literally fulfilled; for no man's property was ever more entirely devoted to the public. The town had, that day, chosen Mr. Hancock into the legislature of the province." (L. John Adams to William Tudor, 1 June 1817: <u>WJA</u>, X, pp. 259-260)

(3-6) "James Otis, Samuel Adams, and John Hancock were the three most essential characters [in making the American Revolution]; and Great Britain knew it, though America does not . . . .

"'<u>Quae ante conditam condendamve urbem, poeticis magis decora fabulis, quam incorruptis rerum gestarum monumentis traduntur, ea' nec possum refellere</u>." (L. John Adams to William Tudor, 5 June 1817: <u>WJA</u>, X, p. 263) The Latin quoted by Pound, <u>magis decora poeticis fabulis</u>, means "more suitable to poetic myths." (<u>Index</u>, p. 134) I have been unable to identify a single passage that brings together the names of Joseph Hawley and John Jay with those of Otis, Samuel Adams, and Hancock, but John Adams clearly admired the other two men as well. Perhaps Pound has put them together for that reason.

(7-8) "He [James Otis] was well versed in Greek and Roman history, philosophy, oratory, poetry, and mythology.

p. 420 (cont.)

His classical studies had been unusually ardent, and his acquisitions uncommonly great. He had composed a treatise on Latin prosody, which he lent to me, and I urged him to print. He consented. It is extant, and may speak for itself. It has been lately reviewed in the Anthology by one of our best scholars, at a mature age, and in a respectable station. He had also composed, with equal skill and great labor, a treatise on Greek prosody." (L. John Adams to H. Niles, 14 January 1818: WJA, X, p. 275)

(9-10) "I had it [the treatise on Greek prosody written by James Otis] six months in my possession, before I returned it. Since my return from Europe, I asked his daughter whether she had found that work among her father's manuscripts. She answered me with a countenance of woe that you may more easily imagine than I can describe, that she 'had not a line from her father's pen; that he had spent much time, and taken great pains, to collect together all his letters and other papers, and, in one of his unhappy moments, committed them all to the flames.' I have used her own expressions." (L. John Adams to William Tudor, 5 June 1817: WJA, X, p. 265)

(11-12) I have been unable to identify a source for these lines. The first Continental Congress met in

p. 420 (cont.)

September of 1774, but I do not know that that is what Pound is referring to in line 12.

(13-18) "When I returned it [the Greek prosody by James Otis], I begged him to print it. He said there were no Greek types in the country, or, if there were, there was no printer who knew how to use them. . . .

"Thus qualified to resist the system of usurpation and despotism, meditated by the British ministry, under the auspices of the Earl of Bute, Mr. Otis resigned his commission from the crown, as Advocate-General, an office very lucrative at that time, and a sure road to the highest favors of government in America, and engaged in the cause of his country without fee or reward . . . .

"Hampden was shot in open field of battle. Otis was basely assassinated in a coffee-house, in the night, by a well-dressed banditti, with a commissioner of the customs at their head. (L. John Adams to H. Niles, 14 January 1818: <u>WJA</u>, X, pp. 275-276)

(19-22) Pound's recapitulation of certain key events in the life of John Adams.

(22-24) "Silver and gold are but commodities, as much as wheat and lumber; the merchants who study the necessity,

p. 420 (cont.)

and feel out the wants of the community, can always import enough to supply the necessary circulating currency, as they can broadcloth or sugar, the trinkets of Birmingham and Manchester, or the hemp of Siberia. . . . I beg leave to refer you to a work which Mr. Jefferson has sent me, translated by himself from a French manuscript of the Count Destutt Tracy. His chapter 'of money' contains the sentiments that I have entertained all my lifetime. I will quote only a few lines from the analytical table, page 21. 'It is to be desired, that coins had never borne other names than those of their weight, and that the arbitrary denominations, called moneys of account, as £, s., d., &c., had never been used. But when these denominations are admitted and employed in transactions, to diminish the quantity of metal to which they answer, by an alteration of the real coins, is to steal; and it is a theft which even injures him who commits it. A theft of greater magnitude and still more ruinous, is the making of paper money; it is greater, because in this money there is absolutely no real value; it is more ruinous, because, by its gradual depreciation during all the time of its existence, it produces the effect which would be produced by an infinity of successive deteriorations of the coins. All these iniquities are founded on the false idea, that money is but a sign." (L. John Adams to John Taylor,

504

p. 420 (cont.)

12 March 1819: <u>WJA</u>, X, pp. 375-376)

(25-27) I have been unable to identify a source for these lines. The <u>Index</u> (p. 148) suggests that "Charlie Mordecai" possibly refers to Karl Marx.

(28-35) "However tedious and painful it may be for you to read, or me to transcribe any part of these
p. 421   dull statutes, we must endure the task, or we
(1-8)   shall never understand the American Revolution. Recollect and listen to the preamble of this statute, of the 7th and 8th of William III. chapter 22d.

"'Whereas, notwithstanding divers acts made for <u>the encouragement of the navigation of this kingdom</u>, and for the better securing and regulating the plantation trade, more especially one act of Parliament made in the 12th year of the reign of the late King Charles II., intituled an act for the increasing of shipping and navigation; another act, made in the 15th year of the reign of his said late Majesty, intituled an act for the encouragement of trade; another act, made in the 22d and 23d years of his said late Majesty's reign, intituled an act to prevent the planting of tobacco in England, and for regulation of the plantation trade; another act, made in the 25th year of the reign of his said late Majesty, intituled an act for the encouragement of the Greenland and Eastland

p. 421 (cont.)

fisheries, and for the better securing the plantation trade, great abuses are daily committed, to the prejudice of the English navigation and the loss of a great part of the plantation trade to this kingdom by the artifice and cunning of ill-disposed persons; for remedy whereof for the future,' &c.

"Will you be so good, Sir, as to pause a moment on this preamble? To what will you liken it? Does it resemble a great, rich, powerful West India planter, Alderman Beckford, for example, preparing and calculating and writing instructions for his overseers? 'You are to have no regard to the health, strength, comfort, natural affections, or moral feelings, or intellectual endowments of my negroes. You are only to consider what subsistence to allow them, and what labor to exact of them will subserve my interest. According to the most accurate calculation I can make, the proportion of subsistence and labor, which will work them up, in six years upon an average, is the most profitable to the planter. And this allowance, surely, is very humane; for we estimate here the lives of our coal-heavers upon an average at only two years, and our fifty thousand girls of the town at three years at most. And our soldiers and seamen no matter what.'

"Is there, Mr. Tudor, in this preamble, or in any statute of Great Britain, in the whole book, the smallest

p. 421 (cont.)

consideration of the health, the comfort, the happiness, the wealth, the growth, the population, the agriculture, the manufactures, the commerce, the fisheries of the American people? All these things are to be sacrificed to British wealth, British commerce, British domination, and the British navy, as the great engine and instrument to accomplish all." (L. John Adams to William Tudor, 6 August 1818: <u>WJA</u>, X, pp. 339-340)

(9-10) I have been unable to identify a source for these two lines. The name of John Hobhouse, described as a "British administrator and liberal pamphleteer" in the <u>Index</u> (p. 94), also appears in Canto 33, page 163, lines 3-6.

(11-16) The Greek quoted by Pound for these lines means "Most honored of the immortals, worshipped under many names, all-powerful always, Zeus, first cause of nature, who govern all things with law." (<u>Index</u>, p. 265) According to the <u>Index</u>, "These are the first two lines (dactylic hexameters, which Pound has divided in his own way) of Cleanthes' Hymn to Zeus, OBGV no. 483."

APPENDIX A

JOHN ADAMS: A CHRONOLOGY

Ezra Pound's elaborate use of repetitions in the "Adams Cantos" produces an ebb and flow of events that is at first confusing, but the narrative takes on greater clarity once the reader knows the chronology of those events.

The <u>Annotated Index</u> of Edwards and Vasse contains, in "Appendix C," a chronology of all dates mentioned in the <u>Cantos</u>, supplemented by additional dates interpolated to provide Pound's chronology a fuller context; it is annotated with brief lines from the <u>Cantos</u> that go with the dates. In the <u>Diary and Autobiography of John Adams</u>, ed. L. H. Butterfield, Leonard C. Faber, and Wendell D. Garrett (Cambridge, Mass.: Harvard Univ. Press, 1961), IV, 257-71, there is a detailed chronology of the life of John Adams. This chronology is the essential source for quick information about what Adams did and when in his long career, but it includes only events in which Adams (or his son John Quincy) is directly involved. One does not find here when the Stamp Act was passed or what it contained, though one does learn what Adams wrote in response to it. Finally, Page Smith, in his eloquent biography, gives the dates of the many important events he recounts in the life of Adams, but these dates, buried in the narrative, are often difficult to ferret out.

The following chronology attempts a concise survey of the life of John Adams, identifying, along with the significant activities of his own career, the controversies that engaged his attention and the major events present in the background of his affairs. This chronology relies greatly on information found in the "Introduction," notes, and chronology of the Butterfield, Faber, and Garrett edition of the Adams <u>Diary</u> and <u>Autobiography</u>. Readers desiring to make a further investigation of the career of John Adams will find this source invaluable.

1735 John Adams born $\frac{19}{30}$ October (old and new style).

1754 Albany Plan of Union, as drafted by Benjamin Franklin to meet a growing threat to British colonies from France, adopted at Albany Congress by the colonies represented but later the various colonial assemblies reject it.
Lords of Trade propose a plan for raising revenue: "Dr. Franklin, who was known to be an active and very able man, and to have great influence in the province of Pennsylvania, was in Boston in the year 1754, and Mr. Shirley communicated to him the profound secret--the great design of taxing the colonies by act of parliament." (Novanglus: WJA, IV, p. 19)

1760-1775 "What do we mean by the revolution? The War? That was no part of the revolution; it was only an effect and consequence of it. The revolution was in the minds of the people, and this was effected from 1760-1775, in the course of fifteen years, before a drop of blood was shed at Lexington." (L. John Adams to Thomas Jefferson, 24 August 1815: WJA, X, p. 172)

1760 Accession of George III, age 22, to the throne of England.

1761 Writs of Assistance, general search warrants authorizing local peace officers to help customs officers locate smuggled goods and collect customs duties on them, opposed by James Otis, who loses his case-- the Writs are judged legal and valid--but raises constitutional issues on which the fight for independence will later be based. Grenville, Chancellor of the Exchequer. The notes John Adams takes during the trial are the only extant record of the trial itself. (See WJA, I, pp. 57-60; II, p. 124n1 and Appendix A)

1763 French and Indian War (Seven Years War in Europe) ends with Treaty of Paris.

1764 Sugar Act passed, bringing higher duties on sugar, lower duties on molassas, and new taxes on wines, silks, and other luxuries. Grenville, Chancellor.
John Adams marries Abigail Smith 25 October.

1765   Stamp Act passes Parliament in March, to go into effect in November. It requires all official and legal documents, newspapers, almanacs, and pamphlets circulated in colonies to carry stamps showing that a tax on them had been paid. Grenville, Chancellor.

Quartering Act passed, requiring colonists to furnish lodging for British troops if local barracks are inadequate. Grenville, Chancellor.

House of Burgesses, in late spring, passes Virginia Resolves drawn up by Patrick Henry condemning Stamp Act because it taxes without consent of the people.

"A Dissertation on Canon and Feudal Law," by John Adams, appears, unsigned, in the Boston Gazette of 12 August, the first of four installments; in this work Adams describes how ecclesiastical and feudal laws had been used to institutionalize a tyrannous power over the common people and concludes with a protest against the Stamp Act.

John Adams drafts "Braintree Instructions" for the town's delegate to the General Court convening in October. These "Instructions" emphasize the unconstitutionality of the Stamp Act and raise objections to trial without jury in Admiralty Courts for those who violate the Act. Draper publishes the "Instructions" in his paper, and they are subsequently adopted by forty other towns in the colony as "Instructions" for their representatives.

Stamp Act Congress meets in New York in October, shortly before Stamp Act goes into effect, at the suggestion of Massachusetts. The first assembly of the colonies whose resolutions receive wide support in the colonies themselves, this Congress formally asserts that the colonies are not represented in Parliament and objects to the unconstitutionality of taxation without representation.

1766   Parliament repeals Stamp Act in March.

Parliament passes Declaratory Act, asserting that King and Parliament can bind colonists in all cases.

"The Earl of Clarendon to William Pym," written by John Adams, appears in Boston Gazette in January to support patriot cause and reply to London writer "Pym" who had argued for Loyalist cause and the legality of the Stamp Act in London papers of 1765.

1767   John Adams publishes "Governor Winthrop to Governor Bradford" in Boston <u>Gazette</u> in January and February, examining the question of whether or not a ruler has the right to decide legality of elections. Adams writes to oppose articles favorable to Governor Bernard signed "Philanthropos."
Townshend Acts passed in June, imposing duties on such items as glass, lead, tea, and paper. Townshend, Chancellor.
John Quincy Adams born 11 July.
John Dickinson begins publishing his <u>Letters from a Farmer in Pennsylvania to the Inhabitants of the British Colonies</u> in November, protesting against the Townshend Acts.

1768   Governor Bernard arranges for Jonathan Sewall to offer John Adams the office of Advocate General in the Court of Admiralty, a lucrative position which Adams refuses because he is unwilling to be obligated to the Crown's policies or to the Crown's point of view.
In June John Adams drafts "Boston Instructions" protesting British seizure of John Hancock's sloop <u>Liberty</u>.
British troops arrive in Boston 29 September.

1768-69   John Adams defends John Hancock against the charge of smuggling wine in his sloop <u>Liberty</u>. Adams's defence decides the case in Hancock's favor and, published in newspapers, becomes an important influence in arousing public feeling against British customs policies.

1769   In May John Adams drafts "Boston Instructions" for the delegates to the General Court, emphasizing, among other things, that the debates of the assembly must be free and that the intimidating presence of British troops around the Court House must be removed.
John Adams defends four sailors charged with murdering Lt. Panton of the British frigate <u>Rose</u> while resisting impressment into service on the British ship. Adams wins acquittal for the sailors.
Colonies begin to form "nonimportation associations" to protest Townshend Acts, forbidding imports of British goods on which duties must be paid. In May House of Burgesses adopts the Virginia Association, the first nonimportation policy officially legitimized by formal vote of the people's elected representatives, in defiance of the Crown's authority.

1770   Lord North becomes Prime Minister in February.
        Boston Massacre occurs 5 March, in which British
           soldiers kill five Boston citizens.
        Townshend Acts, except tea duties, repealed by
           Parliament in April, a conciliatory gesture of
           Lord North.
        John Adams defends Captain Preston, indicted for
           murder in the Boston Massacre, in October, and
           wins a verdict of "not guilty." Three weeks
           later he successfully defends the other British
           soldiers charged in the case.

1773   John Adams, replying to William Brattle's argument
           that judges hold their appointments for life,
           publishes in the Boston Gazette of January and
           February his articles on the "Independence of the
           Judiciary" in which he asserts that an English
           judge holds a commission for life only quamdiu
           se bene gesserit, "during his good behavior." To
           Lord North's plan that the five superior court
           judges appointed by the Crown should also be
           salaried by the Crown rather than by the people
           as they had been previously, Adams responds that
           the executive and judicial branches must remain
           separate.
        Tea Act passes Parliament in the spring. Lord
           North's attempt to help British East India Company
           sell its surplus tea and avoid financial embar-
           rassment, this Act removes duty from tea BEIC
           imports into England and gives the Company a
           monopoly on the transport of tea to America where
           it will be taxed and where it can be sold only by
           Company agents.
        Boston Tea Party occurs 16 December.

1774   John Adams proposes and drafts articles of impeach-
           ment against Chief Justice Peter Oliver who had
           refused to renounce salary grants from the Crown;
           the Massachusetts House of Representatives adopts
           these articles in February. The Council refuses
           to convict, but the impeachment articles are widely
           disseminated through the newspapers. When Superior
           Court sits in Boston for the Suffolk session, the
           grand and petit jurors all refuse to take the
           oaths, saying that they cannot serve as jurors
           while the Chief Justice stands impeached before
           the Council. Jurors in other counties follow suit,
           and the Courts close until after the battle of
           Lexington 19 April 1775.

1774 (cont.) "Intolerable Acts" (Coercive Acts) pass Parliament during the summer; these Acts include the Boston Port Bill, which closes the port of Boston until the tea destroyed the previous December has been paid for, and the Massachusetts Government Act under which a military governor (General Gage) is set up, and under which Town Meetings can meet only with official permission and only for town business. An Administration of Justice Act goes into effect, providing that officers of the Crown accused of capitol offenses may be tried elsewhere at the discretion of the governor, an especially offensive Act in view of the fair trial given the British soldiers after the Boston Massacre.

Intended to isolate Massachusetts, the "Intolerable Acts" have the opposite effect:

First Continental Congress assembles at Philadelphia in September.

Congress adopts Continental Association to boycott both import and export trade with Great Britain.

Congress endorses the Suffolk Resolves of Suffolk County, Massachusetts, thus assuring that the other colonies will support Massachusetts; these Resolves declare the "Intolerable Acts" null and void.

Congress, at the end of September, rejects, by one vote, the Galloway plan of union with Britain which proposed a colonial legislature under the Crown with the powers the House of Commons has in England.

General Gage dissolves the Massachusetts Assembly in the autumn and the Assembly reconvenes in Salem to sit out of his reach as a provincial congress and govern non-Boston Massachusetts through a Committee of Safety that organizes Minutemen, munitions, and supplies.

First Continental Congress adjourns 26 October.

1775 Novanglus articles begin to appear in Boston Gazette in January. Written by John Adams in reply to articles by Daniel Leonard signed "Massachusettensis" which criticized the patriot position, Novanglus contains an elaborate account of the constitutional arguments justifying the patriot cause.

The battles of Lexington and Concord occur 19 April.

Second Continental Congress convenes in May.

John Adams in June nominates George Washington Commander of the Continental Army and Congress votes its approval.

1775 (cont.) In July Congress approves the second petition to the King, the "Olive Branch Petition" proposed by John Dickinson much to John Adams's chagrin in an effort at reconciliation, and sends it to the King.

For the fledgling colonial navy John Adams writes a manual of naval regulations entitled <u>Rules for the Regulation of the Navy of the United Colonies of North America</u>.

1776 John Adams writes "Thoughts on Government" during the first months of 1776, expressing his views on the best design for state constitutions.

Congress opens ports to all countries not subjects of Great Britain.

John Dickinson, on 1 July, makes important speech against the resolution of independence proposed by Richard Henry Lee, arguing that such a drastic step is premature.

John Adams answers Dickinson on the floor of Congress with a persuasive speech in favor of independence.

On 2 July Congress passes Lee's resolution of independence.

On 4 July Congress adopts Jefferson's draft of the Declaration of Independence.

[Of the role John Adams played in winning approval of the independence declaration, Thomas Jefferson later writes: "No man better merited than Mr. John Adams to hold a most conspicuous place in the design. He was the pillar of its support on the floor of Congress, its ablest advocate and defender against the multifarious assaults it encountered; for many excellent persons opposed it on doubts, whether we were provided sufficiently with the means of supporting it, whether the minds of our constituents were yet prepared to receive it, &c., who, after it was decided, united zealously in the measures it called for." (L. Thomas Jefferson to W. P. Gardner, February 1813: <u>WJA</u>, III, p. 57n)]

In September John Adams travels with Benjamin Franklin and Edward Rutledge to visit Admiral Lord Howe on Staten Island.

1777 Congress drafts Articles of Confederation.

Surrender of Burgoyne at Saratoga, New York, in October, wins open support of France and other European countries for the independence struggle.

In November Congress appoints John Adams to join Benjamin Franklin and Arthur Lee as commissioner to France.

Washington occupies Valley Forge in December.

1778   France signs treaty of alliance with United States on 6 February.

With his son John Quincy, John Adams sails to France on frigate Boston in February, beginning his ten-year service in Europe as diplomat for the United States.

Louis XVI, age 24, gives John Adams his first audience in May.

1779   John Adams receives word in February that Congress has relieved him of his commission to the French Court.

In June John Adams, on board French frigate La Sensible, sails from L'Orient for Boston, arriving there 2 August.

John Adams, representing Braintree at constitutional convention for Massachusetts in September, drafts a Report of a Constitution or Form of Government for the Commonwealth of Massachusetts.

In September Congress elects John Adams minister to negotiate treaties of peace and commerce with Great Britain.

In November John Adams sails again for France, taking with him his sons John Quincy and Charles on board La Sensible.

On 8 December, after springing a leak during a storm, La Sensible arrives at Ferrol, Spain. John Adams and his party cross the mountains of northern Spain to France by carriage in winter, leaving from Corunna on 26 December and passing through Lugo, Villafranca, Astorga, Leon, Burgos, Bilboa, Bayonne, Bordeaux, and Angouleme on the way to Paris, a six-week journey of more than a thousand miles, arriving in Paris 9 February 1780.

1780   Massachusetts voters adopt, with some amendments, the draft of the state constitution prepared by John Adams.

Congress in June appoints John Adams to negotiate a Dutch loan.

Not yet knowing of the action of Congress, John Adams in July journeys to Amsterdam on his own initiative to attempt to secure for the United States financial aid from the Dutch.

John Adams writes, 4-27 October, his "Twenty-Six Letters, upon Interesting Subjects, respecting the Revolution of America," at the request of Hendrik Calkoen, a prominent Amsterdam lawyer.

1781   Maryland's adoption completes ratification of the Articles of Confederation.
        Congress in June elects John Adams commissioner, along with Franklin, Jay, Laurens, and Jefferson, to negotiate peace with Great Britain.
        Cornwallis surrenders at Yorktown 19 October.

1782   Lord North resigns as Prime Minister in March.
        In June John Adams secures first Dutch loan, in the amount of 5,000,000 guilders, to the United States. This and the three loans that follow in 1784, 1787, and 1788 as a result of Adams's efforts, ultimately amount to some $3,600,000. They are in effect the only substantial credit available to the government of the Confederation in its most difficult years. [See Samuel F. Bemis, The Diplomacy of the American Revolution (Bloomington: Indiana Univ. Press, 1965), p. 169.]
        John Adams completes treaty with the Netherlands on 8 October.
        John Adams returns to Paris to join the other U. S. commissioners in negotiations with the British in November; there he fights tenaciously for U. S. rights to the North Atlantic fisheries.

1783   Great Britain recognizes the independence of the United States and signs peace treaty at Paris 3 September.

1784   Congress ratifies peace treaty with Great Britain 14 January.
        John Adams, after a harrowing January journey across the North Sea to Amsterdam, negotiates a second Dutch loan in time to save the credit of the United States.
        During the summer Abigail Adams sails from Boston with her daughter to join her husband in Europe. John settles his family at Auteuil in Paris.

1785   In February Congress appoints John Adams first American minister to the Court of St. James, London.
        Congress appoints Thomas Jefferson the following month to succeed Benjamin Franklin at Versailles.
        On 1 June George III grants John Adams an audience.

1786   While visiting London in the spring to negotiate commercial treaties with Tripoli, Portugal, and Great Britain, Jefferson joins John Adams on a tour of the English countryside.

1786 (cont.) John Adams begins work on his <u>Defence of the Constitutions of Government of the United States</u>, written to support the concept of checks and balances in the new state constitutions.

1787 In January John Adams publishes the first volume of his <u>Defence</u>; two additional volumes follow.
The Constitutional Convention meets at Philadelphia 25 May-17 September--John Adams still in England.
John Adams visits Amsterdam in early summer to secure the third Dutch loan.

1788 In March John Adams negotiates his fourth loan from the Dutch to the United States.
Recalled from his assignment to the Court of St. James at his own request, John Adams and his wife sail on the <u>Lucretia</u> in late spring for Boston.

1789 John Adams elected Vice President and presides over the first session of the First Congress; Washington, President.
French Revolution begins with the storming of the Bastille 14 July. In the U. S. Thomas Jefferson and James Monroe will come to be the most prominent advocates of the ideals of the French Revolution.

1790 John Adams begins publishing his <u>Discourses on Davila</u> in Fenno's <u>Gazette of the United States</u>, intending it as a kind of sequel to his <u>Defence</u>.
United States Constitution ratified by Rhode Island, the last state to do so.

1791 John Adams quarrels with Jefferson after Jefferson praises Paine's <u>Rights of Man</u> and John Quincy Adams writes his "Publicola" papers criticizing both Paine and Jefferson.

1793 Louis XVI executed 21 January.
John Adams reelected Vice President; Washington, President.
Citizen Edmond Genet of the new French republic lands in Charleston and calls on the United States to fulfill its 1778 treaty of alliance with France in which the two countries had pledged mutual support in the event that France becomes involved in a defensive war with Great Britain. But in this instance it is France that has declared war on England. Genet attempts to enlist American adventurers in attacks on British shipping, and when he persists in his anti-British campaign, the Washington administration, before even accepting his credentials as ambassador, demands that he be recalled. [See Smith, <u>John Adams</u>, II, pp. 840-841.]

1794	Jay Treaty with Great Britain signed by John Jay and Lord Grenville. It does not satisfy all U. S. grievances--most notably, it says nothing about impressment of American sailors into service in the British navy--but in it Britain does agree to some of the terms previously ignored in the 1783 Treaty of Paris, i. e., to abandon its frontier fur posts by June 1796 and to open ports of British West Indies, under specified conditions, to American shipping.
1795	U. S. Senate ratifies Jay Treaty in June.
1796	John Adams elected President in December despite Hamilton's efforts to deny him a clear majority; Thomas Jefferson, Vice President.
1797-1801	John Adams's term as President.
1797	French Directory, outraged by Jay Treaty, rejects diplomatic mission of Charles Cotesworth Pinckney, who had been sent to Paris to replace James Monroe and instead is ordered off French soil. This is the first major crisis of the Adams administration.
1798	In March John Adams announces that a state of undeclared war, the quasi-war, exists with France. The conflict involves naval contests with warships and commercial shipping. At the request of the House of Representatives John Adams releases XYZ dispatches to the public in April. These dispatches show Talleyrand, now acting for the Directory, attempting to get new U. S. envoys John Marshall and Elbridge Gerry to agree to pay a bribe and also to assure France a loan in return for a favorable treaty with France. In June and July during the anti-French war fever, Congress passes the Federalist-sponsored Alien and Sedition Acts, and John Adams, though he has not asked for them, signs them into law. These laws include: a) a Naturalization Act requiring a fourteen-year residency of aliens before qualifying for U. S. citizenship; b) an Alien Act giving the President authority to remove from the U. S. in time of war or threat of war any aliens who are citizens of the enemy nation; c) a Sedition Act authorizing punishment of fines or imprisonment for any aliens or citizens who

1798 (cont.) oppose the execution of U. S. laws or publish false or malicious writings about the President or about the U. S. government.
These laws hand the Jeffersonian Republicans an immediate issue on which to attack the Federalists, and in later years will be used many times to discredit the administration of John Adams. [See Smith, II, pp. 975-978.]
Vice President Jefferson writes the Kentucky Resolutions and James Madison the Virginia Resolutions, declaring the Alien and Sedition Acts of 1798 null and void because unconstitutional. The Kentucky and Virginia Resolutions assert that the states have the right to prevent the federal government from using excessive powers.

1799 John Adams appoints William Vans Murray, with Oliver Ellsworth and William R. Davie, to a new diplomatic mission to France, an action which provokes anger from Hamiltonian Federalists who are pro-British, and dismay from Jeffersonian Republicans who are pro-French but do not want Adams and the Federalists to win credit for conciliation with France.

1800 In May John Adams dismisses from his cabinet James McHenry and Timothy Pickering, two followers of Hamilton who had attempted to weaken the President's leadership.
John Adams leaves Philadelphia in late spring to visit the site of Washington, the new federal capitol.
In late summer Alexander Hamilton attacks the Presidency of John Adams in his Letter . . . Concerning the Public Conduct and Character of John Adams, Esq.
William Vans Murray's peace mission to France results in a new convention signed 30 September by Napoleon, now First Consul. This convention supersedes the 1778 treaty of alliance and defines new commercial and maritime relations. Although it brings to an end the undeclared war with France, news of the settlement does not reach the United States in time to influence the results of the national election. [See Alexander DeConde, The Quasi-War (New York: Scribner's, 1966), pp. 277-288.]
In December John Adams receives word that he has lost his bid for reelection to the Presidency to Thomas Jefferson and Aaron Burr, both of whom receive 73 votes to 65 for Adams. Jefferson is chosen President after thirty-five ballots in the House of Representatives.

1801	John Adams appoints John Marshall Chief Justice of the Supreme Court in January, and begins appointments of new federal judges. Thomas Jefferson inaugurated President in Washington 4 March. Early that morning, before the ceremony, John Adams leaves Washington to return to Quincy.
1803	Louisiana Purchase conventions signed with France in April; Jefferson, President. John Quincy Adams elected United States senator.
1804	Napoleon crowns himself Emperor at Paris 2 December.
1805	John Adams completes the first part of his autobiography, "John Adams."
1807	John Adams completes the second part of his autobiography, "Travels and Negotiations," and writes the third part, "Peace."
1809	In the spring John Adams begins publishing recollec- of his public career in letters to the <u>Boston Patriot</u>. In June President James Madison appoints John Quincy Adams minister to Russia.
1812	John Adams and Thomas Jefferson become reconciled through the efforts of Benjamin Rush, and resume correspondence. War with Great Britain begins; Madison, President. Napoleon occupies Moscow in September.
1814	Napoleon abdicates in April, accepting exile on the island of Elba. Congress of Vienna opens in autumn to resolve issues created by the downfall of Napoleon. United States and Great Britain agree to peace with the signing of the Treaty of Ghent in December, John Quincy Adams having served as one of the U. S. peace commissioners in the negotiations.
1815	In February President Madison appoints John Quincy Adams minister to Great Britain. In March Napoleon lands in France, beginning his Hundred Days that end in defeat at Waterloo in June. Napoleon exiled to St. Helena in October.
1817	President James Monroe appoints John Quincy Adams Secretary of State, an office he holds during both terms of Monroe's Presidency.

1818   Abigail Adams dies 28 October.

1820   John Adams, representing Quincy, attends the Massachusetts Constitutional Convention of November and December.

1821   Napoleon dies on the island of St. Helena 5 May.

1824   John Quincy Adams receives a minority of electoral votes in the presidential election in December.

1825   On 9 February the House of Representatives elects John Quincy Adams President of the United States.

1826   On 4 July, the fiftieth anniversary of the nation's independence, Thomas Jefferson dies at Monticello; John Adams, in Quincy, dies a few hours later.

APPENDIX B

A NOTE ON THE TEXT

Anyone who examines the sources for the "Adams Cantos" soon finds instances where Pound's text is at variance with the words in <u>WJA</u> from which it is drawn. Spelling differences occur a number of times, as when Pound has "lucerne grass" (p. 355) for "lucern grass" in the source, or "descent" (p. 372) for "decent." No real problem here, because in the first example the spelling has not changed the word, and in the second, the context makes clear what the word should be.

But sometimes a misspelling in the "Adams Cantos," by changing the word, obscures the meaning of the source; this is what happens in Canto 65 (p. 365) when "sharing house" is used instead of "shearing house." Occasionally, a wholly different word turns up that dramatically changes the meaning of the source. In Canto 65 (p. 365) Pound has Mr. Zubly, a representative from Georgia to the Continental Congress, say, "Imperative to open out ports." The source (<u>WJA</u>, II, p. 457) reveals that Zubly said, ". . . therefore it is impracticable to open our ports." "Our" instead of "out"--that change is worth noting, too--but the more important discrepancy is that the Pound line uses "Imperative" where Adams had written "impracticable." Zubly, in fact, was arguing against opening the colonies' ports to foreign trade, but Pound's reader would have every reason to form just the opposite impression.

Names are sometimes misspelled. "Wollaston" appears as "Wollanston," and in the several references to Oxenbridge Thacher, the last name usually shows up as "Thatcher." At times an altogether wrong name appears: the "Dutch vessels" mentioned on p. 379 are "Danish vessels" in the source, and the tax that the Pound text says was "voted in Carolina" (p. 360) turns out to be, according to the source, a duty voted in Virginia on tobacco exports.

Perhaps the most mystifying name in the entire "Adams

Cantos" is "Mihites," in Canto 71 (p. 418). What is, who are, "Mihites"? The <u>Index</u> (p. 144) offers a puzzled guess: "poss. (L) <u>milites</u>: soldiers." The word occurs in a passage (lines 10-14) for which the source is this observation by John Adams (<u>WJA</u>, X, p. 120):

> The Irish, who are very numerous and powerful in Pennsylvania, had been, and still were enthusiasts for the French revolution, extremely exasperated against old England, bitterly prejudiced against New England, strongly inclined in favor of the southern interest and against the northern. . . . The English, Scotch, and Irish Presbyterians, the Methodists, Anabaptists, the Unitarians and Universalists, with Dr. Priestley at their head, and all the other sectaries, even many of the Episcopalians themselves, had been carried away with the French revolution, and firmly believed that Bonaparte was the instrument of Providence to destroy the Pope and introduce the millennium. . . .
> . . . Mr. Jefferson knew them all. These parties had all been making their court to him for fifteen years.

It would seem, then, that "Mihites in Pennsylvania," as Pound has it, should read "Irish in Pennsylvania." This emendation, given the Adams quotation, seems appropriate. Furthermore, given the long-standing antipathy between Irish Catholics and Roman Catholics dating back to the Synod of Whitby (664) and beyond, and between Irish Protestants and any Roman Catholics, which might lead an Irishman of either religious disposition to hope that Bonaparte's rise would mean the Pope's fall, the emendation in this context looks all the more plausible. But perhaps Pound, in his allusive way, has accomplished something more to his purpose by introducing the mysterious word "Mihites." What that purpose might be, I do not know. Thus for the present, with the evidence at hand, I have chosen to list "Mihites" as an error for "Irish."

One discovers dates erroneously recorded in the Pound text. What should be "11 May 1782" according to the source appears as "May 11th 1780" in Canto 69 (p. 405), for example. Dates also raise questions of textual ambiguity at times, a good illustration being the date in the following lines from Canto 62 (p. 344):

> June 7th. approve of committee from the several colonies
> Bowdoin, Cushing, Sam Adams, John A. and Paine (Robert)

The source for these lines is a long paragraph (WJA, I, pp. 144-145) in which Charles Francis Adams speaks of the 7th of June as the day when General Gage, military governor of Massachusetts who had adjourned the House of Representatives, was to allow that body to reconvene. The meeting of the House of Representatives to which Pound's lines refer, the meeting at which John Adams and the others were chosen to attend the congress at Philadelphia, took place on 17 June, not 7 June. Reading Pound's lines, one would very likely assume that 7 June was the day the committee of representatives to the Philadelphia congress was selected, but that assumption would be wrong.

Possibly the date of the Pound line was to have been 17 June all along; perhaps the text shows an error of transcription or an uncorrected typesetter's error. It is also possible, however, that there is no error, that the Pound lines do refer to both events--General Gage's action and the subsequent action of the reconvened House of Representatives--since the first in a sense precipitated the second, General Gage's dissolving and reconvening of the assembly on his own authority being a final provocation which the citizens of Massachusetts could not ignore.

Pound does, after all, shape his sources as well as transcribe them. One must approach the problems raised by discrepancies between Pound's text and his sources with a measure of caution, lest a too-literal-minded criticism of Pound's "accuracy" lead one to misconstrue what his art has accomplished on its own terms. About errors in dates and in the spelling of names--the documentary data of history--there can be no question: where the sources are unambiguously clear, these errors should be identified with the appropriate corrections. But for other discrepancies between text and source one must keep in mind the possibility that the poet is shaping his material. An obvious question to ask of this kind of poem is, has the poet reported the words of his source accurately? But the relevant question may be, what has the source become in his art?

What happens when Pound shapes his material is a subject deserving a book-length investigation, but for the sake of illustration two brief examples may be worth mentioning. In his diary entry of 13 June 1771 (WJA, II, pp. 278-279), John Adams writes of Governor Hutchinson:

> Caesar, by destroying the Roman republic, made himself perpetual dictator. Hutchinson, by countenancing and supporting a system of corruption and all tyranny, has made himself Governor, and by the mad idolatry of the people, always the surest instruments of their own servitude, laid prostrate at the feet of both. With great anxiety and hazard, with continual application to business, with loss of health, reputation, profit, and as fair prospects and opportunities of advancement as others who have greedily embraced them, I have, for ten years together, invariably opposed this system and its fautors.

In Canto 64 (p. 361) Pound's redaction of this passage takes a single line: "not interested in their servitude." The source conclusively reveals that Adams has not used these exact words to describe his own attitude. Yet it is equally clear that these words do describe his attitude, and that Pound, in characterizing Adams's commitments in terms of the negative of what Adams himself has said about Hutchinson, has thereby sharply emphasized the difference between the values of the two men.

The second example concerns Pound's handling of a passage in the Charles Francis Adams biography (WJA, I, p. 171) commenting on members of the Continental Congress who wanted to sit on the fence:

> To acquiesce in further measures of resistance to the British authority was likely to involve the hazard of life and fortune. This was a step further than many

had yet contemplated. In all civil convulsions, there is a class of men who put off taking a side as long as they can, for the purpose of saving a chance to solve the interesting question, which will prove the strongest. This naturally leads them to oppose, with all their might, any and every measure likely to precipitate their decision.

In Canto 62 (p. 344) Pound encapsulates this passage in the following line: "allus them as putts off taking a side." What stands out here is the colloquial idiom that Pound has substituted for the literate prose of his source. The effect is to give the observation the quality of folk-wisdom, a hard-headed realism as old as the earliest communities in which men, unlettered, perhaps, but not unperceptive, have had to make commitments that would bring them to choose sides. The tone of the idiom is what gathers up Charles Francis Adams's words about the timelessness of the problem: "In all civil convulsions, there is a class of men . . . ." Pound's line is not exactly like his source, but it is true to the source. In shaping his material Pound is almost always true to his sources in some important sense that the larger pattern of the "Adams Cantos" sequence makes clear.

Nevertheless, textual discrepancies do exist--some trivial, some significant--and the reader of the "Adams Cantos" should be aware of them. The two lists that follow undertake to provide this information.

I am indebted to Professor William W. Vasse of the University of Michigan at Flint, Michigan, for the permission he has given me to reproduce the list of textual deviations in names and dates that he appended to his article "American History and the Cantos," first printed in The Pound Newsletter, No. 5 (January, 1955), p. 19. For the convenience of the reader, I have substituted the page numbers of the 1970 New Directions edition of the Cantos for those of the edition that Professor Vasse had available, and I have also identified the lines on which the errors occur. I have omitted Professor Vasse's page references for the sources in WJA because the reader can use the page and line of the canto to locate the source in the body of the present book. The actual list, however, including the entries correcting errors in WJA, is Professor Vasse's own, which I have taken from his very helpful essay of twenty years ago.

Professor Vasse's prefatory comment (p. 18) for his list is also appropriate for the supplementary list which I have prepared, and it deserves quotation:

> It should be noted that these deviations from historical fact are not necessarily the responsibility of Pound himself. Many are of the kind to suggest a typographical error, not caught in the proofreading, perhaps because of the rush and uncertainty of things at that time. Cantos LII-LXXI were published early in 1940.

In any event, what the reader of the "Adams Cantos" needs now is an accurate text. Perhaps these two lists will contribute to such a text.

The numbers in the left column identify Canto-page-line in that order: 62 341-15 refers to Canto 62, page 341 of the 1970 New Directions edition of the Cantos, line 15 on page 341.

	"Adams Cantos"	Works of John Adams
62 341-15	Wollanston	Wollaston
62 342-13	baker's boy	barber's boy [now corrected]
62 342-26	Blaydon	Bladen
62 346-10	Flassans	Flassan
62 346-27	Willink	Willink (Frederick Elder: "The Dutch Republic and the American Revolution," Johns Hopkins University Studies in Historical and Political Science, XXIX: "Willinks"
62 348-24	Cotsworth (?) and Pi[n]ckney	(Charles) Cotesworth Pi[n]ckney
62 349-20	Elleswood	Ellesworth
63 352-12	Gordon	Gardiner
63 352-18	Leighton	Lightfoot (Robert)
63 352-30	Van Myden	Van Muyden
63 353-2	Britten	Britton
63 353-2	Fleta on Glanville	Fleta and Glanville

		"Adams Cantos"	Works of John Adams
63	353-9	1788	1798 (C.F.A.'s note from Sabine's *American Loyalists*) (James: *Massachusetts Loyalists* says 1795)
64	355-18	Gridley	Greenleaf
64	355-18	Abingdon	Abington
64	357-20	Thatcher	Thacher
64	358-1	Tuft's	Tufts's
64	359-26	Forest	Forrest
64	362-21	Haworth	Howarth
65	363-21	J. Cabot	Sebastian Cabot
65	364-34	Dickenson	(*DAB*: Dickinson)
65	372-32	d'Agen	d'Ayen
65	374-26	Valcaire	Valcarce
65	376-12	Tholomeno	Theolomico
65	376-19	Rheingrave, de Salm	Rhinegrave de Salm (*Der Grosse Brockhaus*: Rhingrave de Salm)
65	377-2	Vischer	Visscher
66	380-12	Willincks	Willinks
66	381-4	Thompson's	Thomson's
66	381-20	July 18th	July 12th
66	382-14	January 17th, 1768	January 13, 1766
67	388-20	Massachusetts	Massachusettensis
67	389-24	Rourke	Ororic (*DNB*: O'Rourke)
67	389-24	Macmorral	Macmorrogh (*WBD*: MacMurrogh)
67	389-28	Poyning's	Poyning (*DNB*: Poynings)
67	392-5	Bracton	Braxton (Carter)
67	393-18	Philiasia	Phliasia
67	394	[no entry]	
68	401-7	Ven der Kemp	Van der Kemp
69	404-18	Berdsma	Bergsma
69	404-27	Shelbourne	Shelburne
69	404-35	Nollet	Nolet
69	405-26	(J.A. to Jefferson)	John Adams to John Jay
69	406-9	Wopkins	Wopkens
69	406-25	(to Jay, 19 Aug. '85)	10 Aug. 1785
69	407-21	Lawrence	(*DAB*: Laurance)
69	407-21	Carol of Carolton	(*WBD*: Carroll of Carrollton)
71	415-14	Matlock	Matlack
71	418-6	L. Lloyd	James Lloyd
71	418-20	Walcott	Wolcott
71	421-4	Bekford	Beckford

528

The list below supplements Professor Vasse's original list by identifying, in addition to the few errors in names and dates not mentioned by him, other textual discrepancies in vocabulary that his list was not intended to include. I have made a careful effort to see that this list is as complete as possible. There is a matter of judgment involved at times in deciding whether a particular textual deviation is to be taken as an error or as an example of the way the poet has adapted his sources to his art. In such instances other readers may disagree with my conclusions; in fact, some entries on this list remain questionable in my own mind. A definitive list of emendations still awaits a thorough textual analysis.

		"Adams Cantos"	Works of John Adams
62	344-1	month	week
62	346-11	Van Capellen	Van der Capellen
62	346-14	Zeland	Zealand
62	346-14	Gronye	Groningen
62	346-14	Guilderland	Guelderland
62	347-1	Adam Street	Adam's Street
63	351-13	a good deed	a great deal
63	352-11	half after three	half after ten
63	352-26	Thatcher's	Thacher's
63	352-29	country	county
63	354-2	hoarse laugh	horse laugh
63	354-8	Thayer	Thacher
64	355-7	plumes	prunes
64	355-17	lucerne	lucern
64	355-19	ramshorn of straw	ramshorn or straw
64	355-32	instrument	instructions
64	356-25	3rd Inst.	2 Inst.
64	356-33	or avarice	and avarice
64	357-27	to Salem for Boston	from Salem custom-house to Boston
64	358-11	10 o'clock	1 o'clock
64	359-7	Wollanston	Wollaston
64	359-14	Brackett's	Bracket's
64	359-23	toward the end of December so doing	December 1769 refers not to repeal of statute but to a report of the trial John Adams was then reading
64	359-25	baker's boy	[barber's boy: see 62 342-13]
64	360-9	Thatcher	Thacher
64	360-23	he . . . he	I . . . I
64	360-35	Carolina	Virginia
64	361-27	Mrs. Rops	Mrs. Ropes
64	362-27	recourse	recurrences

		"Adams Cantos"	Works of John Adams
65	365-8	sharing house	shearer's house
65	365-12	no account	an account
65	365-24	Imperative	impracticable
65	365-24	out	our
65	365-31	for their artillery	"artillery" not mentioned in the source
65	367-9	powder	powers
65	367-25	Franklin	Franklin not mentioned in the source
65	367-29	fair	frank
65	368-17	dash	Mr. Langdon
65	371-19	bean salad	beans, and salad
65	372-3	grass	grain
65	372-17	descent	decent
65	372-34	louis	livres
65	374-21	St James Campostella	Cathedral at Lugo
65	375-15	Charent	Charente
65	376-24	dan	van
65	376-25	of	op
65	376-34	15s/	16s
65	376-35	OEuvre	ouvrage
65	377-1	16,000 times	1600 times
65	377-14	provide	preserve
65	379-25	Dutch	Danish
65	379-29	17 May '83	17 June
66	381-28	leaves of white oaks	leaves only the white oaks
66	382-30	true	regular
66	383-26	Braintree's representatives	Boston's representatives
66	384-16	direction	discretion
66	384-32	common lay	common law
66	385-20	case	cause
67	387-7	single	simple
67	387-10	latterly	lately
67	387-12	regum	regis
67	387-17	judiciary	justiciary
67	387-19	revocarit	revocaverit
67	388-29	fanatical	fantastical
67	389-18	power	prospect
67	389-20	demand	design
67	389-31	gratiam	gratias
67	389-33	explicavit	exaltavit
67	390-3	militant	martial
67	390-10	*jure*	*jura*
67	390-12	3 knights	2 knights
67	391-14	in	is
67	393-9	representatives	representations

		"Adams Cantos"	Works of John Adams
67	393-27	literature	letters
67	394-20	from	on
67	394-33	officers	offices
68	395-21	transaction	translation
68	396-11	commended	considered
68	396-24	De Klab	De Kalb
68	396-31	some	same
68	397-20	or	of
68	401-4	me	m'ayant
68	401-24	Vloten	Vlooten
69	403-11	Agsterburg	Agterburg
69	403-13	paid in advance	paid as it advances
69	404-6	ou	et
69	404-10	Hollandais	Hollandois
69	405-2	donnent ce repas	donneront un repas
69	405-7	May 11th 1780	11 May 1782
69	405-14	Vloten	Vlooten
69	405-30	some	same
70	409-13	Vervennes	Vergennes
70	412-3	all on system	all upon this principle
70	412-34	'74	1776 [Adams speaking of "fourteen years ago" in a letter written in 1790]
71	414-8	four yeomen	half a dozen, or half a score . . . yeomen
71	415-16	Beaumarchais	La Rochefoucauld
71	418-10	Mihites	Irish
71	420-28	substance	subsistence
71	420-28	extract	exact

LIBRARY OF DAVIDSON COLLEGE